CRITICAL RAVES for
JOHN H. DAVIS

MAFIA DYNASTY
THE RISE AND FALL OF THE GAMBINO CRIME FAMILY

"Mr. Davis tells a fascinating tale of greed, violence, corruption, and betrayal spanning a century. . . . Mr. Davis has done a fine job of putting it all together entertainingly."

—*New York Times Book Review*

"A gripping true-crime history."

—*Kirkus Reviews*

"A lucid, well-crafted account of [New York's] five families."

—*Booklist*

MAFIA KINGFISH
CARLOS MARCELLO AND THE
ASSASSINATION OF JOHN F. KENNEDY

THE KENNEDYS
DYNASTY AND DISASTER

"A carefully researched and highly readable account of the whole Kennedy story."

—*Financial Times*

"John Davis is thorough, insightful, and analytical. . . . Davis does an especially good job of presenting the buildup of hostilities between organized crime and Attorney General Robert F. Kennedy, and the relevance of that war to the assassination of the President."

—Seth Kantor
White House correspondent during
the Kennedy administration

"John H. Davis has produced a book which combines skilled writing and a wealth of material, holding the reader's attention to the last paragraph."

—*The Pittsburgh Press*

THE KENNEDY
CONTRACT
THE MAFIA PLOT TO ASSASSINATE THE
PRESIDENT

"A stunner."

—Liz Smith, Syndicated columnist

ALSO BY JOHN H. DAVIS

The Bouviers: Portrait of an American Family

Venice

The Guggenheims: An American Epic

The Kennedys: Dynasty and Disaster

Mafia Kingfish: Carlos Marcello and the
Assassination of John F. Kennedy

The Kennedy Contract: The Mafia Plot to
Assassinate the President

MAFIA DYNASTY

The Rise and Fall of the Gambino Crime Family

JOHN H. DAVIS

HarperTorch
An Imprint of HarperCollins Publishers

This is a work of fiction. Names, characters, places, and incidents are products of the author's imagination or are used fictitiously and are not to be construed as real. Any resemblance to actual events, locales, organizations, or persons, living or dead, is entirely coincidental.

◆

HARPERTORCH
An Imprint of HarperCollins*Publishers*
10 East 53rd Street
New York, New York 10022-5299

First HarperTorch paperback printing: October 1991
First HarperPaperbacks printing: June 1994
First HarperCollins hardcover printing: February 1993

HarperCollins®, HarperTorch™, and ◆™ are trademarks of HarperCollins Publishers Inc.
Avon Trademark Reg. U.S. Pat. Off. and in Other Countries, Marca Registrada, Hecho en U.S.A.

Printed in the United States of America

Visit HarperTorch on the World Wide Web at
www.harpercollins.com

30 29 28 27 26 25 24 23

FOR

SOHODRA

WITH LOVE

A prince must have no other objective, no other thought, nor take up any profession but that of war, its methods and its discipline, for that is the only art expected of a ruler. And it is of such great value that it not only keeps hereditary princes in power, but often raises men of lowly condition to that rank. It may be noted, on the other hand, that when princes have given more thought to fine living than to arms, they have lost their states. The first cause of losing them is the neglect of this art, just as the first means of gaining them is proficiency in it.

NICCOLÒ MACHIAVELLI, THE PRINCE
(1513)

This life of ours, this is a wonderful life. If you can get through life like this and get away with it, hey, that's great. But it's very unpredictable. There's so many ways you can screw it up.

PAUL CASTELLANO *(1984)*

Contents

Part IV
Building an Empire of Crime
The Rule of Don Carlo
(1957–1976)

Part V
Arrogance, Betrayal, and Murder
The Rule of the Pope
(1976–1985)

Part VI

Drawing Fire

**The Rule of John Gotti
(1986–1992)**

Part VII

The Showdown

**New York, 1992: *The United States v.
John Gotti***

THE GAMBINO CRIME FAMILY
1931–1994

BOSSES:
VINCENT MANGANO
PHILIP MANGANO

UNDERBOSS:
ALBERT ANASTASIA
1931–1951
|
BOSS:
ALBERT ANASTASIA

UNDERBOSS:
FRANK SCALISE
1951–1957
|
BOSS:
CARLO GAMBINO

UNDERBOSSES:
JOE BIONDO (1957–1970)
ANIELLO DELLACROCE (1970–1976)
1957–1976
|
BOSS:
PAUL CASTELLANO

UNDERBOSSES:
ANIELLO DELLACROCE
THOMAS BILOTTI (December 2–14, 1985)
1976–1985
|
BOSS:
JOHN GOTTI

UNDERBOSSES:
FRANK DECICCO (1985–1986)
JOSEPH ARMONE (1986–1989)
SALVATORE GRAVANO (1990–1991)
1985–1994

Prologue

New York, 1992:
The United States v. John Gotti

JOHN GOTTI: It's not a toy. I'm not in the mood for toys, or games, or kidding, no time. I'm not in the mood for clans. I'm not in the mood for gangs. I'm not in the mood for none a that stuff there. And this is gonna be a Cosa Nostra till I die. Be it an hour from now, or be it tonight, or a hundred years from now when I'm in jail. It's gonna be a Cosa Nostra. . . . It's gonna be the way I say it's gonna be, and a Cosa Nostra. A "Cosa Nostra."

JOHN GOTTI: . . . And from now on, I'm telling you if a guy just so mentions "La" . . . he just says "La," the guy, I'm gonna strangle the cocksucker. You know what I mean? He don't have to say "Cosa Nostra," just "La" and they go.

John Gotti's secretly taped conversations with various Gambino crime family underlings were flowing like an open sewer through the headsets and the loudspeakers in a federal courtroom in Brooklyn where the reputed Cosa Nostra boss and his underboss, Frank "Frankie Loc" Locascio, were being tried on charges ranging from racketeering and obstruction of justice to illegal gambling and murder, including the 1985 murder of former Gambino boss, Big Paul Castellano.

The government considered the trial as the final showdown in its long, protracted campaign against John Gotti and the Gambino crime family he ran. Three times Gotti had been indicted and brought to trial over the past seven years and three times he had beaten the case. But this time it was different. This time the government had hundreds of hours of tape recordings of Gotti's self-incriminating conversations and a witness to corroborate them, Gotti's own underboss turned government informant, Salvatore "Sammy the Bull" Gravano.

Only the judge, the defendants, the attorneys, the twelve anonymous, sequestered jurors, and the court reporters had been provided with headsets. I and the other ladies and gentlemen of the newspaper-radio-television press had to rely on two inadequate loudspeakers and the transcripts of the tapes to learn Gotti's thoughts and intentions. Worse off still were the Gambino capos and Gotti relatives and groupies who packed the cramped spectators' section of the high-ceilinged courtroom. Without transcripts, they strained to decipher the blur of Gotti's hoarse, hurried, frequently obscene utterances issuing from the two loudspeakers hanging on the courtroom walls to the right and left of the judge's bench.

Not everyone, however, was straining to make out what was coming over the earphones and loudspeakers. There was a small group in the press section, sitting in the first two rows, who were intent only on observing and rendering the expressions and plumage of the principal defendant, who had refused to put on a headset or even read his unguarded utterances from the printed transcripts provided him. These were the courtroom artists, whose duty it was to portray the trial's cast of characters for print and television.

I observed them as they concentrated on rendering the seemingly most unconcerned man in the room, scrutinizing the immaculately coiffed and attired Mafia don through small binoculars as they applied strokes of colored crayon to large clipboards of drawing paper and traded observations among themselves about the defendant's diamond pinkie ring, his tailor-made, double-breasted suit, the colors and design of his custom-made tie and pocket handkerchief, the starched whiteness of his linen:

"I do believe he uses blueing in his hair. I'm convinced of it. It's the kind of blue you see in the hair of old ladies on upper Park Avenue."

"Will you look at the way he's holding his pinkie ring in the spotlight, so everyone can see it sparkling? He's *flaunting* those diamonds."

"Can you make out the material of his suit?"

"I'd say it's a gray worsted with a light chalk stripe."

"But it shines like silk."

"Everything he has on shines. Did you notice his shoes? I bet he uses them as a mirror."

"And the tie and the handkerchief?"

"It's paisley. A blue and red design. Very busy."

"I wish I knew how his laundry gets his shirts so *white*. Every day he shows up in such gleaming white shirts."

As the artists frantically scratched away, the tapes droned on. Judge I. Leo Glasser, a dour, swarthy, dark-haired man of sixty-eight, listened to them from his eminence on the bench, wearing a long black robe and a consistently sour expression, allowing himself but an occasional nod, or a very faint smile, from time to time. The twelve jurors—seven men and five women—listened to the tapes with varying degrees of concentration and interest. Two or three of them alternately smiled, winced, scowled, strained, and even laughed as the don's inimitable words crackled through their headsets. Others remained expressionless. One or two appeared in danger of dozing off. The prosecution attorneys, U.S. Attorney Andrew J. Maloney and Assistant U.S. Attorney John Gleeson, who had assembled the tapes and were now having them played to the court, listened to them with bored expressions as one would listen to a tape one had heard hundreds of times, which they had. As for the defense attorneys, Albert J. Krieger, John Mitchell, and Anthony M. Cardinale, they dominated the courtroom spectacle, as they had done from the opening bell, keeping up a continuous sideshow of huddles and histrionics, alternately smirking, making loud objections to the prosecutor's questioning of witnesses, exchanging knowing grins, and occasionally indulging in brief whispering conferences with the principal defendant from which all would emerge displaying self-satisfied smiles.

The tapes flowed on, as the trial lurched toward the jury's final decision.

JOHN GOTTI: Fuckin', I tell you what a fuckin' heartbreak. You know you feel like you're being raped with these fuckin' tapes.

SALVATORE GRAVANO: I know. I hate it. I, I listened to a couple of tapes of mine. I was sick.

JOHN GOTTI: We got a game there for twenty years. Is this rat-fucking Greek's name Spiro?

PETER MOSCA: That's right.

JOHN GOTTI: You tell this punk, I, me, John Gotti . . .

PETER MOSCA: I'm meeting him tonight.

JOHN GOTTI: . . . will sever your motherfucking head off! You cocksucker! You're nobody there. Listen to me, tell him. Tell him, "Listen, you know better. He'll sever your motherfucking head off! You know better than to open a game there."

JOHN GOTTI: When Di B got whacked, they told me a story. I was in jail when I whacked him. I knew why it was being done. I done it anyway. I allowed it to be done.

JOHN GOTTI: Every time I turn around there's a new company popping up. Rebars. Building. Consulting. Concrete. And every time we got a partner that don't agree with us, we kill him. You go to the boss and your boss kills him. He kills 'em. He okays it.

JOHN GOTTI: I don't give two fucks about myself going to jail. Don't I know they ain't gonna rest until they put me in jail?

The secretly taped conversations of John Gotti and his men had been recorded by an electronic listening device the FBI had installed in an apartment above the Ravenite Club, the Gambino family headquarters on Mulberry Street in Manhattan's Little Italy. At first the FBI had installed bugs in the club itself, but they were unproductive. Gotti had apparently become aware of them and was keeping his mouth shut in their vicinity.

To confer with his underboss, *consiglière*, and capos in private, Gotti chose a comfortably furnished apartment on a floor above the club which before had been occupied by the widow of a former capo. With great cunning, ingenuity, and daring, members of the FBI's Gambino Squad had succeeded in planting a bug in the apartment one night in 1989, and it soon produced a bonanza for the government. Gotti felt comfortable there. Before long his big mouth and irrepressible vanity were giving away all his secrets.

The bug in the Ravenite apartment revealed, among

other things, what Gotti thought of his former boss, Big Paul Castellano, and why he ordered the murder of Gambino associate Louis DiBono.

GOTTI: That's what made me hate, really, fuckin' Paul. You, ya, you couldn't even get a fuckin' ham sandwich [from him]. . . . He sold the *borgàta* [family] out for fuckin' construction company.

GOTTI: I took Sammy's word that he talked about me behind my back. Louie, did he ever talk to any of you guys?

LOCASCIO: No.

GOTTI: I took Sammy's word. Louie DiBono. And I sat with this guy. I saw the papers and everything. He didn't rob nothin'! You know why he's dying? He's gonna die because he refused to come in when I called. He didn't do nothin' else wrong.

During occasional recesses in the trial proceedings, the media and Gotti's relatives, capos, and assorted supporters would mingle in the fourth-floor hallway outside the courtroom. Prominent among Gotti's men were his older brother, Peter, capo John "Jackie Nose" D'Amico, former defense counsel Bruce Cutler, and Joe DeCicco, uncle of Gotti's former underboss Frankie DeCicco, who had been blown up by a car bomb in 1986.

During one midday break early on in the trial, I watched Peter Gotti approach a group of reporters and astonish them by saying "Hey, you guys, let's go have lunch at Sparks," referring to the Manhattan steak house outside of which former Gambino boss Paul Castellano was murdered in December 1985, allegedly by Peter's brother, John. "Waddaya say?" urged Peter. "I hear they got great steaks over there at Sparks."

"Wait'll you see," chimed in the slim, dapper, silver-haired "Jackie Nose" D'Amico. "Johnny's gonna walk. I'll betcha anything. He's gonna walk again, I'm tellin' ya."

"You know," commented a female television producer, "I used to think John Gotti was the sexiest man alive until I read the transcripts of the tapes. The man's mind is a cesspool. What a turnoff."

"What turns me on," offered a female journalist, "is his walk. He walks like he owns the world. It's the sexiest walk I've ever seen."

"This whole case is nothin' but a government frame-up," remarked Bruce Cutler to a group of reporters, his huge biceps filling out the upper sleeves of his jacket. "The whole case is phony. It's a fantasy."

"What's on the tapes is fantasy?" queried a reporter.

"Who knows how they doctored those tapes?" snorted Cutler, who was himself under investigation for misdemeanor criminal contempt of court at the time.

Back to the courtroom. Back to the tapes.

GOTTI: We had Angelo [Ruggiero] there. We've got to keep him quiet. Keep quiet, don't hum-bar-ramp. I told him, You got to learn, keep your motherfuckin' mouth shut! This is how we get in trouble, we talk.

GOTTI: That's their fucking crew. And he's gotta get whacked! Because he's getting the same, for the same reason that Jelly Belly's getting it. You wanna, you wanna challenge the administration? We'll, we'll meet the challenge, you motherfucker!

This last tape had been played by the prosecution to convince the jurors that John Gotti was indeed the boss of a crime family and if anyone challenged his "administration" he did so at considerable risk.

Throughout the trial the prosecution had gone to great lengths to educate the jurors on the power, organization, and nature of the activities of the Gambino crime family.

The government prosecutors had told them that the Gambino family, now headed by John Gotti, was the richest and most powerful organized crime family in the United States, that it engaged, on a large scale, in such diverse criminal operations as airport cargo hijacking, labor racketeering, extortion, drug trafficking, loan-sharking, bookmaking, illegal restraint of trade, pornography distribution, counterfeiting, car theft, and murder, from which it took in hundreds of millions of dollars a year. They told the jurors that the Gambinos had a virtual stranglehold on New York's concrete industry, the city's garment district trucking industry, and the private garbage carting industry; that because of these strangleholds the Gambinos extracted a mob tax on every drop of concrete poured in the city, and on every garment manufactured in the city, and on every load of garbage picked up and dumped by private garbage carters in the city. Furthermore, the Gambinos controlled the entire Brooklyn waterfront. No ship could load or unload in Brooklyn without paying off the Gambinos.

The prosecutors had further instructed the jurors on the geographical range of Gambino activities, describing the family as a vast crime empire that, in addition to operating in all five boroughs of New York City, conducted criminal enterprises throughout New York State, Connecticut, and New Jersey; was active in Atlantic City, Philadelphia, Las Vegas, and Fort Lauderdale; and did considerable business overseas, from financing heroin factories in Sicily to selling stolen luxury cars in Kuwait.

The jurors had been told that John Gotti had become boss of the Gambino family upon the murder of his predecessor, Paul Castellano, and that the family he led consisted of twenty-three crews numbering three to four hundred "made," or formally inducted, members, and several thousand associates.

In his last trial, held in state supreme court, Gotti had boasted on one of the tapes played by the prosecution:

> "I know what's goin' on. . . . You're oblivious to what's goin' on, but I ain't. I'm in the fuckin' hunt. . . . Me, I'll always be all right.
>
> The law's gonna be tough on us, okay: If they don't put us away . . . for one year or two, that's all we need. . . . But if I get a year, gonna put this thing together where they could never break it, never destroy it. Even if we die, be a good thing.

To which an associate remarked, "It's a helluva legacy to leave."

Gotti went on:

> Well, you know why it would be, ah, because it would be right. Maybe after thirty years it would deteriorate, but it would take that long to fuckin' succumb.

Such unabashed bravado and dogmatic expression of faith in his calling on the part of a Mafia boss the nation had not witnessed since the days of Al Capone in Chicago's Prohibition era, or the heady days of the "Prime Minister of the Underworld," Frank Costello, in the New York of the forties and fifties.

Here was a Mafia boss with style and pizzazz, and seemingly inexhaustible self-confidence. Here was a Mafia boss whose persona could lure television cameras from all the major networks and prompt *Time* magazine to display his portrait, painted by Andy Warhol, on its front cover. Here was a Mafia boss who was a virtual media junkie, who reveled in publicity, courted the press, and would complain when one of his favorite female reporters was missing from the press section at his trial.

"Maybe after thirty years it would deteriorate, but it would take that long to fuckin' succumb." More than likely few persons in the courtroom were aware that the criminal organization John Gotti intended to perpetuate for another thirty years had already been in uninterrupted existence for at least sixty years, that it was already as old as the Chrysler Corporation, or the George Washington Bridge.

The powers behind this hardy institution, a survivor in a world perpetually at war, were the handful of absolute monarchs who had shaped and governed it since its founding in the early 1930s, men like Lucky Luciano, Vincent Mangano, Albert Anastasia, Carlo Gambino, Paul Castellano, and John Gotti.

The roots of these violent and ambitious men were to be found in two separate criminal brotherhoods that had sprung up in and around two ancient Mediterranean cities, Naples and Palermo. One was known as La Camòrra, the other as the Honored Society, or La Mafia. Both could have found no more fertile soil anywhere in which to grow and prosper than in the city in whose underworld John Gotti now reigned supreme.

Part I

Roots

1

San Giuseppe Vesuviano

The vast violet cone of Mount Vesuvius dominates the city of Naples, its shimmering bay, and a wide expanse of some of the loveliest and most fertile farmland in Italy, the plains of what the Romans called Campania Felix.

Below the western, seaward slope of this majestic mass lay the ruins of the ancient cities of Pompeii and Herculaneum, both buried under a sixty-foot-thick avalanche of lava and volcanic ash in the eruption of A.D. 79. Below the eastern slope, on the landward side of the volcano, are nestled a number of small agricultural communities—Somma Vesuviana, Ottaviano, San Giuseppe Vesuviano, Sarno—a string of villages surrounded by terraced vineyards, groves of almond and chestnut trees, flows of jagged black lava, and beds of dark, almost black volcanic soil. It is a landscape of intense natural beauty juxtaposed with scenes of human squalor. Here and there, rising out of the lava fields, tall, slender umbrella pines hold their bright green crowns against the sky, while below, clumps of blazing yellow gentian lick the jagged black rocks like rings of fire. Yet amid this bright and spacious beauty stand crude peasants' huts surrounded by emaciated barefoot children. Hungry pigs and dogs, all ribs and spindly legs, forage futilely among the stones.

Vesuvius and its surrounding plains and towns have been witnesses to much history. It was on the slopes to the north of the volcano that the rebellious Thracian slave, Spartacus, defeated his Roman captors in 71 B.C. It was in what is today called Ottaviano, on the eastern slope, that the emperor Caesar Augustus was born in 27 B.C. Dominating Ottaviano stands a castle that belonged to the great Florentine family, the Medici, when the Medici grand dukes were patrons of Bronzino and Galileo.

Not far from Ottaviano and its former possession, San Giuseppe Vesuviano, is Sant'Agata de'Goti, a village whose name reminds us that Rome's Teutonic invaders, the Goths, who overran the empire in the fifth century, had established themselves in large numbers in the area after their final defeat by the Byzantines in A.D. 555.

The members of this Germanic tribe, famous in antiquity for their stamina and fierceness in battle, were known as Goti.

In the towns and villages girdling the slopes of Vesuvius the names Goti and Gotti are quite common and it is speculated that families bearing these names today may be distant descendants of the ancient Goths who settled around the base of the volcano after their defeat by the Byzantines in the sixth century.

Whatever the case, it was in one of these communities—San Giuseppe Vesuviano—that the father of Gambino Mafia boss John Gotti was born and raised.

His name was John Joseph Gotti and he had the ill

fortune to have grown into manhood during one of
the bleakest times of his part of the world, known as
Il Mezzogiórno, "the Land of Noon." In 1906, when
Gotti was a young boy, Vesuvius awakened from a
twenty-four-year slumber in a titanic eruption that all
but buried San Giuseppe Vesuviano and its surrounding farmland under a thick blanket of volcanic ash.

It took the citizens of San Giuseppe Vesuviano,
mostly poor *contadìni*, who worked the dark volcanic
soil as day laborers, almost a year to dig themselves
out. In the meantime vineyards had been crushed,
farm crops destroyed, farm animals suffocated and
starved to death. The catastrophe could not have happened at a more inopportune time, for the
Campanian region was in the throes of a severe economic depression brought on in part by the Italian
government's all but total neglect of the south. After
San Giuseppe Vesuviano dug out from under its rain
of volcanic ash, the economic situation in the
Mezzogiórno grew steadily worse. The region's principal crop, the grapes from which the celebrated
Vesuvian wine Lachryma Christi is made, had been
destroyed. There was no work and no prospects for
work. There was only one escape from this *misèria:*
emigration. Emigration from Naples and the
Campanian region reached its peak during the years
1890 to 1920, when thousands upon thousands of
southern Italians fled to northern Italy, Switzerland,
North Africa, South America, and the United States
in one of the largest exoduses of a people in
European history.

As soon as he came of age, John Joseph Gotti, a
short, robust young man with strong arms and big
hands, was apprenticed to a builder and began to
learn the trade of mason. But in San Giuseppe
Vesuviano there was almost no construction going on
as young Gotti entered his teens. The *contadìni*, living
in small stucco huts often perched on lava flows,
made repairs and additions to their homes them-

selves to save money. In town, commerce was so slow there was rarely a need to erect new buildings.

But there was more to the *misèria* of southern Italian life than meager economic prospects. There was also the almost total indifference to the people's needs on the part of the fledgling Italian state. The unification of Italy in 1870 had not helped matters much for the chronically malgoverned southern Italians. For ten centuries southern Italy and Sicily had been dominated by despotic foreign powers. The Bourbons' formula for governing the lower orders of southern Italian society epitomized the social policies of all the region's conquerors. It was *fèste, farìna, e fórca*, literally "festivals, bread, and the gallows."

In Naples' principal piazza, immense marble statues of the conquerors and oppressors of southern Italy stare down from arched niches along the Pompeian red facade of the Palazzo Reale, the former courts of the Spanish viceroys and Bourbon kings. Roger II, the Norman, Frederick II of Hohenstaufen, Charles of Anjou, Alphonse of Aragon, Charles V of Spain, Joseph Bonaparte, Gioachino Murat, Ferdinand II of Bourbon, and Victor Emmanuel of Savoy were symbols of ten centuries of despotic indifference to the needs of ordinary people.

To meet those needs, a secret criminal brotherhood sprang into existence in and around Naples in the early nineteenth century that placed itself in direct opposition to the state. It came to be known as the Camòrra, after a Spanish word meaning combat. By the time John Joseph Gotti came of age, the Camòrra had become a *sottogovèrno*, a subgovernment, in his region, more responsive to the needs of average citizens than either the church or the state.

It is not known whether John Joseph Gotti was involved in any way with the Camòrra. Certainly, however, he could not have avoided some contact with members of the brotherhood, for Camòrriste had begun to infiltrate almost every area of a community's commercial and political life by the time John Joseph Gotti came of age, in the period 1915 through 1920.

By the second decade of the twentieth century a certain character had become ubiquitous in the piazzas of Naples and surrounding towns of Campania: a Camorrìsta known popularly as Il Guappo, Neapolitan dialect for 'Il Capo.'

Il Guappo was the local representative of the Camòrra. It was Il Guappo who became the real functioning government in a given community. It was he who drew up and enforced contracts for farmers and merchants, loaned money to people the banks turned down, "protected" shops and farms, taxed lotteries and the auctioneering of livestock at fairs, arranged marriages for unwed mothers, helped take revenge on rapists and the deserters of wives, and, in general, policed the community to which he had been assigned.

A familiar and often flamboyant figure, Il Guappo habitually wore a dark, wide-lapelled, double-breasted, pin-striped suit with an explosion of handkerchief flowing out of his breast pocket. He favored shirts with high starched collars and conspicuous French cuffs. His shoes were always highly polished and he often wore a broad-brimmed black felt hat. He walked about the piazza with an air of bravado and authority more pronounced than anyone else in town, more than the mayor, more than the chief of police, more than the biggest landowner, Il Baróne.

The social and economic conditions resulting from ten centuries of foreign domination also gave rise to a general attitude among the people, a *forma mentis*, as southern Italians like to call it, which was one of ingrained suspicion of the established order, whether that order was perceived as the state, the church, the police, the bank, the courts, or the proprietors. *"Sono tutti una massa di ladri!"* ("They're all a bunch of robbers!") was the people's constant refrain. Any legally constituted authority was, to the *popolino*, as the lower echelons were often called, an enemy. To cheat and outsmart the enemy became a deep-seated, ingrained response of the southern Italian psyche to all the powers that were.

It would not be long before Camòrriste imbued with this mentality began turning up in immigrant Italian neighborhoods in New York: East Harlem, Brooklyn, Manhattan's Little Italy. Il Guappo was making his American debut.

By the end of the second decade of the twentieth century, New York City would become the mecca of thousands upon thousands of southern Italians whose ancestors had been left out of the system for centuries. The names "Nuova York" and "Brookaleen" would become symbols of hope and faith and promise not only to downtrodden peasants and chronically unemployed workers, but to the Camòrriste, who envisioned chances to enrich themselves in America more than they could ever hope to grasp strutting about the piazzas of the Mezzogiórno.

By 1920 the economic and political situation in Italy had degenerated into virtual anarchy. Italy's bitter struggle against Austria in World War I had left the new nation's treasury severely depleted and had also cost Italian families some three hundred thousand sons. Riots were breaking out everywhere. Sudden "lightning" workers' strikes were crippling industry. Bands of disaffected workers and peasants were pilfering factories and farms at will. It was in the midst of this disorder that a young war veteran Benito Mussolini formed the Fascist movement and began his two-year quest for power.

For John Joseph Gotti, who had in the meantime taken a bride, Fannie, life in San Giuseppe Vesuviano at the time Mussolini was recruiting his Black Shirts had become hopeless. There was no work and the foreseeable future held no promise that things would get any better.

The Gottis' days in San Giuseppe Vesuviano had become repetitive, monotonous. The *disoccupàti* [unemployed], like John Joseph Gotti, would congregate every morning in the piazza near the *comùne*, or town hall, to commiserate, rail at the government, and talk about emigrating to America. In New York they needed construction workers. There they were building railroads, tunnels, bridges, and tall apartment and office buildings. There a man could earn more money in one day than he could earn in San Giuseppe Vesuviano in a month. Every day the talk was the same. As were the daily chores of the women: baking bread, drawing water from the fountain, washing clothes in the open-air *lavanderìa*, hanging the laundry out the windows to dry, preparing the same meal every day, spaghetti *cón sàlsa di pomodòro*, tomatoes being the one crop in the region that was in plentiful supply.

By the summer of 1920 it was time for John Joseph and Fannie Gotti to stop complaining and do something about their future. Buying steerage passage with what meager savings the couple had scraped together, the Gottis stuffed all their possessions in two trunks, cried, *"Addìo, arrivedérci"* to a mob of wailing relatives, rode to Naples in a horse cart, boarded a crowded steamer, and sailed for New York.

2

Palermo

As the Gottis of San Giuseppe Vesuviano were sailing for New York, a twenty-year-old Sicilian by the name of Carlo Gambino was making his own plans to escape to America.

The Gambino family of Palermo and its chief ally, the numerous Castellano clan, were by no means as poor and downtrodden as the Gottis. Though not rich, the Gambinos and Castellanos were reasonably prosperous, counting among their members several well-connected members of the Honored Society.

The Honored Society, or Mafia, as it was less often called, was a vast criminal brotherhood that had developed in Palermo and western Sicily independently of the Camòrra of Naples. Like the Camòrra, it had arisen as a reaction to centuries of foreign misrule even more despotic and unresponsive to the needs of the people than that which had prevailed in Naples and southern Italy for a thousand years. By 1920 it had come to dominate entirely the social, political, and economic life of western Sicily.

What distinguished the Mafia from the Camòrra was the rapidity of its advance and the degree to which it had permeated Sicilian society. Whereas the Camòrra had developed relatively slowly and at best had attained but a limited influence in southern Italy, perhaps because the boot of Italy was so much larger than Sicily, the Honored Society took advantage of the political vacuum following the guerrilla leader Garibaldi's "liberation" of Sicily from the Bourbons in 1860 and seized power so rapidly that by 1900 it controlled virtually the entire western third of the island.

Members of the Honored Society had taken control of all local governments in the cities and towns and had forcibly assumed the management of almost all the factories and landed estates. The decrees of the Men of Respect had acquired the force of law. There was scarcely a corner of western Sicilian life that escaped their influence.

The social soil of Sicily had favored the Mafia's rapid rise to power. For, in addition to fulfilling the needs of an abominably governed people by providing services the state had been both unwilling and unable to provide, the Sicilian mentality was eminently *predisposed* to accept the kind of governance the Mafia offered.

For, long before organized criminal brotherhoods began to grow and prosper in western Sicily, the Mafioso outlook, or attitude, had come to dominate the Sicilian consciousness. Centuries of foreign oppression had bred in the Sicilian people a deep-seated antagonism to all legally constituted authority. To be against the ruling establishment gradually became the accepted attitude and to resist it the accepted behavior. To be a Mafioso was to be a man in a certain, well-defined sense, a man who stood up for his rights and those of his family against the incursions and effronteries of the state.

The first time the word *Màfia* began to appear in written Italian in the late eighteenth century, it was as a descriptive term, possibly of Arabic origin, meaning "beauty" or "excellence," with overtones suggesting manly bearing and courage. For centuries the Mafioso type had existed in Sicily as an individual who had attained honor and respect by always standing up for his rights and never shrinking from their defense, even if it meant taking another man's life to achieve his ends or maintain his "honor." It was because of the prevalence in western Sicily of this type of human being, and the code of behavior and way of life he represented, that the criminal organizations of the nineteenth century were able to take such rapid and widespread root in Sicily. In the end, western Sicily had provided the Mafia with a much more fertile social soil than Naples and the Mezzogiórno had provided for the Camòrra.

For a bright, energetic, ambitious young man in early twentieth century Palermo to become a member of the Honored Society was a natural goal. Ambitious young men in Palermo aspired to the Honored Society as their counterparts in late twentieth century New York aspired to Wall Street. It was the thing to do.

Young Carlo Gambino had grown up in an area of Palermo so dominated by the Mafia that it was considered off limits to both the police and the military. As a boy he was accustomed to seeing Men of Respect in their expensive suits walking the calle and piazze of his neighborhood receiving the homage of the people. Men doffed their hats at them and kissed their hands. Women curtsied as they passed. Someday he, Carlo Gambino, would also be a Man of Respect. As a teenager Carlo worshiped a hero of the Honored Society he had vowed to emulate when he grew up. He was the legendary *capo di tutti capi*, the "boss of all bosses," Don Vito Cascio Ferro, regarded as the most powerful man in Sicily in his day.

Since boyhood Carlo had fed on tales of the exploits of the fearless Don Vito: How he had gone to America around 1900 and made a fortune from scratch, then returned to Sicily, after killing a man, to take control of the Honored Society. How powerful bankers, politicians, and magistrates sought his favor. How he was even invited to the villas of the Palermitano aristocracy, the *principi*, *duchi*, and *baroni* who owned vast landed estates in the interior. How he rode through the streets of the poorest districts distributing candies to the children. How he had single-handedly killed the New York police detective Joseph Petrosino, who had come to Palermo to coordinate an attack on the Honored Society with the Sicilian authorities. Someday he, Carlo Gambino, would be a big boss like Don Vito Cascio Ferro.

Carlo's mother was a Castellano. Through her Castellano relatives Carlo was brought to the attention of some Men of Respect as a teenager and they quickly sized him up as a good prospect. He was bright, energetic, a hard worker, and eager to please his elders. Though a bit on the short side—he was only five feet seven—he had a commanding bearing and a striking face: large dark eyebrows, thick dark hair, and a hawk's beak of a nose combined with a perpetual smile that would eventually become his trademark.

Carlo's most cherished dream was finally fulfilled when, one day as he was nearing his twentieth birthday, the Men of Respect initiated him into the Honored Society. Quietly he sat there in the dark candle-lit room at a long table at which ten men wearing black suits were sitting as his pricked right finger bled onto the paper effigy of a saint and the paper was set afire. Picking up the burning paper and holding it in his hands, young Carlo intoned at the prompting of his *padrìno:* "This is the way I will burn if I betray the brotherhood."

Palermo in the year 1920 was, as it is today, a city in which three thousand years of history constantly paraded before one's eyes. There were the remains of Magna Grecia—the urns, statues, and fragments of temples left by the ancient Greeks. There were the ancient Roman remnants—the mosaics, the great marble statues of emperors and gods. To remind the Palermitani that their city had been dominated by North African Arabs for nearly three hundred years there were the mosques and the mosquelike churches such as the church and cloister of San Giovanni Degli Eremiti, with its four small pink Saracenic domes and tower suggestive of a minaret. Proclaiming the Norman domination in the Middle Ages was the vast cathedral of Monreale, with its incomparable Byzantine mosaics and exquisite blending of Romanesque, Norman, and Arabic styles, and the Royal Palatine Chapel of the Normans' greatest king, Roger II. Memorializing the Hohenstaufen domination was the tomb of the Hohenstaufen Holy Roman Emperor, Frederick II, known to his contemporaries as Il Stupor Mundi, "the Wonder of the World." There were French Gothic churches commemorating the Angevin domination and Catalan-style palaces giving evidence of the rule of the Aragonese. And there were the gardens and baroque fountains and palaces of the Spanish Hapsburgs and Bourbons, who held sway over Sicily for three hundred and fifty years.

The effect on the Palermitano psyche of being surrounded by so much palpable history was twofold. On the one hand it bred feelings of superiority and cynicism, and hence inaction. The Sicilians had seen it all. They had experienced directly all the great Mediterranean and European civilizations. Compared to the Sicilians, the other European peoples were uncivilized, barely out of their barbarian infancy. The idealisms of the northern peoples, their belief in popular democracy and the rule of law, the Sicilians looked down upon with disdain. The Sicilians were smarter than anyone else. They were realists. They were more experienced. Being perfect, they did not need to prove themselves. On the other hand, the history of rule by so many peoples also bred feelings of oppression and hopelessness. So much history, so much despotism. Wouldn't it be exhilarating to get out from under it and go to a new land that was not so much immersed in the shadowy grandeurs of the past, that had not had to bear the burden of so much oppression? To the young men of Carlo Gambino's generation, Palermo was an enormous tomb. The place to be was the United States, a nation with a scant history, a nation that was not a prisoner of its past, one that kept its gaze fixed on the future.

Unlike the Gottis of San Giuseppe Vesuviano, Carlo Gambino was already well connected in New York. Several of his mother's Castellano relatives had already settled in Brooklyn. His mother's sister was there. She had married a man by the name of Masotto with connections to the brotherhood, and had a son, Thomas, who had become a made member of the Honored Society in Brooklyn. And two sons of one of his mother's brothers, Peter and Paul Castellano, lived and worked in Brooklyn, where they had begun to make lots of dollars. The Men of Respect of Palermo had remained in close touch with their *paesàns* in New York. They would bring some of their most promising recruits to the attention of their brothers in Brooklyn, hoping to make some good sales. If the money was right, a deal would be made with a freighter captain and the recruit would be smuggled into the states as a stowaway to then join the family of the Man of Respect who had paid for him. By 1920 an entire business had been built up in Brooklyn dealing in the exportation of young Sicilian criminals to New York.

And so, one day in late November 1921, Carlo Gambino, age twenty-one, was smuggled aboard the SS *Vincenzo Florio* at Palermo in the dead of night, bound for Virginia and eventually New York. One of his Castellano relatives would be waiting for him on the dock at Norfolk when his ship arrived.

Part II

The Volcano

3

New York:
The Roaring Twenties

The SS *Vincenzo Florio* docked in Norfolk on
December 23, 1921, laden with a cargo of lemons,
olive oil, anchovies, and Marsala wine, and one passenger, Carlo Gambino.

Legend has it that Gambino decked himself out in
his Sunday best for his entry into the United States: a
new tailor-made dark gray three-piece suit, a black
wide-brimmed fedora, and a pair of narrow, shiny
black shoes. His vest was adorned with the heavy
gold chain of the heirloom watch his father had given
him prior to his departure and a white silk handkerchief exploded out of his breast pocket.

Former New York *Daily News* reporter Paul Meskil,
who interviewed members of the Gambino family in
the sixties, described young Carlo Gambino's illegal
entry into the United States in his book *Don Carlo:
Boss of Bosses.*

As befitting someone with powerful connections,

Carlo was personally escorted to the gangplank by the captain, who had been paid handsomely to transport his only passenger. There was no problem with the immigration and customs officials. They had also been taken care of by Carlo's connections.

Carlo had been told in Palermo to look for a car with flashing lights parked at the end of the dock. Descending the gangplank with a suitcase in either hand, elegant, assured, yet anxious, he peered down the dock through the dense evening fog and there, to his relief, he discerned the blurred headlights of a car blinking on and off. When he got to the car and looked through the driver's window, he immediately recognized a Castellano relative behind the wheel he had not seen for some time. The two embraced and were soon heading for New York.

On the way Carlo was told of all the arrangements his relatives had made in his behalf. They had rented a small apartment for him on Navy Street near the Brooklyn waterfront and had secured a job for him in the Brooklyn trucking firm his first cousins, Peter and Paul Castellano, owned. Another first cousin, Thomas Masotto, son of one of his mother's sisters, had been assigned to introduce him to some Men of Respect. One of his closest childhood friends in Palermo, Tommy Lucchese, who would one day be known as Three-Finger Brown, would introduce him to the burgeoning new world of the illicit liquor trade. The world of basement stills, secret warehouses, bootleggers, and speakeasies had sprung into existence almost overnight with the passage of the Volstead Act two years before Carlo's arrival, banning the manufacture, sale, and transportation of liquor and beer in the United States.

Thus, upon his illegal entry into the United States—Gambino never did become a U.S. citizen—Carlo found himself well taken care of from the very start. Soon after he reported for work at his cousins' garage, his connections landed him another job, a place in New York's most powerful gang dealing in illicit liquor, the outfit run by Giuseppe "Joe the Boss" Masseria, a short, stocky Man of Respect who had fled Sicily in 1903 to escape a murder charge. Before long Carlo would be making more money than he had ever dreamed of back in the narrow alleys of Palermo.

A far less propitious set of circumstances had greeted John Joseph and Fannie Gotti upon their arrival in America roughly a year before Carlo Gambino walked down the gangplank in Norfolk.

The young couple from rural San Giuseppe Vesuviano had landed in a dense, overcrowded Italian immigrant community in the South Bronx surrounded by an immense urban sprawl that engulfed them and made them feel utterly insignificant. Without family connections in the New World, the Gottis had placed themselves at the mercy of a recruiter of construction workers, a familiar figure of the times, who lurked outside the exit gates of the Immigration and Naturalization facility on Ellis Island to capture poor illiterate southern Italian immigrants, find them a place to stay, and put them to work at construction jobs paying $1.25 a day. Not long after their arrival in New York, John Joseph and Fannie Gotti found themselves in a one-room cold-water flat in a tenement in the South Bronx and John Joseph found himself working ten grueling hours a day as a ditchdigger and hod carrier on a trolley line project.

As they assessed their circumstances, John and Fannie Gotti must have often wondered with dismay whether they were any better off in their adopted city than they had been on the slopes of Mount Vesuvius. Alone and isolated in an alien world that scorned their kind, they must have missed the intimate community life of San Giuseppe Vesuviano where they had known everybody and everybody had known them.

"*Buòno giórno,*" "*Buòna séra,*" they had said all day as they made their rounds through the village. Now no one paid the slightest attention to Fannie when she left the apartment in the morning and John Joseph was just another peon in the construction gang he worked with downtown.

Life was also cramped and ugly for the young couple. Used to gazing out over vast distances, up at a towering volcano to the west and down to immense stretches of green farmland to the east, the Gottis must have felt terribly confined in their tenement apartment with no view from the narrow window but the wall of another building across the street. It was a lonely, alienated, pent-up existence. Poor southern Italian immigrants from farming communities were scorned throughout most of the city. Without the polish of the big-city immigrants—the immaculately groomed Men of Respect from Naples and Palermo— they were a laughingstock. In the end, the Gottis of the South Bronx had only one consolation: John Joseph had a job, one that enabled him to bring home as much as $6 to $10 a month if he worked ten hours a day, six days a week. There had been no work at all in San Giuseppe Vesuviano.

Poor, isolated, and scorned, all that was left for the Gottis of the South Bronx to do was to create their own community, found a family that would at least keep them company as they struggled to survive in an alien world. Fannie Gotti would produce thirteen children over the years, seven boys and six girls, two of whom died in infancy. It was the fifth child—a son named John Joseph Gotti, Jr., after his father—who in December 1985 would become, in the words of one mobster, "God's gift to the underworld."

•

The New York in which John Joseph and Fannie Gotti arrived in 1920, followed by Carlo Gambino a year later, was described years later by Mafia boss

Joseph Bonanno as the "Volcano." Bonanno intended the expression to describe the explosive world of Italian immigrants in New York in the twenties, but the expression could well have been an apt description of all of New York society in the age of Prohibition.

New York in the 1920s was a city in continual eruption. The United States had emerged from World War I as a great power, a creditor nation, and an industrial giant, with all that implied in increased responsibilities, opportunities, and pressure. New York was supplanting London as the financial capital of the world. Wall Street was indulging in a virtual orgy of speculation. The old nineteenth century values, manners, and mores were breaking down. New Yorkers now wanted to "have fun," to "get high." They wanted to break free of puritanical repression. They also wanted to make big money. The haves wanted more, and the huge mass of have-not immigrants wanted as much as they could get. New York was a vast free-for-all. "Anything goes" was the credo of the times.

Helping to fuel the Volcano's eruption was the public's insatiable thirst for prohibited liquor and the underworld's frenzied efforts to slake it. By a curious irony the good intentions of the temperance crusaders had resulted in the greatest expansion of criminal activity in U.S. history up to that time, as well as a marked increase in alcohol consumption and alcoholism.

For the Camòrriste and Mafiosi of New York, Prohibition was a godsend, a means of making quick, illicit profits on a scale never before attained in America or Sicily.

While the Gottis of the South Bronx and thousands of *poveracci* like them were plugging away at back-breaking dead-end jobs, slick Sicilian hotshots like Carlo Gambino, Joe Bonanno, Lucky Luciano, and Tommy Lucchese were plunging into the erupting illegal liquor business, setting up stills, warehouses, distribution facilities, and trucking companies; recruiting battalions of bootleggers; and opening up hundreds of speakeasies all over town.

This race for quick riches by the immigrant population of the city would not be seen again until the violent cocaine wars of the 1980s. The Gottis of the South Bronx, and later East Harlem, remained outside this frenzied competition. But the Gambinos and Castellanos of Brooklyn were in the thick of it.

While Carlo Gambino, his Castellano cousins, and Tommy Lucchese were working the liquor business for Joe the Boss Masseria in Brooklyn, another gang, based in Manhattan's Lower East Side, was steadily gaining in power and fearsomeness.

Heading this gang was a tough young immigrant from the small Sicilian village of Lercara Friddi, Salvatore Lucania, later to be known as Lucky Luciano. Lucania had left school and his family's miserable Lower East Side tenement while in his middle teens and had hooked up with a couple of smart Jewish boys, also from the Lower East Side, Polish-born Maier Suchowlijanski, later to be known as Meyer Lansky, and Benjamin "Bugsy" Siegel, son of Russian Jewish immigrants. Later they would be joined by two young toughs from the Naples area, Francesco Castiglia, whom Lucania rechristened Frank Costello, and the brutal Vito Genovese.

These five young gangsters made an unbeatable combination. Lansky and Siegel provided the brains, Lucania the leadership, Costello the art of diplomacy, and Genovese—when he was available, for he often went off on his own—the muscle. The day was not far off when this alliance of talent would come to dominate organized crime in the United States and change its character forever.

With Lansky, the budding financial genius, handling the money, Siegel and Lucania planning and executing the thefts, hijackings, and the transportation and sale of illegal alcohol, and Costello buying protection from the law, the Lower East Side outfit prospered greatly. The demand for alcohol throughout the entire New York metropolitan area always exceeded the supply. Lucania soon realized that if he supplied alcohol to public officials in sufficient quantities he could buy protection at all levels, from the cop on the beat to the precinct captain to the ward heeler all the way to the police commissioner himself, who was paid $10,000 a week to look the other way.

By the mid-twenties Lucania's gang controlled distilleries, fleets of trucks bringing booze down from Canada, teams of hijackers (of rival mobsters' trucks), warehouses, dozens of speakeasies, and as many as a hundred truck drivers, bookies, distillers, distributors, and armed soldiers in Lucania's employ. In his not always wholly reliable autobiography, authored by Martin A. Gosch and Richard Hammer, the gang leader estimated that in 1925 he took in $12 million from booze alone. His hundred-man payroll absorbed $1 million a year. Protection—"grease," as Lucania called it—cost $100,000 a week. That garnered around $4 million to be divided among Lucania, Costello, Lansky, and Siegel.

It was around this time that the two big established bosses from the old school—Joe the Boss Masseria and Salvatore Maranzano—noted the astonishing rise of Lucania's young gang and, fearing it, began courting Lucania with offers to join their organizations.

4

Joe the Boss and Little Caesar

Joe the Boss Masseria was quick to recognize the superior abilities of his new recruit, Carlo Gambino. He had assigned the young immigrant to his bootlegging operation. Just as an executive trainee in a large corporation today is rotated from one department to another to acquaint him with every facet of the business, so Joe the Boss put his young soldier to work for a time in each branch of his complicated liquor business. Carlo tried his hand at making moonshine in the basement stills of Brooklyn; he learned how to smuggle Caribbean rum by speedboat from the "Rum Row" anchorage three miles off the Long Island shore; he tried his hand at hijacking truckloads of a rival gang's liquor shipments; he took a turn at cajoling speakeasy owners into buying exclusively from Masseria.

By the mid-1920s Joe the Boss had become the dominant player in New York's burgeoning illegal liquor trade and was amassing a huge fortune in the process. Working for Masseria with Carlo Gambino were several other up-and-coming young men who would one day play leading roles in the city's underworld: Joe Adonis and Albert Anastasia.

Joe the Boss was a short, squat, fat-faced Palermitano who was called "the Chinese" by his rivals because his puffy cheeks narrowed his eyes. He had a reputation as a glutton, a man who would gobble up half a plate of spaghetti in the time it would take a normal diner to twirl a mouthful around his fork. He was also known for his unkempt appearance and coarse manners. He drooled while he ate and was rude and peremptory in conversation. But his principal reputation was for being a dogged fighter who would not hesitate a second to kill someone who stood in his way.

It wasn't long before a powerful rival appeared on the scene who would challenge Joe the Boss's dominance in New York. His name was Salvatore Maranzano and he had come from the coastal town of Castellammare del Golfo, west of Palermo. There were hundreds of Castellammarese immigrants in New York, mostly in Brooklyn, and hundreds more scattered throughout the United States. They were an intensely clannish bunch, who took special pride in the town of their birth. They had little use for their counterparts from Palermo. The forty-three-year-old Maranzano became their leader. He had been sent to New York by the boss of all bosses in Sicily, Carlo Gambino's hero, Don Vito Cascio Ferro, under orders to organize the American Mafia and bring it, eventually, under Don Vitò's control.

Salvatore Maranzano was a compelling personality. A leader with a commanding presence, he possessed a speaking voice of great persuasiveness and authority and cultivated interests and enthusiasms not commonly found among Men of Respect.

Maranzano professed a deep admiration for Julius

Caesar and knew a great deal about him and his military campaigns. In one room of his Brooklyn house he assembled a sort of shrine to the great Roman general. There, displayed on shelves covering all four walls, he kept his vast collection of books on Caesar, along with several antique marble busts of his hero. Maranzano was a linguist conversant in six languages. When he turned to Caesar's literary works, he read them in Latin.

Another one of Maranzano's heroes was Machiavelli. He was given to declaiming passages from *The Prince* to his troops. He tried to follow Machiavelli's advice in the conduct of his affairs. One of Machiavelli's maxims he took to heart became a key policy of his rule:

> Severities should be dealt out all at once,
> that by their suddenness they may give less
> offense; benefits should be handed out drop
> by drop, that they be relished the more.

A formal, punctilious man, with Old World manners and attitudes, Maranzano had once studied for the priesthood. He may have been the only Mafia boss in America with a college education. One of his lieutenants, future crime boss Joseph Bonanno, characterized him as both an "ascetic intellectual" and a "born warrior." Not long after his arrival in New York he became known throughout the underworld as "Little Caesar."

Once Maranzano had rallied most of the Brooklyn Castellammarese to his banner, he began encroaching on Joe the Boss's bootlegging operations, hijacking truckloads of Masseria booze and strong-arming speakeasies to take Maranzano's product.

As might be expected, Joe the Boss soon retaliated. In 1928 he demanded tribute from the Castellammarese of Brooklyn and, when they refused to pay, promptly had one of the clan murdered.

There followed other killings of Castellammarese in

other cities. Maranzano reacted by intensifying his encroachments on Masseria's bootlegging operations. Losing patience day by day, Joe the Boss eventually made a momentous decision. He passed a death sentence on the entire Castellammarese clan.

Soon cars full of Masseria soldiers were roaming the streets of Castellammarese neighborhoods in Brooklyn shooting up Maranzano's trucks and taking potshots at Maranzano's men in bars, restaurants, and social clubs. What came to be known as the Castellammarese War was on.

Maranzano, belatedly perceiving that a fight to the finish was under way, struck back, inflicting heavy casualties on Masseria's forces. In the first year of the fighting Masseria is said to have lost fifty men.

It was around this time that Lucania, Lansky, Siegel, Costello, and Genovese finally joined forces with Joe the Boss and began operating alongside Albert Anastasia and Carlo Gambino. Maranzano's Castellammarese force of around four hundred men included rising star Joseph Bonanno, future boss Joe Profaci, and the powerful Magaddino clan of Buffalo and Niagara Falls.

These alignments were anything but stable. Many of Masseria's men were biding their time, waiting to see how the tide of battle would run before committing their final loyalties. Before long, as the Masseria gang began suffering heavier and heavier losses, there were defections. One of these was Joe the Boss's bright young soldier Carlo Gambino. It is said that Maranzano, hearing of Gambino's superior abilities, invited him to a secret meeting at which he persuaded Gambino to join his forces and Gambino, sensing Masseria's inevitable defeat, accepted.

As the war ground on and it began to appear that the "born warrior" Maranzano was going to get the best of the gluttonous Masseria, two of Joe the Boss's men, Salvatore Lucania and Vito Genovese, decided to take a daring course of action. They would walk straight into the lion's mouth and agree to destroy Masseria if Maranzano would give them protection and respect after Joe the Boss was eliminated. Maranzano had been trying to persuade Lucania to kill Masseria for some time and Lucania had always refused. For one such refusal Maranzano lured Lucania into a trap where he was given a beating that disfigured his face for life. Lucky to escape alive, he was given the nickname Lucky by Meyer Lansky and henceforth he would be known as Lucky Luciano.

Finally agreeing to destroy Masseria for Maranzano, Luciano in April 1931, lured his boss to a lunch at a Coney Island restaurant, the Nuova Villa Tammaro, where an ambush had been planned. Toward the end of the meal, with Joe the Boss sedated with linguini, veal scallopine, and red wine, Luciano excused himself for a minute and went to the men's room. When he returned to the table he found Masseria's blood-spattered body lying on the floor surrounded by terrified waiters and customers. He had been shot dead by four gunmen—Vito Genovese, Albert Anastasia, Bugsy Siegel, and Joe Adonis—who had already fled.

There followed another spate of killings on both sides but, for all intents and purposes, the Castellammarese War was over. For a brief period chaos ensued in the New York underworld as the Masseria gang began disintegrating and the victorious Salvatore Maranzano began picking up the pieces.

Maranzano was now recognized as the most powerful underworld leader in the nation. To ratify that position and proclaim a new order for the Honored Society, he convened a meeting of all the families in May 1931, at an immense banquet hall on the Grand Concourse in the Bronx.

Around four hundred men from all over the country showed up for the gathering. Maranzano stood alone on a high platform overlooking the crowd.

Directly beneath him on a lower level of the platform sat his crown prince, Lucky Luciano, and the heads of all the families ranged along a table. Those beneath the platform remained standing.

This was Salvatore Maranzano's finest hour. Now he could worship his hero by reincarnating him. Now *he* was Julius Caesar.

"Whatever happened in the past is over," he intoned in a voice that thrilled his listeners. "There is to be no more hatred among us. Those who lost someone in the war must forgive and forget. Even if your own brother was killed, don't try to find out who did it or take revenge. Those who do will pay with their lives."

It was after this preamble that Maranzano then proclaimed himself the "boss of all bosses" and laid down the law for the future organization and functioning of the underworld in the United States.

Speaking in Italian and Sicilian, with occasional bits of Latin thrown in, he defined the new order in the underworld that was to come into existence as Cosa Nostra, literally "Our Thing."

Maranzano then explained that Cosa Nostra would be organized along the lines of Julius Caesar's Roman legions. Cosa Nostra would be divided into well-defined families, each with jurisdiction over a specific territory or business. Each family would be ruled by a boss who would have absolute authority. Directly beneath him would be an underboss, and beneath him would be the *capiregime*, or captains, who would be in charge of individual crews of soldiers. Salvatore Maranzano would function as the *càpo di tùtti i càpi*, the supreme boss of all bosses in the United States, and would receive tribute as such from all the families.

There would be a strict chain of command to ensure discipline and the insulation of the boss from any direct participation in crimes. A soldier could not bring a matter directly to the attention of his boss. He had to bring it to the attention of his *caporegime*, who would then go to the underboss, and if he thought the matter important enough the underboss would bring it before the boss.

That said, Maranzano proceeded to reiterate the familiar laws of the Honored Society which would continue to hold true for Cosa Nostra.

Cosa Nostra was to come first in the life of each member. It was to come before family, friends, church, and country. The penalty for talking about Cosa Nostra to anyone outside it was death without trial. That included talking about Cosa Nostra even with one's wife. Finally an order coming from a boss to an underboss or from an underboss to a *caporegime* or from a *caporegime* to a soldier must be obeyed under penalty of death.

Maranzano also emphasized that a member of a Cosa Nostra family must always obtain permission for an undertaking, whether the undertaking was legal or illegal, and that a boss or underboss should only grant permission if a given undertaking would benefit the family as a whole. Finally membership in a Cosa Nostra family would be open only to men of Italian blood.

After the assembly Maranzano met with the remnants of the Masseria family, the leaders of other families, and his own Castellammarese people to dictate a new order for the New York underworld.

He told the men that from then on there would be five families in New York. The Maranzano family, based in Brooklyn, would be one; its boss would be Joe Bonanno. Another Brooklyn family would be headed by Maranzano's close friend Joe Profaci, with Joe Colombo as underboss. Still another Brooklyn family would be headed by Vincent Mangano, organizer of the Brooklyn waterfront; it would come to include Albert Anastasia and Carlo Gambino. A fourth family would be carved out of the former Masseria gang; its leader would be Lucky Luciano and would include Frank Costello and Vito Genovese. A fifth family would be created out of the former Reina outfit; it would be led by Frank Scalise and Tommy Lucchese. It is an arrangement that has held to this day.

For a while there would be peace. But Maranzano knew he would have to go to war again soon if he was to remain the boss of all bosses. There were too many ambitious young Turks in the other families lusting for more power. After a while Maranzano confided to one of his soldiers, Joe Valachi, that he would have to eliminate some important men. He had composed a list. It included Al Capone, the powerful Chicago mob boss, as well as Frank Costello, Joe Adonis, Vito Genovese, and Lucky Luciano.

5

The Triumph of Lucky Luciano

Although they were both Sicilians and both belonged to Cosa Nostra, there was an enormous gulf between Salvatore Maranzano and Lucky Luciano. Maranzano, in his mid-forties, was a man of the old school who used expressions like "Man of Respect" and "the Honored Society" and spoke Italian as much as he did English. To Luciano, who was twenty years younger and unlike Maranzano, had grown up in America, Maranzano's Old World airs, prating of honor and respect, and Caesarian posturing were all nonsense. It meant nothing to him. What had meaning for Lucky was making money, doing business. Although Maranzano had made him boss of a family, Luciano chafed at the idea of Maranzano, in his self-proclaimed role of boss of all bosses, being in a position of authority over him. It would not be good for business. Luciano had hooked up with a couple of sharp Jewish boys, Bugsy Siegel and Meyer Lansky, who knew how to make money. Maranzano didn't want anything to do with Jews. They were not men of his tradition. But Lansky and Luciano, who had become close friends, knew they could make a lot of money together. Luciano valued his close association with Meyer Lansky and wanted Lansky to be close to Cosa Nostra.

Maranzano had no specific quarrel with Lucky Luciano. He was fully aware that he owed his position to him. Hadn't Luciano eliminated his chief enemy? Still, Maranzano recognized Luciano as a threat to his power. It was well known in the underworld that Lucky Luciano was both ambitious and treacherous, that he would stop at nothing to obtain more power.

Compared to the handsome and imposing Maranzano, with his formal, imperious airs, Luciano was unattractive, even repulsive. Of medium height and somewhat on the skinny side, he had a graceless bearing and few manners. His pockmarked face was further disfigured by scars he had received from a knifing by a Maranzano soldier who had slashed through his right cheek muscles and left him with a drooping right eye.

It wasn't long after the end of the Castellammarese War that Maranzano, eager to solidify his power, decided that the ambitious Americanized Luciano had to go. He then devised a plot to get rid of him and that other ambitious young Turk, Luciano's underboss, Vito Genovese. He would invite Luciano and Genovese to his office in the Grand Central Building for a meeting and have them killed in a hallway as they were leaving the building. To accomplish the double assassination he would hire a non-Italian so Luciano and Genovese would not become suspicious when they encountered him. After some thought, Maranzano settled on a young Irish killer from Hell's Kitchen by the name of Vincent "Mad Dog" Coll.

But Maranzano had unwisely confided his assassination plan to several of his closest associates, one of whom tipped off Luciano. Luciano then set to work devising a plan to kill Maranzano before Maranzano got him. On the day of the scheduled appointment with the boss, Luciano would send to Maranzano's office someone Maranzano knew and trusted, their mutual friend Tommy Lucchese. Following Lucchese would be four killers dressed as treasury agents who would demand to inspect Maranzano's business records for tax purposes. Maranzano would not recognize them because the four men would be hired guns from the Siegel-Lansky mob. Nor would Maranzano be especially suspicious of the uniformed men's desire to inspect his business records, because he had been anticipating a visit from the IRS. He had even told Lucchese he was expecting such a visit and had gone out of his way to have his records in perfect shape.

As it turned out, Luciano's murder plan succeeded brilliantly. Maranzano was unsuspecting when his old friend Tommy Lucchese showed up at his office shortly before Luciano and Genovese were due to appear. While Lucchese was distracting Maranzano in his private office with talk of mutual business, the four uniformed men were lining up Maranzano's bodyguards against a wall in a waiting room and were frisking them. Then, as two of them held the bodyguards at gunpoint, the other two burst into Maranzano's office and shot and stabbed him to death.

As Lucchese and the four killers fled the scene, they ran into Mad Dog Coll in a hallway and told him the cops were coming. They made a clean getaway.

Lucky Luciano was now in control of the Cosa Nostra. Acting swiftly, he ordered a purge of the old guard, the "Mustache Petes," as he contemptuously called them. By the time it was over, sixty Maranzano loyalists had been killed. The triumphant Luciano then called for peace and announced he would hold a meeting of all the fathers to decide on a new deal for the Cosa Nostra.

One of Luciano's first acts after the purge was to notify the heads of all the Cosa Nostra families that the position Maranzano had held and gloried in, boss of all bosses, was abolished. Later on in the fall of 1931 Luciano, now de facto boss of bosses, held a meeting of all the family bosses at which he announced his new plans for the syndicate which, he said in his autobiography, he wanted renamed the "Unione Siciliano."

What Luciano did was create a national crime syndicate that embraced not only the established Italian families but also the Jewish and Irish mobs as nonmember associates. This allowed Luciano to include the Siegel-Lansky gang as a valuable ally of Cosa Nostra. The five New York families that had been formed by Maranzano remained the same, but Luciano insisted on a few innovations. He added the position of *consiglière*, or counselor, to the family hierarchy and established a twelve-member group called the Commission to govern the affairs of the entire crime syndicate. The Commission, composed of twelve family bosses, would function as both a legislature and a court. It would adjudicate disputes among the families and vote on matters of overall policy. It would also negotiate with the non-Italian gangs that had been admitted into association with the syndicate as nonmember allies.

What Luciano accomplished was to Americanize and democratize the old Sicilian Mafia, to replace its elaborate rituals and concepts of honor and respect with efficient business practices and a less formal social structure. Years later Luciano would be credited with having transformed the old Honored Society into a huge, and fearsome, moneymaking machine, one that would prove impervious to the erosions of the Great Depression and would one day do a business equal to that of the nation's ten largest industrial corporations combined.

Part III

Out of Chaos
(1931–1957)

6

Birth of a Mafia Family

By Christmas 1931 a huge sense of relief had settled over the New York underworld. The Castellammarese War and the bloody purges that followed in its wake were over. The two old tyrants Joe the Boss Masseria and Salvatore Maranzano were gone. Now there was peace and the new family chiefs appointed by Maranzano and ratified by Luciano were emerging from chaos to take hold of their fiefdoms and begin shaping their futures.

The family to which Carlo Gambino had become attached in the wake of the Castellammarese War had coalesced around Brooklyn waterfront boss Vince Mangano. It wasn't long before Mangano made Gambino a *caporegime* with a *borgàta*, or crew, of his own.

Also joining Mangano's outfit was Frank Scalise, a former ally of Lucky Luciano, and two young Turks very different in temperament and mind from Carlo

Gambino: the dapper Joe Adonis and the bloodthirsty Albert Anastasia. Whereas Carlo Gambino was essentially a quiet, courteous man who relied on shrewdness and cunning to attain his ends, the handsome, narcissistic Adonis, who had changed his surname from Doto to Adonis in homage to his own beauty, was loud and extroverted and not very subtle. As for Albert Anastasia, his temperamental outbursts and homicidal mania were to become legendary in the underworld. Anastasia at twenty-nine became Mangano's underboss and Adonis, in his early thirties, evolved into sort of an ambassador to Brooklyn's political machine, friend to councilmen, police officials, court officers, and judges, the man who could be trusted with the job of putting in the fix.

Vincent Mangano was a member of the old guard of the Honored Society, a man quite out of step with young Turks like Lucky Luciano, Frank Costello, and Albert Anastasia. He had survived in the underworld by doing favors for Luciano. At the behest of Luciano he had served as a backup gunman in the killing of Joe the Boss Masseria and had helped Luciano in the purge of the "Mustache Petes" following the Castellammarese War. For his loyal service Luciano made Mangano a member of the new Commission.

Vince Mangano's principal theater of operations was the Brooklyn waterfront, which he, his brother Philip, and Albert Anastasia came to control. Working closely with high officials of the International Longshoremen's Association, he made the waterfront his fledgling crime family's principal income producer.

How does a mob boss make money from the waterfront? Largely through extortion, theft, and victimization of the dockworkers. Under threat of preventing a cargo from being loaded or unloaded, a shipping company had to pay the mob a substantial tribute. Only then would a cargo begin to move. And the men who moved the cargo, the dockworkers, had to pay the mob each day in order to work. If you didn't pay, you didn't work. If you rebelled and complained to the police, you might be killed. The mob also extorted money from the shipowners and captains. Mangano's boys would "protect" a ship from harm while it was moored dockside. And then there were all the opportunities for cargo theft. The mob knew the cargo of every ship the dockworkers loaded and unloaded. It could pick and choose what to steal.

The Brooklyn waterfront in the thirties and forties was a tough, lawless place. The docks were full of vicious Mafia soldiers enforcing discipline, collecting payoffs, organizing cargo heists. Many of the dockworkers were poor southern Italian and Sicilian immigrants who lived in miserable shanties in Red Hook and Sheepshead Bay. They had no recourse from the slavery imposed on them by the mob. They could not seek redress of grievances from the International Longshoremen's Association because the organization was controlled by the mob. The mob had a double claim on dockworkers' wages. Vince Mangano's enforcers made them pay to work each day and pay their union dues each month. If a dockworker fell into debt, a Mangano shylock would move in and lend him money at thirty percent interest. The bodies of workers who bucked the system were often never found. They would be taken out to sea and thrown to the sharks. Dockworkers targeted for execution would have cargos accidentally dropped on them in the holds.

Other rackets Mangano and his crime family became involved with were such staples as running numbers, loan-sharking, alien smuggling, truck hijacking, drug smuggling, and bootlegging.

After Prohibition was repealed in 1933, the family continued making high-proof moonshine whiskey, selling it for substantially less than the price of legal brand-name liquor.

Carlo Gambino became particularly adept at man-

aging Mangano's liquor business. The repeal of Prohibition was looked upon by most mobsters as an ill
omen that threatened to put an end to their most
lucrative racket. Carlo Gambino, however, succeeded
in making more money than ever after repeal. Over
the years he had acquired a chain of whiskey stills in
New York, New Jersey, Pennsylvania, and Maryland.
Convinced there would still be a substantial demand
for high-proof, low-priced liquor after repeal, he
bought more stills and more distillery equipment at
bargain prices from other racketeers who had decided
to get out of the business. By the mid-1930s he owned
a virtual monopoly on illegal alcohol within a hun-
dred-mile radius of New York City and was on his
way to making the first of his several fortunes.

Prosperous at thirty, Gambino felt financially secure
enough to get married. His bride was Kathryn Castellano, his first cousin, the daughter of one of his mother's
sisters. Carlo also felt financially well off enough to help
his two brothers, Paolo and Giuseppe, escape from
Palermo (Mussolini was cracking down on the Mafia)
and join him in Brooklyn. He put them to work in his
borgàta and rechristened them Paul and Joe.

By the late thirties the crime family headed by
Vince Mangano, which would someday bear the
Gambino name, was well established. Despite the
stagnant economy of the Great Depression, Man-
gano's rackets prospered, as did those of the other
Cosa Nostra bosses of New York.

One of the keys to Mangano's prosperity was the
resourceful moneymaking ventures of his talented
caporegime, Carlo Gambino. Carlo had the proverbial
Midas touch. He possessed an unfailingly sure
instinct for making money. He was quick in seizing
promising opportunities and tireless in seeing them
through. He quickly acquired responsibilities beyond
the realm of bootlegging liquor.

One of Carlo's most spectacular coups was his
wartime ration stamp racket. When World War II

broke out the federal government announced that gasoline, meat, and certain groceries would be strictly rationed, and created the Office of Price Administration to print and distribute ration stamps. Without ration stamps a motorist could not purchase gasoline, a housewife could not buy a steak for her family. Gambino quickly realized the value of these stamps and set about obtaining huge quantities of them and selling them at stiff prices to distributors. Carlo acquired his first load of stamps by dispatching teams of safecrackers to the vaults of the Office of Price Administration. When OPA officials learned the mob had taken such an interest in their stamps, some of them suddenly realized they could supplement their meager salaries by selling the stamps directly to the mob. Gambino soon found this to be a much safer way of obtaining the stamps than breaking into the OPA's vaults. Before long he was buying hundreds of thousands of stamps from corrupt OPA officials and selling them to his old network of bootlegging distributors. According to Cosa Nostra soldier Joe Valachi's testimony before a Senate committee in 1963, Gambino and his associates were able to realize a $1 million profit from one ration stamp deal alone.

With the huge profits he made selling moonshine liquor and ration stamps, Carlo invested heavily in a broad range of businesses, licit and illicit, all of which proved to be reliable money-makers. He came to own meat markets, fat-rendering companies, importers of olive oil and cheese, bakeries, restaurants and nightclubs, insurance companies, construction companies, fuel oil distribution concerns, carting companies, dress factories, trucking companies, and pizza parlors.

By the time he was forty-five, some twenty-five years after his arrival in the United States, Carlo Gambino, still an illegal alien, was a multimillionaire and the Cosa Nostra family he worked for had become one of the strongest of the five families of New York.

7

Albert Anastasia and Murder Incorporated

Although he was a rising star, Carlo Gambino had to bide his time patiently before he could make a play for real power in the Mangano family. Blocking his way to that power stood the menacing figure of Albert Anastasia, Vince Mangano's underboss and his principal muscle on the waterfront.

But, as Carlo Gambino knew, Albert Anastasia was much more than just Mangano's underboss. He was also the boss of a highly secret organization that came to be known, years later, as Murder Incorporated.

This enforcement arm had been established by Lucky Luciano in 1931 as a separate unit within La Cosa Nostra to carry out contract killings. It was not to be affiliated with any of the Cosa Nostra families. Designed to insulate the bosses of the families from murders, it was to have its own independent structure and personnel.

Luciano had chosen the Jewish labor racketeer, Louis Lepke, to run Murder Incorporated in tandem with Albert Anastasia. Working for Lepke and Anastasia would be a cadre of Italian and Jewish killers who would each be paid a salary of $200 a week as a retainer. These killers could not, in turn, work for anyone else. They were to be available at all times to carry out a contract murder. Their headquarters was a candy store in the Brownsville–East New York section of Brooklyn, Midnight Rose's, that remained open twenty-four hours a day. When a contract was made, one of the killers would be told who the victim would be, where he lived, and what his daily habits were. Then he would be sent to perform the hit under strict instructions to return to home base immediately after the deed was done.

Lucky Luciano was at the head of the chain of command. A boss would tell Luciano who he wanted hit, then Luciano would consult with Meyer Lansky and Frank Costello to receive their approval. If neither one objected, the contract would then be turned over to Louis Lepke or Albert Anastasia, who would select the killer and send him on his way.

Helping Lucky Luciano run Murder Incorporated gave Anastasia immense power in the underworld. By the late thirties he had become perhaps the most feared member of Cosa Nostra. People called him the "Mad Hatter," the "Earthquake," and the "Lord High Executioner."

Albert Anastasia was born in Calabria, the rugged mountainous toe of the Italian boot, famous for its *cinghiàle* hams and its *'ndrangheta*, a secret criminal society every bit as vicious as the Sicilian Mafia. He was brought to the United States as a child by his parents, along with his eight brothers. One of his brothers became a priest. Another, his younger brother Anthony, or "Tough Tony," became a labor leader, rising to become a vice president of the International Longshoremen's Association.

Albert Anastasia, a robust, barrel-chested, hirsute man of medium height with a dark complexion and curly black hair, was known for his rapid-fire, Cagneyesque speech, intimidating stare, and sheer brutality. It was said that his solution to almost every problem was homicide, and that he especially enjoyed killing with his bare hands.

Albert prided himself on being Vince Mangano's muscle on the Brooklyn waterfront. Contributing not a little to that muscle was Tough Tony Anastasio,* probably the most powerful man on the New York waterfront in the forties and fifties. Tony was not affiliated with any Cosa Nostra family. He was a legitimate union leader, vice president of the International Longshoremen's Association and head of Local 1814, the largest and most powerful waterfront local in Brooklyn. Though he was not, strictly speaking, in the mob, Tony derived considerable power from the fact that it was well known throughout the waterfront he was the brother of the feared Albert Anastasia.

The presence of the two Anastasia brothers on a Brooklyn dock would inspire terror in everyone around them. The dockworkers knew what happened to men who crossed an Anastasia. They knew that the strangled body of rebel Peter Panto had been found buried in a chicken yard in New Jersey, and that the body of another rebel had been found in an Ohio lime pit.

Picture the Anastasia brothers on a Brooklyn dock, a scene out of Marlon Brando's *On the Waterfront*. The ferocious Albert swaggering around, head up, chest out, barking out orders to a foreman in that machine-gun delivery of his, pleased with the look of terror on the dockworkers' faces. He is followed, a few paces behind, by his brother, Tough Tony, wear-

---

*Tough Tony spelled his surname Anastasio, perhaps to distance himself, in the public mind, from his murderous brother.

ing his trademark custom-made, wide-lapelled, double-breasted suit with white tie and white carnation. Tough Tony was known for his expensive wardrobe, flashy cars, and Broadway showgirl companions, all paid for by the toil of his waterfront slaves, who numbered in the thousands.

Meanwhile, as the Anastasias' power steadily increased, Meyer Lansky, now functioning as a financial consultant to the syndicate, made a daring move in Cuba. He journeyed to Havana, met with dictator Fulgencio Batista, and came away with gambling rights to the island. According to Lucky Luciano's autobiography, Lansky had to give Batista $3 million up front and guarantee him $3 million a year. The mob's penetration of the Caribbean had begun.

Lansky's success in Cuba came at a time when his closest associates in New York were beginning to suffer considerable pressure from law enforcement. In 1936 Albert Anastasia and the rest of the underworld were jolted by the successful prosecution of Lucky Luciano on charges brought against him by Thomas E. Dewey, special prosecutor for the state of New York. Luciano was sentenced to thirty to fifty years in prison for running a huge statewide prostitution ring. From his cell in Dannemora he continued running the affairs of his own crime family and those of Murder Incorporated.

Even though Luciano was able to function from Dannemora, it made the Anastasia brothers nervous to have him in prison. What could be done to free him? Finally, early in 1942, a few months after the United States entered World War II, the brothers hit upon a clever scheme. The U.S. Navy was concerned about the dangers of possible acts of sabotage against warships berthed at Brooklyn and Manhattan docks. Both the Navy and the police were fully aware that the mob controlled those docks. Cognizant of all of this, the Anastasia brothers hit upon the idea of making a deal with the Navy for the release of Luciano. In return for his release, the mob would guarantee the safety of the docks as far as the Navy's interests were concerned.

But how to get the Navy worried enough so it would fall for the idea?

Create a maritime disaster. This was the preposterous idea Tough Tony eventually hit upon according to Lucky Luciano's posthumous autobiography. Create a disaster on the docks that would shake up the Navy so much it would persuade the government to make a deal with the mob over Lucky Luciano.

Tony Anastasio was aware that over the past few months agents of naval intelligence had been scouting the Brooklyn and Manhattan waterfront looking for Italians and Germans who might be involved in a plot to sabotage Navy shipping.

Not only U.S. naval vessels were at risk, but also ships of Allied nations. One of these was the French luxury liner *Normandie*, which was being hastily converted into a troop transport and was docked at a Hudson River pier. The Anastasia brothers decided to sabotage the *Normandie*.

The fire that broke out the afternoon of February 9, 1942, was one of the most spectacular in New York City's history. For hours the mighty *Normandie* burned, until, listing heavily to port from all the water she had taken on, she finally capsized along the pier.

The destruction of the *Normandie* convulsed the Navy high command in Washington and prompted it to approach the mob, which it knew had absolute control over the New York waterfront. What the Navy wanted was a firm guarantee that there would be no sabotaging of shipping in New York Harbor.

After making a few discreet inquiries, the Navy was informed that only Lucky Luciano, then an inmate in Dannemora prison, had the authority to deliver such a guarantee.

What followed was a spectacular triumph for La Cosa Nostra. The U.S. government entered into a virtual alliance with the underworld to ensure the safety of naval shipping in New York Harbor—and later to ensure the cooperation of the Mafia in Sicily at the time of the Allied invasion of the island in June 1943.

As a reward for his "patriotic" support Luciano was transferred from maximum-security Dannemora prison to Great Meadow prison, a minimum-security facility. From Great Meadow, with its liberal visitors' policy, Luciano was able to resume effective control of the national crime syndicate and also help the United States' war effort. As it turned out, the successful Allied invasion of Sicily was made possible, in small part, by the cooperation of the Honored Society secured by Luciano. Luciano had told the Sicilian Mafia bosses that if they cooperated with the American invaders they would be rewarded by them, which they were. Several military commanders appointed Mafia bosses mayors of cities they liberated. Luciano received his final reward in February 1946, when he was released from prison and escorted to a ship docked in Brooklyn that would take him to permanent exile in Italy.

Meanwhile, Murder Incorporated had been discovered by the law, thanks to the testimony of one of its killers turned canary, Abe "Kid Twist" Reles, who began singing in 1940 about its atrocities in order to escape the electric chair. Reles, whose specialty was murder by ice pick, gave testimony that led the police to the solution of some forty murders. Soon other Murder Incorporated killers began talking to save their skins and the homicide count attributed to the organization went up and up. In the end it was estimated that Murder Incorporated had fulfilled from four hundred to five hundred contracts, perhaps many more.

The exposure of the activities of Murder Incorporated shocked New Yorkers as few crime stories in the city's history ever had. For weeks it was front page news. New Yorkers were horrified. But, thanks to the timely disappearances of key witnesses, law enforcement was never able to connect the organization to Cosa Nostra (which was known only to the law as "the combination" at the time), and so Lucky Luciano and Albert Anastasia were never implicated in its crimes.

By the end of the war, Albert Anastasia found himself stronger than ever. He and his brother had forced the government into freeing Lucky Luciano and Albert had survived the investigation of Murder Incorporated unscathed. In the streets of Brooklyn the name Anastasia was held in awe. Albert had become the most feared man in the city.

As Albert Anastasia's power grew, he began chafing under the rule of old Vince Mangano and his brother Philip. It was a vexing situation. The real, effective powers in the family were Anastasia, Joe Adonis, and Carlo Gambino, with Meyer Lansky dispensing advice from the sidelines. They were the big money-makers. All Vince and Phil Mangano did was confiscate the money they earned.

Vince Mangano sometimes became so enraged with his underboss that he would attack him physically. Albert, the younger man, would always get the best of him. An underboss beating up a boss was an unthinkable infraction of discipline, but it was Mangano who brought these humiliations on himself.

Anastasia had always been closer to Lucky Luciano and Frank Costello than he had been with his boss, Vince Mangano. Now, as hostilities between boss and underboss mounted, Anastasia began moving closer and closer to Frank Costello.

Lucky Luciano, Vito Genovese, and Frank Costello had taken over what was left of the old Masseria gang after the Castellammarese War. Luciano was then sent to prison in 1936. Two years later Vito Genovese fled to Italy to escape a murder charge brought against him by Luciano's nemesis, Thomas E. Dewey. That left Frank Costello acting boss of the family. Throughout the forties Costello consolidated his power, achieving a unique status in the underworld. He became La Cosa Nostra's chief politician, the mob's representative to the upperworld. As such he consorted with top politicians, police brass, leading bankers, and judges, earning in the process the sobriquet "Prime Minister of the Underworld."

Anastasia and Costello made a powerful pair. Their closeness was a source of constant irritation to Vince Mangano. Who did Albert think his boss was, Frank Costello?

Then something happened that profoundly affected the balance of power among Cosa Nostra bosses. Vito Genovese returned from his nine-year exile in Italy. Upon his return he immediately sought control of the family he, Luciano, and Costello had taken over following the Castellammarese War, trying to edge out acting boss Costello.

This had the effect of strengthening the Costello-Anastasia alliance, for Costello needed Anastasia's power now more than ever to counter the ambitions of Genovese.

As Anastasia drew closer and closer to Costello, Vince Mangano became more and more enraged at his underboss, berating him whenever he got a chance. Rumors began circulating that Mangano was out to kill Anastasia.

It was while this jockeying for power was going on that Frank Costello began to goad Anastasia into taking over the Mangano family. Costello needed Albert Anastasia, with an entire family behind him, as an ally against Genovese.

What happened next is still shrouded in mystery. On April 19, 1951, the body of Phil Mangano was found in a marshland near Sheepshead Bay. He had been shot three times in the back of the head and in both cheeks.

When the police went to find his brother they learned Vincent had disappeared. No one around the boss seemed to know where he was. A few days later he failed to show up at his brother's funeral. Weeks passed. Months. Vince Mangano remained missing.

When the belief finally sank in that both Phil and Vince Mangano had been murdered, the bosses held a sit-down in Manhattan to hear Albert Anastasia's explanation.

Albert told them he had learned that Mangano had been plotting against him. Costello backed up this contention. But Anastasia did not admit to killing the Mangano brothers. The meeting ended with the bosses ordaining Albert Anastasia as head of the Mangano family.

Returning to Brooklyn, Anastasia met with his top men and told them what had happened at the sit-down. He then made Frank Scalise and Joe Adonis his underbosses and beefed up *caporegime* Carlo Gambino's *borgàta*. With his brother in command of the New York waterfront, and with Frank Costello a close ally, Albert Anastasia was now on his way to becoming the most powerful Mafia boss in New York.

8

The Gottis of East New York

Less than a year after the rubout of the Mangano brothers, John Joseph Gotti moved his family from the South Bronx to an apartment in East New York, a tough working-class district bordering on Brooklyn's Brownsville section.

The Gotti family had moved to Brooklyn because John Joseph Gotti had landed a civil service job with the Sanitation Department and could therefore afford better housing for his family than that which he and Fannie had had to put up with in the South Bronx.

A fiefdom of Albert Anastasia, East New York was a lawless, brawling community so wide open that the rackets were conducted in the streets in full view of the public and the police.

In the Gottis' predominantly Italian and Jewish neighborhood, the streets were lined with pool halls, numbers joints, bars, card game parlors, bookie offices, whorehouses, and stores that openly fenced goods stolen from the waterfront. Interspersed among these houses of temptation were outdoor cafés and storefront social clubs with chairs and tables out on the sidewalks peopled by sleek, well-groomed men in double-breasted suits and fedoras known in the area as *gli amìci*, the friends. They were the men of Albert Anastasia.

At first the Gottis had moved to a two-story house in Brooklyn's Sheepshead Bay district, not far from Coney Island and the ocean. But soon they were forced out by a developer who planned to tear down all the houses on their block to erect a high-rise apartment building.

By the time the Gotti family moved to East New York Fannie Gotti had produced five more sons: John, Jr., Carmine, Vincent, Gene, and Richard. John Gotti, Jr., born on October 27, 1940, was twelve at the time of the move. The boy had had a troubled childhood. He had grown up in a family so poor that an item of clothing was considered almost a luxury. As a child Gotti went about in shorts and an undershirt. On a construction worker's meager pay the Gotti family lived on a near subsistence economy. There was only enough money around for rent, electricity, food, and drink. More often than not, meals consisted solely of pasta, cheese, and fruit. Meat was a luxury to be tasted only once a week. Whether this life of deprivation was at the root of young John Gotti's problems is open to speculation. All we know is that troubled he most surely was.

New York *Daily News* reporters, Gene Mustain and Jerry Capeci, researched Gotti's youth in detail for their 1989 book, *Mob Star: The Story of John Gotti*. At P.S. 113 in the South Bronx, young Gotti had impressed his teachers as having an uncontrollable temper; he seemed to be in a constant rage. He would react violently to the older boys who tried to extract dimes and quarters from him for "protection," slugging it out with them in the hallways of the school. At

P.S. 209 in Sheepshead Bay, Gotti soon acquired a reputation for being a kid you wouldn't cross. He was continually getting into fistfights. A teacher at his junior high, P.S. 178 in East New York, remembers Gotti as a bright boy who always seemed enraged over something and who easily dominated his schoolmates. Once P.S. 178 had to suspend him briefly for fracturing a fellow student's skull in a fight.

What contact did this tough, troubled young kid have with the world he would one day lead? We can be certain that from his earliest years Gotti was able to observe the *amìci*, the Men of Respect, at close range. When he was growing up in the South Bronx he and his brothers would often go down to Italian East Harlem, where Sicilian and southern Italian immigrants had created a Little Italy in an attempt to duplicate the communities they had left behind. There, along with the espresso bars, the *salumerie*, and the outdoor stands of fruit and vegetables and fish, he could not have escaped the Palma Boys Club, the most important storefront social club in East Harlem, the place where the biggest mobsters hung out. There on chairs scattered along the sidewalk young Gotti was able to observe prosperous-looking men in expensive tailor-made suits with wide lapels wearing wide-brimmed black fedoras and bright shiny shoes. They wore diamond rings on their pinky fingers and drove big black gleaming new cars. They were men of apparent leisure. Gotti must have wondered why these men of the rackets looked so at ease and so well off while his poor father labored long, hard hours on the construction gangs for such meager rewards.

Since he was alert to what was going on around him, Gotti, at the age of eleven, could not have failed to take note of the big Mafia boss, Frank Costello, whose defiant face was on the front page of every newspaper in the country in connection with the sensational Kefauver Senate Committee hearings on organized crime. He could have also seen the mobster's fidgeting hands on television, for the Kefauver hearings were televised nationally and could have been watched in the bars of East Harlem and East New York. Costello, the star of the show, had insisted that his face not appear on the screen. So the cameras focused exclusively on his hands, prompting endless comment in the press on Costello's "hand ballet."

When he reached East New York at the age of twelve and began hanging around with some of the street gangs on Livonia Avenue, young John Gotti heard talk of the legendary Lucky Luciano and the current Lord of Brooklyn, Albert Anastasia, and his brother, Tough Tony of the docks. He was guided to one of the social clubs where one could gawk at the *amici* in all their glory, sipping espresso and talking business in the morning. There they were in their flashy double-breasted pin-striped suits and gleaming stiletto shoes, their sleek new cars double-parked out in front of the club.

Young Gotti was dazzled by these lieutenants of the all-powerful Anastasia. He watched them take huge bankrolls out of their pockets, watched them swagger down the streets receiving bows from passersby, watched them usher beautiful Manhattan showgirls into their shiny new cars.

He was also fascinated by the stories he had heard on the street about Anastasia's Murder Incorporated and its hired killers, Abe "Kid Twist" Reles, Vito "Chicken Head" Gurino, and Frank "the Dasher" Abbandando. Their headquarters, Midnight Rose's Candy Store, was on the boundary between East New York and Brownsville and Gotti and his new pals would go there to hang out and act tough.

By the time John Gotti dropped out of P.S. 178 at the age of sixteen, the mighty Anastasia had become his idol, the man on whom he wanted to model his own life. The year was 1956 and Albert Anastasia was at the summit of his power.

While at P.S. 178 John Gotti had joined a street gang called The Fulton-Rockaway Boys, recruited by his older brother Peter. One of the members was a fat chatterbox of a boy, Angelo "Quack Quack" Ruggiero, who became Gotti's close friend and a partner in his future crimes.

The Brooklyn street gangs at the time were dedicated to petty thievery and the defense of their local turf. Clashes with other gangs, called "rumbles," could occur if a member of a gang invaded a rival gang's territory without obtaining permission, or if, per *l'amor di dio*, a gang tried to make a *score* on a rival's turf.

John Gotti, at sixteen, took to the street gang life with gusto. Aware that street gangs were training grounds for the big time—joining one of the five Mafia families—Gotti worked hard and eventually attracted the attention of a made man from no less than the family of Albert Anastasia.

Starting out with the Fulton-Rockaway Boys as a bookmaker and collector for one of the gang's loan sharks, Gotti soon acquired the reputation of a no-nonsense guy who got things done.

One day in the spring of 1957, after he had been rebuked by a debtor upon making an attempt to collect on a loan, he became so enraged that he went to the club where the debtor was known to play cards, burst in unannounced, overturned the table on which the debtor and his friends were playing poker, and beat him into a bloody pulp. A riot ensued, the cops were called, and Gotti was arrested for disorderly conduct, the first of his many arrests as a young street gang punk.

The incident came to the attention of a soldier in Anastasia's family, one Angelo Bruno, who was looking for someone of Gotti's caliber. He needed a tough young man who knew how to be brutal when the moment demanded drastic action. Bruno began giving Gotti and his gang odd jobs, and he promised he would introduce him to his capo, the man who bossed East New York for Albert Anastasia, Carmine "Charlie Wagons" Fatico.

For young Gotti meeting, and favorably impressing, one of Anastasia's top lieutenants would be a decisive event in his life. It would open the door to his eventual conquest of the family.

9

The Plot to Kill Anastasia

With the Manganos eliminated, Albert Anastasia and his triumvirate of Frank Scalise, Joe Adonis, and Carlo Gambino worked to take charge of the rackets formerly controlled by Vince Mangano. Chief of these were certain areas of the Brooklyn waterfront where Mangano's influence had been both strong and exclusive. It wasn't long before Albert and his men, working in tandem with Tough Tony Anastasio, were in virtual control of all the docks of New York: more than three hundred deep-water berths and forty thousand longshoremen. This meant that Anastasia's crime family controlled the point of entry for the vast majority of imports entering the United States in the 1950s. It also meant that Anastasia could import illegal substances, like heroin, with impunity. The opportunities for making money under this dispensation were limitless.

Although Albert Anastasia relished his new power,

it soon began to go to his head, leading him to underestimate the ambitions of the other bosses in New York, and some of the men in his own family.

What was the state of the New York underworld in 1951, twenty years after Lucky Luciano had established the national crime syndicate?

Luciano was living in Italy, to which he had been deported by the U.S. government in 1946. He maintained his headquarters and home in Naples and remained in close touch, by courier, with his chief allies in the States, Frank Costello and Meyer Lansky.

In October 1946 Luciano took the risk of traveling to Cuba to preside over a huge convention he had called of syndicate bosses in Havana. It was a risk because under terms of his deportation order he was not to leave Italy. Among the delegates who showed up in Havana were Vito Genovese, Joe Adonis, Albert Anastasia, Frank Costello, Tommy Lucchese, Joe Bonanno, Joe Profaci, Tony Accardo, Carlos Marcello, and Santos Trafficante, and the Fischetti brothers with Frank Sinatra in tow. Meyer Lansky also showed up, as a nonvoting associate. Among the items on the agenda were the division of the casino gambling spoils and the establishment of new routes to facilitate the importation of hard drugs from Europe into the United States. It is said that during the meeting the bosses became alarmed over Anastasia's excessive greed.

Although Dictator Fulgencio Batista had been forced to step down in 1944, largely due to pressure from President Franklin Roosevelt, he nevertheless remained the de facto boss of the island nation, even though he was often compelled to give out orders from temporary exile in Miami. Because of the alliance Meyer Lansky had struck with Batista in the thirties, Havana was considered a safe place to hold a Mafia summit.

However, the mob summit was discovered by agents of the Federal Bureau of Narcotics, and

Bureau Chief Harry Anslinger moved to exert pressure on the Cuban government to deport Luciano back to Italy. But since Batista was still being "greased" by Luciano and Lansky, the caretaker government, still taking orders from Batista, did nothing about it. Finally news of Luciano's presence in Havana broke in the New York papers and the State Department, responding to the public outcry, persuaded the Cuban government to deport Luciano. By the end of April Lucky was back in Italy.

The five New York families established by Maranzano and reorganized by Luciano were now coexisting quite peacefully. By 1951, Vito Genovese had taken control of the Luciano family, having edged aside Frank Costello. Tommy "Three-Finger Brown" Lucchese ran his own family in Manhattan, specializing in garment district rackets. The huge borough of Brooklyn was divided up into three families: two small ones run by Joe Profaci and Joe Bonanno, respectively, and the largest one, with interests also in Manhattan, run by Albert Anastasia.

Although relative peace between the five families prevailed, Vito Genovese, anxious to become boss of bosses, was looking for new worlds to conquer. This led Frank Costello and Albert Anastasia to draw closer together. With the ferocious Vito Genovese on the rampage, no one was entirely safe.

Then came the Kefauver Committee hearings on organized crime in interstate commerce. Held in fourteen cities, the hearings brought Frank Costello's large, beefy face onto page one of every newspaper in the country and his fidgeting hands onto every television screen. Because Costello had a certain flair, wore expensive tailor-made clothes, and because the press had labeled him the "Prime Minister of the Underworld," Costello became the focus of Senator Kefauver's traveling committee hearings in both New Orleans, where Costello operated thousands of slot machines, and New York. The experience was disastrous for Costello, causing more erosion of his power within the Luciano family and ultimately leading to his prosecution by the government for contempt of the U.S. Senate. The contempt charge had arisen over Costello's repeated refusal to answer questions from Kefauver Committee counsel. Convicted on the charges, Costello was sentenced in the summer of 1952 to eighteen months in jail.

Having such a loyal and powerful ally as Costello in prison was unsettling to Albert Anastasia, who did not disguise his fear of Vito Genovese. The people around Anastasia sensed the boss was under pressure, as he began throwing more tantrums than ever. Then Albert did something that led some to believe he was going off the deep end.

The story was told to the McClellan Senate Committee on organized crime by Genovese soldier Joe Valachi in September 1963.

Albert Anastasia was watching television at home one evening in April 1953 when, as part of a newscast, he saw a young Brooklyn clothing salesman, Arnold Schuster, being congratulated for notifying the police he had just seen notorious bank robber at large Willie Sutton on a Brooklyn street. The notification led to Sutton's arrest and Schuster became an instant hero.

As Anastasia watched Schuster being congratulated by top police brass on television, he went into one of his famed rages. Leaping to his feet in front of his set, he yelled "I hate squealers!" then ordered one of his hired guns, Frederick "Chappy" Tenuto, to hit Arnold Schuster. A few days later Tenuto shot the young salesman to death as he was walking home.

The murder outraged the city. There were calls for a crackdown on the mob. In fact, the Schuster murder went against one of the Mafia's own cardinal rules: Kill only for good reason; never kill out of caprice. That Anastasia broke that rule led some to believe he was losing his grip. Anastasia's blood lust seemed boundless. Aware that Tenuto was the only person who could tie him to the murder, he called for Tenuto to come to his office and promptly killed him.

It was an unstable time. Upon Costello's release from prison on October 29, 1953, Vito Genovese immediately began plotting against him. He began spreading the word throughout the underworld that because of the massive publicity he had received during the Kefauver hearings, Costello was now too hot. It would only be a matter of time before the feds would expand their investigation of Costello to the family he worked for. Something had to be done.

Around this time, the power-hungry, conniving Genovese heard rumors that Albert Anastasia and his underboss, Frank Scalise, were committing serious infractions of the Cosa Nostra code by selling memberships in the Cosa Nostra for $50,000 each. The Commission had recently decided to open the books, closed since 1931, and initiate a limited number of new applicants. Anastasia and Scalise had hit on the Commission's decision as a way to make some quick, easy money. Rumor had it they had already sold a hundred new memberships, netting a cool $5 million. The code of Cosa Nostra expressly forbade selling memberships. Outraged over these infractions, Genovese let it be known among his intimates that something also had to be done about Scalise and Anastasia.

By 1956 Albert Anastasia was feeling more uneasy than ever over what was happening in his world. According to his intelligence sources, Vito Genovese was planning a move against him, Scalise, and Costello. He was beginning to feel vulnerable. Then, suddenly, he lost Joe Adonis.

For years the government had been trying to deport Adonis without success. Joe was too well connected. Then, finally, in 1956, the Immigration and Naturalization Service succeeded, and Adonis was dispatched to Italy. Losing Adonis was a blow for

Anastasia. It had been Adonis who, through his friends in high places, had been keeping away the heat.

Not long after Joe Adonis was shipped off to Italy, Vito Genovese called a meeting of the Commission and announced that Frank Costello would be dropped from the body. Since he could no longer be considered capo of the Luciano family, Genovese having assumed that position, Costello no longer had any right to sit on the Commission.

Genovese's decision greatly increased Anastasia's sense of vulnerability. He opposed the move vehemently. But the other bosses all agreed Costello had to go. Finally Anastasia had to acquiesce. He did so with extreme reluctance. He was losing his strongest ally on the Commission.

Anastasia continued to stick by Costello, meeting him secretly from time to time. Eventually Genovese learned of the meetings and concluded that Costello and Anastasia were plotting against him.

Despite his ouster from Cosa Nostra's supreme court, Frank Costello continued going about his business, which meant making a lot of money out of a lot of rackets, especially casino gambling in Havana and Las Vegas. Then, without warning, something happened that shook the underworld to its foundations and made front page headlines across the nation. Frank Costello was shot in the head in the lobby of his apartment building. He was not killed. He was only slightly wounded; the bullet had grazed his scalp.

Given Vito Genovese's recent action against Costello, Albert Anastasia suspected Genovese was also behind the attempt to kill Costello. If it was true that Genovese was behind it, then it meant no one was safe.

As it turned out, Anastasia was correct in his suspicions. Six years later Genovese soldier turned informant Joe Valachi told the McClellan Committee in

Washington that Genovese had indeed ordered the hit on Costello. Selected to carry out the murder was Genovese soldier Vincent "The Chin" Gigante, a hulking ex-boxer, known for his eccentricities, who went on to take control of the Genovese family in 1987 upon the conviction of its boss, Fat Tony Salerno, and who still runs the family today.

It was now clear to the powers in the New York underworld that Genovese would not rest until he had eliminated all opposition to his rule. Who would be next?

Albert Anastasia was taking no chances. He had abandoned his house in Brooklyn and was now living in a huge fortified mansion surrounded by a high wrought-iron fence in Fort Lee, overlooking the Hudson, not far from the George Washington Bridge. Here he lived and conducted his business, rarely venturing into the city.

Who would be next? To Albert Anastasia's rage and horror, it was his underboss, Frank Scalise. Scalise was buying fruit one day in a large Italian market on Arthur Avenue in the Bronx when his killer came up to him and pumped four bullets into his neck and head. Although the murder was never solved, it is believed it was carried out by Genovese soldier Jimmy Squillante on orders from his boss.

It has long been a practice in the Mafia to eliminate a family's underboss before going after the boss himself. Albert Anastasia, well aware of this, became more reclusive than ever, rarely venturing from his fortress on the cliffs of Fort Lee, with its spiked iron fence and pack of ferocious Dobermans roaming the grounds. He also let it be known that he planned to avenge the shootings of Costello and Scalise.

Anastasia had every reason to be apprehensive. Not long after the murder of Scalise, the plotting against him began in earnest.

In a sense, the plot to kill Albert Anastasia had been unfolding for the past three years. The deposing from the Commission and attempted murder of Frank Costello had been part of it. The greed for profits off drugs and casino gambling he had expressed at the Havana summit of 1946 had also been a part of it. As had been the rubout of Frank Scalise. Vito Genovese had acted shrewdly and deliberately. First you have to kill off your enemy's friends before you go after *him*.

With Joe Adonis deported and Frank Scalise dead, Carlo Gambino emerged as Anastasia's second in command. Wealthy, talented, ambitious, Gambino at fifty-five was ripe for the top job himself. Vito Genovese knew this. In fact, for the past three years Genovese had been cultivating Gambino, meeting with him secretly from time to time.

Albert Anastasia was about the same age as Carlo Gambino. A robust man, Anastasia looked after his health. Barring an act of God, he still had quite a few good years ahead of him. By tradition a Mafia boss retains his position until his death. That left little room for the ambition of Carlo Gambino.

Gradually, with the quiet cunning of an Iago, Vito Genovese insinuated himself into the consciousness of Gambino, slowly leading him to believe that the only way he could ever become boss of his family would be by eliminating Albert Anastasia.

To justify the murder of Anastasia, the sixty-year-old Genovese listed wrongdoings that he planned to bring to the attention of the Commission after Anastasia was gone: the capricious murder of Arnold Schuster; the selling of Cosa Nostra memberships; evidence that Anastasia was trying to muscle in on other bosses' rackets, especially in Havana; Anastasia's attempt to monopolize the entire New York waterfront; and Anastasia's vow to avenge the shootings of Costello and Scalise.

Finally, to clinch his argument, Genovese assured Gambino he would fully support his ordination as boss at a meeting of the Commission he planned to hold after Anastasia's demise.

Carlo Gambino pondered Genovese's arguments, then came up with an assassination plan that would insulate himself and Genovese from the commission of the crime. He would approach his old friend Joe Profaci, boss of one of the lesser Brooklyn families and a man who detested Anastasia, and see if he would accept the job of arranging for Anastasia's end. Genovese gave his blessing. Profaci then accepted and gave the murder contract to three of his wildest killers, the Gallo brothers: Crazy Joe, Louie, and Kid Blast.

Albert Anastasia did not journey into Manhattan very often from his Fort Lee bastion, but it was well known in the underworld that when he did, he always stopped at his favorite barbershop in the Hotel Park Sheraton at Seventh Avenue and Fifty-fifth Street for a trim and a shave. He liked the whole ritual of the hot and cold towels. It relaxed him.

When, at 10:15 A.M. on October 25, 1957, Anastasia arrived at the Park Sheraton barbershop, the Gallo brothers were waiting for him in the lobby near the entrance to the barbershop. Patiently they waited for the burly mobster to hang up his coat, hat, and jacket and settle into the barber's chair. Then, when the barber cranked the chair back and laid a hot towel over Anastasia's face, covering his eyes, two of them entered the shop from the hotel lobby and, setting upon Anastasia from the rear, blew the boss out of the barber's chair with five shots to his head and back. With some life still in him, Anastasia lunged at his killers' reflection in the mirror, then collapsed on the floor in a pool of blood.

Word of Anastasia's execution spread quickly throughout the underworld. In the cafés and social clubs of East New York Anastasia's men were stunned. It was inconceivable that the mighty Lord of Brooklyn had been brought down. One of Anastasia's most trusted *caporegimes*, Aniello Dellacroce, vowed he would find out who was behind the killing and take revenge.

Among the Anastasia loyalists who were most affected by the murder was seventeen-year-old John Gotti, who was hoping to join Anastasia's family one day. Anastasia had been his idol. It is said that he had even begun to strut like Anastasia, glare like him, and copy the rapid-fire staccato of his speech. Now his hero was gone. Who could replace such a titan? Would it be Aniello Dellacroce, Paul Castellano, Joe Biondo, Carlo Gambino? Soon all East New York was speculating on that question.

Part IV

Building an Empire of Crime

The Rule of Don Carlo (1957–1976)

> *The Prince of Darkness is a gentleman.*
>
> *Shakespeare,*
> KING LEAR

10

Fiasco at Apalachin

On the morning of November 14, 1957, Carlo Gambino, and four of his men, including his cousin and brother-in-law, Paul Castellano, got into a Chrysler Imperial and drove toward upstate New York, bound for the estate of Joseph Barbara, near the village of Apalachin in the western part of the state.

Gambino and his men were driving north to attend what promised to be the largest Cosa Nostra sit-down in history, a meeting of nearly one hundred bosses, underbosses, *caporegimes*, and labor union officials called by Vito Genovese to settle the most pressing issues facing La Cosa Nostra at the time.

One of the issues to be settled was the question of who was going to succeed Albert Anastasia as boss of the crime family he had led since the disappearance of Vince Mangano six years before. Was Carlo Gambino going to be Albert's successor? Vito Genovese had already assured him he would, and he had the support of the other bosses.

There were other issues to be discussed at the sit-down besides the anointing of Carlo Gambino. Vito Genovese and other top bosses had agreed on an agenda a week or so before the meeting was to be held, which was then communicated to the other leading conferees. The agenda was first publicly revealed by Genovese soldier Joseph Valachi during the McClellan Committee hearings of September 1963. Later, in 1979, the House Select Committee on Assassinations added some fresh new information, based on FBI wiretaps, to Valachi's testimony.

There were to be four major items on the agenda. The most pressing would be concerned with the violence over the past six months resulting in changes of leadership. The bosses were worried about the apparent breakdown of discipline among the New York families. They wanted explanations for the shooting of Frank Costello in May, the killing of Frank Scalise in July, and the murder of Albert Anastasia in October. They wanted to discuss the question of who was going to succeed Anastasia as boss of his family.

The second item on the agenda was to be a discussion of Cosa Nostra membership. Membership rolls were to be pruned. Dead wood had to be cleared out. And those who had paid fees to Anastasia and Scalise for initiation into the brotherhood were to be excluded and the practice of selling memberships condemned.

A third item had to do with Cosa Nostra policy on drugs. In 1956 Congress had passed the Narcotics Control Act, which took effect on July 1, 1957. The new legislation made it a federal offense to deal in drugs and facilitated the arrest of high-level heroin importers. In view of this new federal pressure the bosses wanted to discuss the possibility of prohibiting Cosa Nostra families from trafficking in drugs.

A fourth item on the agenda had to do with various labor problems in New York and Pennsylvania;

specifically, policy was to be laid down on how to deal with nonunion labor that threatened the jobs of unionized labor under Cosa Nostra control.

A fifth, undeclared item was going to be raised by Vito Genovese himself. He was going to crown himself boss of all bosses, the title Salvatore Maranzano had created and Lucky Luciano had subsequently abolished. For the egomaniacal Genovese, this was the principal reason for the conference.

As it turned out, the delegates to the Apalachin convention were prevented from formally considering this agenda by the New York State Police.

The meeting was to be held at the 150-acre hilltop estate of Joseph Barbara, a *caporegime* in Stefano Magaddino's crime family headquartered in Buffalo. Born in Castellammare, Barbara had been a follower of Salvatore Maranzano and was close to fellow Castellammarese Joseph Bonanno, boss of one of the Brooklyn families. Barbara had grown wealthy as a soft drink distributor in upstate New York, having secured exclusive franchises through his underworld connections.

Other high-level Cosa Nostra meetings had been held at Joe Barbara's place, as recently as 1956. The isolated hilltop estate was considered safe since it was Joe Barbara's practice to take good care of the police.

However, according to Joseph Bonanno's 1980 autobiography, the police of late had been getting greedy and Barbara had reacted by cutting down on his handouts. Bonanno believed this was why the police decided to raid Barbara's estate during the Cosa Nostra conclave.

Whether Barbara's holding back payments to the police was in fact behind the disruption of the Cosa Nostra conclave at Apalachin is not known. The state trooper who led the raid on the Barbara estate, Sergeant Edgar G. Croswell, gave a different reason for the raid in his testimony before the McClellan Committee in 1959. He said that quite by accident he was in a local motel when he noticed Joe Barbara's son, Joseph, Jr., making reservations for three rooms on November 13 and 14, telling the clerk that he did not know who was going to occupy the rooms, and asking for the room keys in advance.

Then, on the evening of the thirteenth, Croswell went back to the motel and found that a car belonging to Cleveland boss John Scalish was parked outside. Earlier, other state troopers had observed several expensive-looking cars with out-of-state plates driving up to the Barbara estate. Suspicious that some sort of underworld meeting was about to take place, Sergeant Croswell decided to pay a visit to the Barbara estate the following day.

When shortly after noon the troopers converged on the estate, the conferees were all outdoors standing around a huge barbecue pit. Big thick steaks flown in from the Armour Company in Chicago were sizzling on the grill. First the mobsters would have lunch alfresco, then they would get down to business inside.

Milling around the barbecue pit and standing in clusters near the garage were some of the most powerful and vicious Cosa Nostra leaders in the nation. There was Sam Giancana from Chicago; Frank de Simone from California; Joseph Civello from Dallas; John Scalish from Cleveland; Gerardo Catena and Frank Majuri from New Jersey; Santos Trafficante, Jr., from Tampa and Havana; and Carlo Gambino, Joseph Profaci, Tommy Lucchese, and Vito Genovese from New York.

Gambino and Paul Castellano had driven up to the convention with three ranking men in the family Carlo hoped to lead: *caporegime* Carmine "The Doctor" Lombardozzi, soldier Salvatore Chiri, and Joe Riccobono, a candidate for the position of *consiglière*. Since it was already well known among the conferees that Vito Genovese was going to crown Carlo boss after lunch, Gambino was treated with special deference. As he and his men stood by the barbecue pit, mobsters from other parts of the country kept coming up to him to pay their respects.

When the troopers arrived at the estate, a sprawling ranch-style house in brown and gray stone, they found ten cars parked in front of the main house and over twenty-five parked near a barn. Many of them had out-of-state plates. Immediately the troopers began taking down license numbers. As they were making their rounds, they observed a group of men talking near a garage. All of them were wearing expensive-looking dark suits, shirts with jeweled cuff links, and shiny black shoes, not the sort of dress one would expect to find in such rural surroundings. It was at this point that the troopers heard a female voice shouting from a window: "Hey, there's the state troopers, the troopers are here!" It was Mrs. Barbara warning the guests.

Immediately pandemonium broke out. Some mobsters fled to their cars. Others found refuge in a barn. Others took off through the woods and fields.

Thinking quickly, Sergeant Croswell ran to his car with another trooper and, tearing down the hill, established a roadblock and checkpoint on Route 17 near the intersection of the road leading up to the Barbara estate.

The occupant of the first car they stopped was Vito Genovese. Then came Santos Trafficante, Jr., Joe Profaci, Gerardo Catena, Frank de Simone, Joe Civello, and Carlo Gambino, with his driver Paul Castellano.

In all, fifty-eight of the conferees were detained, identified, and questioned, including a prominent businessman from Buffalo and an attorney from California. The state troopers not only checked driver's licenses, they also inspected the contents of wallets. The fifty-eight detainees were found to be carrying a combined total of around $300,000 in cash on them, or around $5,200 apiece.

Among those who escaped detection was Sam Giancana, who had fled through the woods, tearing his silk suit on brambles and thorns, and Carmine "The Cigar" Galante, boss of the Bonanno family, who had also taken to the woods. Frank Costello did not attend, nor did his ally in New Orleans, Carlos Marcello. Also noticeably absent were invitees Meyer Lansky and his Las Vegas associate, Joseph "Doc" Stacher.

Eventually twenty-seven of the conferees were indicted on obstruction of justice charges, and twenty of these including Paul Castellano, were convicted for refusing to tell law enforcement authorities what the meeting was all about. As a consequence of his refusal to talk, Castellano was sent to prison for a year.

The debacle at Apalachin proved to be a fiasco of enormous magnitude for La Cosa Nostra. The day after the event, news of the abortive "gangland" conference made front page headlines across the nation. The mob was held up to public embarrassment on a scale never seen before or since. The incident also brought about increased heat from the Justice Department. Sergeant Croswell had given the feds their greatest intelligence breakthrough concerning the leadership of organized crime. Soon all the bosses would be feeling stepped-up pressure from the Justice Department.

And so Carlo Gambino, Paul Castellano, and the other men who had accompanied them to Apalachin returned to Brooklyn empty-handed. The promised ordination had been aborted. Carlo would return to Brooklyn not in victory, but in limbo.

Vito Genovese and his men also returned to New York. Genovese returned not from his coronation as boss of all bosses, but from a humiliating roadblock of the New York State Police. Throughout the underworld the great Genovese had become an immediate laughingstock, a disgrace. Apalachin would prove to be the beginning of his decline, as others who felt threatened by him seized upon his momentary weakness to begin plotting against him.

11

The Crowning of Carlo Gambino

Though seriously hampered, Vito Genovese was still not without power. Once back at his head-quarters in New York, he promptly called for a sit-down of the New York families to discuss the agenda he had planned to present to the conferees at Apalachin.

Genovese conducted the meeting briskly and the bosses, underbosses, and *consiglièri*, actual and future, came to quick and firm decisions.

There would be no dealing in drugs. Any member of a family caught dealing in drugs would face death without trial. The decree had nothing to do with morality, and everything to do with expediency. The new Narcotics Control Act was in effect. If Cosa Nostra got involved with the international heroin trade, it could bring the full weight of the federal government down upon it. This had to be avoided at all cost.

As for the question of Cosa Nostra memberships, the rolls were to be temporarily closed and all those who had paid for their initiations had to renounce their places.

The New York bosses adopted a tough stance on nonunion labor. If nonunion labor threatened to undercut unionized labor controlled by Cosa Nostra, warnings would be issued to the leaders, and if they were ignored, executions would follow.

On the matter of Albert Anastasia's murder and who would succeed him as boss, Vito Genovese explained that Anastasia was getting too reckless and powerful and had come to pose a threat to all the other families. He had killed out of caprice. He had sold memberships to Cosa Nostra. He had encroached on another boss's territory—that of Santos Trafficante, Jr.—in Florida and Havana. And he had become too powerful on the waterfront, virtually monopolizing the waterfront rackets. Genovese then told the bosses that Carlo Gambino would be the new capo of the family formerly led by Anastasia. Carlo was then approved by acclamation and Genovese also appointed him to the Commission. From now on, Gambino would be known as Don Carlo.

Carlo Gambino, at fifty-seven, had finally realized the ambition he had formed as a young mafioso in Palermo thirty-seven years before. Returning to Brooklyn, Gambino made *caporegime* Joe Biondo his underboss; Joe Riccobono his *consiglière;* and his brother, Paul Gambino, and cousin, Paul Castellano, *caporegimes.* Together they would build the crime family they inherited from Anastasia into the largest and most powerful one in the United States.

Gambino at the time was a fifty-seven-year-old father of three sons, Thomas, Joseph, and Carl, and a daughter, Phyllis. He had sent Thomas off to prep school at New York Military Academy at Cornwall-

on-Hudson, near West Point, where he had mingled
with future leaders of the upperworld, and had then
arranged for him to marry Frances Lucchese, the
daughter of fellow Cosa Nostra boss Tommy
Lucchese, who had attended the Sacred Heart
Convent School at Ninety-first Street in Manhattan.
Joseph and Carl he put to work in the garment center
and Phyllis married a well-known New York physician. From all accounts, Carlo remained the devoted
husband to his wife and first cousin, Kathryn, and a
model family man.

Carlo Gambino had risen to power with the aid of
Vito Genovese, but had never felt comfortable with
him. Vito was ambitious and treacherous. He could
not be trusted. Not long after his investiture as boss,
Carlo began plotting against him.

It is conceivable that Carlo Gambino had already
begun plotting against Genovese even before the
Apalachin debacle. In fact, a good case could be
made that Gambino and others—Frank Costello,
Meyer Lansky—had conspired to sabotage the
Apalachin conclave in order to bring about the downfall of Genovese.

The reasoning went something like this: Why didn't
invitees Frank Costello, Carlos Marcello, Meyer
Lansky, and Joseph "Doc" Stacher, a Lansky associate, show up? Answer: Because they knew the conclave would be raided and didn't want their names
taken down by the police. How did they know the
meeting would be raided? Because they, in concert
with Carlo Gambino, planned the police raid themselves.

Such has been the speculation of those who have
studied the Apalachin conclave and its aftermath in
some depth.

Vito Genovese calls a conference to have himself
crowned boss of bosses. His enemies then tip off the
New York State Police about the meeting to sabotage
Genovese's plans. Consider who did not show up at

the conference: Frank Costello, a sworn enemy of Genovese whom Genovese had tried to kill. Carlos Marcello, Costello's partner in crime in Louisiana. Meyer Lansky, close ally of the exiled Luciano and of Frank Costello and Carlos Marcello. Doc Stacher, Lansky's man in Las Vegas and an ally of Luciano and Costello. Given the loyalties of these nonattendees at Apalachin, the theory of their conspiring to undermine Genovese by sabotaging his convention begins to appear plausible. But what of Carlo Gambino? Why should he have risked his name being taken down by the state troopers by participating in a plot to tip off the troopers in order to ruin Genovese, even considering that Genovese was going to crown Carlo Gambino a boss at the conference? Answer: It was worth the risk to ensure the undermining of Genovese. Almost *anything* was worth the risk if it would diminish Genovese's power and curb his ambitions.

But the wounding of Genovese's prestige at Apalachin was only the beginning. Once he took control of Anastasia's family, Carlo Gambino began plotting the total ruin of the man who had been so instrumental to his advance.

First, however, Carlo had to deal with two former Anastasia loyalists, John "Johnny Roberts" Robilotto, a *caporegime* under Anastasia, and Armand "Tommy" Rava, a soldier in his crew. Both had been overheard muttering things about avenging Anastasia's murder. When Gambino learned of their intentions, he acted coolly and deliberately. Johnny Roberts was shot four times in the head in the East Flatbush section of Brooklyn. Two weeks later Tommy Rava received eighteen bullets while playing cards in a Brooklyn social club. According to Joe Valachi's Senate testimony, "Everything was peaceful after that."

Turning his attention back to Genovese, the wily Gambino entered into a conspiracy with Frank Costello, Meyer Lansky, and Lucky Luciano to get

Genovese involved in a multimillion-dollar international heroin smuggling operation which would be conveniently discovered by the feds. Even though Genovese had outlawed all drug trafficking in La Cosa Nostra under penalty of death, he, the self-styled boss of bosses, evidently felt himself exempt from the stricture. How Gambino, Lansky, Costello, and Luciano set Genovese up was explained by Lucky Luciano in his autobiography, which may or may not represent the whole truth.

A minor Puerto Rican hoodlum, Nelson Cantellops, was serving time on a narcotics charge in Sing Sing. He had worked for both Sam Giancana and Meyer Lansky and was known to Carlo Gambino.

Gambino proposed that Cantellops be bribed to testify that he had been a witness to Vito Genovese making buys of large quantities of heroin. Luciano, Costello, and Lansky accepted the plan and pledged $50,000 toward the bribe. Gambino then kicked in another $50,000. Cantellops accepted the $100,000 and agreed to testify against Genovese. "We had to grease him pretty good," wrote Luciano in his autobiography.

An anonymous tip was then transmitted to the New York Narcotics Bureau that Nelson Cantellops was willing to make a trade with the government. He would be willing to testify in court that he saw Vito Genovese buying large shipments of "junk" in return for a suspended sentence and release from Sing Sing.

The Narcotics Bureau had suspected Genovese was heavily involved in drug trafficking but could never get anything on him. Genovese was so feared in the underworld that no one would dare risk testifying against him. The bureau decided to take a chance on Cantellops and he then delivered enough reliable information to warrant an indictment against Genovese and others. In 1958 Genovese and twenty-four of his confederates were arrested for violation of the new Narcotics Control Act.

Nelson Cantellops was the star witness at the 1959 federal trial. He testified he was an eyewitness to Genovese and his associates making many buys. On the basis of Cantellops's testimony, all were convicted.

Genovese was sentenced to fifteen years in a federal prison. This was enough to finish him off for good. He died in prison ten years later.

With the Anastasia loyalists silenced and Vito Genovese removed from the scene, Don Carlo was free to operate unchallenged. Fifteen years of rule as a family boss now lay before him.

12

Kennedy, Hoover,
and Gambino

No sooner had Carlo Gambino consolidated his
hold on Anastasia's family than a president was
elected who had sworn to destroy people like him
and rid the nation of the scourge of organized crime.

"We have only one rule around here," Senator John
F. Kennedy had declared at a McClellan Committee
hearing in 1959. "If they're crooks, we don't wound
'em, we kill 'em." Later, John Kennedy's brother,
Robert, upon taking office in 1961 as attorney general of the United States, stated, "If we do not, on a
national scale, attack organized criminals with
weapons and techniques as effective as their own
they will destroy us."

The Kennedy brothers' remarks represented a new
attitude toward organized crime on the part of the
executive branch of the U.S. government. Before the
Kennedys' accession to power, presidents and attorneys general did not place high priority on fighting

organized crime. Harry Truman had even opposed the Kefauver Committee's investigation and Eisenhower did not encourage the McClellan Committee's investigation. Part of the blame for this oversight lay in a general lack of public awareness of the power, even the existence, of organized crime in the United States. Until the fifties most Americans, let alone those who ran the federal government, had no idea such a thing as the Mafia existed.

A good deal of blame for why the federal government remained ignorant of the Mafia for so long can be laid on the peculiar mind-set of the man who directed the FBI since 1924, J. Edgar Hoover. For reasons that will be explored later, J. Edgar Hoover's private and public position on the Mafia was that it did not exist.

Not even the discovery of the Apalachin conclave of November 1957 persuaded Hoover that organized crime existed. His reaction to news of the conclave remains the classic example of the director's attitude toward organized crime.

In the wake of the Apalachin revelations Deputy FBI Director William Sullivan and his assistant, Charles Peck, drew up a report on the conclave and the known activities and affiliations of most of its attendees. Twenty-five numbered copies were printed up and distributed to the top twenty-five law enforcement officials in the government. Upon reading his own copy, Hoover ordered all copies recalled and destroyed, telling Sullivan the report was "baloney." The report was never mentioned at FBI headquarters again.

It wasn't until the Valachi Senate hearings of September 1963 that Hoover finally had to admit publicly that such a thing as organized crime did, in fact, exist. But even then he refused to call it the Mafia. Joe Valachi, in his Senate testimony, had called it Cosa Nostra, "Our Thing." The Cosa Nostra would translate into La Cosa Nostra, the acronym for which would be LCN. Hoover felt comfortable with this little acronym. It did not smack of the hated words "organized crime" and "Mafia." From October 1963 on, he would have the FBI use the term in all its dispatches having to do with organized crime, as in "LCN hoodlum Carlo Gambino" or "LCN meeting at La Stella restaurant."

As might be expected, there was no meeting of minds whatsoever between the thirty-five-year-old Attorney General Robert Kennedy and his subordinate in the Justice Department, the sixty-six-year-old FBI Director J. Edgar Hoover, regarding policy on organized crime. While Kennedy wanted to launch the most massive attack on organized crime in the nation's history, his FBI director, who was supposed to lead the attack, refused to believe organized crime even existed.

Despite his FBI director's obtuseness, Robert Kennedy went ahead with his promised campaign. He and his aides in the Justice Department drew up a list of forty priority targets among Cosa Nostra bosses, underbosses, and mob-influenced labor union leaders. Topping the list was Teamsters President Jimmy Hoffa. Then came Louisiana boss Carlos Marcello, followed by Florida boss Santos Trafficante, Jr., Chicago boss Sam Giancana, and Philadelphia boss Angelo Bruno. Carlo Gambino was somewhere in the middle of the list.

During the first year of Kennedy's war against organized crime, 121 mob defendants were indicted and 73 convicted of various crimes. By the end of 1962, 350 had been indicted and 138 convicted. And by the end of 1963, 615 had been indicted and 288 convicted. Clearly Kennedy's campaign was a success. For the first time in its history organized crime was on the run.

FBI electronic surveillance of various Cosa Nostra leaders throughout the nation initiated by Kennedy in 1962 revealed that Robert Kennedy's pressure was causing the mob considerable grief. On May 2, 1962, two members of the Profaci crime family in Brooklyn, Michelino Clemente and Sal Profaci, were taped complaining about the Kennedy crackdown.

CLEMENTE: Bob Kennedy won't stop today until he puts us all in jail all over the country. Until the Commission meets and puts its foot down things will be at a standstill. When we meet, we all got to shake hands, and sit down and talk, and, if there is any trouble with a regime, it's got to be kept secret.

On February 17, 1962, the FBI picked up a conversation between Angelo Bruno, boss of the Philadelphia family, and two in-laws and associates, Mario and Peter Maggio.

MAGGIO: . . . Kennedy is going to leave, they are going to make a special assistant to the president out of him. They want him out of the way, he is too much, he is starting to hurt too many people, like unions. He is not only hurting the racket guys, but others, antitrust . . . I think that he is going to leave. But the only reason he won't leave, which I heard before, you see he wants Edgar Hoover out. . . .
BRUNO: Edgar Hoover?
MAGGIO: He wants Edgar Hoover out of the FBI because he is a fairy, you know he is a fairy. . . .
BRUNO: Who?
MAGGIO: Edgar Hoover is a fairy. . . .
BRUNO: Who would ever listen to that bullshit?

On February 8, 1962, Angelo Bruno and a business associate, Willie Weisburg, were taped discussing the Kennedys.

WEISBURG: See what Kennedy done. With a Kennedy, a guy should take a knife, like one of them other guys, and stab and kill the fucker, where he is now. Someone should kill the fucker. I mean it. This is true. Honest to God. It's about time to go. But I'll tell you something. I hope I get a week's notice. I'll kill. Right in the fuckin' White House. Somebody's got to get rid of this fucker.

In May 1963, the FBI finally got around to eavesdropping on members of the Gambino family. The surveillance was a direct result of an assault by a young Gambino associate on an FBI agent.

In April the father of one of Carlo Gambino's most valuable capos, Carmine "The Doctor" Lombardozzi, the family's principal Wall Street operative and financial adviser, died, and the mob turned out in full force for his funeral and wake in Brooklyn. As usual for such events, several FBI agents were assigned to cover the wake and funeral and to take down names and license plate numbers and observe the family's ritualistic demonstrations of respect. As the funeral cortege was entering the church, two young men, one of whom, Danny Marino, was a relative of the Lombardozzis, suddenly broke from the cortege and attacked one of the agents who was carrying an attaché case fitted with a hidden camera. The agent, John Foley, was knocked down and was severely kicked and beaten as he lay on the sidewalk in front of the church.

The unprecedented assault—it is a rule of La Cosa Nostra that members are never to attack FBI agents—brought about an apparent conversion to belief in the existence of organized crime on the part of Hoover and a flurry of electronic surveillance of Gambino family members.

In early May 1963 an FBI wiretap picked up a conversation between Pete Ferrara, a Gambino capo, and Mike Scandifia, an acting capo.

SCANDIFIA: Well, I would say, right now, they [the

FBI] are giving you the zing. Actually what it boils down to, they're looking to use a stick. But now we'll go on midnight raids. We'll do this, we'll do that, we'll do the other thing. You're a captain. You belong to Carl's family. They want to get you.

FERRARA: Well, previous to that he [the FBI agent] hands me Carlo's picture. "You know him?" he asks. "Sure I know him," I said. "How long you know him?" "I know him twenty, thirty years."

SCANDIFIA: They didn't expect you to say nothin'.

FERRARA: He says, "Can you tell us anything about him?" I said, "The only thing I could tell you about him is that he is a businessman, been in business all his life. Brought up four kids. They had a good education. They're all in business. They all went to college and married a profession." I said, "What else could you ask for? He's got a nice family."

See what they fuckin' do. They want to get a message through. There's no question about it.

SCANDIFIA: They want to put the heat on you, me.

FERRARA: Yeah.

SCANDIFIA: And they call them "Captains." One guy said "Foreman." And the other guy said "Capo Regina." I mean they're going right to each head.

FERRARA: [Referring to the fact that his daughter is a nun and the FBI threatened to embarrass her about her father at her convent] What are they going to embarrass me for? What can they do? Go up there?

SCANDIFIA: Well, God forbid! They can't, fuckin' they can't throw her out.

FERRARA: No.

SCANDIFIA: [Referring to one of Albert Anastasia's brothers, who was a priest] They couldn't throw Albert's brother out. How are they going to throw her out?

FERRARA: Nah, they can't throw her out.

SCANDIFIA: Embarrassment, that your daughter is a nun. I mean, Jesus Christ! It's supposed to be an honor.

FERRARA: They can't do nothin'. They won't do nothin'.

SCANDIFIA: Dirty bastards. Now that they bring out everything, Pete, the Cosa Nostra is a wide-open thing.

FERRARA: Yeah.

SCANDIFIA: It's an open book.

FERRARA: It's an open book.

News of the FBI's interrogation of the two Gambino capos traveled fast in the underworld. A week later, on May 20, Angelo Bruno, the boss of the Philadelphia mob, was overheard by an electronic listening device mentioning it at a meeting with Joe Magliocco, a *caporegime* in the Profaci family, and two cousins, Peter and Salvatore Maggio.

BRUNO: They [the FBI] went to Carlo and named all his capos to him and named Joe Biondo as his underboss and Joe Riccobono as his *consiglière*.

MAGLIOCCO: Yeah?

FERRARA: The FBI asked him: "Did you change the laws in your family, that you could hit FBI men, punch and kick them? Well, this is the test, that if you change the laws, and now you are going to hit FBI men, every time we pick up one of your people we are going to break their heads for them."

And, really, they picked up our guy, they almost killed him, the FBI. They don't do that, you know. But they picked up one of his fellows and crippled him. They said: "This is an example. Now, the next time anyone lays a hand on an FBI man, that's just a warning. There's nothing else we have got to tell you." And they went away.

Then, about two weeks later, on June 3, an FBI listening device picked up a brief conversation between Stefano Magaddino, boss of the Buffalo Cosa Nostra family, and two of his aides, that alluded to the FBI's recent interrogation of Carlo Gambino.

MAGADDINO: They know everyone's name. They know who's boss. They know who is on the Commission. They know *amici nostro*.

    They asked [Gambino]: "What was your *caporegime* doing here? What did he come to tell you?"

    To Carlo Gambino they said: "This is your underboss, this is your *caporegime*, this is your *consiglière*."

UNKNOWN MALE: They talk as if they belonged.

If it had not been for the incident at the Lombardozzi funeral, the FBI would probably not have brought much heat on the Gambino family, for Justice Department records disclose that during Robert Kennedy's brief term as attorney general the FBI did not pursue Carlo Gambino to any significant extent, despite Kennedy's having identified him as a priority target in his war on organized crime.

Curiously, FBI records show that Attorney General Kennedy seemed to be more concerned about the incestuous marriages in the Gambino blood family than he was about Carlo's criminal activities. It had been brought to his attention that Carlo Gambino had married his Castellano first cousin, the daughter of his mother's sister, and that there had been other marriages between first cousins among the Gambinos and Castellanos in Brooklyn and Palermo. As a practicing Catholic, young Kennedy was appalled by these incestuous unions, which violated the doctrine of his church, and directed the FBI to inform the Archdiocese of New York about them. That, and the brief flurry of activity over the Lombardozzi incident, was about the extent of the heat brought on Gambino by the FBI during the Kennedy administration.

But Gambino was not alone among the bosses in escaping FBI pressure during the Kennedy years. In 1979 the House Select Committee on Assassinations established that the FBI had failed to adequately investigate Kennedy's number two priority target, Carlos Marcello, boss of Louisiana and Texas, even though Kennedy had specifically urged Hoover to step up his investigation of the Gulf Coast chieftain.

What might have been behind the FBI's failure to carry out Robert Kennedy's directives in regard to the investigations of Gambino and Marcello?

Was there a reason why J. Edgar Hoover had shied away from going after these two powerful bosses? Had someone put in the fix with no less a power than the head of the FBI?

In recent years it has come to light that, in all probability, someone high in La Cosa Nostra brotherhood had indeed neutralized J. Edgar Hoover and kept him from turning the heat on some of his friends. He was Frank Costello.

The genial and outwardly gentlemanly Costello had functioned as the mob's principal fixer throughout the forties and fifties until Vincent "The Chin" Gigante, on orders from Vito Genovese, creased his scalp with a bullet in May 1957. After that close call the Prime Minister of the Underworld went into semi-retirement at his Sands Point estate on Long Island, which was next to the opulent Falaise, the estate of Harry Guggenheim, president of the Guggenheim Museum and founding owner of the newspaper *Newsday*. Semi-retirement, because he still held court in the Waldorf-Astoria several mornings a week, arranging deals and settling disputes among mobsters and politicians until his death in 1973.

Among Costello's closest allies in the mob were Carlo Gambino and Carlos Marcello. Costello had helped Gambino frame the hated Genovese on a narcotics charge, sending him away to prison for what turned out to be the rest of his life. Costello enjoyed an equally friendly relationship with Marcello, for, after Costello's slot machines were banned in New York by Mayor Fiorello La Guardia, they found a friendly and profitable home in Louisiana with the cooperation of Marcello. Another ally of Costello's was FBI Director J. Edgar Hoover.

Many reasons have been advanced to explain J. Edgar Hoover's self-induced blind spot in regard to organized crime. Hoover knew organized crime had grown immensely prosperous during Prohibition and was therefore in a position to buy cops, politicians, even judges and police commissioners at will. He did not want to subject his agents to that kind of corruption. He wanted to keep them free of mob entanglements so they could concentrate on going after Hoover's favorite domestic enemy, the Communists; the "commies" and "pinkos" didn't have enough money to corrupt his men. Hoover was very publicity-conscious and was always striving to improve his image as a fearless "G-Man" before the Congress, which appropriated funds for the FBI every year. He therefore went after criminals not affiliated with organized crime whose spectacular captures would make front page headlines in the papers. Criminals described in those days as "Public Enemy Number One" included John Dillinger, Pretty Boy Floyd, and Baby Face Nelson. On his retirement from the number two job at the bureau, William Sullivan wrote in his memoirs, "The whole of the FBI's main thrust was not investigation but public relations and propaganda designed to glorify its director."

These reasons notwithstanding, there remains the disconcerting fact that J. Edgar Hoover, director of the FBI, and Frank Costello, the so-called Prime Minister of the Underworld, were friends and met often in Washington and New York.

For years there had been rumors of a Costello-Hoover relationship. People had reported sighting the two together on a bench in Central Park, in the lobby of the Waldorf-Astoria, and at the track. That the relationship did, in fact, exist was confirmed to me in an interview with William G. Hundley, former head of the Organized Crime and Racketeering section of the Justice Department under Attorney General Kennedy.

When Hundley was in New York he used to stay at the apartment of his friend the noted attorney Edward Bennett Williams, who was Frank Costello's principal counsel. One day in the early fifties Hundley and Williams were having breakfast together when in came Frank Costello. Over coffee Hundley confronted Costello with the rumors he had heard that he and J. Edgar Hoover were friends and had met frequently throughout the years. Costello was happy to oblige. In the hoarse, gravelly voice he had made famous during the Kefauver hearings, Costello launched into a series of anecdotes and stories about his encounters with Hoover that Hundley believed sounded too complicated and authentic to be invented over morning coffee.

Costello told Hundley that whenever Hoover came to New York the two would often meet. Sometimes it would be at a mutual friend's apartment, sometimes on a bench in Central Park. Costello led Hundley to believe that he and the FBI director had reached a mutual understanding, an "entente," over "business," which meant that if Costello did Hoover an occasional favor, Hoover would reciprocate as best he could.

But what favors could Costello do for the director of the FBI outside of giving him information on the underworld, which Costello would never do? (He had even refused to identify Vincent "The Chin" Gigante to the police as his attacker after his attempted murder.) As banal as it may seem, what Costello could do for

Hoover was give him hot and reliable tips on the horses. J. Edgar loved the track and was an inveterate bettor on the races. When William Hundley asked Costello if it was true that he and Hoover often went to the track together, Costello laughed and exclaimed: "The *horse* races! You'll never know how many races I had to fix for those lousy ten-dollar bets of Hoover's."

William Sullivan has testified to Hoover's penchant for betting on the horses. He wrote in his memoirs that it amounted to a veritable addiction. To protect his image he would allow himself to be photographed by the press placing bets at the $2 window while agents who had accompanied him to the track placed his real bets at the $100 window.

But how did Frank Costello get his tips on the "sure" races and how was he able to transmit them to Hoover? According to sources close to the intrigue, the pipeline ran from top bookmaker Frank Erickson, who knew which races were fixed, to gossip columnist Walter Winchell, who passed them on to his good friend Frank Costello, who passed them on to J. Edgar Hoover. Erickson's tips never failed. They were a source of much joy and satisfaction to the harried, and addicted, director of the FBI.

Though publicly professing an ignorance of the very existence of organized crime, J. Edgar Hoover had to have been fully aware of his friend Frank Costello's close relationship with New York boss Carlo Gambino and New Orleans boss Carlos Marcello.

Would Hoover countenance the idea of jeopardizing his huge advantage at the track, of risking the satisfaction of his primary addiction, by going after the friends of his benefactor, Frank Costello? Not for a minute.

And so Carlo Gambino was spared intensive pressure from Hoover's FBI during the Kennedy administration. Only when one of the director's agents was beaten up by a Gambino hotblood did he take any action against the family, and that action would have been tacitly condoned by both Gambino and Costello, since the assault of the FBI agent had been a violation of the code of La Cosa Nostra.

And thus, too, was Costello's close ally in New Orleans, Carlos Marcello, spared FBI investigation during the short-lived Kennedy administration. Herein, however, larger issues lie, since in 1979 a committee of the U.S. Congress, the Select Committee on Assassinations, concluded, after a two-year reinvestigation of the assassination of President Kennedy, that the most likely Mafia boss to have participated in a unilateral plan to kill the president (without Commission approval) was Carlos Marcello.

As it turned out, the assassination of President Kennedy effectively neutralized the power of his brother, the attorney general. When, after an interval of two months, Robert Kennedy returned to his office in the Justice Department, he found himself cold-shouldered by President Johnson and ignored by J. Edgar Hoover; the director would not even return his calls.

As a consequence, Kennedy's war on organized crime began to wind down. Without the power of the presidency behind him and without the cooperation of his FBI director below him, Kennedy's crusade lost momentum rapidly and soon ran out of steam. Before long it would be business as usual for the mob, as bosses like Carlo Gambino and Carlos Marcello, who would rise to be number one and two in the national Cosa Nostra hierarchy, set about building their crime empires into enormous conglomerates with annual takes in the billions.

13

Gambino Incorporated

L'appetito viene mangiando.
NEAPOLITAN PROVERB

On March 5, 1963, three thousand longshoremen lined the Brooklyn waterfront to pay their last respects to Anthony "Tough Tony" Anastasio, as the forty-eight cars in his funeral procession drove slowly past the docks on the way to the high requiem mass at St. Stephen's Church.

Eight thousand Brooklyn dockworkers had showed up for work that windy, mist-shrouded morning, but out of respect for the most powerful International Longshoremen's Association leader in the history of the New York waterfront they did not labor at any tasks.

When the funeral cortege, with its eleven flower cars, reached the vicinity of the church, it passed through a corridor of several hundred dockers, heads bowed, lining both sides of the street. The funeral mass was said by Tough Tony's brother, Father Salvatore Anastasia. Among the six hundred mourners cramming the church—leading politicians, high union officials, relatives, and in-laws—was Tough Tony's engaging twenty-nine-year-old son-in-law, Anthony "Young Tony" Scotto, who would soon inherit the New York waterfront and become a *caporegime* in the crime family bossed by Carlo Gambino.

Gambino had not found Tough Tony to be as cooperative as he would have liked after the murder of his brother, Albert, in the barbershop of the Park Sheraton Hotel. Tony, suspicious that Gambino had been behind his brother's murder, had withheld from Gambino substantial sums of money derived from his waterfront rackets. And so, when Carlo took over Anastasia's family after Apalachin, he did not immediately receive the waterfront as a legacy. But with the passing of Tough Tony and the accession of Scotto to power, he would finally win control of the most lucrative arena of labor racketeering in New York.

When Anthony Scotto took over Local 1814 and was elected a vice president of the sixteen-thousand-member ILA, he was a handsome six-foot-two thirty-one-year-old with a political science degree from Brooklyn College, who was known for his charm and intelligence. Carlo Gambino was delighted to have someone of his class in his organization.

Carlo was further delighted when Scotto began ingratiating himself with some of the nation's leading politicians. He was pleased with newspaper accounts of Young Tony conferring with New York's Mayor John V. Lindsay at City Hall and with President Lyndon B. Johnson in the White House. These high-level contacts augured well for all of Carlo's criminal operations.

The New York waterfront was but one of the big prizes Carlo Gambino acquired in the sixties. With all the vigor, ambition, and intelligence of a CEO of a vast multinational corporate empire, Gambino forged ahead throughout the decade to assemble the richest and most diversified crime conglomerate in U.S. history.

The prizes to be won in this exercise of sustained empire building ranged from air cargo theft at JFK International Airport to private garbage disposal throughout the five boroughs of New York, from securities markets fraud on Wall Street to major construction projects in Manhattan, from heroin smuggling out of Sicily to trucking and loan-sharking operations in Manhattan's garment district.

By the mid-1960s, Carlo Gambino was devoting more and more attention to the illicit moneymaking opportunities offered by the John F. Kennedy International Airport in Queens. The huge airport had begun to replace the waterfront as the principal entryway for foreign imports into the country. It has been estimated that by 1966 from $20 billion to $30 billion worth of goods was arriving at JFK per year. Air freight had become big business.

From his experience with the waterfront, Carlo Gambino quickly realized that to make big money at Kennedy he first had to take control of the unions that handled the unloading of cargo from the planes and the trucking of that cargo out of the airport.

Local 295 of the International Brotherhood of Teamsters, representing fifteen hundred cargo handlers, controlled the loading and unloading of air freight at JFK, and the National Association of Air Freight handled the trucking of that freight in and out of the airport. If Gambino could gain control of the leaders of these organizations, he could hijack air cargoes at will.

For years the Teamsters had been the most corrupt labor union in the United States. In the fifties Teamsters President Dave Beck was found guilty of grand larceny—he had helped himself to $370,000 in union pension funds—and tax evasion, and was sent to prison. Beck's successor, Jimmy Hoffa, was found by the McClellan Committee in 1959 to be in close association with two powerful Lucchese family *caporegimes*, Anthony "Tony Ducks" Corallo and John "Johnny Dio" Dioguardi. When Robert Kennedy became attorney general in 1961, he named Hoffa as his number one target in his war on organized crime and, during the course of the Justice Department's successful prosecution of the Teamsters chief for fraud and jury tampering, discovered more links between Hoffa and the mob. Hoffa's successor, Frank Fitzsimmons, proved even more corrupt than Hoffa, if that was possible. Under Fitzsimmons's presidency the infamous boss of Local 560, Anthony "Tony Pro" Provenzano, flourished, the man whom the Justice Department believes was responsible for the mysterious disappearance of Jimmy Hoffa in 1975. During Provenzano's trial for extortion in 1966, witnesses testified that no truckload of cargo could pass through New Jersey without Tony Pro's approval.

The first of the New York bosses to gain a foothold in Teamsters Local 295 and the National Association of Air Freight at JFK International Airport was Carlo Gambino's good friend, and father-in-law to his son, Tommy Lucchese, working through his powerful *caporegimes* Tony Ducks Corallo and John Dioguardi. Soon Lucchese was cutting his friend Carlo in on the action, and when Lucchese died of a brain tumor in 1967, Kennedy Airport became one of Gambino's most lucrative theaters of criminal operations.

How does a Cosa Nostra family make money off air cargo operations at an airport? The same way it makes money on the waterfront. It corrupts the unions handling the loading, unloading, and trucking of the cargoes. Kickbacks to shop stewards and foremen make them look the other way when bribes are offered to "spotters"—cargo handlers who would locate valuable shipments—and truck drivers, who would divert a load of valuable goods to a family hijacker or directly to a fence. The fence, in turn, would pay forty percent of the value of a shipment received to the family and would then sell the goods to legitimate businesses at prices they couldn't refuse.

In addition to air shipments of durable goods Gambino also dealt in shipments of stocks and bonds coming into JFK by mail and pouch. Gambino's spotters would identify a promising consignment of securities, and a bribed cargo handler would then get hold of the shipment and pass it on to a bribed trucker, who would then deliver it to one of Gambino's men. Eventually the shipment would end up in the hands of Gambino *caporegime* Carmine "The Doctor" Lombardozzi, one of whose most valued specialties was fencing stolen securities.

It has long been myth about the Mafia that the big bosses did not deal in hard drugs. Mario Puzo's 1969 novel *The Godfather* and its film adaptation helped publicize the myth, as did Joe Bonanno's 1980 autobiography, *A Man of Honor*. But the truth is that La Cosa Nostra families have been active in the drug trade since the late forties and Carlo Gambino was in the thick of it. The bosses may have banned their family underlings from dealing in drugs, under penalty of "death without trial," but the ban did not apply to the bosses themselves.

Federal investigators have concluded that Lucky Luciano, while in exile, got Gambino involved in bigtime heroin smuggling. Luciano had realized that the appetite of Americans for illegal drugs would probably exceed that for illegal alcohol during Prohibition.

The manufacture of heroin base from poppy seeds imported from the Middle East had been a cottage industry in Sicily for some time. On a trip to Sicily from his Neapolitan exile, Luciano concluded that it would not be difficult to obtain considerable quantities of poppy seeds from Turkey and to process them into heroin in Sicily and in certain pharmaceutical firms in northern Italy that manufactured morphine for medicinal use. Getting the finished product to the States would be the easiest phase of the venture.

Summoned by Luciano, Carlo Gambino took the risk of journeying to Palermo in 1948 to discuss with Luciano and others the importation of heroin from Sicily into the United States. The trip was risky for Gambino, since, as an illegal alien subject to deportation, if his presence in Sicily was discovered, he might never be able to return to the States again.

Traveling from New York to Canada with his brother Paul, Gambino took a freighter from Toronto to Palermo, met Luciano as planned, and agreed to help Luciano export heroin to New York. Later Gambino put his underboss, Joseph "Joe Banty" Biondo, in charge of his heroin-smuggling operation. Federal investigators believe that Gambino's heroin trade became his second most lucrative business after gambling. Cargo hijacking operations on the waterfront and at Kennedy Airport ranked third in profitability.

But there were scores of other businesses, licit and illicit, in Carlo Gambino's constantly expanding empire.

There were the garment district rackets, among others. By the mid-sixties, seventy percent of all clothing sold in the country was designed and manufactured in a seven-block area of midtown Manhattan. Vast fortunes were being won and lost in this crowded, frenzied maelstrom of humming factories, frantic executives, jammed showrooms, and side streets congested with double-parked tractor-trailer trucks, vans, and hundreds of hand-pushed racks of clothes.

How does a Cosa Nostra family make money off the garment district? Again, primarily through control of the labor unions involved in the manufacture and trucking of wearing apparel. Carlo Gambino's son, Thomas, had, as we know, married Tommy Lucchese's daughter, Frances. When Lucchese took control of the Teamsters locals operating in the garment district, he made his son-in-law, Thomas Gambino, a vice president of one of his trucking firms, Consolidated Carrier Corporation, the largest in the district. With this foothold, it was only a matter of time before Carlo would extend his hegemony over other trucking operations in the garment center. Until he pleaded guilty to restraint of trade in a case brought against him by the Manhattan District Attorney in 1992, Thomas owned the six largest trucking companies doing business in the garment district and was reputed by the Manhattan District Attorney's office to possess a personal fortune of approximately $100 million.

Other rackets, other businesses. According to the grand jury testimony of New Jersey Cosa Nostra boss Samuel DeCavalcante, Carlo Gambino had by 1965 acquired total control of all private garbage disposal in New York City and was expanding into the suburbs of New Jersey, and Westchester and Nassau counties. On Wall Street, Gambino put his trusty lieutenant Carmine "The Doctor" Lombardozzi in charge of securities theft and stock price manipulation, rackets that earned his family millions no matter how the stock market was behaving. Then there were such mob staples as loan-sharking, alien smuggling (from Sicily), pornography distribution, topless bars (where a $12 glass of "champagne" consisted of one part sparkling wine and three parts water), monopolization of vending machine distribution, and contract murder.

In the less profitable realm of legitimate business, Gambino gained a lucrative foothold in Castro Convertibles furniture (exclusive control of mattresses used in Castro beds, and the trucking of Castro furniture from factory to showroom to retail outlets), Pride Meat Supermarkets (run by his cousin and brother-in-law, Paul Castellano), fuel oil trucking, pizza parlor equipment concerns, meat packing companies—the list was endless. So adept at business did Gambino become that he was persuaded to go into partnership with two consultants, Henry Saltzstein and George Schiller, to form Saltzstein, Gambino, and Schiller, SGS Associates, consultants to private enterprise, especially in the field of labor relations. Gambino's fees began at $40,000 a consultation.

All of this far-flung, intricate, and dangerous business was overseen by one quiet, unprepossessing man of modest habits, an uneducated illegal alien, aided by an underboss, a counselor, twenty-four *caporegimes*, and crews, some numbering as many as one hundred soldiers. In all, around four thousand people worked for Gambino, of whom no more than four hundred were "made" members of La Cosa Nostra. The rest were associates, mostly businessmen and union officials who were not strictly speaking members of the family. Unlike the highly organized high-tech business corporations of today, the Gambinos did their business with limited use of the telephone and without computers, files, records, or even bank accounts. Theirs were largely cash businesses and the fewer the records of transactions, the better. And yet the businesses were taking in billions a year.

It had taken Carlo Gambino twenty-eight years as a subordinate and twelve as a boss to put together this vast American rackets empire, and yet he had never graduated from high school (Liceo in Sicily), gone to college, become an American citizen, or even mastered the English language. (He preferred to speak in Sicilian dialect.) It was a journalistic cliché in his day, but nonetheless valid, that had Gambino obtained the rudiments of an education and entered legitimate business, he could have soared to the summit of corporate America and enjoyed a career worthy of a Rockefeller or a Getty.

But could he have? Wouldn't the fact that he was a Sicilian have militated against his advancement in a business world dominated by WASPs? Was not the great engine of Carlo Gambino's ambition fueled by his *opposition* to the WASP establishment? Hadn't the dynamic of that ever-present opposition been at least partially responsible for goading him on to the relentless acquisition of more, and more, and more?

What is curious about Don Carlo's phenomenal career is that he did not seem ruthlessly aggressive enough to have achieved what he did. By all accounts, Carlo Gambino remained an essentially mild-mannered, quiet, courteous man, helpful to his neighbors, generous with advice and financial assistance, disdainful of show and ostentation, and much devoted to his wife, Kathryn, and their four children.

By 1971, at the age of sixty, Carlo Gambino was a slim man of medium height who walked with a slight stoop and spoke English, not Italian, with a lisp. His preferred Italian was a Sicilian dialect that would be all but incomprehensible to a Florentine or a Venetian. Antique Sicilian poetry was his favorite reading. He was unfailingly soft-spoken and mannerly and people often referred to him as kind. He had some strange mannerisms. Noticing that he seemed to be constantly nodding his head during conversation, people called him "the nodding don." As he grew older, his large Pinocchio nose came to dominate his thinning face more and more as it hooked down over the upper lip of his perpetual smile. People meeting Gambino for the first time were always struck by his smile. They likened it to a mask and to the proverbial inscrutable smile on the face of Leonardo's *Mona Lisa*. It was a smile that said nothing in particular. It was just there, always there.

Gambino's personality mystified the other Mafia bosses. They continually misread him. In his 1980 autobiography, Joseph Bonanno had this to say about him:

> He was not a warrior. Given a choice he avoided violence. He was a squirrel of a man, a servile and cringing individual. When Anastasia was alive, Albert used to use Gambino as his gopher, to go on errands for him. I once saw Albert get so angry at Carlo for bungling a simple assignment that Albert raised his hand and almost slapped him. In my tradition, a slap on the face is tantamount to a mortal offense. Another man would have not tolerated such a public humiliation. Carlo responded with a fawning grin.

Joseph Cantalupo, former Colombo soldier turned government informant, once worked as a secretary and notary for Gambino. Gambino struck him as "a small, deceptively mild-mannered man" who one would think would be incapable of wielding great power.

"Gambino, unlike Colombo," Cantalupo said, "was very low-key, very quiet, and very private. He didn't wear a lot of rings like Colombo, or drive a flashy Cadillac, and he wore inexpensive suits." Although he was utterly ruthless, capable of ordering the killing of a man by simply nodding his head, he was unfailingly courteous in the presence of others.

Law enforcement officials were well aware of Carlo's deceptively mild exterior. Albert Seedman, chief of detectives of the New York Police, once said of him, "Gambino was like the hog snake, which rolls over and plays dead until the trouble passes."

What very few people were able to perceive in Gambino were the deep wells of cunning, guile, and murderous ambition that lay beneath his perpetual smile and gentle manner. Gambino's most formidable weapon in his long climb to power was not muscle, but brains, not bluster, but *furberìa*, an Italian word meaning a wary cleverness, a slyness, the astuteness of one who figures out all the angles before he makes a move.

14

Luciano in Exile

Carlo Gambino may have become the most powerful Mafia boss in New York, but until Lucky Luciano's death in 1962, Luciano remained the ultimate boss of organized crime in America, even though he was living in exile in Italy.

It will be recalled that in 1946 the government granted Luciano his freedom as a reward for his assuring the safety of naval vessels on the mob-controlled New York waterfront during World War II and getting the Mafia in Sicily to cooperate with the Allies in their invasion of Nazi-held Sicily in 1943.

After the war Luciano was released from prison and deported to Italy. Boarding the Liberty ship USS *Laura Keene* in Brooklyn on February 9, 1946, he was given a lavish send-off by his fellow mobsters. According to Luciano's autobiography, Meyer Lansky and Frank Costello threw big farewell parties for him. Among those who came aboard ship to wish him well were Carlo Gambino, Albert Anastasia, and Tommy Lucchese. Luciano's bon voyage envelope contained $165,000 in cash.

Luciano had been exiled to his native village in Sicily, a dusty, poverty-stricken place inland from Palermo called Lercara Friddi. Although welcomed there by the mayor and the villagers as a hero, Luciano soon outgrew his stay and appealed to the authorities to be given permission to live on the mainland. Somehow he managed to get himself transferred to Rome, where he holed up for a while in the expensive Hotel Excelsior on Via Veneto. In the end he wound up in Naples, living in splendor in a luxurious penthouse apartment on a hill overlooking the vast, shimmering expanse of Naples Bay.

Naples was still reeling from World War II when Luciano arrived. The masts of sunken ships still poked up above the harbor waters. Many buildings near the waterfront were still in ruins. There were shortages of everything. A huge black market had sprung up in a maze of narrow alleys in Vecchia Napoli, known as La Forcella. The city was ripe for someone like Lucky Luciano who knew how to profit from shortages.

I had occasion to meet Lucky Luciano when I was a naval officer with the U.S. Sixth Fleet in the Mediterranean. I was then navigator of an auxiliary and we used to put into Naples regularly between fleet exercises.

At the time I had no idea "Looky," as the Neapolitans pronounced his name, had been the father of organized crime as it came to be structured in the United States. I knew only that he was a deported New York gangster who owned an American-style restaurant in Naples called the California, where you could get a genuine cheeseburger with Heinz tomato ketchup. To those of us on liberty in Naples, Luciano was just one of many deported Italian mobsters scrounging around the city trying to make a buck off U.S. military personnel, who had access to the local gold mine, the PX.

Later I learned that Luciano had positioned himself as the chief middleman between the PX and the huge, burgeoning black market in Naples. It was he who had bought the radios, cameras, phonographs, cigarettes, and whiskey from the military that we would see spread out for sale over the cobblestoned alleys of La Forcella.

Later, when I returned to Naples to study Italian history on a Fulbright scholarship, I felt grateful, in a way, to Lucky Luciano. Since I no longer enjoyed PX privileges, La Forcella was the only place in Naples where I could buy such indispensables as Colgate toothpaste, Listerine, and a bottle of Jack Daniels.

Naples was an exciting city in the mid-fifties. The nightmare of the war was ten years in the past, and the city and its charming environs, spurred by infusions of Marshall Plan funds, had been recovering at a rapid pace. The bombed-out Palazzo Reale and Teàtro San Carlo had been restored to their former glory. Destroyed factories on the outskirts were humming again. The tourist trade was bustling, with tens of thousands of northern Europeans and Americans descending on the city to head off for Sorrento, Capri, Ischia, and the Amalfi coast. When the U.S. Sixth Fleet was in port, its vessels disgorged thousands of cash-laden, liquor-thirsty, sex-starved sailors into the streets to the immense profit of the bars, nightclubs, and bordellos. Fashionable shops and boutiques—Pucci, Ferragamo, Valentino—were beginning to appear in the chic residential areas of town, the Via Calabritto and Via Dei Mille. Vittorio De Sica's *Gold of Naples*, starring Sophia Loren, Silvano Mangamo, and De Sica was playing at the Grande Cinema Delle Palme. "Il Miracolo Economico," which was transforming the North into an industrial powerhouse, was finally beginning to inch south.

And then, as a backdrop to this dynamic scenario, there were the surviving relics of three thousand years of Neapolitan history. Ancient walls dating from the Greek city of Neapolis in 600 B.C., stately Roman columns encrusted in sixteenth century Renaissance palaces, soaring Angevin Gothic churches and cathedrals, ornate Spanish baroque palaces, the monumental structures of the eighteenth century Bourbons.

By the mid-fifties the boss of the American underworld was a familiar figure in these surroundings. One would bump into "Looky" Luciano continually in his restaurant California; in his favorite restaurants in the Santa Lucia boat basin, Zi Teresa and Transatlantico; in the nightclubs along Via Partenope; on the ferries heading for Capri and Ischia. And he was by far the most famous American in town. Few people knew the name of the commander-in-chief of NATO forces, Southern Europe, who lived in a villa not far from Luciano's. But everyone knew who "Looky" Luciano was. He had become a living legend. The Neapolitans gossiped about his supposedly hidden millions and his special charities, like all the unwed mothers, and impecunious Italian deportees he was reputedly supporting.

Luciano, who was receiving around $25,000 in cash a month from the mob in the States, was as active as ever in the high councils of organized crime even though in Naples he was over five thousand miles from New York.

In October 1946 he had presided over the huge Cosa Nostra conference in Havana that had cemented the mob's control of all gambling casinos in Cuba and authorized new routes for the smuggling of Sicilian heroin into the United States. In 1947 he sanctioned the murder of his old friend Bugsy Siegel in Siegel's Beverly Hills home as a punishment for losing syndicate money in his Las Vegas casino venture. In the early fifties he was horrified watching the squirming hands of his friend Frank Costello on television during the Kefauver hearings, and seeing the faces of Meyer Lansky, Joe Adonis, and Albert Anastasia on the front pages of the papers during those same hearings. Luciano was consulted after Frank Costello's head was creased by a bullet fired by Vito Genovese's henchman Vincent "The Chin" Gigante. He advised the courier sent to him after the assassination attempt, Tommy Eboli, to call a meeting of the Commission to decide how to punish Genovese. He was in his penthouse apartment on Via Tasso when he was given news of the murder of Albert Anastasia and he was enjoying a plate of spaghetti with butter and cheese at the Transatlantico Restaurant in Santa Lucia when word reached him about the disastrous conclave at Apalachin.

It was shortly after this fiasco that Carlo Gambino, now a family boss, went to Naples to consult with Luciano about what to do next. Gambino had already consulted with Lansky and Costello. Now he and Luciano worked out the details of what was to be the successful framing of Vito Genovese.

The imprisonment of Genovese vastly increased the power of Lucky Luciano and Carlo Gambino. Now the two ran the American Cosa Nostra in tandem with Meyer Lansky with no significant opposition. Couriers bearing messages and cash traveled back and forth between Gambino in New York and Luciano in Naples at least once a month. In all major disputes among the families Luciano still had the last word.

I was unaware of all this when I first met Lucky Luciano as a young naval officer, and later when I interviewed him as a graduate student. On board ship rumor had it that Luciano was the father of organized crime in the United States. On the streets of Naples he was spoken of in reverent tones as *il càpo di tùtti càpi,* and the former head of Murder Incorporated. These rumors were all I had to go on.

Given his exalted reputation, Luciano disappointed me when I first met him in the California on liberty from my ship. He was sitting in a green vinyl booth in the restaurant, which was organized along the lines of a typical American cafeteria, signing menus for the sailors who constantly importuned him for his autograph. Lucky Luciano's autograph was one of the most prized trophies a sailor could take back home after a tour of duty in the Med with the Sixth Fleet.

One afternoon, during a lull in the autographing, I went up to Luciano's booth and asked the mobster if I could sit down with him a minute.

"Sure, Lieutenant," he said.

"You've been signing menus for all my men," I explained, "now *I* want to get a chance to talk with you."

"Sure, okay."

I scrutinized him as he sat there in the half-light of a late fall afternoon, with a glass of Coca-Cola in front of him. He was a small man with narrow sloping shoulders and a repulsive face. One of his half-closed eyes drooped and he had some deep scars on one cheek and on one side of his mouth. His general expression was deadpan and his mood sullen. I noticed he had surprisingly thick wrists for a man his size and very large, powerful hands.

"How do you like living in Naples?" I asked him.

"Dis place is a dump," he replied.

"A lot of us in the Navy find it very beautiful. The bay. Vesuvius. The islands. Capri."

"Listen, there ain't nuttin' like the States."

"You miss it?"

"I sure do. I'd do anythin' to get back."

"Are you keeping busy?"

"Yeah, I've got a few things goin'. I ain't got no problem with that."

There was a lull in our conversation and I sensed he wanted out. So I stood up and told him I was glad to have met him, but I had to go.

"Hey, don't ya want my autograph, Lieutenant?" he asked.

"Oh, yes," I said, "I forgot," and I picked up a menu and put it in front of him.

He signed. "There. Okay. Pleased to meet ya."

As I slid out of the booth, two sailors came up, menus and pens in hand.

From then on Luciano would nod to me whenever I went to the California for a hamburger or passed by him on the street. He apparently liked to be on good terms with the officers of the Sixth Fleet. The only time I ever saw him seeming to really enjoy himself was one evening in the California when I spotted him talking with a full captain. It seemed to elate him that he was with an officer with four big gold stripes on his sleeve and scrambled eggs on his hat. In the company of lesser mortals Luciano was usually morose. Unlike his fellow Italians, Luciano rarely smiled or gestured with his hands and almost never laughed. And he did not carry himself the way one would expect of a boss of bosses. He did not strut, Anastasia style. He scuttled around Naples, head down, trying to look as inconspicuous as possible, as if he felt every corner held a potential ambush. A Neapolitan friend of mine who knew Luciano once told me that the boss was only relaxed in a car with a driver.

On leaving the Navy I returned to New York for a year, then went back to Naples again, this time on a Fulbright scholarship to study Italian history and literature at the Italian Institute for Historical Studies, a graduate institute founded by the late Neapolitan philosopher and historian Benedetto Croce. The rarefied institute, lodged in a sixteenth century Renaissance palazzo in the heart of Vecchia Napoli, was light-years from the docks of Naples harbor and fleet exercises in the central Mediterranean.

When, upon my return to Naples, I paid my first visit to the California, it was business as usual. There was Lucky Luciano, boss of bosses, in his customary booth autographing menus for officers and sailors of the Sixth Fleet. Our eyes met and he looked quizzical. Soon he got up to leave. As he passed the counter, where I was munching on a cheeseburger, he turned toward me and said, "So, Lieutenant, you're outa de Navy?"

"Yes," I said, "hello."

"Ya gotta job here now? Maybe with de government?"

"No."

"Well, I'm tellin' ya, if you're back here to make money, forget about it. There ain't none to make," and he left.

Later I learned something about Luciano's life in Naples around the time of my return. When he turned fifty Lucky had fallen in love with a beautiful young Milanese woman of twenty-six, Igea Lissoni, a former dancer, who became his mistress and the center of his life. Together they lived in Lucky's Naples penthouse and traveled regularly to Capri, Ischia, Amalfi, and the resort town of Taormina on Sicily's eastern coast. People who knew her in Naples speak highly of Igea. They say she was very much a lady and was utterly devoted to Luciano.

Apparently Luciano mellowed somewhat during this period. He told a friend of mine, who owns a villa on the Amalfi coast, that he had decided to "go straight" and get into some legitimate businesses. Ironically, his attempt to "go straight" was, in the end, thwarted by the government.

According to my friend, Lucky first went into the tomato paste business, long a traditional business of the Naples area. He opened up a cannery on the outskirts of Naples and soon truckloads of tomatoes were arriving from the fertile soil of Campania to be processed into paste and canned. Luciano was proud of the product he was making and personally escorted the first shipment to the docks for export to New York.

The police, however, were still watching Luciano's every move. Suspicious that Luciano was packing his cans with more than tomato paste, they punctured every can in the shipment without finding so much as a grain of heroin. With the entire shipment ruined, Luciano turned to other ways to go straight.

Another traditional Neapolitan business was the manufacture of confetti. The white candy was made with almonds harvested from the Campanian plains encircling Mount Vesuvius and was much prized throughout Europe and the United States. Soon truckloads of almonds and sacks of sugar were arriving at Luciano's cannery. Before making his first shipment Lucky called the police and told them not to worry, that his confetti business was legit.

But the police didn't believe him and when Luciano's crates of confetti arrived on the docks the customs police opened them up and smashed all the candies in another vain search for Luciano heroin.

Discouraged, Luciano closed his cannery and returned to his old ways. Through his vast chain of contacts he opened up some new routes for the smuggling of heroin from Palermo to New York. The payoffs were expensive—Lucky had to grease everybody along his routes, from dockmaster to ship's captain—but they turned out to be worth it. Once again Luciano was in the money.

Luciano even indulged in some charitable causes during his long exile in Naples. He got to know the parish priest of a little village on the western slope of Mount Vesuvius, Father Francesco Scarpato, whose church had been damaged in the furious eruption of 1944. Luciano gave him enough money for a new altar and new stained-glass windows and made a special donation to help the padre fight the new Communist mayor of his village.

Running into Luciano as often as I did, and hearing so many rumors about him, I became curious about his role in organized crime in the States and decided to interview him about it. One afternoon in the California he agreed.

I remember I felt quite uneasy when I sat down in the California to question Lucky Luciano. When you encountered Luciano you always remembered he was once the reputed boss of Murder Incorporated. His appearance that afternoon did nothing to lessen my sense of unease. There he was, with his eyes half closed, his expression leaden, a man who had killed a few with his own hands and scores of others with but a nod to a subordinate.

"Thanks for letting me interview you," I opened. "How's the menu-signing business today?"

"Slow, but before we start I wanna know if you're writin' some kind of a book."

"No, I'm not, but who knows, I might write one in the future, far in the future."

"Okay, then. Shoot."

"Well, first, I'd like to know something about your role in organized crime back in the States."

"Hey, you're not some kind of an intelligence guy, are you? FBI? CIA?"

I shook my head. "No."

"You better not be," he said. "Okay, well, back in Prohibition there was no national syndicate, it was just a bunch of gangs each goin' its own way. They was killin' each other off in gang wars. So after the Big War I organized the national syndicate. I divided the guys up into families and gave 'em some rules. Then I created the Commission, the top council, with the big bosses as members, to arbitrate disputes among the families and keep order. That's what I done. But I'm outa that now. I'm goin' straight."

"You must be a very good organizer," I observed.

"You gotta be a pretty tough guy," he replied.

"What is this I hear that you were once the head of Murder Incorporated? How do you feel about that now? I've been told around eight hundred people were killed by that organization."

Luciano tossed his head to one side. "What the hell, it was just a business like any other. They performed a service and got paid for it. That's all there was to it."

"I remember when I was in the Navy and talked with you once you told me you missed the States a lot. What do you miss about it?"

"Well, I'm kinda gettin' used to it here in Naples now. I got me a real nice girl. But there's nuttin' like the States. I was raised poor as dirt on the Lower East Side. The States made me rich. I owe everything to the USA. In the old days I ate in the best restaurants, wore the best hand-tailored suits, and got to know top people, like Walter Chrysler, you know, the automobile guy? He used to gamble in my club in Saratoga and I okayed his markers. And I was pals with all the big politicians. Like the Mayor, Bill O'Dwyer. He come in a fireboat to see me off when I left for Italy. What I'm tellin' ya is I had a big career back in the States. What would have happened to me if my family had remained in Sicily?"

That was a difficult question to answer. I fell silent for a moment.

Then Luciano said: "Hey, what about you? What you doin' over here?"

"I'm studying at the Italian Institute for Historical Studies. I'm on a scholarship."

"A scholarship. That sounds like some kinda racket. You get paid for doin' nuttin'."

"You might say that."

"Well, if you're thinkin' of makin' any money around here, forget it. I was in two legitimate businesses here and lost my shirt. . . . Hey, there's a whole bunch of sailors behind you with menus. I guess I gotta give 'em my autograph. See ya around." And he dismissed me with a toss of his head.

That turned out to be my last conversation with Lucky Luciano. Although we continued to greet each other on the street and in the California, I did not feel like talking with him at length again. I remained curious about him, but the man made me too uncomfortable in a one-on-one situation.

My encounters with Luciano did teach me one thing: There is nothing romantic about a Mafia boss, that the idealized image of the Mafioso personified by Don Vito Corleone in Mario Puzo's *The Godfather* is wholly unrealistic, a fiction—in a word, a lie.

Lucky Luciano thrived in Naples, though he was always homesick for the United States, until 1959. On January 1 of that year an event occurred that shook the underworld to its foundations: Fidel Castro, victorious in his revolution against the Batista government, took over as president of Cuba and Fulgencio Batista and his aides fled the island for Florida. One of Castro's first acts as president was to close down the gambling casinos in Havana and expel from Cuba the mobsters who owned and operated them. From this time on Luciano's fortunes went into decline.

Batista had returned from temporary exile to full power in 1952 and had struck a deal with Meyer Lansky whereby the mob and the Cuban government would be partners in developing gambling and tourism on the island. Batista would match syndicate investment in Havana dollar for dollar.

It was Lansky who determined who got the major gambling concessions. In the end Cleveland's Moe Dalitz got the old Hotel Nacional. Meyer's brother, Jake, would be pit boss. Charlie "The Blade" Tourine, a Lansky associate, got the Capri. Its host would be the actor George Raft. The $24 million Havana Hilton went to Las Vegas front man Eddie Levinson, another Lansky associate. Santos Trafficante was given the Sans Souci and was allowed shares in the Capri, Hilton, and Hotel Commodoro. Lansky built himself the lavish $14 million Hotel Riviera. Lucky Luciano held shares in the Sans Souci and the

Riviera. The revenue from these and other, lesser gambling establishments was vast beyond the bosses' wildest imaginings.

Then, suddenly, it all came to an end. In one bold stroke Castro had deprived organized crime of one of its largest sources of income. Suddenly the mob's treasury was deprived of millions upon millions of future dollars. Castro's deed sent the bosses back in the States into a frenzy. It sent Meyer Lansky off to the Bahamas to try to establish casinos there. It dealt severe blows to Santos Trafficante, Carlos Marcello, Sam Giancana, and Lucky Luciano, all of whom had substantial investments in the Havana casinos and the hotels in which they operated.

In his autobiography Luciano wrote that Castro's coup caused gambling empires to collapse overnight. He also wrote that Meyer Lansky confided to him that he helped the now exiled Batista transfer $300 million into secret numbered Swiss bank accounts. Later Lansky would get Batista to invest those funds in casino gambling in the Bahamas, Beirut, and London.

Not long after Castro's gigantic affront to the mob and to the U.S. government, which had supported Batista, Lucky Luciano suffered a heart attack, the first of several.

It had been a relatively mild attack, a "warning," as his doctor explained to him, that put him out of action for only a couple of weeks.

Then, as he was recovering, a courier arrived from the States with his monthly envelope. Opening it, Luciano was horrified to note that it did not contain the usual $25,000, but a much smaller amount.

Telling the courier that he found the envelope "a little short," Luciano remonstrated, according to his autobiography, that "Lansky was startin' to slice me into a fuckin' two bit pension."

Shortly after receiving this disappointment Luciano suffered a massive coronary occlusion and was hospitalized. His doctors told him he was under too much pressure and had to cut down on his business responsibilities. Luciano consulted with a good friend who was living in Taormina, Chinky Vitaliti, and Vitaliti advised him to retire.

It was around this time that a courier arrived in Naples from New York bringing terrible news: Vito Genovese had let out a contract on Luciano from prison. Who knew when the hired guns would turn up in Naples?

Time was beginning to run out for Lucky Luciano. In addition to health problems and the Genovese contract, he had begun to suffer financially. Contrary to what people thought, Luciano did not have a large amount of money salted away. His trial had cost him almost $2 million in legal fees, thereby consuming most of his savings. The funds Lansky sent him from New York were dwindling, but he was still having to support quite a few people in Naples, a number of prostitutes and many penniless American deportees, and he was committed to helping Father Scarpato build his clinic on Mount Vesuvius. He had to make some money fast, but he wanted to make it legitimately, without pressure. In the end he decided to make a film on his life.

Through contacts in Spain, Luciano was put in touch with Martin Gosch, a former Hollywood producer and screenwriter who had established his own production company in Madrid. Gosch agreed to write a screenplay based on Luciano's years of exile in Italy, which would also contain scenes of underworld events in the States, such as the shooting of Frank Costello and the murder of Albert Anastasia.

Fortunately, Gosch made considerable progress with the screenplay, winning Luciano's approval of it, and before long he was ready to go into production. Meanwhile, Luciano had given courier Pat Eboli a message to take to Lansky and Gambino informing them he had made a deal to have a picture made on his life. After the message was delivered, Luciano got word that there were no objections.

Gosch's choice of actor to play Luciano was Dean Martin, an idea that excited Luciano because he knew he could get to Martin via his old friend Frank Sinatra. For Luciano, the film project was going well. He liked the screenplay. The boys back in New York had raised no objections. There was a good chance he could land Dean Martin for the title role and Gosch had the financing already lined up in London and Paris.

Then, unexpectedly, the ax fell. Luciano received a visitor from New York, Tommy Eboli, who did not bring cash but a message from Vito Genovese, Meyer Lansky, Joe Bonanno, Tommy Lucchese, and Carlo Gambino. The five mob leaders had reconsidered Luciano's film project and had decided against it. The last thing they wanted was a movie based on the life of a Sicilian-born gangster who had established the structure of organized crime in America and had been its de facto boss of bosses ever since. The film would focus too much light on the mob today.

In his autobiography Luciano wrote: "Tommy told me that this was not a request from nobody; he was givin' me orders. He talked to me like I was some young punk. . . . He told me not to get sore at the time, because he was only deliverin' a message—that if I didn't give up the picture, I was gonna be cut off complete. Or maybe I wouldn't even be around to enjoy the profits."

Luciano was devastated. This was a direct affront to his authority, a challenge to his position as de facto boss of organized crime in the United States.

The message from New York begged the question: Was he still the boss?

After recoiling momentarily from the initial blow, Luciano summoned what strength he had left and mounted a counterattack. He decided he would take control of the entire supply and distribution of heroin in Europe and the United States. He had the contacts, the growers, shippers, processers, and sellers. Now he would control an empire that would enable him to paralyze his onetime associates in the States if he so chose. All of them would be forced to come to him for supplies. They would not be able to acquire "junk" from any other source.

The reaction from the States was swift. The bosses spoke in unison. Luciano had to be hit, and hit soon. Luciano suspected that Genovese would also mount an attempt to frame him in a phony drug deal.

Luciano realized he was losing his grip as head of the Commission and went into seclusion in his penthouse on Via Tasso. Soon his chest pains returned, his blood pressure rose, and he began living off pills as he had following his first heart attack.

Then, in December 1961, Luciano suffered severe heart failure and had to be hospitalized again. He had barely recovered when, on January 17, 1962, Pat Eboli arrived from New York to inform him that the Commission had met and had sanctioned his murder. Carlo Gambino had already taken Luciano's place as de facto chairman of the Commission. According to Eboli, the Commission had concluded, after lengthy discussions, that Luciano had become a danger to the organization he founded, that as long as he lived nobody was safe.

Pat Eboli told Luciano that there had been much discussion of the movie about Luciano's life at the meeting of the Commission. The bosses had the feeling that as long as the signed filmscript was in existence there was a danger that the movie would eventually be made.

This situation provided a last ray of hope for Lucky Luciano. Eboli put forth the idea that if Luciano could obtain the original copy of the screenplay, the one he had signed and approved, and send it back to New York, it might placate the bosses on the Commission and save his life.

Immediately Luciano phoned Martin Gosch in Madrid and told him to come to Naples with the script. Police were monitoring both Gosch's and Luciano's phones and interpreted the word "script" as a code word for heroin, prompting the Naples police to haul Luciano in for questioning and temporary detention.

Luciano was released on January 25 and the next day he went to Naples' Capodichino Airport to meet Gosch's plane.

When Gosch reached the terminal, Luciano went up to him and said, "I fucked myself, Marty, they're goin' to kill me."

"Who's going to kill you?"

"All of 'em, all of 'em. . . . I'm not gonna even end up the king of junk. . . . Lansky's gonna wind up with all the money."

By the time Eboli, Gosch, and Luciano arrived in the parking lot, Luciano was feeling terribly weak and had to hold on to Eboli's arm. He was breathing heavily. Then the attack came, sending Luciano crashing to the pavement. The sixty-four-year-old boss of bosses heaved and gasped, writhing on the pavement. Then suddenly he lay still. Gosch bent over and felt his wrist. There was no pulse. Luciano was dead.

Pat Eboli telephoned the news to New York. The bosses received it with a sense of relief. Especially Carlo Gambino. Gambino was now head of the Commission. Without challengers, he was now the most powerful Mafia boss in the United States.

15

Summit at La Stella

In early 1966 Tommy Lucchese, boss of the crime family bearing his name and close ally of Carlo Gambino, was found to have an inoperable brain cancer and could not be expected to live for more than three to six months.

Knowledge of Lucchese's ill health led police to the discovery of the most important known Cosa Nostra conclave held since Apalachin, the meeting of thirteen mobsters, including four family bosses, at the La Stella Restaurant in Queens on September 22, 1966.

New York police detectives had reasoned that, in the event of Lucchese's incapacitation or death, a new boss of his family would have to be chosen and the choice ratified by the Commission. Consequently, a meeting of top bosses would have to be held, preferably in New York, to consider the Lucchese succession and whatever else might have been of pressing importance to the Cosa Nostra families at the time.

On that assumption detectives began trailing high-level members of the New York families who would be most likely to attend such a meeting. One of these was Mike Miranda, who was serving as one of the three de facto bosses of the Genovese family in the absence of the imprisoned boss Vito Genovese.

Shortly after noon on September 22, the detective assigned to trail Mike Miranda spotted him entering the La Stella Restaurant in Queens followed by Carlo Gambino and one of Gambino's *caporegimes*, Joseph N. Gallo. Shortly after that, another officer on the same detail, who had run into Florida boss Santos Trafficante before, observed Trafficante get out of a car and head for the same restaurant. The two detectives quickly concluded that a high-level meeting of La Cosa Nostra was about to take place and called headquarters for instructions. They were told to go to the restaurant and arrest all the attendees.

When the officers arrived inside, they found, in a private basement dining room, thirteen men seated at a long table the restaurant had assembled by joining four tables together. Bottles of wine were scattered over the white tablecloth, together with baskets of Italian bread and plates of antipasti. The meal was apparently just beginning. Before making any arrests the officers wisely told the diners to stay put and then quickly sketched a diagram of the seating arrangement at the table.

Organized crime authority Ralph Salerno told the House Select Committee on Assassinations in a 1978 executive session hearing that the seating arrangement at La Stella was "as formal as it could be if the chief of protocol of the State Department had, in fact, put place cards there."

At the head of the table sat Genovese acting co-boss Mike Miranda, the host of the luncheon. To his right sat Joe Colombo, boss of his own family; Tommy Eboli, another acting co-boss of the Genovese family; and Dominick Alongi, a Genovese soldier who was

Eboli's driver and a cousin of one of the diners, Frank Gagliano. To Miranda's left sat three major bosses, Carlo Gambino, Carlos Marcello, and Santos Trafficante, Jr., in that order. Six lower-echelon mobsters sat at the opposite end of the table: Joseph Marcello, Jr., Carlos's brother; Aniello Dellacroce, Gambino's new underboss; Joseph N. Gallo, Gambino's future *consiglière;* Anthony Carolla, a New Orleans rival of the Marcello brothers; Frank Gagliano, a supporter of Carolla; and Genovese soldier Anthony Cirillo. Salerno pointed out in his testimony that Cirillo probably picked up the check, since "the bosses never pay when these people get together. It is always the henchmen."

Salerno believed that the formal meeting had already taken place at another location and that the luncheon was simply an informal celebration of the agreements reached at the meeting.

After taking down the seating arrangement, the two police officers quickly called for reinforcements, then arrested all thirteen men, charged them with "consorting with known criminals," handcuffed them, took them off to a bail hearing, where bail was set at $1,300,000—$100,000 each—then locked them up in a civil jail in Queens for the night. The next day a bail bondsman put up the $1,300,000 bail on no collateral—the mobsters' word was sufficient—and the thirteen were released.

What was the La Stella sit-down all about? Law enforcement officials have offered various explanations.

Former FBI special agent Harold Hughes of the New Orleans office told me that he had learned from reliable informants that one of the purposes of the summit was to mediate a dispute between the Marcello and Carolla families of New Orleans over the spoils of Carlos Marcello's criminal operations in Louisiana and Texas. Anthony Carolla, whose father, "Silver Dollar" Sam Carolla, had preceded Carlos Marcello as boss of the Gulf Coast underworld, had demanded a greater share of the action. In the end the New York dons sided with Carlos Marcello and his brother, ruling that Carolla was not entitled to more than he was now receiving.

But the dispute between Carolla and Marcello was, more than likely, a minor subject of discussion at the meeting that preceded the La Stella luncheon. The burning questions in the Cosa Nostra at the moment were what to do about a recent federal crackdown on illegal gambling and drug dealing in New Orleans, Atlanta, Tampa, and Miami, and what would happen to the terminally ill Tommy Lucchese's vast drug-smuggling operation after the boss died.

Police intelligence officials studying the invitees, the timing of the meeting, and the state of the underworld concluded that the main purpose of the La Stella sit-down was to divide up and reorganize Lucchese's widespread crime empire, not to name his probable successor. As Lucchese's closest friend, Carlo Gambino asserted a caretaker's claim to the Lucchese crime family's interests and the other attendees assented. When, months later, in July 1967, Tommy Lucchese finally died, Gambino quickly named a figurehead successor, one Carmine Tramunti, and began running the family in tandem with his own.

With Lucchese's passing, two enormous legacies fell to Carlo Gambino: control of Teamsters Local 295 at Kennedy Airport and control of the unions involved in trucking seventy percent of the clothing apparel sold in the United States out of the garment district in midtown Manhattan.

Don Carlo now controlled two of the New York families—his and Lucchese's—and exercised considerable influence over a third, the Colombo family, whose current boss, Joe Colombo, he had hand-picked. Then, a year and a half after Lucchese's demise, Vito Genovese died at the Medical Center for Federal Prisoners in Springfield, Missouri, and Carlo quickly asserted de facto control also over the Genovese mob, which had been inefficiently run by a feuding troika of co-bosses since Genovese's imprisonment in 1959.

Thus by 1970 Carlo Gambino had emerged supreme in the New York underworld. He was in virtual control of two of the five families and exercised a predominant influence in two others. Soon a convulsion in the Colombo family would give him a chance to place a godson at its head, thereby strengthening his hold on four of the five New York families.

16

The Apprenticeship of John Gotti

As Carlo Gambino consolidated his hold on the family he had inherited from the murdered Albert Anastasia and maneuvered to dominate the other four families in New York, John Gotti, the young tough who would one day become boss of the family, was learning the gangster's trade from one of Gambino's twenty-four *caporegimes*, Carmine "Charlie Wagons" Fatico. The year was 1966.

Fatico, a short, slim man with more brains than brawn, whose nickname alluded to his penchant for hijacking trucks, had been put in charge of all criminal operations in the East New York section of Brooklyn by Albert Anastasia and had been kept on in that position by Carlo Gambino. As the boss of the East New York crew, Fatico commanded a force of made and not-yet-made captains, soldiers, and associates numbering around 120 men. Operating out of an unpretentious storefront social club in East New

York known locally as "The Club," Fatico held court every morning behind a desk in a back room, giving out orders to his men and receiving applicants for jobs in his crew and supplicants from East New Yorkers who needed his help for one reason or another. The *caporegime* of a Cosa Nostra crew was not merely an instigator of crimes and an administrator of various established rackets; he was also a source of advice, a dispenser of financial assistance, and an informal court of justice for the community.

Carmine Fatico had become a leading capo in the Gambino family by following the basic rules for an aspirant to a high place in a crime family. He was unfailingly loyal and obedient to his boss and was a tireless and innovative earner for the family. It has been estimated that his crew grossed around $30 million a year. A violent, even sadistic man, Fatico had acquired a reputation as a brutal killer when the occasion demanded the ultimate penalty. This also stood him in good stead with the Gambino family. For the most appreciated talent of all in a Cosa Nostra family was the ability to kill efficiently and silently, leaving no trail of evidence or talk that could lead investigators back to the source of the crime.

Before joining Fatico's crew at the age of twenty-six, John Gotti had led the unstable life of a petty crook and unskilled worker who was repeatedly in trouble with the law and almost always broke. He had tried everything. He had tried burglary and failed. Once he attempted to steal copper wire from a construction firm, was caught and arrested and put on probation. He tried his hand as a presser in a Brooklyn coat factory and quit, finding the work beneath him. He had tried gambling and had lost consistently. He had even tried marriage and had come within a hair's breadth of losing his bride.

It was in late 1960, when Gotti was twenty years old and working as a presser that he met an attractive dark-haired teenager, Victoria DiGiorgio, the daughter of an Italian sanitation worker and his Jewish wife. Like John, she had dropped out of high school and was now hanging around the house and with other teenagers on the streets of East New York. Before long Gotti got her pregnant and their first child, a daughter, Angela, was born in April 1961. Three more children followed in the next four years.

John Gotti at the time was a robust young man of five feet nine and around 170 pounds, well muscled, with rugged good looks and long, thick black hair. He had kept the rapid-fire speech and swaggering gait he had learned from Albert Anastasia and was already displaying a liking for flashy clothes.

But for all his panache Gotti did not do very well as a provider in the first years of his marriage. Carmine Fatico had assigned him several common burglaries and he blew at least three of them. He and his partner, Salvatore Ruggiero, were arrested for trying to steal an Avis rental car and later he was sent to prison for six months for another attempted burglary. It was then that his independent-minded wife, Victoria, sued him for nonsupport in domestic relations court, an intolerable affront to the dignity of an aspiring Mafioso.

When Gotti was released from prison, he went straight back to The Club in East New York to see what Carmine Fatico had for him next. To his surprise and relief, Charlie Wagons assigned him to the hijacking operation at Kennedy International Airport. Gotti must have been pleased because everyone in his crew was well aware the boss Carlo Gambino was beefing up operations at JFK as freighter traffic on the waterfront was beginning to dwindle. This might be Gotti's big chance.

As it turned out, it was not. As with everything else he had tried so far, Gotti failed also in the art of hijacking. He and his brother Gene had started modestly. Armed with forged freight documents and using a truck they borrowed, they drove into the

United Airlines air freight terminal one day in 1969, submitted the documents to a clerk, and drove off with a load of women's clothing and imported electronic devices. The little operation had been so easy that they foolishly tried the exact same ploy with the same terminal, United Airlines. This time they were caught, arrested, and freed on bail. A few weeks later Gotti, his brother Gene, and fellow member of the Fatico crew, Angelo Ruggiero, were caught trying to hijack two trucks on the New Jersey Turnpike. They were arrested, tried, convicted, and sentenced to four years in the federal prison at Lewisburg.

Lewisburg, like other federal prisons, was officially run by a government of wardens, clerical personnel, and guards, and unofficially by an invisible network of Mafiosi inmates. The two groups worked in tandem. This system made it easier on both inmates and prison employees and tended to prevent such unpleasant things as prison riots. As it turned out, what young Gotti received at Lewisburg was not so much punishment but an education in the ways of organized crime and an introduction to important members of the brotherhood he would probably not have had much of a chance to meet on the outside. The most powerful of these was the tough, ruthless fifty-seven-year-old boss of the Bonanno family, Carmine Galante. Doing time with him at Lewisburg was no less a towering figure than ex-Teamsters boss Jimmy Hoffa, sent to Lewisburg through the dogged efforts of Bobby Kennedy. (In 1967 Lewisburg prison informants told the FBI that Jimmy Hoffa had talked with a fellow inmate, perhaps Galante, about a plot to kill Bobby Kennedy.) At a far lower level, Lewisburg had become home also to John Gotti's close friend Angelo Ruggiero and a convicted heroin dealer, Anthony Rampino, who would one day become John Gotti's personal chauffeur and be known as Tony Roach.

Gotti learned as much as he could from the four hundred Mafiosi of varying rank at Lewisburg and even won the admiration, and a job offer from Carmine Galante. Gotti was flattered, but, reminded by another inmate that he belonged to Charlie Wagons Fatico, he had to refuse Galante. Galante took no offense and continued to see Gotti and make sure he received his share of prison privileges. As it turned out, Gotti spent most of his term at Lewisburg working one hour a day and dividing the rest of his time exercising and pumping iron in the gym and learning as much as he could from the older inmates. If the government had consciously devised a program of physical fitness and expert instruction in how to commit crimes, it could not have done better than to have dumped budding Mafioso John Gotti in Lewisburg's Mafia Row for two years.

17

The Problem of Joe Colombo

ITALIAN POWER; ITALIANS ARE BEAUTIFUL; WE WANT EQUAL RIGHTS; THE FBI FRAMES ITALIAN-AMERICANS; ITALIANS UNITE! So proclaimed the signs, placards, and badges boss Joe Colombo and his men paraded in front of the New York office of the FBI on Sixty-ninth street and Third Avenue in the spring of 1970.

Two months later, on June 29, the signs, placards, and badges were out again in far greater numbers, as seventy thousand of Colombo's supporters flooded into Columbus Circle to celebrate Colombo's brain-child, Italian Unity Day. They came from all over, from Buffalo, Detroit, Philadelphia, Trenton, Newark, but most came from the five boroughs of New York City and from Nassau County on the Island. In deference to boss Colombo's wishes, hundreds of Italian stores, cafés, and restaurants in the Italian neighborhoods of Brooklyn and Manhattan's Lower East Side had closed down for the day and had bedecked their storefronts with red, white, and green bunting and signs proclaiming the first Italian Unity Day.

Reluctantly, Carlo Gambino had agreed to have his man on the docks, Anthony Scotto, shut down the New York waterfront for a day and allow red, white, and green bunting and flags to decorate the piers and warehouses he controlled.

At his grand Columbus Circle rally Joe Colombo stood on a podium surmounted by a statue of Christopher Columbus and received those politicians who had dared risk having their pictures taken in the company of a known gangster: Deputy Mayor Richard Aurelio, Congressmen Adam Clayton Powell and Mario Biaggi, former Mayor Vincent Impellitteri. Then Colombo launched into a speech telling his screaming, flag-waving audience that they were finally organized, united, and free and could not be pushed around anymore. The raucous meeting ended with a parade down Sixty-ninth Street to the FBI offices.

Law enforcement took due notice of Colombo's theatrics. A month after the rally the Nassau district attorney indicted Colombo and twenty-three of his men on charges of criminal contempt, loan-sharking, and illegal gambling. By the end of the year the FBI had twenty percent of Colombo's men under indictment. But the arm of the law did not stop with Colombo. Carlo Gambino's new underboss, Aniello Dellacroce, was summoned before grand juries in Manhattan and Brooklyn, and, after refusing to testify, even under immunity, was jailed for a year.

These events made Carlo Gambino uneasy. A quiet man who believed in secrecy, anonymity, and invisibility, he quickly perceived his error in cooperating with Colombo by shutting down the waterfront for Italian Unity Day. Colombo's sensational public posturing was not going to be good for Colombo, his family, and the other families. It was only going to bring the heat on everyone. In the months that followed, as Colombo's new Italian-American Civil Rights League grew and prospered, and became more and more vociferous, Carlo began giving more and more thought to how he could sabotage the entire movement, kill it off with one stroke.

Italian-Americans had just cause to feel resentment over the way they had come to be treated by the public and the media. Largely because of the enormous amount of publicity the Mafia had received throughout the fifties and sixties, ordinary law-abiding Italian-Americans felt threatened. In 1951, 1957, and 1959 Americans saw a gallery of gangsters with Italian names parading across their television screens as the Kefauver and McClellan Committee hearings unfolded and the Apalachin conclave was discovered. Then, in 1963, the public absorbed the horrendous tales of La Cosa Nostra as narrated by soldier-turned-informant Joseph Valachi. From then on the Mafia, La Cosa Nostra, or whatever it was called was constantly in the news and on film, the process reaching its apogee in 1969 with the publication of Mario Puzo's *The Godfather*, which in that year became the fastest-selling novel in U.S. publishing history. By then Italian-Americans had had enough. A tiny minority of their population, less than one hundredth of one percent, had besmirched the good name of millions of honest, hardworking men and women bearing Italian names.

Paradoxically, in a sense the American upperworld had been celebrating the best of Italy for the past sixty years, but this had not impinged on the American consciousness nearly as much as the outrageous activities of the Italian underworld.

While poor southern Italian and Sicilian immigrants were setting up their forlorn storefront social clubs in the alleys and streets of East Harlem, south Brooklyn, and Manhattan's Lower East Side, the lords of the upperworld were building magnificent palaces for themselves in the grand style of the Italian Renaissance.

J. P. Morgan, the most powerful financier of his day, had his architects build a splendid Florentine palazzo in the manner of Brunelleschi, for himself on Thirty-eighth Street off Madison Avenue, which he filled with Italian Renaissance paintings, drawings, and furnishings. The city's finest men's clubs—the Metropolitan Club, the University Club, and the Century Association—were all erecting imitations of sixteenth century Italian palazzi. The Metropolitan built a Florentine palazzo worthy of a Medici grand duke on Fifth Avenue and Sixtieth Street. The Century put up a splendid Veronese palazzo on Forty-third Street off Fifth. And the University Club erected an enlarged copy of Florence's magnificent Palazzo Strozzi at Fifth and Fifty-fourth Street.

But the New York upperworld's celebration of things Italian was not confined to architecture. Delmonico's Restaurant, with its exquisite northern Italian *cucìna*, was the favorite of the Wall Street crowd. Thousands of New Yorkers waited in line for hours outside the Metropolitan Opera House on Thirty-ninth Street to attend performances of their favorite operatic composers, Verdi and Puccini. Arturo Toscanini, appointed principal conductor of the New York Philharmonic in 1928, became the toast of New York as the Castellammarese War raged on in the Italian ghettos.

How ironic, then, that it was a Mafia boss who was leading the movement to gain respect for the vast Italian-American community. As journalist Nicholas Pileggi wrote in *New York* magazine at the time, Colombo had "made allies of his own victims."

The stated purpose of the Italian-American Civil Rights League was "to fight the gangster stereotype in the media, make Italian-Americans proud of their heritage, fight, on all fronts, the victimization of

Italian-Americans, and persuade the media to refrain from using the terms Mafia and Cosa Nostra."

At first Colombo's program enjoyed a number of notable successes. Colombo's men put so much pressure on the advertisers of the television series *The FBI* that the producers agreed to stop using the expressions "Mafia" and "Cosa Nostra" on the show. Because of the growing numbers of his supporters, and the potential political clout they represented, Colombo was even able to get Nixon's attorney general John Mitchell to refrain from using the two terms in the Justice Department's public pronouncements. Finally, he strong-armed the producers of Mario Puzo's movie *The Godfather* to force them to delete the word "Mafia" from the script wherever it appeared. Not only that, but in return for labor peace, Colombo even got *The Godfather* producers to hire his men for bit parts in the movie. Even the *New York Times* agreed not to use the words "Mafia" and "Cosa Nostra" in its articles on organized crime.

According to Colombo soldier Joseph Cantalupo, all these public relations successes went straight to Colombo's head, and the Mafia boss began conceiving of himself as *the* leader of all Italian-Americans in the country and possibly a future candidate for high political office.

Encouraged by the success of his first Italian Unity Day rally, Joe Colombo began planning his next extravaganza. For this one he was expecting a turnout of one hundred thousand in Columbus Circle and adjacent Central Park that would include all the leading politicians in New York and New Jersey and such big-time celebrities as Frank Sinatra and Sammy Davis, Jr. The rally was planned for June 28, 1971.

News of Colombo's plans was not received well by either his friends or his foes. The other bosses worried about the pressure they knew all the publicity would bring down upon them, and the FBI, still outraged over Colombo's picketing of their New York office a year ago, stepped up its investigation of the Colombo mob and the other families.

For the first time since he had taken over as boss of his family, Carlo Gambino felt severely threatened. Joe Colombo's grandiose plans were sure to bring reprisals from the FBI. He had warned Colombo of this, advising him to step down and turn the Italian-American Civil Rights League over to a professional politician, but Colombo had not heeded his advice and had even insulted him at the time. Gambino decided to do something drastic. Quietly the cunning Sicilian began plotting the ruination of Colombo and his league. He wanted to publicly humiliate the entire movement.

When Joe Colombo arrived at Columbus Circle at 11:30 A.M. on June 28, 1971, he was gratified to see such a large turnout of his faithful. There, crowded into Columbus Circle, were thousands of Italian-Americans waving red, white, and green banners and displaying ITALIAN POWER! badges on their chests.

The size of the multitude encouraged Colombo, for he had received nothing but bad news earlier in the morning. He had ordered posters advertising the second annual Italian Unity Day rally to be displayed in every storefront and café in the Italian neighborhoods of East Harlem, Brooklyn, lower Manhattan, and Staten Island. Many store owners had put them up, but when Carlo Gambino gave the order that they be taken down, most were taken down. Then came word that Tony Scotto, Gambino's waterfront boss, had refused to shut down the waterfront on orders from Don Carlo. What was behind these moves of Gambino's? So disconcerting were they that several of Colombo's aides tried to persuade Joe not to go to Columbus Circle, to call the rally off. Maybe they're setting a trap for you, one aide counseled. But, like Caesar, Joseph Colombo did not heed the doomsayers.

Now he was standing among a crowd of worshipers, receiving handshakes, embraces and kisses, with his bodyguards looking on. It was a bright, sunny day. A sea of red, white, and green banners fluttered in the light June breeze.

A few minutes after his appearance in Columbus Circle, press photographers began to close in on the burly Joe Colombo, who was dressed informally in a sports shirt and slacks. One of the photographers with press credentials was a young black man with a 16mm Bolex moving picture camera. He was filming Colombo being greeted by well-wishers when, at a certain point, he lowered his camera, walked behind the boss, and suddenly pulled out a 7.65mm automatic and pumped three bullets into Colombo's head. Gravely wounded, but not dead, Colombo collapsed on the pavement, and as he did, a bodyguard identified only as "Chubby" opened an attaché case, took out a Smith & Wesson revolver, and shot the attacker dead.

After five hours of surgery at Roosevelt Hospital, Joe Colombo was declared to be out of danger but no longer in command of his faculties. Part of his brain had been destroyed. He was semi-paralyzed and unable to walk, hear, or speak. Colombo would linger on in this vegetative state for the next seven years.

Initial suspicions as to who might have been behind the attack were focused on Crazy Joe Gallo, a longtime enemy of Colombo who had recently been released from prison and was out to avenge past wrongs. Among other things, Gallo was known to have cultivated relationships with black gangsters in Harlem.

Joe Colombo's attacker was found to be Jerome A. Johnson, a twenty-five-year-old black with a prison record. Police detectives went to work with the idea of tying Johnson to Joey Gallo. But they were unable to make the link. Scores of street informants in Harlem were questioned, but no one had ever seen Gallo and Johnson together or heard anything about them being together or knowing the same people.

The deeper the detectives delved into the shooting, the more it became apparent that the only white mobsters Jerome Johnson was known to deal with were members of the Gambino family. The detectives found out that Johnson used to frequent a gay establishment on Christopher Street in Greenwich Village owned by Gambino soldier Paul DiBella and managed by a Gambino associate Michael Umbers, a known dealer in pornography. Johnson and Umbers had been seen together at the after-hours place during the weeks prior to the attack on Colombo.

But for all their expert sleuthing, the New York police were unable to link Jerome Johnson to the man the police were now convinced ordered the hit, Carlo Gambino.

Meanwhile, in the wake of the assault on Colombo, Gambino had slyly won a beachhead within the leaderless Colombo family itself. By 1971 Carlo had become the ranking member of the Commission. At a meeting of the Commission called to discuss the Colombo assault and decide on a successor to the totally disabled boss, Carlo once more displayed his mastery of Machiavellian politics.

As it happened, Carlo had a close friend and ally in the Colombo family. He was Vincent Aloi, a thirty-eight-year-old godson of Gambino's who ran a garment district trucking firm and was friendly with Carlo's son, Tommy. Back when Colombo and Gambino were friends, Carlo had persuaded Colombo to make his godson a *caporegime* and it was done. Now Carlo proposed that Vinnie Aloi be made acting head of the Colombo family while Colombo was "convalescing." Such was the power now held by Carlo Gambino that no one on the Commission was strong enough to deny Gambino his wish. Aloi was duly anointed.

Joe Colombo never recovered from the head wounds inflicted on him by Jerome B. Johnson, nor did the Italian-American Civil Rights League recover from the loss of its leader. In the months following the shooting the League became as vegetative as its founder and, like poor old Joe, eventually died.

With Colombo and his league silenced and Gambino's godson running Colombo's family, Carlo Gambino now reigned supreme in the New York underworld. Although in his understated way Gambino never ascribed to himself the august title of *càpo di tùtti càpi*, Carlo had become just that. His position in the Cosa Nostra was now unassailable. His word on the Commission was law.

18

The Making of
John Gotti

On Lewisburg Prison's Mafia Row, news of the shooting of Joe Colombo provoked a mixture of laughter and rage, the laughter coming from those who thought Colombo's Italian-American Civil Rights League a joke, the rage directed at the prison's black population.

It was around this time that word soon reached John Gotti and Angelo Ruggiero that the government was dismissing one of its indictments against them, paving the way for their release in six months.

John Gotti was thirty-one when he was released from Lewisburg in January 1972. He returned to a twenty-nine-year-old wife with four kids ranging in age from four to ten. Victoria Gotti, in her small Canarsie apartment, had been supporting her family on handouts from her parents and part-time jobs. Life had not been easy.

John Gotti's prospects were not particularly bright

as he returned to life on the outside. He had told his parole officer he was going to go to work for his father-in-law, Francesco DiGiorgio, who had retired from the Sanitation Department to found his own firm, Century Construction. Gotti would work as a superintendent for Century at $300 a month.

But Gotti had little intention of working at a straight job for his father-in-law. Soon after his release from Lewisburg some of his friends from Carmine Fatico's crew beckoned and he answered the call.

Fatico had moved his crew out of East New York, because blacks had taken over the area, and had reestablished it in Ozone Park, Queens, a quiet, middle-class neighborhood inhabited mostly by people of Polish and Italian ancestry. Fatico's new headquarters were two storefront locations on 101st Avenue, which he named, for reasons that are still unclear, the Bergin Hunt and Fish Club. The first consisted of a social room in the front, furnished with card tables and a bar, and an office in the back where Fatico would hold forth from behind a large desk with scattered chairs. The other storefront was used mostly for storage and telephone conversations. It had two pay phones near the entrance that Fatico and his men believed were immune to bugging.

Out of these unpretentious premises Gambino capo Carmine Fatico conducted a variety of criminal operations: hijacking cargoes at Kennedy Airport and on the waterfront, fencing stolen property, loan-sharking, bookmaking, numbers, floating dice games, illegal casinos, betting on professional football and boxing, and push-button poker machines. Two of John Gotti's brothers, Gene and Peter, had joined Fatico's crew while John was in Lewisburg. Gotti's best friend, Angelo Ruggiero, had gone straight to Fatico as soon as he got out of Lewisburg. It was only a matter of time before John Gotti gave up working for his father-in-law and became a full-time crook in

Fatico's Ozone Park gang. They were a rough and greedy lot, the 120 or so men who gravitated around the Bergin Hunt and Fish Club. Thanks to one of them, an FBI informant code-named Wahoo, or Source BQ 5558-TE, we know a good deal about what went on behind its forlorn fake brick facade.

We know, among other things, that when John Gotti returned to full-time activity in Fatico's crew, Fatico put him in charge of all gambling operations. It was a demanding position. The Gambino family's gambling network was a multimillion-dollar enterprise employing thousands of people, from squads of numbers runners to the managers of illegal casinos in Manhattan and Queens, where roulette, blackjack, and craps were played for high stakes. Each of the twenty-four Gambino crews had its own territory. The Fatico crew's turf was eastern Queens. To govern Fatico's share of the Gambino gambling network required superior management skills, strong leadership, and the ability to enforce discipline, especially when it came to forcing gamblers to make good on their debts.

It was this latter ability that endeared Gotti most to his boss, Carmine Fatico. No one in a Cosa Nostra regime is more admired than the man who brings in the money, especially money from recalcitrant debtors. Gotti soon became known for the vicious beatings he administered to gamblers who tried to welsh on a bet.

Yet for all his hard work and toughness, John Gotti was fully aware that he would go nowhere in the Gambino family until he was formally inducted into the Honored Society, until the Mafia fathers decided he should be made.

To a promising young soldier in a Cosa Nostra family, being made was as coveted a career goal as a young attorney in a law firm making partner. But the ascent to such recognition in the mob was fraught with many more obstacles and uncertainties than the climb to partnership in a law firm. For one thing, young attorneys in law firms had more opportunities to rub elbows with the partners than young hoodlums in the mob had to come into direct contact with the boss and underboss of a Cosa Nostra family.

Gotti finally got his chance to move up when in 1972 Carmine Fatico, now sixty-two, was indicted in Suffolk County for loan-sharking. Occupied with preparing for his trial and not wanting to draw the attention of the law to his activities at the Bergin, Fatico made Gotti acting boss of the Bergin crew, which meant Gotti had to report now to Gambino underboss Aniello Dellacroce at his headquarters in Little Italy, the Ravenite Club at 239 Mulberry Street.

Aniello Dellacroce, a veteran of the Anastasia years, had a reputation as one of the toughest and shrewdest mobsters in New York. Carlo Gambino had such faith in him that he had given him virtual autonomy in running the rackets under his command.

For a while Gotti and Dellacroce saw a good deal of one another and Gotti impressed his boss by making several big scores. Wahoo reported to the FBI that Gotti had become a big-time hijacker, that in 1972 he and his crew had successfully seized a truck containing $100,000 worth of mink pelts, and that a year later he had made off with fifty-seven thousand watches from JFK Airport. But then Dellacroce began to have *his* troubles: He was indicted and convicted on tax evasion charges. Now the thirty-three-year-old John Gotti would be reporting to Carlo Gambino.

It was around this time—in the early seventies—that a nephew of Gambino's, the twenty-nine-year-old Emmanuel "Manny" Gambino, was kidnapped by a gang of Irish mobsters from the West Side's Hell's Kitchen. These wild young Irish hoodlums, led by a hothead named James McBratney, had been preying on low-level associates of the Gambino organization for some time, kidnapping bookies and loan sharks and not releasing them until a $100,000 ransom had been paid.

Negotiations for Manny Gambino's release took several months. Finally the $350,000 ransom demand was bargained down to $100,000 and paid to McBratney. An ailing Carlo Gambino waited for his nephew's release. But a few months later, in January 1973, the police, on a tip, dug up Manny Gambino's body from a New Jersey dump.

Reacting to the affront to his family's honor, Carlo Gambino immediately put out a contract on James McBratney's life. The contract was given to a team of three men: the up-and-coming John Gotti, Angelo Ruggiero, and one of the Bergin hijackers, Ralph Galione. Here was John Gotti's main chance.

Mafia bosses often entrust contract murders to veteran but unmade associates because they know such men would have more incentive than others to get the job done. It was also likely that a man with many years service in the family would not be an undercover cop. The incentive, of course, would be promotion to made status if the murder was accomplished efficiently.

Gotti, Ruggiero, and Galione devised a plan first to kidnap McBratney, then to take him to a location that would serve as both a torture and execution chamber. The killing of a boss's nephew demanded no less a punishment.

Gotti and his cohorts located McBratney at a bar and restaurant on Staten Island called Snoope's. The place was well lit and there were quite a few people besides McBratney present. Pretending to be plainclothesmen, the Bergin trio erupted into the bar one evening and told McBratney he was under arrest. When they tried to handcuff him, a furious struggle followed. McBratney, a powerful man himself, was not fooled and put up a brave fight. In front of several startled witnesses he dragged Gotti, Ruggiero, and Galione down the bar until Gotti and Ruggiero finally immobilized him against a wall. In full view of the barmaid, Galione then fired three shots into McBratney at close range, killing him instantly. The three hit men then escaped into the night.

It had been a sloppy job, but the end had been achieved. Carlo Gambino had avenged his nephew's murder. In the eyes of the underworld, honor had been restored to the family.

Not long after the hit, Ralph Galione was himself murdered near his apartment, it is thought by associates of McBratney. John Gotti and Angelo Ruggiero laid low for a while, but Gotti's habit of bragging about his crimes spread word of the McBratney rubout within the Bergin and that word reached the ears of Wahoo, who immediately reported it to the FBI and was paid $600 for the information. At a state grand jury hearing all the witnesses in Snoope's Bar who saw the shooting identified Gotti from police mug shots as one of the team that had killed McBratney.

On a further tip from Wahoo, Gotti was arrested in a Queens bar on June 3, 1974, and held on $150,000 bail. Victoria Gotti's parents had by then bought their daughter an eight-room Cape Cod house in Howard Beach, Queens, near Jamaica Bay. The house was put up as bond to secure John Gotti's release.

Gotti now faced certain imprisonment. It remained for Carlo Gambino's attorneys to work out some sort of a deal. Until that deal was made and Gotti had served his time, he could not be formally inducted into the Honored Society. But that he would be made, in due time, was now assured.

19

Death of a Don

About a month after Joe Colombo was shot at his Italian Unity Day rally, Carlo Gambino's wife of forty-two years, Kathryn, died of cancer at the Gambino home on 2230 Ocean Parkway in the Sheepshead Bay area of Brooklyn. She had been in poor health for some time.

Kathryn Castellano Gambino, niece of Carlo's mother, and first cousin to her husband and his brothers and sisters, was also the sister of the Castellano brothers who had settled in Brooklyn before Carlo had arrived from Palermo. It had been a tightly knit blood family. The Gambinos and Castellanos had wanted it that way. Loyalty was assured, above all, by blood. *Sàngue di mìo sàngue,* "blood of my blood," was, to a Sicilian, the most sacred bond of all.

By all accounts Kathryn Gambino had led an exemplary life and had been much beloved by her family and friends. A quiet, courteous woman with Old

World manners and feminine charm, she greeted all visitors to her two-story Brooklyn house with the same warm hospitality, whether they were FBI agents or her husband's henchmen.

Joseph Cantalupo, former notary and secretary of Carlo Gambino, later turned government informant, remembers Kathryn Gambino well. When he went to the two-story house to see the boss, she would receive him in a parlor on the second floor and would immediately offer him an espresso in a dainty little Sicilian porcelain cup. Cantalupo remembers the spacious wood-paneled parlor was mostly furnished with Italian provincial tables and chairs and that there were many plants scattered here and there in brightly colored ceramic pots. Long damask curtains fell from the high floor-to-ceiling windows and there were paintings of Sicilian palaces and churches on the walls. It could have been a parlor in any number of patrician houses in Palermo.

Cantalupo recalls that the first thing Mrs. Gambino would do when he called would be to inquire of members of his family, his father, mother, brothers, and sisters. She seemed to take a genuine interest in all of them, whom she, of course, had known for years.

When one of her husband's underlings finally appeared to escort Cantalupo into the presence of the great man, Mrs. Gambino would always make sure to have herself remembered to Joe's dear mother and sweet sister. As he took her leave and headed for the boss's office, Kathryn Gambino would stand there with her hands clasped in front of her long dress, displaying a faint smile, her head slightly bowed, following him with her eyes until he disappeared inside.

FBI agents visiting the Gambino home to question Carlo about his alleged criminal activities or to hand him a subpoena encountered similar treatment from Mrs. Gambino. A burly, officious agent coming to accuse the boss would be completely disarmed by this slight, fine-featured, graceful gray-haired lady offering him a little cup of espresso and asking him about his wife and family. "And where does your dear little daughter attend school these days? Oh, at a convent school, how nice."

For years Kathryn Gambino had played this role for her husband. Angry men would erupt into the Gambino homes bursting with urgent business, and by the time they reached the boss, a lot of their afflatus had died down. Subdued, they would then enter a room dominated by a long conference table to encounter a lean, slightly stooped gentleman with thinning white hair, who would wave them to their seats with what appeared to be a withered hand, smile, nod his head up and down several times, then, still smiling and nodding, ask them, in a quiet voice, with a faint lisp, "Gentlemen, what can I do for you?"

Now, with the passing of Kathryn, the routine would be changed. Kathryn's sister, Providencia, and her husband, Philip Villano, would take up residence on the first floor of the big Brooklyn house and share the honor of receiving visitors.

Thousands of mourners turned out for the Mass of Resurrection at the Church of Our Lady of Grace, where Kathryn had attended mass every Sunday of her life. Among the mourners filling the front rows were her husband, sons Thomas, Joseph, and Carl, daughter Phyllis, their spouses and children, two sisters, and a half dozen Castellano nieces and nephews.

Remembering the disorder and confusion that had spoiled some of the brotherhood's funerals in the past, most notably the violent disruption of the funeral of Carmine Lombardozzi's father, Carlo Gambino had seen to it that his wife's funeral was strictly policed by his own men and by the New York City Police Department. Uninvited guests, onlookers, and snooping FBI agents were kept at a considerable distance from the church in areas that had been cordoned off the night before. As a result, the funeral went off without incident.

Because of Mrs. Gambino's illness that summer of 1971, Carlo had called off the traditional Fourth of July celebration he always gave for his men and their families at his summer home in Massapequa, Long Island, on an inlet of South Oyster Bay. The entire neighborhood used to attend these noisy fiestas at which, in addition to fireworks, Gambino had his men distribute free hot dogs and sausages, salami and provolone sandwiches, sugar dusted *zeppole*, cannoli, pizzas, candy, and wine and beer. That Gambino had never bothered to become an American citizen and had consistently defied the U.S. Constitution all his life was irrelevant. Business was everything for Carlo Gambino and his Fourth of July celebrations were just good business. It made the community believe he was a fine American patriot.

That is not to say there was not a genuinely benevolent side to the now legendary Mafia patriarch. There was. For, in addition to his principal job of piling up more and more money for himself and his crime family, Carlo also fulfilled the traditional role of the Mafia don as head of an invisible government that administered to the mundane needs of the neighborhoods he controlled.

Stories of Carlo Gambino's generosity of spirit and purse among the poor of the city's Italian ghettos are legion and can still be heard today in certain sections of Brooklyn and Manhattan's Little Italy.

Carlo Gambino would appear on Little Italy's Mulberry Street without warning, and within minutes the "street telegraph," or word of mouth, would have alerted every family within ten blocks that Don Carlo had arrived and was receiving his *amìci* at the Café Biondo.

Soon, from the windows and doorways of Mulberry, Grand, and Hester streets, shrill cries would be heard from the women: *"O' padrino sta ca'!"*

"É venuto Don Carlo!" "É qui, é qui, Don Carlo sta qui, al Café!"

Then a crowd would begin to collect outside the café: old men wearing black knickers and black hats, old women in black shawls, buxom middle-aged housewives with their aprons still on and sleeves rolled up, tough young men with long greased black hair, gesturing wildly with their hands and speaking a heavy Sicilian dialect. storekeepers, café owners, landlords, tenants, fathers of teenage unwed mothers.

Don Carlo would settle at a table in the very center of the café accompanied by a bodyguard and a secretary. Two other bodyguards would take a table directly behind him, one from which all entrances and exits could be watched. A fourth man would stand at the main entrance to the restaurant. Then the protracted audience and tribunal would begin.

A supplicant would approach the man at the door, who would decide whether he or she would be permitted to see the don. Once passed on, the petitioner would be admitted to Gambino's table.

An elderly man, dressed in black, with hat in hand, would sit down and tell Don Carlo that his wife of fifty years was very ill and he had no savings or insurance to pay her medical bills.

A stern-looking father, a butcher by trade, dressed up in a fine suit with white shirt and tie and brightly polished shoes, would confront the don in hushed tones about his teenage daughter's pregnancy, her dishonor, and how he knew who the boy was and how he had to restore his daughter's honor.

An elderly widow with a black shawl over her head and shoulders was ill and had no money. Her two sons would not help her. Soon she would be evicted from her one-room apartment on Spring Street. What would she do?

. A heavyset middle-aged housewife with four kids in school had just been abandoned by her husband. He left no money for her, nobody knew where he was, and she had no means of support.

As these petitioners pled their cases, Don Carlo's white head would nod up and down, up and down, his perpetual grin only occasionally broken by a whispered comment to the secretary sitting by with pad and pencil. The audience would invariably end with a broadly smiling Don Carlo telling his supplicant that he would look into the matter and try to do what he could.

Such informal audiences in the Italian ghettos of New York won Don Carlo a huge constituency of devoted followers. Add to these the hundreds more won over by his twenty-seven *caporegimes* who also held court and heard grievances in their respective neighborhoods. By the dawn of the seventies Carlo Gambino had thousands and thousands of people who owed him favors. Who among his favored petitioners would not go out of his way to repay Don Carlo if he needed him—at a grand jury hearing, at a trial?

Carlo Gambino also endeared himself to his people by appearing regularly in the Italian neighborhoods of the city just to stroll about with his wife shopping and talking with his old friends on the streets.

He liked to stop in at Ferrara's on Grand Street to have a pastry and a cappuccino, then go on to Alleva's, also on Grand Street, to buy fresh mozzarella, *fiòre di làtte*, and Sicilian salami. As he sauntered about the narrow streets he would buy fruit and flowers from the outdoor stands and talk in dialect with his favorite vendors, attracting a crowd of admirers wherever he went. None of the other bosses behaved this way. Barricaded in their fortresses on Bay Ridge, Staten Island, and the Jersey Palisades, with armed bodyguards on twenty-four-hour alert, they made themselves as inaccessible as possible.

Carlo also went out of his way to get in the good graces of his Brooklyn parish priest, Father Lo Gatto, who happened to be a member of Mayor John Lindsay's Human Rights Commission. One night thieves broke into Lo Gatto's church and made away with all the parish's treasures, its jeweled mitres and icons, gold and silver crucifixes, chalices, incense burners, and communion vessels and plates.

Father Lo Gatto reported the theft to the police and got no results. He then paid a call on Gambino in his Brooklyn apartment and was assured by the aging don his men were not responsible, but that he needn't be concerned; his men would soon find the thieves and return the stolen items to the church.

The next day, true to his word, one of Carlo's capos returned all the stolen treasures to Father Lo Gatto. Amid effusions of gratitude, the priest asked the mobster if he had reported the recovery of the treasures to the police. The Gambino capo replied that he had not, that there was no need to, the thieves had been punished enough. With his parish priest on his side, Don Carlo had a character witness available who could conceivably be of great help to him in his inevitable skirmishes with the law.

But life for Carlo Gambino in the seventies was not all holding audiences and tribunals in Little Italy, browsing the flower and fruit stands of Mulberry Street, and doing favors for his parish priest. Carlo was still relentlessly pursued by the law and he himself had plenty of brutal family business to look after. As he confronted these challenges, his health began to fail.

In March 1970, a police detail swooped down on Carlo as he was sauntering along a Brooklyn street with his wife, handcuffed him, and charged him with masterminding a scheme to steal $30 million in cash from an armored truck company in the Bronx. A noted Boston armored car hijacker had implicated him in the plot. By then it had become common to blame Gambino for every big criminal conspiracy that came to light in the city. Later a federal grand jury indicted him for conspiring to rob an armored truck company, but the case was never brought to trial.

The following year the Justice Department renewed its efforts to deport Gambino. A deportation order had been issued against him in 1966, but had never been implemented. Now the government sought to implement it. But Carlo suffered one of his heart attacks days before the government planned to escort him out of the country. U.S. Public Health Service doctors examined the ailing don and confirmed that he did, in fact, have a heart condition. The deportation order was stayed. That heart condition took a turn for the worse in 1972 when, as a result of a severe attack, Carlo was rushed by ambulance to Columbus Hospital in Manhattan. But Gambino soon recovered and was back at his home on Ocean Parkway again attending to business.

It was around this time that Gambino got sucked into helping finance a narcotics deal to the tune of $4 million in partnership with Thomas "Tommy Ryan" Eboli, one of the ineffectual acting bosses of the Genovese family, and a certain Louis Civillo, believed by federal authorities to be the largest narcotics wholesaler in the nation. Somehow the deal went bad. Civillo's plan was discovered, he was arrested, and Carlo lost his $4 million investment. Rather than push hard to recover his investment, Don Carlo conceived of a better idea. He would get rid of Eboli and install his own man as boss of the Genovese family.

Eboli was shot dead one night as he was leaving the Crown Heights apartment of one of his mistresses. At a subsequent meeting of the Commission Don Carlo quietly elevated his dear old friend, Genovese *caporegime* Francesco Alphonse "Funzi" Tieri, to boss the Genovese family. Carlo was at the pinnacle of his power in New York, for he now controlled all five of New York's Cosa Nostra families.

Then there was the annoying matter of the kidnapping of one of Carlo's nephews, the twenty-nine-year-old Emmanuel "Manny" Gambino, in May 1972. What a messy business for a sick old man to have to deal with.

From then on Don Carlo's health began to fail him seriously and he retired to the house at 2230 Ocean Parkway to live out his last years. Here, in his sanctuary, he was insulated from the world by two layers of supporters. The inner layer consisted of his closest blood relatives, his brothers Joe and Paul, his sons Tommy, Carl, and Joe, his cousins Peter and Paul Castellano. The outer layer was staffed by two dozen or so Sicilian aliens Carlo had recently imported into New York from Palermo who were totally dependent on him financially and were also at the total mercy of the INS. The only money these "greasers" had came from Don Carlo and if they did something that displeased the don, all Carlo had to do was put in a call to the INS and the offenders would be out of the country within seventy-two hours.

In 1974, with Gambino's health speedily deteriorating, the government discovered that Don Carlo had been engaging in a huge alien smuggling operation over the past ten years that had been responsible for bringing several thousand Sicilians into the country illegally. Many were brought down from Canada. Others came in via the Gambino-controlled Brooklyn waterfront. Among them was Sicilian heroin smuggler and enforcer, Tommaso Buschetta, who would become notorious in the eighties. Law enforcement authorities believed Gambino had been collecting from $150,000 to $200,000 dues a year from his smuggled aliens. It was in 1974 also that the government finally learned from reliable informants that Gambino had been behind the murder of Joe Colombo on Italian Unity Day in June 1971.

The year 1975 brought a further deterioration of Don Carlo's heart condition and he began to make plans for his succession. The most powerful of his underbosses was the tough, ruthless killer, Aniello Dellacroce, who held forth from the Ravenite Social Club on Mulberry Street in Little Italy. Dellacroce was in command of some of the most powerful *regimes* in the Gambino family, among which was Carmine Fatico's crew at the Bergin Hunt and Fish Club in Queens. Dellacroce was a logical successor to Gambino.

But then there was Carlo's cousin, Paul Castellano, the son of his mother's sister, who had been through so many wars with him. Paul, or Big Paulie, as he was called, had taken a one-year prison term after Apalachin rather than reveal to a grand jury what had been said at the conclave. Big Paul was blood, *sàngue del sàngue*. Carlo and Paul had been like brothers for the past fifty years.

In the end Gambino chose his cousin Paul to succeed him, with the further proviso that Castellano, in turn, would turn the family over to Carlo's son Tommy upon Paul's death or incapacitation. Years later Castellano told two FBI agents that he made a solemn deathbed promise to his uncle Carlo to carry on after he was gone.

But what about the powerful Dellacroce? To ease the irascible man's inevitable disappointment, Carlo awarded him a huge consolation prize: near absolute control of all the family's most lucrative Manhattan rackets. This amounted to creating a family within a family, a possibly dangerous situation, but it did serve the cause of peace. Dellacroce was appeased and he and Castellano would go on to run the family in the late seventies and early eighties with a minimum of friction.

Carlo Gambino suffered his final heart attack on October 15, 1976, in his summer home at Massapequa, Long Island. Before long his blood family was at his bedside: sons Tommy, Carl, and Joe and their wives; daughter Phyllis and her husband; brothers

Paul and Joe; cousins Peter and Paul Castellano; and his sister-in-law, Providencia Villano, and her husband. It turned out to be not a very long vigil. After the Reverend Dominick A. Sclafani administered the last rights, he declared that Gambino had died "in a state of grace." He had died in his sleep and in his own bed, a rarity indeed among Sicilian Mafia bosses.

People in Brooklyn still talk about Don Carlo's funeral. The hundred cars in his cortege. The long line of weeping old men and women, immigrants from the old country whom Carlo had saved from penury. All the political big shots and high police brass, braving the inevitable innuendos in the next morning's press. The long line of cars winding toward the cemetery for the burial.

Years later Don Carlo was memorialized in film as the Mafia boss in John Huston's *Prizzi's Honor*, in which the bent, white-haired old man with the nodding head, perpetual smile, and lisping speech was resurrected before our eyes. It was a magnificent re-creation. His previous reincarnation, as Don Vito Corleone in Mario Puzo's *The Godfather*, had been all wrong. Marlon Brando did not resemble Carlo Gambino in the slightest. Brando was tall and muscular. Gambino was short and slim. But a few details of his performance rang true, such as holding the popular tribunals in Little Italy.

In 1982, the editors of the book *The Timetables of History—A Horizontal Linkage of People and Events* published by Simon & Schuster with a foreword by Daniel J. Boorstin, Pulitzer Prize winner and former Librarian of Congress, bestowed a signal, though doubtless unintentional, honor on Carlo Gambino. A perusal of the book's eighty-two page index reveals the name of no other Mafia figure but that of Carlo Gambino. His name appears under the Daily Life heading for 1976. There he is listed as one of the three notable world figures who died in that year. The others are Howard Hughes and J. Paul Getty.

Carlo Gambino had left an enduring imprint on organized crime in the United States and a huge festering tumor in his chosen city. The criminal enterprise he had led for almost twenty years had become the largest and richest of all the nation's Cosa Nostra families, a force for corruption of incalculable dimensions. The mayhem and suffering that accompanied Gambino's rise to power and that would continue unabated in the rule of his successors throughout the eighties cannot be adequately measured, only imagined. Gambino's legacy, in the end, was wholesale subversion of private business and public institutions and environmental havoc on a scale never before seen in New York City. It was countless ruined lives: decimated families, legions of addict slaves. To combat this monstrous parasite the government had spent millions with little result. What Gambino left New York was a tax on all its citizens.

Part V

Arrogance, Betrayal, and Murder

The Rule of the Pope (1976–1985)

20

Big Paul Takes Over

*If the president of the United States, if he's smart, if he
needs help, he'd come. I could do a favor for the
president. . . . You understand, Gloria?*

Paul Castellano, boss of the richest and most powerful crime family in the United States, was talking casually with his maid, and mistress, Gloria
Olarte, in the kitchen of his $3.5 million seventeen
room Staten Island mansion, known locally as the
White House. His boast was being recorded by an
FBI electronic listening device that had been planted
in his kitchen in March 1983. By then Big Paul had
become powerful enough to make such a boast without sounding unduly fatuous. Presidents of billion-
dollar corporations, heads of major labor unions,
and bosses of other Cosa Nostra families were regularly seeking his counsel. In terms of sheer power, he
possessed more effective authority than the mayor of
his city, for he could shut down the ports of
Brooklyn and Manhattan with a phone call, halt the
construction of a major building project with a command to a union official, and then, of course, he held

the ultimate power of life or death over his men and the people he did business with.

Big Paul had acquired this immense power in early December 1976, about a month and a half after the death of his predecessor, his cousin and brother-in-law, Carlo Gambino. Immediately after Gambino's death speculation was rife within the family that Carlo's experienced and ruthless underboss Aniello Dellacroce was going to take over, but, as we know, Gambino had made it clear before his death that cousin Paul would be boss and within hours of that death family *consiglière* Joe N. Gallo and two of the most powerful *caporegimes* in the family, James Failla and Ettore Zappi, had proclaimed their allegiance to Castellano. Dellacroce was in prison at the time, as was his protégé, John Gotti, and was therefore not in much of a position to mount a successful challenge to Castellano. Big Paul's backers respectfully waited for Dellacroce's release from confinement, which fell on Thanksgiving Day, before calling the sit-down at which Castellano would be officially confirmed boss.

The sit-down took place on November 24 at the modest Bensonhurst home of veteran Gambino capo Anthony "Nino" Gaggi, chosen to host the confirmation proceedings so as not to draw the attention of the law to the event. Present at the formalities, in addition to Castellano and Gaggi, were rival Aniello Dellacroce and loyalists Gallo, Failla, Zappi, Lombardozzi, and a few other high-ranking capos. John Gotti's immediate boss, Carmine Fatico, had not been invited to attend.

Big Paul's job was to placate the ambitious Dellacroce, who had been offended by Gambino's decision not to make him his successor, and lay down the law to his capos on some fundamental issues. To placate Dellacroce he confirmed his control over some of the family's most lucrative rackets and moneymaking crews in Queens and Manhattan, a control that, as we know, Carlo Gambino had awarded him before his death. Among these was the extremely prosperous Gotti-Fatico crew that operated out of the Bergin Hunt and Fish Club in Ozone Park. Gotti, still in prison for his complicity in the McBratney murder, was due to be released the following summer. These concessions seemed to appease the veteran Dellacroce, who had faithfully served three dons—Mangano, Anastasia, and Gambino—because he knew he would make a good deal of money out of them. The Dellacroce pacification presumably taken care of, Big Paul then told his capos that under his leadership there would be no cop killing and no dealing in drugs under penalty of death without trial. The last thing Big Paul wanted during his reign was heat from the law, especially from the feds. A relatively peace-loving man who scrupulously avoided publicity, Castellano wanted his men to devote their talents and energies to such more or less safe crimes as loansharking; numbers; construction job shakedowns; labor racketeering in cartage, meat, and garment industries; waterfront extortion; and car theft. So brisk were the formalities of Big Paul's confirmation and inaugural address that the entire sit-down took less than a half hour.

Although Big Paul believed he had successfully placated his underboss Aniello Dellacroce, in reality he had not. As Carlo Gambino's second-in-command, Dellacroce, according to the Cosa Nostra's unwritten code, should have succeeded Gambino as boss. In naming his cousin and brother-in-law his successor, Gambino had indulged in flagrant nepotism, a practice generally frowned upon not so much by the Sicilian Mafia as by its American counterpart, La Cosa Nostra. Since the sixty-two-year-old Dellacroce was a mobster of the old school, believing that a boss should never be challenged, that his orders should always be respected and obeyed, he swallowed his pride at being passed over, but the slight nevertheless rankled him and embittered his relations with Big Paul. Gambino's nepotism also irritated most of Castellano's capos and soldiers. They were suspicious that Castellano might indulge in nepotism himself, showing favoritism to his three sons or to Carlo Gambino's son Tommy. An ambitious young soldier like John Gotti wanted to rise in the family on his own merits and not have to worry about some relative of Big Paul's being promoted over him.

Paul Castellano was a very different species of Mafia don than the three men who had bossed the family before he took over. He was much more of a diplomat than they had been, was more polished and soft-spoken, and cultivated a more elegant appearance. A tall—six-foot-three—rugged man with a large, imposing head, big, meaty features, and thick, graying dark hair, he wore heavy black-rimmed spectacles, expensive custom-made, double-breasted suits, and hand-tailored mohair overcoats. When someone told him he looked more like a businessman than a mobster, it pleased him no end.

But a mobster he most surely was. Born in Brooklyn in 1915, the son of Sicilian immigrants (his father had been a butcher and a small-time numbers operator), he had dropped out of school after eighth grade, helped in his father's lottery and meat businesses, had joined Vince Mangano's outfit in his early twenties; had served Albert Anastasia during his thirties; had driven his cousin Carlo to the abortive Apalachin conclave at the age of forty-two; had served Carlo loyally throughout his fifties; and had acceded to bossdom of the nation's most powerful crime family at the age of sixty-one.

By the time he had risen to the top of his profession, Big Paul had acquired a liking for expensive clothes, dining in the finest restaurants—his favorites in Manhattan were the Palm on Second Avenue and Forty-fourth and Sparks Steak House on Third and Forty-sixth—and being driven around town by his chauffeur in his black Lincoln Town Car. Considering himself first and foremost a businessman, he disliked violence, had never been arrested in an actual shooting—though he would order many killings during his rule—did not carry a gun, and often expressed a dislike for the "shooters" in the family he had come to boss. He harbored a special detestation for the violent Dellacroce, who, it was said, enjoyed watching his victims die. Known by his minions variously as Paulie, Big Paul, Big Paulie, Uncle Paul, and the Pope, Castellano was somewhat averse to the latter sobriquet because he felt it carried overtones of ridicule and disrespect.

Yet there *was* something papal about Big Paul Castellano. He was a man with a weighty air of authority about him whose markedly Italianate profile with its huge vulturine nose recalled those of some of the infamous Renaissance popes. He also had a tendency to remain somewhat aloof from the capos, soldiers, and associates of the crime family he bossed, and carried himself with a similar haughtiness in the company of the members of the Commission of the five New York Cosa Nostra families over whom he presided, much to their irritation. In his self-ordained role of businessman, he was at his happiest at a meeting or a meal with a distinguished legitimate corporate executive. Among those he did business with were supermarket chain owners Ira Waldbaum of Waldbaum's; Pasquale Conte of Key Foods; Julie Miron, president of the Miron Lumber Company of Brooklyn; Robert Matthews, owner and president of Matthews Industrial Piping; and the "chicken king," Frank Perdue. To Waldbaum he dispensed advice on a regular basis for a fee. Matthews had sought him out to give him a $100,000 payoff for union peace on the $10 million oil pipeline reconstruction project he was building at Port Mobil, Staten Island. Frank Perdue had sought his advice on distributing his chickens in supermarket chains in which Castellano and his sons had influence and on obtaining labor peace at his huge nonunion chicken processing plant in Accomac, Virginia.

Paul Castellano had a certain air of privilege about him. The Castellanos had been a respected family in Palermo and had done well in New York over the past sixty years, especially in the meat business. And, of course, his sister Kathryn had married his cousin, Carlo Gambino. To be both the cousin and brother-in-law of the man regarded as the foremost criminal genius in the United States had conferred a certain status on Big Paul. For years—ever since Apalachin—he had known he was an heir apparent, the Prince of Wales of the Gambino family.

It was perhaps Paul Castellano's feelings of privileged status that ultimately undid him. He felt too secure in his power. He was not given to be suspicious enough of his own capos and the bosses of the other major New York families, all of whom came to detest him. Mafia bosses are known for their paranoia. Castellano was the opposite. He had a reputation of being too trusting of others.

Like his predecessor, Big Paul was also very much a family man. He had been close to his older sister, Kathryn Gambino, and her children, especially her firstborn son, Tommy, who was eventually supposed to inherit his crown. And he was devoted to his wife, three sons, and extraordinarily beautiful daughter, Connie. Two of those sons, Joseph and Paul, Jr., he had set up as president and secretary-treasurer, respectively of the P&H Rendering Company of Brooklyn, a prosperous fat-rendering concern that did a considerable business with the supermarkets of New York. Later he bought them a majority interest in the Dial Poultry Company, the business that helped Frank Perdue distribute his chickens in supermarket chains along the East Coast more efficiently than before. By the early eighties he considered himself practically the "de facto" boss of Waldbaum's supermarkets ("You know Waldbaum's . . . the super-markets?" he asked his maid in a conversation taped by the FBI in 1984, "I'm almost the boss of Wald-baum's now.").

Later on in his reign Castellano proved to be partic-ularly adept at infiltrating legitimate businesses and bringing them under the control of his crime family.

By Christmas 1976 Big Paul Castellano was reason-ably pleased with how things had gone during the transition from his cousin Carlo's rule to his. Recently released ex-convict Dellacroce had been temporarily placated and was beginning to make money again. The family's various rackets continued to be productive and his own legitimate business interests in New York State, and in New Jersey and Pennsylvania, were thriving. His appearances in his favorite restaurants in Brooklyn and Manhattan caused maître d's and waiters to stage opera buffa scenes of fawning obeisance when he would arrive, usually accompanied by a small entourage, for a meal. About the only misfortune he had suffered in this, the most important year of his life, was the onset of diabetes, an illness that would plague him for the rest of his life.

To memorialize and proclaim his new high status, Big Paul decided to build himself a splendid man-sion, surrounded by a park, on Staten Island, which would not only symbolize his position but would also insulate him and his immediate family from various undesirables. As a site for his new home he chose, as did the feudal lords of yore, the highest land on the island, a wooded hill the original Dutch settlers had named Todt Hill, or Death Hill, because of the casu-alties they had suffered in capturing the mound from the Indians who had occupied it for centuries.

Upon this hill—the highest elevation on the Atlantic seaboard between Maine and Florida—the chieftain of the nation's most powerful crime family chose to have built a large stone and stucco mansion, painted white, whose curved entrance portico, supported by two tall, slender fluted white columns, was suggestive of the south portico of the White House. With a frontage over 120 feet long, the great house was secluded from the road by majestic stands of pine, spruce, maple, and oak and by a wrought-iron fence high enough to both discourage intruders and prevent his ferocious Doberman pinscher guard dogs from leaping to freedom over its spikes.

The interior of the seventeen-room Castellano White House was spacious. A thirty-foot-long entrance hall, decorated with huge gilt framed mirrors, led to a graceful spiral staircase ascending to the second floor. The other ground-floor rooms were large and airy. Huge gilded lamps, sculpted in the style of the high Renaissance, rested on dark mahogany tables. The high-ceilinged living room and dining room each measured twenty by thirty feet. The huge mahogany dining room table seated twenty. Off the living room there was a small den, or study, with a fireplace. The kitchen was immense, containing huge freezers, a long counter, and a dining nook table that could seat ten. Upstairs there were four bedrooms, and there were eight bathrooms throughout the house, two of which contained ten-foot-square bathtubs. To ensure the safety of his domain, Big Paul had installed the finest, state-of-the-art security system his illegal earnings could buy.

The walled-in area in back of the house contained a small park with an Olympic-sized swimming pool and tennis and bocce courts. Huge terra-cotta urns sprouting flowering plants were scattered here and there. From the upstairs windows, each giving way to a balcony with a wrought-iron railing, breathtaking views could be enjoyed of the Atlantic Ocean and New York Harbor. Big Paul was particularly fond of the view from his bedroom window, which framed the graceful Verrazano Narrows Bridge, connecting Staten Island with Brooklyn, named after the first European to enter what became New York Harbor, the Italian navigator Giovanni da Verrazano, who sailed past Todt Hill in 1524.

It would be from this safe, stately, patrician setting that Big Paul would direct the intricate business of the vast crime conglomerate his cousin, Carlo, had assembled during a lifetime of illegal activity.

Yes, it was a seemingly impregnable fortress-residence that Big Paul had built for himself on Staten Island, a sanctum sanctorum in which the Pope could conduct business in maximum safety, comfort, and security.

Yet in only three years from its erection the ears of the FBI would become part of his bastion's electrical infrastructure, listening to Big Paul's conversations with family members and subordinates in his kitchen dining nook, where, as he was having his maid and lover, Gloria, prepare him a sandwich one evening, FBI monitors overheard him boast about how much he could do for the president of the United States.

21

The Return of John Gotti

As Big Paul was settling into his splendid White House on Todt Hill, one of his soldiers, John Gotti, was preparing to leave Green Haven State Prison, two years after having been confined there for having participated in the murder of James McBratney, alleged kidnapper of Carlo Gambino's nephew, Manny Gambino.

Gotti had been given an unusually light sentence for his role in the McBratney murder, thanks to the attorney Carlo Gambino had hired to represent him, the brilliant, ambitious, and well-connected Roy Cohn.

Cohn, the precocious son of a New York judge, had graduated from Columbia Law School at the age of eighteen and had gone on to develop, among his many and varied clienteles something of a mob practice over the years. Among his clients were Genovese boss Fat Tony Salerno, Bonanno boss Carmine "Nino" Galante, and Gambino family members

Carmine Fatico, Aniello Dellacroce, Tommy and Joe
Gambino, Angelo Ruggiero, and John Gotti. A crucial
component of this practice was Cohn's network of
compliant law enforcement officials, judges, prosecutors, and district attorneys.

Conferring with Gambino over the problem of how
to handle the charges against Gotti in the McBratney
murder case, Roy Cohn came up with what turned
out to be a brilliant solution. Gotti was to plead guilty
to participation in the crime—he had held McBratney
while Galione shot him—and plea-bargain his way to
a light sentence. Cohn then persuaded the Staten
Island district attorney to accept a Gotti plea of guilt
for attempted manslaughter, a charge carrying a sentence of only four years, which meant two if the prisoner remained on good behavior.

Proving himself to be a model prisoner, Gotti was
released from Green Haven on July 28, 1977, after
serving barely two years.

And so he returned to his home in Howard Beach
and his wife and four children, and to his niche at the
Bergin Hunt and Fish Club in Ozone Park, with his
trusty *"gumbahs"*—companions in crime—Angelo
Ruggiero, Tony "Roach" Rampino, Willie Boy Johnson, and brothers Gene and Peter.

Gene Gotti and Angelo Ruggiero had been made, or
straightened out, as the mob phrases induction into
its ranks, while John Gotti had been in prison, and
now John was anxious to become a made guy himself.
One night, a couple of months or so after his release
from Green Haven, his wish was fulfilled. He and
eight other men were initiated into La Cosa Nostra in
a secret ceremony it is believed was conducted by Neil
Dellacroce. Dellacroce then appointed Gotti capo of
the Bergin Hunt and Fish Club crew, formerly run by
Carmine "Charlie Wagons" Fatico, who was standing
trial for loan-sharking and tax evasion at the time.
Before long Gotti and his men became the highest-
earning crew under Dellacroce's supervision, making

huge profits off such staples as gambling, loan-sharking, and hijacking. Appreciating the energy and drive of the thirty-seven-year-old Gotti, Dellacroce became his mentor and protector, grooming him for ever more lucrative future responsibilities.

It is not known whether, in the fall of 1977, Big Paul Castellano was fully aware of the Dellacroce-Gotti bond and what it meant for the family he bossed. Remaining essentially remote from the Dellacroce faction within his family, Big Paul kept to himself in his secluded White House on Todt Hill, seeing mostly certain trusted capos also based on Staten Island, men like the wiley James "Jimmy Brown" Failla, a veteran Castellano loyalist active in the carting and waste disposal business; Failla's protégé, Frankie DeCicco; and the pugnacious, hotheaded Thomas Bilotti, an official in his Scara-Mix Concrete Company, who was to become his aide-de-camp, chief confidant, and chauffeur. Another frequent visitor to the White House was the *consiglière* of the Gambino family, the astute, philosophical, and aging Joe N. Gallo.

Delegating enormous authority to the virtually autonomous Dellacroce and his crews, and leaving routine criminal operations in the crews under his immediate supervision up to his capos, Big Paul conducted his business from the kitchen of his Todt Hill mansion and from his office at Dial Poultry in Brooklyn, concentrating on his own pet concerns: the infiltration of legitimate businesses and control of key labor unions.

One day tapes of Big Paul's remarks, recorded on an FBI bug planted in his White House kitchen, would reveal the extent of his control of the International Longshoremen's Association, through his capo, Anthony Scotto, whom he was promoting for the union's presidency. "We were making him advance in our union," he told a visitor to the White House one day, "Go up, up, up the ladder. And what it was, what's gonna happen, we're gonna have a president!"

The White House tapes would also reveal Big Paul's grip on the construction unions, through which he controlled the ready-mix concrete industry in New York. From every gob of concrete poured to erect the Manhattan skyline of the eighties Big Paul took his cut, and in so doing helped make construction costs in New York the highest in the nation.

Big Paul's policy of isolating himself from John Gotti and the Dellacroce faction did not mean that he isolated himself from the money Gotti's crew was making. As Boss, Big Paul was entitled to his share of the Gotti crew's profits, as he was to shares of the other twenty-two crews' net earnings, and he made sure he received his due, sometimes more than his due, for Big Paul was a greedy man who struck his capos and fellow Commission members as being always on the take.

Isolating himself from personal contact with Gotti and his *gumbahs* in the Bergin crew, but taking a slice of the profits nevertheless, Castellano inevitably aroused Gotti's ire. As time passed, FBI informants within the Bergin Hunt and Fish Club would report an ever-growing disaffection between Gotti and his boss. Who did Big Paul think he was to remain so aloof, to disdain contact with such a big earner as he was? It was around this time that an informant told the FBI that Gotti was referring contemptuously to Castellano as the Pope.

Shortly before John Gotti was formally inducted into the Cosa Nostra and appointed captain of the Bergin crew, the FBI turned a Gotti associate within the Bergin Hunt and Fish Club and hired him as a paid informant. The informant was given the designation source BQ 11766-OC. Another FBI informant within the Bergin, BQ 5558-TE, also known as

Wahoo, had been informing on Gotti since 1966. Thus, unbeknownst to the new captain of the Bergin crew, practically everything that Gotti did or said at the Bergin was routinely reported to the FBI.

One of the consequences of the FBI intelligence operation against John Gotti was to focus the bureau's attention on Gotti's chief sponsor, Aniello "Neil" Dellacroce. The two sources BQ (the letters stood for "Brooklyn Queens") had informed the FBI that Gotti visited Dellacroce at least once a week at his Little Italy headquarters, the Ravenite Club on Mulberry Street. Soon the FBI would be installing bugs near the Ravenite and keeping the club under twenty-four-hour surveillance.

The Bergin informants told the FBI of the unusually heavy gambling John Gotti himself indulged in. Gotti, it was learned, bet on everything—numbers, horses, fights, college and pro football games—risking considerable sums, as much as $30,000 in one weekend. According to Wahoo, Gotti regularly sustained huge losses from gambling. So relentlessly did he gamble away his money that FBI investigators began to conclude that Gotti had a serious, uncontrollable addiction to betting.

Gotti's personal finances became so depleted from gambling that, according to Wahoo, Gotti had to resort to drug dealing to make up for his losses, even though Big Paul had banned drug trafficking in his family under pain of death and Gotti himself had ordered his Bergin crew not to deal drugs. To insulate himself from the actual buying and selling of heroin and cocaine, Gotti became simply an investor in drugs such as heroin and cocaine. According to Wahoo he would put up money for a buy and the money would go through several hands before the buy was actually made. Similarly, sales were made for Gotti by people three rungs removed from the actual transaction. And the money would get back to Gotti after having passed through several hands.

Gotti's gambling habit was putting him at considerable risk. If Big Paul found out he was trying to make up his gambling losses by pushing dope, he would most certainly order Gotti killed.

But despite his gambling and drug dealing, John Gotti proved to be a very capable captain of the Bergin crew and a much valued partner of the powerful Dellacroce. Gotti's crew earned a lot of money for Neil, and Dellacroce loved money. As the months passed, detectives spotted Gotti entering the Ravenite Club, where Dellacroce held court every day, with ever-increasing frequency. This could only mean one thing. Gotti and Dellacroce were growing closer and closer and Dellacroce was giving his protégé jobs beyond the range of his Bergin responsibilities.

As his power and influence grew, Gotti began wearing expensive tailor-made suits and his gait took on a swagger which reminded the old-timers in the family of the lordly strut of Gotti's boyhood idol, Albert Anastasia.

Was Gotti trying to imitate Anastasia? the old-timers wondered. For the Bergin capo's violent outbursts of rage were also reminiscent of the uncontrollable Mad Hatter. The sources BQ frequently reported to the FBI on Gotti's tirades, threats, and tongue-lashings. He bossed his crew around at the Bergin, insulting and shouting obscenities at them over the slightest infractions. When a subordinate did not return his phone calls, he threatened to blow up his house. He would threaten to have a man killed at the slightest provocation. And if a subordinate, or an associate, did not accord him proper respect, he would fly into a rage, order the offender out of his sight, and tell him that if he ever showed such a lack of respect again he would kill him. Clearly John Gotti was not a man to be trifled with.

Everyone in the Gambino family was aware of how tough and merciless and unforgiving John Gotti was. But it was not until the third year of his leadership of the Bergin that the full and dire extent of his brutality became fully appreciated.

In the spring of 1980 John Gotti's youngest son, Frank, a twelve-year-old who was a good student and had done well in sports, was struck by a car as he was riding a minibike near his parents' home, and was instantly killed. The driver of the car, John Favara, was a fifty-one-year-old service manager at a Castro Convertibles furniture plant on his way home after work. He had not seen the minibike suddenly shoot out from behind a garbage Dumpster until it was too late. The police ruled the boy's death an accident.

Frank Gotti had been the apple of his father's eye, the son for whom he had the highest hopes. His sudden death crushed John Gotti and drove his wife, Victoria, into prolonged despair. No one had ever seen the normally insensitive Bergin capo so upset. For days following the accident John Gotti appeared utterly distraught, almost breaking down during his son's funeral and burial.

Almost equally disturbed was the hapless John Favara, who knew the Gotti family and whose son had played with young Frank. Not long after the accident Favara began receiving threats. Immediately after an anonymous caller phoned the local police precinct and said, "The driver of the car that killed Frank Gotti will be killed," Favara found a written death threat in his mailbox. Later Favara's car was stolen and was found abandoned on a street about a mile from Favara's home. One day Favara opened his mailbox to find a funeral card bearing a photograph of Frank Gotti inside.

Meanwhile, John Gotti had erected shrines to his lost son in both the Bergin Club and his home in Howard Beach, and was observed frequently staring blankly at the framed photograph of Frank that hung in the Bergin shrine.

John Favara, deeply worried that John Gotti might try to avenge his son's death, began asking around for advice. A Gambino soldier who knew John Gotti advised Favara to slip away, to sell his house and car and move out of the neighborhood. Still Favara could not believe anyone would take revenge over what everyone, including the police, knew was just an unfortunate accident.

One day in late May he paid a visit to the Gotti home to offer his apologies and condolences and was greeted at the door by a wild-eyed Victoria Gotti, who promptly picked up a baseball bat and smashed Favara over the head with it. After being treated for injuries at a nearby hospital, Favara and his wife put their house up for sale.

Two months later, as the Favaras were about to move out of their house, John and Victoria Gotti left for a week's vacation in Florida. Later Gotti explained that he wanted his still grief-stricken wife to get some rest and distraction.

Three days later John Favara left the Castro Convertibles factory where he worked and was walking toward his car, which was parked in front of a diner, when a tall, brawny man came up to him and smashed him over the head with a club, knocking him unconscious. The assailant then picked Favara up, threw him into the back of a blue van, and drove off, followed by a green car that had arrived in front of the diner with the van.

A witness from the diner reported the apparent kidnapping to the police and the next day Favara's wife told the police her husband was missing. Police detectives then went to the diner and showed a photograph of John Favara to the diner's owner, Leon Papon. Papon recognized the man he had seen abducted as Favara. As the police proceeded with their investigation, three powerfully built men walked into Papon's diner, sat down, and fixed Papon with steady stares. Papon got the message, refused to talk anymore to the police, sold his diner, and moved out of town.

John Favara was never seen again and was officially declared dead six years later.

The police naturally suspected that John Gotti had had a hand in the abduction and probable murder of John Favara and were appalled by what they imagined Gotti had done. Police traffic accident investigators had reported that Favara had broken no laws—he was not exceeding the speed limit or running a red light—and obviously did not see the boy on the minibike when he struck him. To take revenge on a man who had merely caused a tragic accident was barbaric in the extreme.

Later Wahoo reported to the FBI that John Gotti had ordered Favara's death and that he and his wife had gone to Florida to establish an alibi.

But the police were never able to get to the bottom of the crime. When questioned by the police upon his return from Florida, John Gotti pleaded innocent, telling the police that he certainly wouldn't do something as foolish as that. Later the police received an unconfirmed report that Favara had been slaughtered by means of a chain saw and his body parts placed in a wrecked car that was then compacted into a cube of metal and bone.

Writers have speculated that the killing of Favara was carried out by Gotti's closest associates from the Bergin: Angelo Ruggiero, Tony "Roach" Rampino, and Willie Boy Johnson. Another theory posited the murderous Gambino soldier Roy DeMeo, street boss of the family's car-theft ring, as Favara's killer. Although most investigators, official and unofficial, believe John Gotti was behind the murder, the crime remains unsolved.

The Favara killing showed the world how tough and unforgiving the up-and-coming Bergin capo could be. Most of the men in the Gambino family got the message. John Gotti was not someone you could trifle with, not even accidentally. Among the few who did not get the message was Paul Castellano.

22

The Troubles of the Pope

Big Paul Castellano's assumption of leadership of the Gambinos was so quiet and invisible that it took months for the press to discover it. In *Time* magazine's May 16, 1977, cover story on the Mafia, published almost six months after Castellano took command, Aniello Dellacroce was reported to be boss of the Gambino family. More than likely, Big Paul was delighted with *Time*'s error. The last thing he would have wanted was the mention of his name in *Time* as a Mafia boss. It would have been embarrassing. How would all those respectable legitimate businessmen he dealt with have reacted to it? No, Big Paul liked to live and work in the shadows. The spotlight was abhorrent to him.

The messier side of his role as a crime boss was distasteful to him as well—the enforcing, the disciplining, the killing. Although Big Paul was most comfortable working out a lucrative agreement with a legitimate businessman over a steak at Sparks, he still could not avoid dealing with some pretty nasty people. For example, not long after he assumed command of the Gambinos he had to sit down with such lowlifes as the Westies and the Zips.

The Westies were a wild, bloodthirsty gang of Irish criminals who operated in Manhattan's Hell's Kitchen, a West Side, low-income neighborhood extending roughly from West Thirty-fourth Street to West Fifty-seventh Street between Eighth Avenue and the Hudson River. Leading the gang was a greedy, ruthless young tough with choirboy looks—blond hair, rosy cheeks, blue eyes—by the name of Jimmy Coonan, son of Irish immigrants. There were around twenty-four men working for Coonan during the sixties and seventies, including such infamous murderers as Mickey Featherstone (another choirboy), Jimmy McElroy, and Kevin Kelly. Among their criminal operations were loan-sharking, labor racketeering, extortion, numbers, counterfeiting, narcotics distribution, and murder for hire. Tales of how the Westies dismembered the corpses of their victims and disposed of the remains in city dumps and sewage treatment plants had spread terror throughout Hell's Kitchen for twenty years. "No corpus delicti, no crime, no police investigation" was the cornerstone of Jimmy Coonan's criminal philosophy, so he and his boys made sure the bodies of the people he and his gang killed were never found.

The victims were chopped up, usually in bathtubs, and the parts placed in several garbage bags and taken to various locations for elimination. A favorite final destination was a sewage treatment plant on Ward's Island in the East River where a cooperative worker accepted the bags for a price and consigned their contents to the sewage being treated that day.

By the late seventies the gang had become so inebriated with financial success—Coonan himself had salted away millions—that they became audacious enough to start roughing up, robbing, kidnapping, and killing made Mafia guys, including a Gambino loan shark. When this was brought to Big Paul's attention it so disturbed him that he called for a sit-down with Jimmy Coonan. Perhaps he could cut some sort of deal with him to keep the crazy killer in check. Having him murdered was out of the question because Jimmy and his followers had the reputation of being even more vengeful than La Cosa Nostra.

As unpleasant as this sort of encounter was for a man of Big Paul's fastidious sensibilities, he arranged to meet with Jimmy Coonan at a restaurant in the Bay Ridge section of Brooklyn called Tommaso's. The place was on Gambino turf, next door to a Gambino social club known as the Veterans and Friends, head-quarters of the powerful capo Jimmy Failla.

When Jimmy Coonan and his second-in-command, Mickey Featherstone, arrived at Tommaso's for the sit-down they were surprised to find that the boss was accompanied by a sizable entourage of Gambino brass. The two Westies had been met near the restaurant's entrance by Gambino car-theft chief Roy DeMeo and taken to a back room, where, seated around a large horseshoe-shaped table, they beheld Big Paul, his underboss Aniello Dellacroce, his *consiglière* Joe N. Gallo, and two of his most powerful *caporegimes*, Carmine Lombardozzi and Anthony "Nino" Gaggi. Also present was a representative of the Genovese family, underboss Frank "Funzi" Tieri, an ally of Paul Castellano's.

Big Paul was not taking any chances with the Irish mob. Aware of their mad-dog capriciousness and brutality, he had wanted to present to these upstarts as much power as he could to take the edge off their audacity.

After the food was served and small talk exchanged, Funzi Tieri whispered something in Big Paul's ear and Castellano reacted by asking Coonan whether he knew anything about the killing of one of his associates, a shylock, and what had happened to the shylock's "black book" that contained records of millions of dollars' worth of loans.

Coonan, who had been responsible for the killing of the loan shark, pleaded innocent, claimed he didn't know anything about the black book, and, in response to questions about his business dealings with the loan shark, admitted he had borrowed money from him, but had paid back all loans in full.

There were more questions about the murdered loan shark from the other diners; then the matter was dropped and Big Paul spoke up again. He told Jimmy Coonan that from now on he and his gang would be allied with Castellano and his men, that they could no longer act independently "like cowboys, like wild men."

From now on, Castellano insisted, if Coonan wanted anybody "removed" he had to get permission from either Nino Gaggi or Roy DeMeo. He also told Coonan he could use the Gambino name on the West Side but from now on he had to give Castellano ten percent of all the money he and his gang made. Coonan agreed. Being associated with the Gambinos vastly increased his prestige.

Later, over drinks and cigars at the nearby Veterans and Friends club, where around forty mobsters were carousing, Castellano took Coonan aside and told him that if he was ever called to Brooklyn, he had to come, no questions asked. The implication was that Big Paul was planning to use Coonan and his Westies to carry out hits for the Gambinos.

As it would turn out, the Westies would perform contract murders for the Gambinos and go a step further. They would introduce the family to their master corpse eliminator, Eddie "The Butcher" Cummiskey, who taught a few Gambino soldiers how to dismember a murder victim and make his remains vanish from the face of the earth.

The Gambino soldier selected by Big Paul to keep the Westies in line and collect their tribute was the deadly Roy DeMeo. Every Wednesday DeMeo would travel from Brooklyn to the West Side to meet with one of Coonan's soldiers, Tommy Collins, discuss ongoing business, and collect ten percent of everything the Westies had brought in since his last visit.

When, not long after the sit-down at Tommaso's, Castellano was questioned about his relationship with the Westies by Joseph Coffey, commander of the New York Police Department's Organized Crime Homicide Task Force, Big Paul went so far as to tell Coffey that he had met with Jimmy Coonan and Mickey Featherstone, referring to them as "two nice Irish kids," but said nothing much had come of it. Privately, among his own men, Castellano confided he did not feel very comfortable with the two Westy leaders.

Another bunch of disagreeable wild dogs Castellano was compelled to deal with were the Zips, Sicilian nationals who took orders from the Sicilian Mafia in Palermo. They had begun to infest certain areas of Brooklyn—Bushwick and Bensonhurst—and had begun to play a major role in the Sicily–New York heroin trade. On October 6, 1980, Big Paul had his first and only sit-down with the Zips. It took place over lunch at Martini's Seafood Restaurant in Bay Ridge.

The Sicilians—dubbed Zips by their American counterparts, who also called them, contemptuously, Geeps and Siggies—had become a problem for Big Paul because they were brazenly engaging in criminal activities in his family's territory without his consent. Furthermore, they had let it be known that they answered to no one but their *cosca*, or clan, in Sicily. The Zips were getting so rich off the burgeoning Sicilian heroin trade that they were becoming more powerful in Brooklyn than Castellano's own men.

Law enforcement authorities agree that the birth of the Sicilian heroin cartel occurred at a summit meeting between two dozen or so Sicilian and American Mafiosi held at the Grand Hotel des Palmes in Palermo in 1957.

Among the Americans present at the conference were Lucky Luciano, Joe Bonanno, with two of his top capos, Carmine Galante and John Bonventre, and the Magaddino brothers from Buffalo. Among the Sicilians were Don Giuseppe Genco Russo, then one of the most powerful bosses on the island; Salvatore Greco, member of one of Palermo's wealthiest Mafia families; and Gaetano Badalamenti, destined to be head of the Sicilian Mafia commission known as the Cupola and later a key figure in the Pizza Connection heroin distribution conspiracy. After protracted discussions in the sumptuous art nouveau salons of the des Palmes, it was agreed that the two Mafias would work together, while retaining separate identities, to market heroin in the United States.

The Sicilians would import the morphine base from the Middle East, refine it on the island, ship it to New York, and distribute it there and throughout the rest of the nation. All the Americans had to do was provide certain support services and, of course, the territory once the product arrived in the United States, for which the Sicilians would pay the Americans a "rent." This way the Americans would make money off heroin without ever getting their hands dirty touching the stuff.

It took a while for this arrangement to be worked out in practice. It was not until the late sixties and early seventies that Zips began turning up in Brooklyn in large numbers and the Sicilian heroin refining and exporting machine got into high gear. By the early eighties the sale of Sicilian heroin in the United States was bringing in billions, perhaps as much as $15 billion a year. It had become a major industry and had begun to cause a lot of disruptions within La Cosa Nostra families.

Trafficking in narcotics was a federal offense in the

United States and so the American bosses had shied away from the trade for years, ordering their men not to deal in drugs under penalty of death. But by the late seventies and early eighties the profits that could be made from drugs were so vast that many in La Cosa Nostra families could not resist the temptation of dealing in them. This, in turn, brought internal havoc to several families.

The staggering profits to be made off heroin also proved to be too tempting for at least one Cosa Nostra boss, Carmine Galante, now head of Brooklyn's Bonanno family and one of the attendees at the 1957 Palermo summit. A greedy man and a vicious killer, Galante plunged into the heroin trade as soon as he got out of prison (he had done twelve years at Lewisburg on a narcotics conviction), becoming a collaborator with the Zips, many of whom he himself had imported from Sicily, and forming a close alliance with their leader in New York, also a Sicilian national, Salvatore "Toto" Catalano.

Galante was soon challenging the power of the other New York dons. On his orders several obstreperous members of the Genovese and Gambino families were gunned down. The greedy Galante was out to monopolize the drug trade in New York. He wanted it all for himself.

Galante's ambitions soon became intolerable to the other dons and they started conspiring against him. By the summer of 1979 a plot had been hatched to do away with him. On board were Santos Trafficante, Jr., from Florida, and Frank "Funzi" Tieri, Jerry Catena, Aniello Dellacroce, and Paul Castellano from New York.

In one of the most spectacular hits in mob history, Carmine Galante was taken out in broad daylight while eating lunch in the open-air garden patio of Joe and Mary's Restaurant in the Bushwick section of Brooklyn. Galante was finishing his meal when three masked gunmen erupted into the place and blasted him to death with two shotguns. It was later rumored that some disaffected Zips had been hired to carry out the assault.

With Galante gone the American end of the heroin trade was now up for grabs. Some investigators, including two Justice Department attorneys, believe that is why Big Paul Castellano sat down with the Zips in Bay Ridge once the smoke had cleared.

Paul Castellano was, like Galante, a greedy boss who avoided sharing his spoils with his capos and soldiers whenever he felt he could get away with it, which was more often than not. Certainly he was not about to share the enormous profits to be made off the Sicilian heroin trade with the other New York bosses. As chairman of the Commission, he felt he was entitled to the entire pie.

According to Richard Martin, assistant U.S. attorney for the southern district of New York and lead prosecutor in the 1985 Pizza Connection trial, Big Paul Castellano sat down with Salvatore Catalano and his Zips at Martini's Restaurant in Bay Ridge to "work out the new terms of payment for the heroin franchise. . . . Carmine Galante was out of the way; now the money would go straight to Castellano himself." One of Martin's colleagues, Louis Freeh, also an assistant U.S. attorney, agreed: "We know that the Sicilians have been paying off the U.S. bosses on the heroin all along. . . . Paul Castellano got paid, in spite of threatening others with death for dealing."

With the Westies and the Zips now in the Gambino fold, Big Paul could conduct his various criminal enterprises knowing that between the Irishmen and the Sicilians he had a pool of killers at his disposal who, being outside the family, could help further insulate him from complicity in whatever murders he might order.

Not that he needed more killers at his command. With the homicidal DeMeo crew operating from within his own family, he did not lack hit men.

Roy DeMeo was the street leader of a band of Gambino killers, extortionists, loan sharks, drug traffickers, and auto thieves who were responsible for at least twenty-five murders during the period January 1975 through June 1982, probably many more. To read the federal RICO indictment that was handed down in early 1984 against Big Paul and twenty members of this crew is to sense the full horror and depravity of what went on in the crime family Big Paul led for nine years. Investigators now believe that DeMeo, who lived grandly in a luxurious home in Massapequa Park, may have been responsible for killing more people than any other killer in U.S. history. The indictment alleged that there was a direct connection between Roy DeMeo, under whose day-to-day direction all this murder and mayhem was carried out, and Paul Castellano. It held that DeMeo reported directly to defendant Anthony "Nino" Gaggi, "who served as captain of the crew," and Gaggi reported to Castellano, "who acted as boss."

Some of the more active members of the crew were Gambino soldiers Joey Testa, Ronnie Ustica, Paul "Paulie Pinto" Dordal, Henry Borelli, Anthony Senter, Ronald "Bulldog" Turekian, and Edward "Fast Eddie" Rendini.

The purpose of the crew, the indictment asserted, was "to obtain income from murders, thefts, loan-sharking, fraud, drug trafficking, selling stolen property, and promoting prostitution."

The principal activity of the crew was stealing expensive, luxury automobiles from streets, parking lots, used car lots, even showrooms, altering them, if necessary, to make them appear brand new, giving them false registrations, and transporting them to the Middle East, principally to Kuwait, where they would be sold as new to Kuwaiti sheikhs and businessmen at cut-rate prices. One New York City police detective, sent to Kuwait City to find out what happened to the stolen cars, found that some were being used by the Kuwaiti police force.

Roy DeMeo let no one stand in his way. Potential witnesses and potential competitors to the enterprise were quickly eliminated. Most of DeMeo's victims were mobsters; some were members of his own crew. Others were entirely innocent bystanders who happened to be in the wrong place at the wrong time. One twenty-year-old bystander, who happened to be at the scene of one of DeMeo's killings, was himself killed. Even persons close to suspected informers were shown no mercy. DeMeo had the nineteen-year-old girlfriend of a suspected informer shot to death. When Nino Gaggi was on trial in 1979 on racketeering charges, DeMeo's crew coolly rubbed out three government witnesses due to testify, including a New York Housing police officer, and kidnapped and killed two of the jurors hearing the case. DeMeo also rubbed out a supposed Middle Eastern competitor, a Jordanian Khaled Fahd Darwish Daoud, known as "The Arab," whom DeMeo believed was also shipping stolen cars to Kuwait.

As a sideline, unrelated to the car-theft operation, DeMeo and his men carried out select hits for their ultimate boss, Big Paul Castellano. One of the most shocking was the killing of Big Paul's son-in-law and Gambino soldier Frank Amato, a hijacker and butcher at Dial Poultry, who was married to Castellano's gorgeous daughter Constance. Big Paul had heard on good authority that Frank Amato was fooling around with other women and periodically beating up his pregnant wife. Connie had become aware of her husband's infidelities and, deeply disturbed, suffered a miscarriage. That was enough for Big Paul. He ordered DeMeo to get rid of his son-in-law. Frank Amato disappeared on September 20, 1980, and was never seen again. DeMeo, Nino Gaggi, Joey Testa, and others were charged with the crime.

Key witness Dominick Montiglio testified to the

horror of the DeMeo operation. He told the court that many killings took place in a Brooklyn apartment that served as both an execution chamber and a butchery for dismembering human bodies.

"When the person would walk in," said Montiglio, "somebody would shoot him in the head with a silencer, somebody would wrap a towel around his head to stop the blood, and somebody would stab him in the heart to stop the blood from pumping."

"They would then drag him into the bathroom," Montiglio went on, "put him in the shower, bleed him, pull him out, put him on a pool liner in the living room, take him apart, and package him."

The body parts, according to Montiglio, were wrapped in plastic bags and placed in cardboard boxes that were tied up and taken to a city dump controlled by the Gambinos. The DeMeo crew also dealt heavily in drugs, despite Big Paul's ban. The 1984 indictment charged them with possession, with intent to sell, of 23.4 tons of marijuana, 499,000 Quaalude tablets, and 25 pounds of cocaine.

By late 1982 the DeMeo crew's wholesale killings and drug dealing had begun to trouble Big Paul. Word had gotten back to him that federal agents had begun investigating the crew's activities. One of DeMeo's victims found and identified by the police had been stuffed in a barrel, a clumsy method of elimination. Sensing that DeMeo may have drifted out of control, Castellano called the mobster to a sitdown. DeMeo never showed up. Around this time, an FBI bug in Big Paul's Staten Island mansion picked up a conversation in which Castellano seemed to be feeling out the Gotti crew about killing DeMeo. Later a bug in the Bergin Hunt and Fish Club overheard Gene Gotti telling his brother John that DeMeo had killed at least thirty-seven people.

But in the end Big Paul turned to his trusted capo Nino Gaggi, DeMeo's immediate superior, to get rid of his wayward soldier. "Take care of him, Nino," an

FBI bug heard Big Paul tell Gaggi one morning. Gaggi did as he was told. On January 10, 1983, the murderous career of Roy DeMeo came to an end. His body was found in the trunk of his own car. Ralph Scopo, a soldier in the Colombo family, was taped by the FBI delivering DeMeo's epitaph: "The guy had cast-iron balls."

But for Big Paul it was too late. The cat was already out of the bag. By the time of the DeMeo murder, the U.S. attorney for the southern district of New York, Rudolph Giuliani, was assembling a case against him, Nino Gaggi, and most of the men who had worked for DeMeo. Early in 1984 Big Paul would find himself and twenty of his men indicted on fifty-one counts of racketeering in connection with the activities of the DeMeo crew. And that was only the beginning of what the U.S. attorney had in store for him.

23

The Giuliani Crusade

Big Paul Castellano had not the remotest idea what an adversary he had in Rudolph Giuliani. For the first time since the days of Bobby Kennedy there was someone at Justice prepared to take on the mob with crusading zeal. When Giuliani finally struck with full force, Big Paul and the other New York bosses were taken by storm. For almost two decades they had gotten away with so much. Fatuous and overconfident, they proved totally unprepared for Giuliani's massive assault.

Prior to becoming U.S. attorney for the southern district of New York, Rudolph Giuliani had held the number three position in the Justice Department in Washington. At thirty-four he was associate attorney general under William French Smith in charge of the criminal division. In this capacity he singlehandedly persuaded the Reagan administration to launch what turned out to be the most intensive onslaught against organized crime since Bobby Kennedy had taken on the mob in the early sixties.

It was in the fall of 1981, in the first year of the Reagan presidency, that Giuliani seized a chance to get Ronald Reagan's ear. The occasion was a Cabinet meeting at the White House he had attended at the side of Attorney General Smith. Officials of Giuliani's rank usually attend Cabinet meetings with their bosses to listen and learn, not speak up and advance ideas or programs of their own. But at this meeting, the young and impetuous associate attorney general broke the rule and, addressing the president and his Cabinet, urged Ronald Reagan, in an impassioned plea, to mount a concerted effort against organized crime.

Giuliani's urging bore fruit about a year later when, on October 14, 1982, President Reagan went to the Justice Department and delivered a nationally televised address in which he announced a $100 million crackdown on the drug trade and organized crime.

The president delivered his address in the department's vast auditorium before an audience of hundreds of FBI, INS, and DEA agents, U.S. attorneys from all over the nation, the entire Justice Department staff, and administrative employees of the various law enforcement agencies. Flanking the president on the stage were Attorney General Smith, FBI Director William Webster, and Associate Attorney General Rudolph Giuliani.

In his address Ronald Reagan delighted his audience of crime fighters by talking tough. His ultimate aim was "to eliminate this confederation of professional criminals, this dark, evil enemy within." To accomplish this required a total commitment. He would mount a virtual war against organized crime, which, he told his audience, was costing the nation billions of dollars and thousands of ruined lives every year. "What kind of people are we," he asked, "if we continue to tolerate in our midst an invisible lawless empire?"

Getting down to details, the president announced he would soon establish twelve new drug and organized crime task forces in the nation's major cities and hire nine hundred new FBI agents and two hundred new assistant U.S. attorneys. To pay for the coming onslaught he was going to ask the Congress for $100 million.

Three months later Rudolph Giuliani's Organized Crime Drug Enforcement Task Force, armed with $100 million and a new Justice Department ruling allowing for increased use of electronic surveillance, was in place, primed for its attack on the mob.

But Giuliani would not remain in Washington long. In the spring of 1984 the position of U.S. attorney for the southern district of New York suddenly opened up, due to the resignation of the incumbent, John Martin, Jr., and Giuliani was quick to volunteer for it. In New York, where five organized crime families operated, he would be on the cutting edge of the Reagan administration's crackdown on the mob. Instead of pushing papers from a command center in Washington, he would be on the front lines in New York.

Once installed in his Manhattan office at One Saint Andrew's Plaza, it did not take Giuliani long to become the most zealous, and successful, prosecutor of Mafiosi in the city's history.

There was a special dimension to Giuliani's personality that had been lacking in his predecessors. He was more motivated than they had been. As an Italian-American, he had long held a strong repugnance for the Mafia. As a young boy growing up in Brooklyn he had listened to his maternal grandmother's stories of how one of his great-grandfathers had been persecuted by the Black Hand, the Cosa Nostra's precursor. His father, who ran a pizza restaurant in Brooklyn, and one of his aunts used to continually rail against the Mafia, complaining how unfair it was that this small segment of the Italian-American community slandered the reputation of the vast majority, who were honest and hardworking and abided by Christian principles of morality. Giuliani was the first U.S. attorney in New York of Italian ancestry. Most of his predecessors had been WASPs. Battling the Mafia had been just a job for the WASP prosecutors. For the Italian Giuliani it was a mission.

That was part of his heightened motivation. There was also the priestly side of his personality in the equation. Brought up in a strict Catholic household, young Rudy Giuliani went to Catholic parochial schools, where he fell under the influence of the rigorously intellectual Christian Brothers, went on retreats to a Trappist monastery, and aspired to the priesthood. He was about to enter the Montfort Seminary on Long Island when, after much agonizing, he decided against it, entering Manhattan College in the Bronx, and then New York University Law School in Manhattan, graduating *cum laude* in 1968. Yet the sacerdotal side to his personality remained. His serious, ascetic chalk-white face is suggestive of fifteenth century frescoes depicting Florentine monks. Writers have already likened him to the Franciscan monk and religious reformer Girolamo Savonarola, who attacked what he perceived was the greed and licentiousness of Medicean Florence and consigned hundreds of "profane" paintings and books to the flames in the conflagration that came to be known as the Bonfire of the Vanities. Giuliani possessed the zeal of the dedicated priest. His detestation of corruption had a religious fervor to it. Perhaps this aspect of Giuliani's character had something to do with his ancestry. For, unlike the mobsters he prosecuted, all of whom came from impoverished areas of southern Italy and Sicily, Giuliani's paternal grandfather came from Tuscany, specifically from the prosperous province of Lucca, about seventy miles from Florence, an area known for its stern Roman Catholicism, its skilled weavers of wool and silk, its fine olive oil, its ancient churches, and its most famous son, the great opera composer, Giacomo Puccini.

When Giuliani took over as U.S. attorney, he soon learned that the New York FBI office had been assembling "enterprise evidence" against each of the five Cosa Nostra families in the city using the RICO statute as a guide in their investigations, and that much of the evidence had been gathered from wire-taps and electronic listening devices.

He also learned that the New York State Organized Crime Task Force, headed by Deputy State Attorney General Ronald Goldstock, had succeeded in bugging the Jaguar that Lucchese family boss, Anthony "Tony Ducks" Corallo, used in his travels around town.

In reviewing the transcripts of the FBI and state task force tapes, Giuliani quickly realized that not only was there sufficient evidence for RICO cases against the five families, but also for a RICO case against the Cosa Nostra's ruling body, the Commission.

The RICO statute was the brainchild of Notre Dame Law Professor G. Robert Blakey and was enacted into law in 1970. Standing for Racketeer-Influenced and Corrupt Organizations, RICO provided for the prosecution of entire criminal organizations, as well as their leaders, and provided also for the forfeiture of money, businesses, and property accumulated as a result of criminal activity. Under RICO the very existence of a Mafia family is a crime, and the family's ill-gotten gains are subject to confiscation.

Although RICO became law in 1970, it took federal prosecutors years to apply it to actual criminal cases. During the seventies the Justice Department's efforts against La Cosa Nostra had been hampered by a sclerotic J. Edgar Hoover, the turmoil over Watergate (which saw an attorney general go to prison), and the Church Committee's revelations of the government's alliance with certain Mafia bosses to plot the assassination of Fidel Castro. By 1979 only two hundred RICO cases had been tried, and not one of them had involved the mob. It was to Rudolph Giuliani's credit that he did not hesitate a minute to use the statute to prosecute the Cosa Nostra families of New York.

Paul Castellano was the first to feel the sting of a Giuliani RICO indictment. He and twenty members of the Gambino family's DeMeo crew were indicted in the fall of 1984 on fifty-one counts of racketeering. Next came the indictment of eleven high-ranking members of the Lucchese family, including its boss, Tony Ducks Corallo. Then, in February 1985, the bosses and underbosses of the five New York Cosa Nostra families were indicted under the RICO act for conspiring to operate an illegal enterprise, the Commission. Named in the indictment were Paul Castellano and Aniello Dellacroce of the Gambino family, Anthony "Fat Tony" Salerno of the Genovese family, Carmine "The Snake" Persico of the Colombo family, Anthony "Tony Ducks" Corallo of the Lucchese family, Philip "Rusty" Rastelli of the Bonanno family, and old Joe Bonanno himself, retired in Arizona. Later in 1985 Castellano was also indicted for conspiring to murder former Bonanno family boss Carmine Galante.

But these cases were only the first round of Giuliani's massive assault on the mob. Still to come were the so-called Pizza Connection heroin-smuggling indictment, involving twenty-two members of the Bonanno family, including several Sicilian Zips; the RICO indictment of Gambino *consiglière* Joe N. Gallo and *caporegime* Joseph Armone; the indictment of Gambino *caporegime* and Gotti intimate Angelo Ruggiero and ten others for racketeering and narcotics trafficking; and the indictment of Paul Castellano and Aniello Dellacroce for running the vast criminal enterprise that was the Gambino family.

By 1985 it finally dawned on Big Paul Castellano what an implacable foe he had in Rudolph Giuliani.

He was under no fewer than four federal indictments brought against him by the relentless prosecutor from One Saint Andrew's Plaza.

Giuliani had struck a bonanza of evidence against the mob in New York. The FBI had bugged Paul Castellano's White House on Staten Island; Dellacroce's house, also on Staten Island; Dellacroce's headquarters in Little Italy, the Ravenite Club; John Gotti's headquarters in Queens, the Bergin Hunt and Fish Club; and Fat Tony Salerno's East Harlem headquarters, the Palma Boy Club. And the State Organized Crime Task Force had bugged Gotti associate Angelo Ruggiero's home in Cedarhurst, Long Island, and the car Tony Ducks Corallo used in his travels around town.

Armed with one hundred thousand pages of transcripts of the FBI's and state task force's tapes, and the RICO statute, Giuliani was finally able to vent his abhorrence of the Cosa Nostra by inflicting the worst setback on the brotherhood in its seventy-year history in America. By the time Giuliani's assault was over, he would send half the Cosa Nostra's top leadership to jail.

24

The Ruggiero Tapes

In April 1982 FBI agents, in a daring operation, broke into Gambino soldier Angelo Ruggiero's house in Cedarhurst, Long Island, and planted bugs in the mobster's basement den, kitchen, and dining room. Since Ruggiero was a married man with children, the break-in was particularly risky. Yet the bugging of Ruggiero's home turned out to be an FBI masterpiece. By placing the bugs in three strategic locations, the monitoring agents were able to eavesdrop on Angelo as he walked about his house, following him upstairs and downstairs, rarely letting him get out of earshot.

The FBI had decided to bug Ruggiero's house because an informant at the Bergin Hunt and Fish Club, the headquarters of the Gotti-Fatico crew to which Angelo belonged, had told the FBI he believed Ruggiero was dealing in heroin—*babania*, as it was called by the mob—on a large scale. Ruggiero, the informant told the FBI, was part of a heroin-dealing ring operating out of the Bergin and Ruggiero's home that included Gambino soldier John Carneglia; John Gotti's brother, Gene; and eleven others. The informant, and intimate of John Gotti known as "Willie Boy" Johnson, also gave the FBI a blueprint of Ruggiero's Long Island home and advised them on the best places to plant the bugs.

It wasn't long before FBI agents, monitoring Ruggiero around the clock, had accumulated an enormous store of information about Ruggiero's heroin operation. They learned that Ruggiero and his men distributed large quantities of high-grade Sicilian heroin over a vast area that included Michigan, Wisconsin, and the Canadian provinces of Manitoba and Ontario; that the ring earned around $2 million every four months; and that Ruggiero was desperately fearful Big Paul Castellano would get wind of the operation and impose a death sentence on him.

Angelo Ruggiero was a plump, voluble extrovert who could never keep his mouth shut. He was called "Quack Quack" by his colleagues at the Bergin. Never dreaming that the FBI would ever succeed in bugging his house, he ran his heroin operation from his eat-in kitchen, where he met with a steady stream of accomplices and talked with others incessantly over the phone. It was the FBI's kitchen bug that accumulated most of the evidence against him.

In the conversations the FBI taped, Ruggiero frequently expressed concern that Big Paul Castellano might find out about his drug dealing. One such conversation between Ruggiero and one of his heroin ring partners, Eddie Lino, concerned the fate of Pete Tambone, a Gambino soldier whom Big Paul suspected was dealing in heroin.

Apparently Castellano had summoned John Gotti and Aniello "Neil" Dellacroce to a meeting at which he told them that two friends of theirs had informed him one of his soldiers, Pete Tambone, was trading in *babania*. Big Paul then reminded Gotti and Dellacroce that if one of his made men got caught dealing drugs, he would be killed.

The somewhat cryptic conversation between Ruggiero and Eddie Lino on the Tambone problem was recorded by the bug in Ruggiero's kitchen.

RUGGIERO: . . . John was excited. . . .

LINO: So what do I care? . . .

RUGGIERO: Bad, bad. . . . So Paul [Castellano] told, uh, Johnny [Gotti], he says, I want you. . . . He says you know anybody that's straightened out that moves *babania* [heroin] gets it . . . he says, from now on.

LINO: Really.

RUGGIERO: This kid Jo Jo told us. Is he [Pete Tambone] in the junk business? And I said, "Listen, ah, I can't say that, no. As far as I know the kid's been a bookmaker all his life." He says, "Where does he get his one hundred thousand, two hundred thousand to push out?" John [Gotti] said, "I don't know." So he says to Johnny, "What do you got to say about it?" He said he [Tambone] shouldn't be a friend of ours. He says, that's it. That's it.

LINO: What?

RUGGIERO: I don't know. Johnny gave him [Paul Castellano] some off-the-wall shit. Paul says, okay. He said, "John, whatever you told me, you don't have to tell him that." John says, "Don't worry about it. 'Cause after I leave here, I'm going to see Neil." Went right to Neil's house. I understand Neil had a bad argument with Paul. Joe Gallo wants to hit Jo Jo. So Johnny went to his fucking house. . . . I told you who ratted, uh, Little Pete out, right?

LINO: Yeah, the wolf and Frank the Wop.

RUGGIERO: What do you think Pete told me yesterday?

This stays between me and you.

LINO: You should whack 'em.

RUGGIERO: Me and Johnny are gonna whack 'em.

Having disposed of the Pete Tambone matter—for the time being, at least—the discussion turned to heroin smuggling.

LINO: I'm going to Florida. I'm gonna get away from all this bullshit. I don't need it.

RUGGIERO: [low voice] I can get planes.

LINO: We can get it, too. How much you got?

RUGGIERO: [low voice] Six. Yeah, well, I can give it to you for about sixty. . . .

LINO: Yeah. Well, I'll ask him.

RUGGIERO: [low voice] So listen. I'll give you one. You let me know if you want them. Then do what you want. I'll give it to you every week, whatever you want.

LINO: Okay.

RUGGIERO: [low voice] It's got to be a hundred thousand or higher a week.

LINO: All right.

RUGGIERO: So, if you want them, let me know.

LINO: You look whatever I say. Go full out or back off. . . . Go full out.

The Pete Tambone problem was an acute one, not only for Tambone and Castellano, but also for Ruggiero and the Gotti brothers, who feared that Castellano's discovery of their old friend's drug dealing would lead Big Paul to be suspicious they, too, might be pushing junk.

Castellano had informed John Gotti that he was going to the Commission to obtain approval to kill Pete Tambone. He told Gotti that getting rid of Tambone would be a lesson to everyone in the family: If you deal in drugs, you pay for it with your life.

Big Paul maintained a double standard. It was all

right for him to profit from the heroin trade indirectly, through the Zips. That would not bring any heat from the feds. But it was not all right for one of his men to deal junk in the streets with all the undercover agents out making buys. That could invite a federal investigation.

Ruggiero and the Gotti brothers were in a difficult position. They had been close to Tambone for years. Now they were being called upon by their boss to sanction Tambone's murder, perhaps even carry it out themselves.

As it turned out, Castellano eventually decided that Pete Tambone would not be killed, but would be expelled from the family. Although the resolution of the crisis had been peaceful, it nevertheless served to increase tension between the Gotti-Dellacroce faction of the Gambino family and the Castellano faction.

That tension would be heightened to the brink of war when in 1983 a federal indictment was handed down against Angelo Ruggiero, Gene Gotti, John Carneglia, and eleven others, charging them with trafficking in narcotics and revealing the existence of the Ruggiero tapes upon which evidence the indictment was based. When Big Paul Castellano learned of the tapes, he flew into a rage and demanded to see transcripts of them, or else. Ruggiero refused. As a defendant in a federal case the law required that Ruggiero be given transcripts of his taped conversations.

A conversation about the Ruggiero tapes between Angelo Ruggiero and Gambino underboss Aniello Dellacroce, who was Ruggiero's uncle, recorded by an FBI bug planted in Dellacroce's Staten Island home, revealed how imminent hostilities between the two factions were.

RUGGIERO: All these months that . . . no excuse . . . there's no shame over here.
DELLACROCE: I've been tryin' to make you get away

with these tapes. But Jesus Christ Almighty, I can't stop the guy [Castellano] from always bringin' it up. Unless I, un', un', unless I tell the guy, "Hey, why don't you go fuck yourself, and stop bringin' these tapes, tapes up." Then you, then we know what we gotta do then, we, we, go and roll it up and go to war. I don't know, if that's what you want.

RUGGIERO: I don't want that. No, I don't want that, no, I don't want that.

DELLACROCE: I'm sure you don't want it, because . . .

RUGGIERO: I don't want, I don't want that, no. I don't want that at all.

DELLACROCE: I mean, that, that's what I, I told you last week, you say, "What should I?" I told you, that's, that's in the last stage. Let's, let's wait, let's take it easy, that's the last stage. If, if it has to come to that, it'll come to that. But let it come to that. Let's not just talk about it, because you don't wanna give the guy the tapes. I'm, for Christ sake. I ain't sayin' you're wrong. Don't forget, don't only consider yourself. You know, you got a lot of other fel—you know, fellas, too, that you like. And a lot of other fellas'll get hurt, too. Not only, you could get hurt, I could get hurt, he could get hurt. A, a lot of other fellas could, could, could get hurt. For what? For what? Over, over because you don't wanna show him the tapes.

Angelo Ruggiero had no intention of giving up the tapes to Big Paul Castellano, even though that refusal might precipitate war between the two factions. There were conversations on those tapes that represented infractions of the Cosa Nostra code and Ruggiero knew it. One was a discussion Angelo had had with Eddie Lino about high-level Commission business Ruggiero had been privy to. If Big Paul read a transcript of that tape, he most certainly would have handed down a death sentence against his overtalkative Bergin soldier.

Meanwhile, as Big Paul was fuming over Angelo Ruggiero's indiscretions, putting pressure on Angelo's boss, Dellacroce, and close friend, John Gotti, to make Angelo hand over the tapes, the FBI, in an operation that surpassed the break-in of Ruggiero's house, succeeded in invading none other than Big Paul's stronghold on Staten Island.

25

The Bugging of the Pope

Big Paul's seventeen-room Staten Island mansion on Todt Hill stood on some of the most desirable, and expensive, real estate in New York City. Rising 410 feet above sea level, Todt Hill provided its residents with groves of ancient trees, lush green lawns, and spectacular views of New York Harbor and the Manhattan skyline. One hundred and thirty-five acres of the hill were taken up by the fairways and greens of the Richmond Country Club, the only privately owned golf course in the city. For neighbors Big Paul had two secluded Roman Catholic seminaries, a twelve-acre private prep school, and such distinguished public servants as borough president Guy V. Molinari and James F. Regan, chairman of New York State's Commission on Pension and Retirement Systems. Another neighbor, the old Moravian Church cemetery, held the remains of the great nineteenth century steamship and railroad magnate Cornelius

Vanderbilt, who upon his death was reported to have been the richest man in America, if not in the world.

For the FBI to invade this secluded residential sanctuary, plant a bug in Castellano's White House, and not be detected was an extraordinary feat of daring and professional expertise.

Complicating the procedure was the fact that Big Paul's wife, Nina, was in residence, and his maid and mistress Gloria rarely left the house except to do a little shopping in the morning.

The White House was something of a fortress. Big Paul had installed a closed-circuit television camera security system whose screens could be monitored in an office on the ground floor, and which was in turn connected to a Staten Island security firm with a capability of almost instantaneous response. And outside, within the confines of a high wrought-iron fence, two fierce Doberman pinschers roamed at will.

It was in 1981, five years after Big Paul had taken over the Gambino family, that the FBI decided to concentrate on nailing Castellano. During the first five years of his reign, Big Paul had led the most restrained and inconspicuous life of any of the five New York bosses. Well insulated from his crimes by several layers of middle management, it was hard to get anything concrete on him. It was hard to even *see* Big Paul, for more and more he had begun to remain within the confines of the White House, rarely venturing out into the traffic snarls, crowded streets, and foul air of Brooklyn and Manhattan.

All this was most frustrating to the New York FBI, especially to Bruce Mouw, supervisor of the Gambino Squad of the Brooklyn-Queens FBI office, and the two special agents he had assigned to investigate the Gambinos, Andris Kurins and Joseph O'Brien. Something had to be done about Big Paul Castellano.

Putting their heads together, Mouw, Kurins, and O'Brien devised two plans of harassment, one they dubbed Operation Wreak Havoc and the other Operation Meathead. Through Wreak Havoc they would accost, pester, annoy, and intimidate every capo and soldier in the Gambino family they could locate, with the idea that the harassment would eventually get back to Big Paul and possibly cause him to make a careless move that would invite FBI investigation. Through Operation Meathead they would harass Castellano in his most cherished arena, the meat business, by, among other things, asking a lot of embarrassing questions of people Big Paul did business with, like the chicken magnate Frank Perdue.

For a while the two operations proceeded according to plan and agents Kurins and O'Brien succeeded in stirring up a lot of trouble within the Gambino family. But they were still unable to get to the boss. The two FBI agents got Gambino underlings to talk about a lot of things. But one thing no one would talk about was Big Paul. Most of the capos and street soldiers the agents talked to said they never heard of the guy.

Then something happened that opened up a new perspective on the investigation of Castellano. The FBI had gotten wind of a $500,000 open contract on Special Agent Joe Pistone who had been operating undercover for six years using the alias Donnie Brasco. Since 1976 he had so infiltrated the Bonanno crime family that he had become accepted as a virtual member of the family. Joe Pistone knew a lot and when he finally came back up to the surface he became a marked man. Any wiseguy, from any family, could collect $500,000 for killing him.

This was an intolerable situation for the FBI brotherhood. The contract had to be canceled and there was only one person who could cancel it: the head of the Commission, Big Paul Castellano. Special Agents Joe O'Brien and Frank Spero decided to go to the White House and speak with the boss about it.

After announcing themselves to Castellano's maid, Gloria, through the intercom, the two agents waited on the steps beneath the White House's high-columned portico for a few minutes, then were surprised to behold Big Paul himself bursting out of his front door and quickly slamming it behind him. He was dressed in a scarlet satin bathrobe over blue silk pajamas and was wearing black velvet slippers. Later the agents learned from Castellano's maid that this was the boss's preferred at-home dress. He only got into one of his $2,000 tailor-made, double-breasted suits when he received a distinguished visitor or drove into the city for an appointment.

Standing there under his stately portico with the two FBI agents, his scarlet and blue satin and silk contrasting stridently with the agents' drab gray and brown, Big Paul asked the agents what he could do for them.

Frank Spero explained the situation with the contract on FBI man Pistone and advised Castellano that if any harm came to Agent Pistone, or any member of his family, "the full resources of the FBI and the Department of Justice will be brought to bear against you and your associates."

"I understand your concern," said Castellano.

Spero then told the boss he wanted more than concern, he wanted "assurances."

After a brief pause, Big Paul obliged. "Gentlemen," he said, "if you know anything at all about me, you know that I would never go along with anything like this."

Joseph Pistone, whose testimony in several trials was responsible for putting more than a hundred high-level wiseguys behind bars, has survived.

Joe O'Brien and his colleague Frank Spero had gotten as close to Paul Castellano's bastion as any law enforcement official had ever been. They had even talked with the boss on his front porch.

A few weeks later O'Brien and another agent, Wally Ticano, got even closer. Ordered to serve a subpoena on Big Paul in relation to a case involving a Gambino soldier in Florida, they were admitted into the White House by Castellano's aging wife, Nina, and beautiful daughter, Connie, in order to make a telephone call to Big Paul's attorney, James LaRossa, about the subpoena.

The phone was attached to a wall in the Castellanos' enormous kitchen. When O'Brien reached the room he found the maid, Gloria, cooking dinner. She was sautéing mushrooms and onions in a pan and preparing a thick sirloin steak for the fire. Quickly scanning the room, O'Brien noticed the boss's high-backed chair at the head of the dining nook's long blond wood table and a tall decorative chrome lamp standing nearby. This was where the boss probably conducted his business, he mused as he placed his call.

By now Bruce Mouw of the FBI's Brooklyn-Queens office had decided that the only way to get enough on Big Paul Castellano to prosecute him was to bug his Todt Hill White House. Accordingly, a court order authorizing the installation of the bug was painstakingly prepared and obtained. The burning question then became: Where to install the device?

The story of the bugging of the Castellano White House was first revealed by agents Kurins and O'Brien in their 1991 book, *Boss of Bosses*.

Joe O'Brien had noted Big Paul's kitchen dining nook, with his high-backed papal chair at the head of the table and chrome lamp and telephone nearby. Sensing this was where the boss conducted most of his business, he sought confirmation of his intuition from a business associate of Castellano's, Julie Miron, head of the Miron Lumber Company, who had been observed by surveillance agents making a visit to the White House at least once a month. Adroitly leading Miron, a would-be architect, into a discussion of the interior of Big Paul's mansion, O'Brien learned from the lumber merchant—who, it was later found, handled payoffs and kickbacks on Gambino construction projects—that Castellano spent most of his time in the dining nook of his kitchen. This, then, would be where the FBI would have to install the bug.

Special Agents Kurins and O'Brien, the men Bruce

Mouw chose to supervise the White House bugging, were given thirty days by the authorizing judge to install the electronic listening device. As it turned out, it would take four more affadavits and four more months for Kurins, O'Brien, and their team of eight to effect the bugging.

One of the first things Kurins and O'Brien did was establish a command center in a house not far from the Castellano mansion on Todt Hill. From here the agents would keep the White House under surveillance and, once the bug was installed, would monitor whatever conversations it picked up.

The Castellano White House boasted a complex and very sensitive security system. There was a powerful electric bullhorn alarm mounted on the roof. Security cameras panned back and forth under the portico and at all other points of entry to the house and the six-car garage. Delicate motion sensor wires were attached to every window and door in the house. All door locks were purportedly tamperproof. The entire security system was hooked up with a local firm, Community Security System, run by a registered private detective, Salvatore Barbato, a part-time chauffeur for Big Paul, who could respond to a White House break-in anytime, day or night, within twelve to fifteen minutes of the tripping of the alarm. Chances were that before Barbato's men arrived, the two Dobermans would have already immobilized the intruders.

And so a complicated plan was devised to defeat Big Paul's security system, including the two Doberman pinschers. But, of course, before the plan could be put into effect, most of the occupants of the White House had to have left.

That much-anticipated moment came in mid-March 1983, when unexpectedly the godfather embarked on a Florida vacation with his maid and paramour Gloria and his trusted aide-de-camp Tommy Bilotti. Surveillance agents observed the exodus with glee. Later the FBI office in Miami confirmed that Big Paul and his entourage were ensconced in his luxurious condominium apartment in Pompano Beach. Castellano, Gloria, and Bilotti had been observed sailing over the local golf course in a golf cart. The only person left in the White House was Castellano's long-suffering wife, Nina.

It was time to move. The date was March 17, 1983. One of the most consequential buggings of a Mafia boss's house in U.S. history was about to begin.

Phase one: the drugging of the Dobermans. Two FBI men, dressed as gardeners, carrying pruning shears, rakes, burlap sacks, and two sirloin steaks impregnated with sleep-inducing drugs, puttered about in the shrubs lapping at the White House wrought-iron fence, listening to a spotter in an FBI surveillance plane hovering overhead tell them where the Dobermans were located and what they were doing. At 5:22 P.M. the two gardeners, stationed forty feet from one another, received the order to heave, and the two steaks flew over the fence. They were immediately grabbed by the dogs, who were roughly forty feet apart, each patrolling its own territory. In approximately six hours the drugs would take effect and the animals would fall into a deep sleep that would last another six hours. That, of course, meant that the break-in would have to be effected between 11:22 P.M. March 17, and 5:22 A.M. March 18.

Phase two: prelude to the break-in. First the orders to the two FBI sanitation workers in their New York Department of Sanitation garbage truck. If the alarm is tripped the truck will station itself broadside at the intersection of Todt Hill and Four Corners Road and effectively block access to the White House to the Community Security System people responding to the alarm. Second, the orders to the agent following the break-in team to climb immediately to the roof and stuff the alarm bullhorn with a thick foam that would reduce its voice to an impotent splutter. Third, the orders to the two FBI men wearing jeans and leather jackets in the lead van to circle around the block surrounding the White House and look for lights turned on in the mansion and report them, if they are observed, to the break-in team immediately.

Phase three: the actual break-in. Following instructions from agents Kurins and O'Brien, three FBI technicians—or "techies," as they are called—got out of a van at 1:30 A.M. half a block from the White House and proceeded toward the mansion. Wearing black from head to toe and carrying walkie-talkies, small bore automatic pistols, and a poison dart gun for a possibly awake Doberman, they scaled the fence and made their way to the garage. One of the techies, an expert locksmith, picked the lock to the garage's pedestrian entrance door and within seconds the two FBI men found themselves among a Jaguar, a Cadillac, a Mercedes, a Datsun, and two slumbering Dobermans. Waiting twenty-five seconds for the third techie to climb to the roof and stuff the bullhorn with foam, they picked the lock of the door leading from the garage to the house in thirty seconds, entered the mansion, and headed straight to the enormous Castellano kitchen. On the way they deactivated the security system using a computerized digital selector.

Once in the kitchen, the two FBI technicians worked fast. Arriving at the head of Big Paul's dining nook table, one agent took the chrome lamp near the boss's high-backed chair, laid it on the floor, unscrewed its base, and replaced it with a base containing an omnidirectional microphone and power pack. The newly enhanced lamp was put back in its usual position. Then, after checking for any debris accidentally left behind, they reactivated the mansion's security system, locked the doors, and made it back to the waiting van half a block down the street. The entire operation took only twelve and a half minutes.

Soon the White House bug was transmitting conversations between Big Paul, his minions, his mistress, and his wife that Kurins and O'Brien and their superiors found very interesting. And amusing. Not long after the FBI team broke into his house, Big Paul was recorded boasting, "No one comes to Staten Island unless I say so!"

The tapes also confirmed law enforcement's belief that one of Paul Castellano's major criminal activities was labor racketeering, especially in the construction industry. For years the Gambino family had used control of the supply of labor to extract huge sums from the construction industry through extortion and the solicitation of bribes. One taped conversation showed how fully Castellano understood the importance to his organization of controlling labor. "Our job is to run the unions," he instructed one of his capos in a conversation taped on May 5, 1983, about a month and a half after the FBI had bugged his house.

Construction industry business had been one of the first items on Big Paul's agenda when he and Gloria returned from their vacation at Pompano Beach.

The leading families of the New York Cosa Nostra had long controlled New York's construction industry through their influence in certain key construction workers' unions. By controlling these unions the mob controlled the labor supply at a given construction site and also the supply of building materials such as concrete and steel girders.

The Cosa Nostra's highest governing body, the Commission, had organized the principal building contractors into what they called a "club." If a given contractor was not in "the club," he could not even bid on a construction job. He was entirely left out. According to the State Organized Crime Task Force, "On all concrete pouring contracts up to two million dollars, the Colombo family extorted a one percent kickback. Contracts from two to fifteen million dollars were reserved to a 'club' of contractors selected by the Commission. These contractors were required to kick back two percent of the contract price to the Commission," whose members would split the kickback four ways. That meant that on a $15 million job, four Commission members would divide up a kickback of $300,000, or $75,000 apiece. The Commission was able to enforce this arrangement through bribery, intimidation, and violence, including murder.

Big Paul Castellano, besides sitting as chairman of the Commission, was in a most favorable position to make money from the construction industry. For years he had controlled the head of Teamsters Local 282, John Cody, a corrupt union official (eventually sent to jail) who derived his power from controlling the trucking of supplies and materials to major building sites. If a contractor needed cement, Cody would have his trucks deliver it at a price. If you wanted bricks and stone and steel girders delivered to a building under construction, you paid Cody and the material would be delivered. Castellano, in turn, took a cut of everything Cody extorted from the suppliers.

Beginning their morning monitoring routine, on March 24, a week after the bug had been installed, and a few days after the boss's return, agents Kurins and O'Brien lucked into an initially arcane and eventually most rewarding conversation between Castellano, his impetuous aide and chauffeur Tommy Bilotti, and Gambino bagman Alphonse "Funzi" Mosca, interrupted occasionally by the ever-hovering Gloria, about the division of the spoils in a major Manhattan building project.

The conversation about an unnamed construction project that agents Kurins and O'Brien picked up was carried on in a kind of code language and went like this:

CASTELLANO: He gotta pay. And he, he gotta be clued in. Over two, forget it, he sits out. That's club. Under a deuce, we talk. Maybe he gets some. But he pays the two points. First. None of this "you'll have it in a few days" bullshit.

MOSCA: You want I should talk to the fat guy?

CASTELLANO: Talk to the fucking president for all I care . . . just get me my money.

BILOTTI: I don't see where this fucking guy should get nothing. We set it up. We did the work.

CASTELLANO: If you're calling the fat guy, call the Chin.

GLORIA: Mister Tommy. You finish all the cookies.

MOSCA: So he says take it for six million nine. Cody says take it for six seven-fifty, a hundred seventy-five grand under. Something like that. Plus some jobs.

CASTELLANO: Twelve men, fifteen days.

BILOTTI: Yeah, twelve. Fifteen.

CASTELLANO: And the money comes up thirty percent. We do things on our own. We gotta think of our own. Tell it to the fat guy. Tell Chin.

MOSCA: It might get a little raw.

CASTELLANO: It does, it does. What are they gonna do, sue me?

Agents Kurins and O'Brien were able to decipher this strange discussion as follows. Their topic was about constructing a skyscraper on a major building site in midtown Manhattan. Bagman Funzi Mosca was being sent as an emissary to Genovese family boss, Anthony "Fat Tony" Salerno and his powerful underboss, Vincent "The Chin" Gigante, to negotiate the division of the payoffs on the multimillion-dollar construction project. If there was money to be collected for Big Paul, and it appeared there was, Mosca would bring it back to him.

That was only the beginning.

During its four-and-a-half-month life the bug in the Castellano kitchen recorded over six hundred hours of conversations. These alluded to construction industry bid rigging and kickbacks in Manhattan; garbage hauling on Long Island; wholesale meat rackets in Brooklyn and Manhattan; controlling supermarket chains; controlling unions—the longshoremen, the Teamsters, the painters, a dozen miscellaneous building trade locals; controlling garment industry trucking; selling pornography; shaking down restaurants and nightclubs by controlling supplies of liquor, linen, and guarantees of labor peace; stock frauds, insurance frauds, endless petty corruptions— all enforced, in the end, by threat of murder. Go along with Big Paul and his men and you live and prosper. Oppose him and you and your business die.

The tapes also revealed that three of the most frequent visitors to the White House were Big Paul's nephew, Thomas Gambino; one of Castellano's sons, Paul, Jr.; and Thomas Bilotti.

On one tape Big Paul reminisced with his nephew and son about the Apalachin Cosa Nostra summit of 1957. Castellano had driven his brother-in-law, Carlo Gambino, to the conference in upstate New York.

During the course of the conversation Castellano revealed that two of the most important items on the Apalachin agenda were strict rulings on drugs and cop killing. These issues were discussed by the conferees at the open-air barbecue that was disrupted by the state police. At the general meeting that was supposed to follow, dealing in drugs and killing cops were going to be forbidden on pain of death without trial. The godfathers wanted their men to refrain from any criminal activities that would bring about a crackdown from the law.

On another tape, recording a discussion between Big Paul and his aging *consiglière* Joe N. Gallo, Big Paul asked his *consiglière* what he should do with men in the family who deal with drugs. Gallo advised him to kill them.

In May 1983, the FBI picked up a conversation between Big Paul, Tommy Gambino, and Tommy Bilotti in which Castellano expressed his strong dislike of John Gotti, but admitted he respected his toughness. "He knows how to lay down the law [to a union official]," he told the two younger men.

Big Paul went on to discuss with his nephew certain problems Gambino was having in Manhattan's garment district. The discussion revealed that the Gambino family wielded considerable influence in the district, controlling, along with the Lucchese family, all trucking in the garment industry.

On one of Tommy Gambino's subsequent visits he and his uncle Paul and Joe Gallo talked about Joseph Bonanno's recently published autobiography, *A Man of Honor.*

CASTELLANO: I tried to take ten minutes of that fucking book. I thought it would be interesting, you know, what with knowing a lot of the people. But fuck, I can't read this shit.

GALLO: It makes you wonder. Is this son of a bitch senile, or is he just a fucking nut? . . . What the fuck. This is a new kind of plea bargain, or what? Go to the slammer or write your memoirs and make your friends look lousy?

CASTELLANO: The memory. That's what gets me. The fucking guy acts like he remembers every word ever said to him since 1972.

GALLO: But that's the remarkable thing about these cocksuckers, Paul. Maybe they can't read or write, but they can remember. It's like they have another sense. It's unbelievable. You know this guy . . . Joe Soderik . . . can't read, can't write. But he can sing you an entire opera, word for word. All the parts. Fucking soprano shit.

But Big Paul was not particularly interested in Gallo's analysis of Bonanno's memory. What interested, and shocked, him most about the book was Bonanno's detailed explanation of the Commission, the Cosa Nostra's ruling body and supreme court. Big Paul complained to his nephew and heir apparent about what Bonanno had written. "He don't know what the government is looking for," he railed. "The government is looking to make us one tremendous conspiracy. And anybody that they know who is a member, they can lock him up on conspiracy. . . . This guy's explaining the Commission!"

Coincidentally at about the same time Big Paul was complaining about Bonanno's mention of the Commission in his book, two other bugged mobsters were expressing similar concern over Bonanno's indiscretions. They were Lucchese capos Salvatore Santoro and Salvatore Avellino. Their conversation about *A Man of Honor* was recorded by a bug the State Organized Crime Task Force had installed in Avellino's Jaguar.

AVELLINO: I was shocked. What is he tryin' to prove, that he's a man of honor? But he's admitting— he, he actually admitted that he has a fam—that he was the boss of a family.

SANTORO: Right. Right. Right. Right.

AVELLINO: Even though he says, "This was my family, I was like the father."

SANTORO: . . . He's trying to . . . away from the image of a gangster.

AVELLINO: Yeah.

SANTORO: His father was friend of ours in Italy. See, 'cause the town he come from when he came here. He's full of shit, 'cause I know he was a phony . . . you know he was. . . . Like, he says he ain't never been in narcotics, he's full of shit. His own fucking rules . . . he was makin' piles of money, ah. What's his name was in the junk business. . . . They were in the junk business and they were partners, like, with him.

AVELLINO: Right.

SANTORO: You know. Anyway. Actually what he was trying to say: "I'm misunderstood. They got me down that I'm a gangster, I'm a boss in the Maf—" See he didn't want to use the word Mafia. See? Although he is admitting that there is a . . .

AVELLINO: Family.

SANTORO: . . . Well, wait until, wait until you read the whole . . .

AVELLINO: Now there's gonna be a part two?

SANTORO: Yeah.

AVELLINO: Mike Wallace says, "We'll continue about his kidnapping."

SANTORO: This cocksucker, you, what he's gonna make, this cocksucker? You know how much money he's gonna make now, his book?

AVELLINO: Is it out already? I knew that they were writing it.

SANTORO: Yeah, it's comin' out, it's comin' out. Because he's quoting from the book, from the . . .

AVELLINO: Mike Wallace's questions were from the book.

SANTORO: . . . Were from the book, right.

AVELLINO: About what he's . . . about killing people.

SANTORO: Right, right. Now right, now what's gonna happen, Hollywood is gonna come along . . .

AVELLINO: And make a movie.

SANTORO: Make a movie and this guy's gonna be like the technical director. Forget about it, this cocksucker will make a fortune.

AVELLINO: This will be like the, ah, now they'll say: "We have the original godfather."

SANTORO: Yeah. Yeah.

AVELLINO: "We really have a godfather now."

SANTORO: Right, right.

AVELLINO: What did he say about Carl [Gambino]? He says, "I used to tell him . . ."

SANTORO: He was full of shit.

AVELLINO: Yeah, he says that Carl was full of shit, like he didn't, ahhh.

SANTORO: Carl was no gangster.

AVELLINO: But he said it on the TV! . . .

SANTORO: Yeah, they had arguments, him and Carl used to argue, 'cause Carl—money, money, money, you know, everything was over money.

AVELLINO: Yeah.

SANTORO: You know, we don't know. . . . You see, when he said the Commission can't tell a family what to do.

AVELLINO: So that means he was even, was saying that about a Commission.

SANTORO: Yeah.

AVELLINO: He was admitting that there was a Commission!

SANTORO: He did.

AVELLINO: Yeah.

SANTORO: He says, you see, the Commission that first started, Charlie Lucky [Luciano] . . .

AVELLINO: Right.

SANTORO: . . . And, ah, five, five bosses of New York.

AVELLINO: Right. Joe Profaci.

SANTORO: Yeah, that was the original Commission.

AVELLINO: Right.

SANTORO: Then they took in Chicago, then they took in, you know, they were making 'em all . . . Oh, he admits, he don't call it La Cosa Nostra, he don't call it a Maf—I don't know in the book . . .

Bonanno's book had also been of great interest to crime fighter Rudolph Giuliani. After *A Man of Honor* came out, Giuliani told friends he was galled by the book. He thought Joe Bonanno had nerve to claim that the precepts and way of life of the Sicilian Mafia he had imbibed as a young man in Castellammare del Golfo had made him "a man of honor." To Giuliani it was "a way of life that perpetuated a slander on law-abiding Italian-Americans."

Giuliani was particularly interested in Bonanno's chapter on the Commission. It was the first time a Cosa Nostra boss had ever admitted there was such an institution as the Commission, much less explained its functions and named its past members. Later Giuliani confided to his associates that Bonanno's chapter on the Commission had such a profound influence on him that it helped spur him on in his ambition to bring a RICO indictment against the present Commission members. As it turned out, it was primarily information from the Castellano tapes, introduced as evidence in the Commission trial, that sent the entire Commission to jail.

Some of the most revealing discussions picked up by the White House bug were between Big Paul and his nephew and heir apparent, Tommy Gambino.

One such discussion showed how tough and imperious on money matters Big Paul could on occasion be. Gambino and his uncle were talking about the division of spoils in the garment district rackets, and how the Chinese and the Jews also wanted their shares.

CASTELLANO: So what's the fucking story on the money, Tommy?

GAMBINO: Their guy gets six-fifty a week and a car. Our guy gets four-fifty and no car.

CASTELLANO: You're telling me that their guys get more fucking money than you and I?

GAMBINO: Yeah . . . yeah, yeah.

CASTELLANO: What the fuck! . . . Well, here's how it seems to me. If it's thirds, it's thirds and cut the bullshit excuses. Look, we got a third of the jobs, and I want a third of the money. A third of the jobs and a third of the responsibility. I want a third of everything, get it? It's rightfully mine and I want it. Fuck the Chinese, fuck the Jews, and fuck the fucking *paisans* who are grabbing more than their share. It's our association to reap the benefits.

Big Paul and his nephew also talked about contract murder.

CASTELLANO: So what did they want?

GAMBINO: They wanted eight grand. . . . Now what do you do? I say to Pete, fifty to a hundred thousand instead to get him killed. . . . Hey, that's too much money, what are you doing? I said to Arnold, let's give him fifty, I'll get Pete, and Paul has to agree, okay? But I'll let you know, but keep your mouth shut. Don't say anything . . . because it's my ass if Tommy said hundred thousand to kill a guy from Paul. . . . It may sink us all. . . . Whether it's ready or not, it's coming down . . . now play with it. That's the end of the problem.

But Big Paul did not always go along with murder as the solution to a given problem. Once he and trusted capo Joe "Piney" Armone were discussing the practicality of authorizing a contract murder. Armone was one of the gentler members of the Gambino family. He had earned his nickname from coercing Christmas tree vendors on the Lower East Side to give small pine trees to the poor for free.

CASTELLANO: Look, when we sit down to clip a guy, we have to remember what's at stake here. There's some hazard. Guys forget that. They get a guy behind in his vig payments, they get a hard-on about it, right away they want to whack him. Why? Just because they're pissed off, they're aggravated. But what I say is: "Hey, you're making a living with this guy. He gets you aggravated, and right away you want to use the hammer? How do you get your fucking money *then*?"

ARMONE: It's means and ends. The idea is to collect. But you know, Paul, I think some guys just take so much pleasure from breaking heads that they'd almost rather not get paid.

CASTELLANO: Yeah, yeah. We got some guys like that. Dick-fists, I call 'em. I'm always sayin' to 'em, "Just to take a guy out, that ain't the point." Because I'll tell ya', Piney, anytime I can remember that we knocked guys out, it cost us. It's like there's a tax on it or some shit. Some-

THE BUGGING OF THE POPE   ■   237

body gets arrested. Or there's a fuckup, which means we gotta clip *another* guy, maybe a guy we don't wanna lose.

Later on in the discussion Castellano philosophized with Joe Piney about life in the mob.

CASTELLANO: This life of ours, this is a wonderful life. If you can get through life like this and get away with it, hey, that's great. But it's very, very unpredictable. There's so many ways you can screw it up. So you gotta think, ya gotta be patient. A lotta guys, they're yanking their zipper before their dick is put away, and they don't know when to zipper their fucking mouths shut, either. I tell 'em: "You listen, you learn. You talk, you teach." Am I right, Piney?
ARMONE: Yeah, Paul, you're right.
CASTELLANO: Because there's just so many fucking things that can blow up on you.
ARMONE: Yeah, Paul, there are.
CASTELLANO: There's so many fucking ways they can get to you.

The Castellano tapes also confirmed there were two opposing factions within the Gambino crime family that might conceivably go to war against each other. Big Paul continually betrayed his liking of and trust in tough, violent, but loyal Tommy Bilotti, who he was thinking of grooming to be his future underboss, and his nephew, Tommy Gambino, who he wanted to succeed him as boss once he died or if he went to prison. Correspondingly, the tapes revealed he had little use for the faction headed by his current underboss, Aniello "Neil" Dellacroce, and Dellacroce's protégé, John Gotti. When he first heard about Angelo Ruggiero's involvement with *babania*, Big Paul summoned Gotti to the White House and admonished him: "Listen, Johnny, you better prove you weren't involved." Later, when Gotti's friend Ruggiero refused to turn over transcripts of the tapes recorded in his Cedarhurst house to Big Paul, Castellano told Gotti if he didn't receive the transcripts soon he was going to do something drastic, like take out Angelo Ruggiero and remove Gotti from his position as capo of the Fatico crew and reassign him to another crew.

In expressing his irritation over the Ruggiero tapes, Big Paul had been oblivious to the fact that his own house had been bugged and soon transcripts of his taped conversations would be circulating throughout the law offices and courtrooms of New York.

It fell to FBI agents Kurins and O'Brien to break the awful news to Big Paul, or rather, as it turned out, subject him to the news, on the evening of March 25, 1985, when they arrested the godfather at the White House in connection with the Commission case.

For months the State Organized Crime Task Force, the FBI, and the U.S. attorney for the southern district had been assembling a massive case against the Mafia Commission. The bosses of the five New York families would all be indicted on RICO conspiracy charges. The purpose was to knock out the Mafia's entire ruling body in one bold stroke.

Big Paul was rendered speechless when agents Kurins and O'Brien told him he was being arrested on RICO conspiracy charges. It appeared to the two FBI agents, as he let them in the White House door, that he hadn't the slightest idea what the charges were about. Silently the tall, hulking godfather led the agents through the house and into the kitchen, where Gloria was preparing a roast beef dinner in the company of Castellano's personal physician.

Once in the kitchen Big Paul, still looking nonplussed, asked his captors if he could change into a suit, and they gave him their permission. The aging godfather then left the kitchen accompanied by his doctor and Gloria.

While he was changing clothes Castellano's wife,

Nina, suddenly showed up with her daughter, Connie, and Connie's husband, who was holding their baby. When Big Paul reappeared in the kitchen, resplendent in a navy-blue double-breasted suit, he greeted his family absently, kissing only his little granddaughter, and then both Gloria and Nina began to cry. This quickly got on Big Paul's nerves, prompting him to lead the agents out of the kitchen and finally out of the house and into a waiting government car.

While Big Paul was being arrested, FBI agents were simultaneously arresting Fat Tony Salerno, boss of the Genovese family; Lucchese boss Tony Ducks Corallo; Colombo godfather Carmine "The Snake" Persico; Rusty Rastelli, de facto boss of the Bonannos; Joseph Bonanno, retired head of the clan bearing his name; and various underbosses, including Big Paul's own Aniello Dellacroce. The eighty-two-year-old Bonanno was pinched in his retirement home in Tucson. Seldom in history had a man's autobiography had such catastrophic consequences for its author.

According to Kurins and O'Brien, Big Paul first learned his White House had been bugged from the radio as he was being escorted to his arraignment in Manhattan in a government car.

The news over the radio caused the diabetic godfather to feel suddenly ill and ask his captors to stop for some Tums and a Snickers candy bar.

Castellano recovered his poise midway over the Verrazano Bridge. He guessed that the bug had been planted while he had been in Florida and expressed an anguished dismay that the electronic device might have also picked up his conversations with Gloria. O'Brien calmed him down momentarily by telling him they did not listen to any "personal stuff."

The next day, as Big Paul awaited his 3 P.M. bail hearing, Kurins and O'Brien ushered their charge into an office in the federal courthouse, where, according to the FBI agents' account, the godfather waxed philosophical with them.

Hey, I know you disapprove. That's why we're here, after all, isn't it? So the United States government can make the point that *we do not approve of how certain guineas make their living*. Okay. Fair enough. If I was the government I'd put my ass in jail for a thousand years. . . . But not because I'm *wrong*. You see, that's the part I object to—this idea that the law is right and that's the end of the story. Come on. We're not children here. The law is—how should I put it?—a convenience. Or a convenience for some people and an inconvenience for other people.

At the bail hearing Big Paul found himself sitting next to his attorney, James LaRossa, with Fat Tony Salerno and his attorney, Roy Cohn, nearby. Among the spectators were Nina Castellano, her daughter, Connie, and her three sons, Joe, Phil, and Paul, Jr. The two-and-a-half-hour hearing resulted in the underbosses having to put up $1 million bail and the bosses $2 million each. Since Big Paul had already put up $2 million bail in the car-theft ring case, his freedom was now costing him $4 million.

Big Paul's circumstances had changed dramatically in the last forty-eight hours. Driving back to the White House with his wife and daughter, with Tommy Bilotti at the wheel, Castellano must have been besieged with thoughts of the consequences of the White House bugging. He was the biggest boss of all, the chairman of the Commission. And his vaunted state-of-the-art security system had not thwarted the FBI from bugging his home. Not only that, but he had said things within earshot of the bug that were vain, foolish, adolescent, and even highly uncomplimentary about his fellow members of the Commission. What a humiliation. Now what would happen to his respect?

26

The Ménage à Trois

Big Paul Castellano was equally concerned, and embarrassed, over what the bugging of his house would reveal about his bizarre private life, about his relationship with his wife of almost thirty years, Nina Manno Castellano, and with his thirty-five-year-old Colombian maid and mistress, Gloria Olarte.

The public airing of his ménage à trois, if it would ever come to pass, threatened to inflict on him a fate worse than death—that of making him into a national laughingstock.

Gloria had come to the White House to work as the Castellanos' maid in the fall of 1979. She was a thirty-year-old newly arrived immigrant from Colombia, and Big Paul, sixty-four, was the proud new owner of a just-completed seventeen-room mansion on Staten Island's fashionable Todt Hill.

The story of Paul Castellano's relationship with Gloria Olarte became known to law enforcement after transcripts of Castellano's bugged conversations began circulating in law offices and courtrooms in late 1983 and early 1984. For Gloria's interjected remarks— "Mister Joe, you like more coffee?" "Mister Tommy, take more cookies"—appeared throughout the reams of mob talk with a frequency that suggested she occupied a position in the Castellano household a notch or two above that of maidservant. But the nature of the relationship was not revealed in all its ripeness until FBI agents Andris Kurins and Joseph O'Brien wrote their book about Big Paul, *Boss of Bosses*, in 1991.

It was a firm rule in the FBI that when agents monitoring bugged conversations between Mafiosi came across talk that was strictly personal—that had nothing to do with crime—they would remove their headsets and not listen in. Furthermore, when a transcript was made of a given tape containing remarks of a personal nature, those remarks would not be included in the transcript. In this way transcripts of tapes circulating in law offices and courtrooms would never present information of a personal nature—only evidence of the planning and commission of crimes. In the FBI this practice was known as "minimization." As a fillip to the bugged mobster's right of privacy, the bureau would minimize his conversations of a personal nature. "There's this thing called minimization," Joe O'Brien had reassured Big Paul Castellano after they had told him his house had been bugged. "We try not to listen to the personal stuff."

Agents Kurins and O'Brien, however, breached the minimization rule. From what appears in their book, *Boss of Bosses*, it is evident that they listened to *everything*, business and personal, that went on within earshot of the White House bug, and recorded everything as well. From this practice they were able to piece together intimate details of Castellano's relationships with his wife and maid/mistress that other law enforcement agencies, such as the State Organized Crime Task Force, had only the barest inkling of.

Joseph "Joe The Boss" Masseria (1879–1931). Boss of New York's Lower East Side underworld from 1920 to 1931. Carlo Gambino, Frank Costello, Albert Anastasia, and Lucky Luciano helped him run a huge illegal liquor business during Prohibition and battle rival boss, Salvatore Maranzano. Murdered by Lucky Luciano in a Coney Island restaurant in April, 1931. (*UPI Bettmann*)

Salvatore "Little Caesar" Maranzano (1868–1931). Old-fashioned Sicilian "Man of Honor" who challenged leadership of Joe The Boss Masseria in the Castellammarese War. Founded modern U.S. Mafia, La Cosa Nostra ("our thing"), with himself as "Boss of All Bosses." Murdered by Lucky Luciano in September, 1931.

Vincent "Vince" Mangano (1888–1951). Appointed boss of what was to become the Gambino crime family by Lucky Luciano in 1931. Carlo Gambino and Albert Anastasia joined the family as soldiers. Murdered by Anastasia in April, 1951. (*Collection of the Municipal Archives of the City of New York*)

Charles "Lucky" Luciano (1897–1962). Organized the national crime syndicate of the 1930s, after the end of the Castellammarese War, appointing the bosses of all the crime families and establishing the Commission. Remained the "de facto" Boss of All Bosses until his death from a heart attack in Naples in January, 1962. (*UPI Bettmann Newsphotos*)

Carlo Gambino (1902–1976) at thirty-three. Starting as a soldier in the family run by Vince Mangano, Gambino became boss of the family in 1957 after arranging the murder of his immediate predecessor, Albert Anastasia. Built the family that eventually came to bear his name into the largest and most powerful in the United States. (*AP/Wide World Photos*)

Thomas "Three Finger Brown" Lucchese (1900–1967). Founder of the crime family bearing his name and close associate of Carlo Gambino. His daughter, Frances, married Carlo Gambino's son, Thomas. Lucchese controlled the trucking industry in New York's garment center, a racket he passed on to his son-in-law, Thomas Gambino. (*UPI Bettmann*)

Meyer Lansky (Maier Suchowljansky) (1902–1983). Jewish gangster who, with Benjamin "Bugsy" Siegel, allied himself with Lucky Luciano and Carlo Gambino and became the financial genius of the national crime syndicate. (*UPI Bettmann Newsphotos*)

Frank Costello (Francisco Castiglia) (1891–1973). The national crime syndicate's chief "fixer," or payoff man, known as "the Prime Minister of the Underworld" and the Cosa Nostra's "elder statesman." A close ally of Carlo Gambino, Lucky Luciano, Carlos Marcello, and Meyer Lansky, he was shot in the head by Genovese soldier Vincent "The Chin" Gigante in 1957 and survived. (*AP/Wide World Photos*)

Anthony "Tough Tony" Anastasio (1906–1963) (*center*) and his brother Jerry (*right*), brothers of Albert, with Frank Russo (*left*), business agent for Local 327 of the International Longshoremen's Association, on the Brooklyn waterfront, surrounded by striking Longshoremen who refused to return to work, 1951. (*AP/Wide World Photos*)

Frank Costello after he was shot in the head by Gigante in the lobby of his New York apartment building. After the wounding Costello retired to his estate on Long Island where he died of natural causes at eighty-two. (*AP/Wide World Photos*)

Vito "Don Vitone" Genovese (1897–1969). Boss of the crime family bearing his name, the nation's second largest, from 1946 until his death in the Federal Penitentiary in Atlanta at seventy-one. A vicious killer, it was Genovese who had ordered Gigante to murder Frank Costello. (*UPI Bettmann Newsphotos*)

Albert "The Mad Hatter" Anastasia (1903–1957). Also known as "the Earthquake" and "the Lord High Executioner." While boss of the crime family formerly run by Vince Mangano, he and Lucky Luciano created an enforcement arm for La Cosa Nostra that came to be known as "Murder Incorporated," responsible for from 700 to 1000 murders. He and his brother, Tough Tony, controlled the Brooklyn waterfront for almost a decade. (*AP/Wide World Photos*)

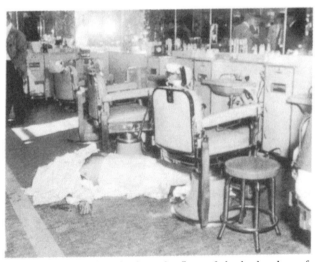

Albert Anastasia lies dead on the floor of the barbershop of the Park Sheraton Hotel in New York where he was ambushed by the Gallo brothers acting on orders from Carlo Gambino, who succeeded Anastasia as boss of the crime family founded by Lucky Luciano and Vince Mangano in 1931. (*AP/Wide World Photos*)

The funeral procession of Tough Tony Anastasio, March, 1963. Thousands of dock-workers line a South Brooklyn street to view the procession to the church, where Father Salvatore Anastasia held a funeral mass for his brother. The procession included fifty limousines and fifteen flower cars. (*UPI Bettmann*)

Paul Castellano (1915–1985), Carlo Gambino's cousin and brother-in-law, and future boss of the Gambino crime family, at forty-five, upon his arrest for attending the Cosa Nostra crime conclave at Apalachin, New York, in 1957. (*AP/Wide World Photos*)

Carlo Gambino (1902–1976), boss of the nation's largest and most powerful Cosa Nostra family, flanked by FBI agents upon his arrest in 1970 for plotting to rob the crew of an armored car containing $6 million. The charges were dropped. Gambino died in 1976 of natural causes. (*UPI Bettmann Newsphotos*)

Joseph Colombo (1914–1978). Boss of the crime family bearing his name and founder of the Italian-American Civil Rights League designed to combat the harassing of Italian-Americans and the government's "myth of the Mafia." The other bosses, notably Carlo Gambino, vehemently opposed Colombo's posturing on behalf of Italian-Americans. (*UPI Bettmann Newsphotos*)

Joseph Colombo being loaded into an ambulance, having been shot in the head during an Italian-American Unity Day rally he organized at Columbus Circle, New York, in 1971. Colombo survived the attack, lingering in a vegetative coma for seven years. It is believed Carlo Gambino was behind the assassination attempt. (*AP/Wide World Photos*)

Paul Castellano (far left, standing) and his brother-in-law, Carlo Gambino (third from right, standing), at the Westchester Premier Theater in 1976. Others included, from left to right, Gregory de Palma, Frank Sinatra, Thomas Marson, Jimmy "The Weasel" Frattiano, Salvatore Spatola. Bottom row: Carlo's brother, Joe Gambino, and Richard Fusco. (*Government photo*)

"The White House," Paul Castellano's lavish mansion on Todt Hill, Staten Island. From here Big Paul ran the Gambino crime family for eight years. In 1983 the FBI bugged "the White House." The recorded conversations led to two federal indictments against Castellano. (*Government photo*)

Rudolph Giuliani, U.S. Attorney for the Southern District of New York, who indicted Paul Castellano in 1984 for racketeering and being a member of the Cosa Nostra Commission. (*Ron Galella, Ltd.*)

Castellano, sixty-eight, indicted for racketeering by Rudolph Giuliani in 1984, is being led into federal court by Detective Kenneth McCabe of the New York Police Department. (*AP/Wide World Photos*)

The murder of Gambino boss, Paul Castellano, and his underboss and driver, Thomas Bilotti, in front of Sparks Steak House on East 46th Street, Manhattan, December 16, 1985. In 1992 Castellano's successor, John Gotti, was convicted of orchestrating the assassination. (©New York Post)

The body of Big Paul Castellano lies on the sidewalk in front of Sparks Steak House after being shot six times in the head by Gambino gunmen under the command of John Gotti. (*Government photo*)

John Gotti (1940–), successor of Paul Castellano as boss of the Gambino crime family, leaving Manhattan federal court in February, 1990. He is followed by his brother, Peter (*left*), and attorney, Bruce Cutler (*right*). (*Randy Bauer/Galella, Ltd.*)

John "Junior" Gotti, son of John Gotti, leaving Manhattan federal court, in February, 1990, with one of his father's attorneys, Gerald Shargel. (*Randy Bauer/Galella, Ltd.*)

Victoria Gotti, John Gotti's wife, at the door of the Gottis' house in Howard Beach, Queens, which was guarded by a huge Neapolitan mastiff watchdog. (©New York Post/ *Mary McLoughlin*)

Gambino boss, John Gotti, wearing one of his $2,000 tailor-made suits, with his principal attorney, Bruce Cutler, in courtroom during his 1990 trial for ordering an assault on a Carpenters Union official. (*UPI/Bettmann*)

John Gotti, with new underboss, Salvatore "Sammy the Bull" Gravano (1945–), emerging from Gambino headquarters, the Ravenite Club in Little Italy, after having been acquitted in the 1990 assault trial. Two years later Gotti would be convicted of five murders, and suspected of six more, and Gravano would confess to nineteen murders as a member of the Gambino crime family.(© New York Post)

United States Attorney for the Eastern District, Andrew J. Maloney, who successfully led the prosecution team to victory over John Gotti in Gotti's 1992 federal racketeering trial, at his desk in Brooklyn Federal Courthouse. (*AP/Wide World Photos*)

Andrew J. Maloney (*second from left*) and Assistant U.S. Attorney, John Gleeson (*center*), hold a press conference in Brooklyn Federal Court after a jury found John Gotti guilty of all charges, including the murder of Big Paul Castellano, in his 1992 federal racketeering trial. Flanking John Gleeson are J. Bruce Mouw, head of the FBI's Gambino squad (*left*), FBI agent Joseph Schilitro, and James E. Fox, Chief of the FBI's New York office. In June, 1992, John Gotti was sentenced to life in prison with no chance of parole. (*Dith Pran*/New York Times)

John Gotti's attorneys, Albert Krieger (*foreground*) and Bruce Cutler, leaving Brooklyn Federal Court after a grim session of Gotti's 1992 racketeering trial at which Sammy the Bull Gravano was the government's star witness against Gotti. (*Monica Almeida*/New York Times)

Joseph (*left*) and Thomas Gambino, sons of Carlo Gambino, at a 1991 ceremony at Long Island Jewish Medical Center's Children's Hospital marking the Gambino brothers' $2 million donation to the Center's bone marrow transplantation unit for children with cancer. Despite these good works, government investigations continued. In 1992, Thomas Gambino pleaded guilty to restraint of trade in his garment district trucking business. He agreed to pay a $13 million fine and get out of the trucking business. In return, all other state charges were dropped. (©1991 Newsday/Don Jacobsen)

Danny Marino, a Gambino family "capo," believed to be acting boss of the Gambino crime family in the absence of imprisoned boss, John Gotti. (*Kevin Cohen*/NewYork Post)

For their infringement of one of the FBI's most stringent regulations, Kurins and O'Brien were reprimanded by the FBI and were forbidden to receive royalties from their book. After a brief dispute, the two agents decided they would rather collect royalties from their book than remain in the FBI and both resigned from the bureau.

Paul Castellano had married his childhood sweetheart, Nina Manno, in 1937, when he was twenty-two and she was a teenager. Nina was a sister-in-law of the rising mobster Carlo Gambino, who, in turn, was first cousin of Castellano. For Paul Castellano the marriage was a shrewd and ultimately fruitful union. For one, it reinforced his relationship with one of the cleverest Mafiosi on the New York scene, a made member of Vince Mangano's family who was destined to take over that family twenty years later. For another, Nina bore Paul four healthy children and brought them up as well as she could, given the unpredictability of the family income in the initial years of their marriage, and the perils of her husband's chosen profession.

Nina gave Big Paul three sons: Paul, Jr., Joseph, and Philip. Nina had wanted them all to go to college and enter some respectable profession. She had emphatically not wanted them to have anything to do with the professions of her brother-in-law and husband.

But Paul, Jr., her eldest—a tall, handsome young man with a head for business—dropped out of college early, preferring to join one of this father's enterprises, Blue Ribbon Meat, the company that eventually developed into the prosperous, and slightly shady, Dial Poultry. Joseph, the middle son, took the same route as his older brother. And Philip, the youngest, was set up by his father in his Scara-Mix Concrete Company on Staten Island, a concern run by people like Tommy Bilotti and known to possess an uncanny ability to win lucrative construction contracts in New York City. Big Paul liked to boast that he had made all his three sons millionaires. This was true. But they had not become millionaires via the route their mother had wanted.

Nina's fourth child, the tall, slender, and ravishingly beautiful Constance, known as Connie, the apple of her father's eye, disappointed her mother by marrying within the mob. Nina had wanted her to marry a fine, college-educated, unconnected man with a solid profession, a doctor or a lawyer. Instead she had married Frank Amato, a hijacker for a Gambino crew and a butcher at Dial Poultry, who soon took to beating her up and fooling around on the side with other women, much to her parents' displeasure. After their divorce in 1973 Frank Amato disappeared and has not been seen since. Connie later remarried a man her father had set up in the construction business, Joe Catalonotti. The couple gave Nina and Paul a granddaughter and Big Paul gave them a fine house on Todt Hill not far from his own.

Nina Manno Castellano was an imposing, handsome woman who carried herself with dignity and was much respected by the rank and file of the organization her husband grew up in and eventually achieved command of. She had been a loyal, dedicated wife, mother, and grandmother, known by all as a proud, patient, and religious woman. The last thing she needed as she approached her sixtieth year was the intrusion into her life of the likes of Gloria Olarte.

That intrusion was, to say the least, a chance event. Somehow it came to the attention of the Colombian immigrant community in Queens that a wealthy Staten Island couple needed a maid. A young, bright-eyed Colombian girl, newly arrived in the United States, who knew no English, applied and was granted an interview in the White House with Mrs. Nina Castellano and her daughter, Connie. Even though she couldn't speak English, Gloria sufficiently impressed the Castellano women to be awarded the job. She would live in the White House and remain on duty from morning until night six days a week. When Nina and Connie introduced her to Mr. Castellano, Big Paul struck her as "a sad and bitter man."

It became Gloria's job not so much to serve Big Paul as to cheer him up.

For the Castellanos, dealing with Gloria was awkward at first because of the language barrier. Nina and Connie had to go into virtual contortions of sign language to explain to Gloria what they wanted done. Frustrated, they eventually had to resort to a handheld bilingual computer to get their ideas across to the confused and harried Colombian girl.

Curiously, it was the bilingual computer that became the first vehicle by which Big Paul was able to flirt with young Gloria. It was several months after she had been hired that Gloria began to notice readouts that had nothing to do with performing menial household chores, but were compliments on her eyes and smile. Surely these did not emanate from the taskmistress, Mrs. Castellano.

At home most of the day, sometimes seven days a week, in his comfortable and stately White House, Big Paul, the old satyr, found ample time to observe his sweet little South American maid, and spend some precious moments with her alone. After all, Nina and Connie liked to shop, and Big Paul made sure they had plenty of money to shop with. It was when the two Castellano women were out shopping that Big Paul would get up enough nerve to make amorous passes at his little *Camarista*.

At first these passes were not much more than putting an arm around her waist or stroking her long, black, shiny hair. Soon he graduated to kissing her, patting her on her behind, and running a hand up her leg. Along with these displays of affection Big Paul also showered Gloria with gifts—dresses, shoes, accessories—which she would proudly display to her sister Nellie in Queens on her day off.

Still, for all the fondling, petting, and gifts, Gloria became extremely confused over the fact that Mister Paul, as she called him, never tried to make love to her. It had become acutely frustrating for her. All the foreplay leading up to nothing.

What Gloria didn't know was that Mister Paul had been afflicted with diabetes for many years and his constitution was of a type that suffered sexual impotence from the disease. By the time Gloria came into Big Paul's life, he had been unable to achieve an erection for almost four years.

But while Gloria was wondering why her master always stopped short of intercourse, Big Paul was working on a way to overcome his disability by surgical means. He had already scheduled the operation—a penile implant—that would enable him to consummate his love affair with the young woman who had become the light of his life.

For it had become apparent to all who were close to Big Paul—humiliatingly apparent to his wife, bemusedly apparent to Tommy Bilotti—that Gloria Olarte had indeed brought a new happiness to the otherwise sad and world-weary boss.

Now Big Paul would smile when a picture of him was taken. Before Gloria, he had usually appeared glum in photographs. Now his capos and associates would often find him in relatively high spirits at their meetings with him, even when nasty business was on the agenda.

Big Paul was clearly enjoying a "second spring" with Gloria under his roof. Schlepping around his huge mansion in his scarlet robe and blue pajamas, he doted on his beloved Colombian maid, denying her nothing, watching her swim nude in his huge swimming pool with adolescent glee.

Before long Big Paul began taking silly risks in his relationship with Gloria. He openly flirted with her in front of his wife, and did not disguise his affection for her in front of his minions. Big Paul and several of his capos would be sitting around the long table in the kitchen discussing important affairs of state and Gloria would be hovering over the gathering all the time, welcoming new arrivals to the meeting—"Good morning, Mister Joe, how feelin' today?"—continuously pouring cups of coffee for the boys and receiving a little pat on her behind from the boss for her efforts. Castellano's men recalled that Big Paul's wife, Nina, never came near a business meeting. The closest she ever came was greeting a visitor at the front door.

As Big Paul became more and more infatuated with his Colombian paramour, and less and less reluctant to display that infatuation to others, Nina Manno Castellano became more and more disgusted with her husband, who, she believed, was making a fool out of himself before his business associates. The consequences could be disastrous.

Nina soon proved to be right. As Big Paul's and Gloria's relationship grew agents Kurins and O'Brien began noticing hints of disapproval from senior members of the Gambino organization, such as seventy-year-old Joe "Piney" Armone, who, like others of his generation, had known and respected Nina Castellano for many years and were outraged by Big Paul's treatment of her. To cast her aside in the twilight of her life, after all she had gone through with him, after all the sacrifices she had made, to defile the sacred marriage bed with this impish servant girl who was clearly taking the boss for a ride, was outrageous. This behavior was a clear violation of the code they had all lived by since their inductions into the Cosa Nostra three decades ago.

But Big Paul, luxuriating in his second spring, was oblivious to the growing disapproval he was receiving, albeit guardedly, from his family and associates. He was used to arguing with his wife. He was used to arguing with his men. In most arguments he prevailed, by default.

Big Paul could no longer impress those who had been close to him since he took over the family in 1976. But he felt he needed to dazzle people with his power and importance. Here is where Gloria came in. He could boast of his influence and she would listen and applaud. Such an occasion came up at the beginning of their relationship. The conversation was taped by agents Kurins and O'Brien.

CASTELLANO: You know Waldbaum's, Gloria? The supermarkets? I'm almost the boss of Waldbaum's now. They pay me. You know why? Because of my influence. When I sit down, I talk to a man. "Oh, Paul," they say, "how ya feel? How's everything?" And I say to them, "Look, now, I want you to be nice to my boys. And I want my boys to be nice to you. When they don't do that, you come see me. I'll straighten it out. 'Cause, listen, while I'm alive this is my business." "Paul," they say, "don't worry. We have got a lot of respect for you. When we need help, we'll come to you."

So they come, Gloria. Waldbaum's, they come. The unions, they come. Frank Perdue, the big chicken man, he comes. I don't care who he is. If the president of the United States, if he's smart, if he needed help, he'd come. I could do a favor for him.

GLORIA: Mister Paul is just like the president.

Gloria's adulation of her Mister Paul, whether feigned or genuine, eventually paid off for her. In early 1984 Nina Manno Castellano moved out of the White House and into an apartment of her own and Gloria triumphantly told Special Agent Joe O'Brien, "Mister Paul and Gloria we live there all alone now."

27

When Sorrows Come

"When sorrows come, they come not single spies, but in battalions," complained the murderous King Claudius in Shakespeare's *Hamlet*.

Big Paul's sorrows began coming in 1984, as he was approaching his seventieth birthday. It was early in that year that Rudolph Giuliani hit him with fifty-one counts of racketeering in the case involving the murderous DeMeo crew and its international car-theft operation. It was rotten publicity for him, not good at all for the legitimate businessman image he had been trying so hard to project to his corporate associates. Sanctioning the killing of twenty-five people, stealing cars, pushing dope. This was the first time he was ever up on such demeaning charges.

As it would turn out, the car-theft-ring trial would generate perhaps the worst publicity Big Paul's Mafia family had suffered since Murder Incorporated was brought to light in the days of Albert Anastasia.

Witness Vito Arena, a homosexual member of the DeMeo car-theft crew, dubbed "the Gay Hit Man" by the press, told of the brutal slayings of rival stolen car dealers Ronald Falcaro and Khaled Fahd Darwish "The Arab" Daoud by crew member Henry Borelli, and how DeMeo ordered the two corpses "cut up" after the shootings, telling Arena, in the same breath, to go out and "buy some pizzas and frankfurters." After returning with the food, Arena continued, crew member Freddie DiNome dismembered the two bodies with small saws and boning knives, and Arena and Borelli then bagged the body parts in plastic garbage bags. Continuing, Arena testified that DiNome had gotten so "carried away" in dismembering the bodies, "cutting off their private parts and ears," that one ear fell through a crack in the floor, causing crew leader DeMeo to fly into a rage.

The "Gay Hit Man" also told the court of the killing of nineteen-year-old Cherie Golden, girlfriend of a suspected informer, by crew members Joey Testa and Anthony Senter. According to Arena, the two men flanked the petrified young girl in a car, and while Joey Testa drew her attention toward him by talking with her, Anthony blew her brains out from the other side.

And how did Big Paul fit into this scenario? A nephew of car-theft ring capo Nino Gaggi, Dominick Montiglio, dubbed "the Smoking Nephew" by the press, told the court how he brought cash payments from the car-theft-ring profits, which amounted to $20,000 a week, from his uncle Nino Gaggi to Big Paul at Castellano's "meat palace," or warehouse, in Brooklyn, and also drove his cash-laden uncle to meet with Big Paul at Dial Poultry, the Castellano family's chicken distribution firm. There was no doubt, the prosecution contended, that defendant Paul Castellano profited from the car-theft-ring's operations and sanctioned all the killings that accompanied it.

It was about a year after receiving the car-theft-ring indictment and the very day he was hit by the Commission case indictment that Big Paul learned his house on Staten Island had been bugged. Since the bug had yielded evidence that led to the Commission case indictment, the federal authorities were obligated by law to turn over transcripts of the tapes to the bugged defendants. If the DeMeo crew racketeering indictment had been an embarrassment, the Commission case indictment was nothing less than a mortification. For now the other bosses on the Commission, Big Paul's fellow indictees, would be given transcripts of the Castellano tapes in which Big Paul made disparaging remarks about all of them.

The year 1985 would finally see Big Paul's sorrows coming "in battalions." Not only would he be hit with two more federal indictments, but he would also be afflicted with serious challenges and dissensions within his own organization and his own blood family, the latter rent by his affair with Gloria Olarte.

For some time his irascible underboss Aniello Dellacroce, who was stricken with terminal cancer, had been chafing under Castellano's rule. In contravention of Big Paul's explicit ban on drug dealing, Dellacroce had been helping finance a group of Zips who were running a huge heroin-smuggling operation out of the Bensonhurst section of Brooklyn. Known to law enforcement as the Cherry Hill Gambinos (because they also operated out of a house they owned in Cherry Hill, New Jersey) John, Rosario, and Giuseppe Gambino were distant cousins of Carlo Gambino, Sicilian nationals who answered only to their boss in Palermo.

Dellacroce went to considerable pains to distance himself from his involvement with the Cherry Hill Gambinos' heroin operation. He rarely dealt with them directly, delegating that responsibility to two of his capos. During the Pizza Connection trial, testimony was heard about how Dellacroce operated.

"Don't tell me what it is," he would bark at one of the capos he had assigned to deal with the Cherry Hill Gambinos, "just give me back one and a half million for one million."

In time Big Paul learned from one of his men that at least two of Dellacroce's capos were dealing in heroin. FBI bugs planted in Dellacroce's Little Italy headquarters, the Ravenite Club, and in his Grasmere, Staten Island, home revealed that Big Paul told his underboss he would have the two capos killed. Castellano was now suspicious that his underboss was also dealing drugs, that the two capos were dealing with the Cherry Hill Gambinos for him. Just as he was suspicious that John Gotti was involved in the Ruggiero–Gene Gotti–Carneglia heroin operation.

Dellacroce, a dying man in the spring of 1985, knew that if Big Paul executed the two capos he had dealing with the Cherry Hill Gambinos, he would lose a major source of income. Either that or he would have to take the enormous risk of dealing directly with the Cherry Hill Gambinos himself. If Big Paul, who, as we know, was on friendly terms with several Zips, including their leader, Toto Catalano, found out that Dellacroce was dealing in heroin with the Sicilians, there would probably be war. Big Paul would have no choice but to mount an assault against the Dellacroce faction in his family. Reluctantly he would have to kill at least a dozen people. Among them would be Dellacroce himself, the two capos who dealt with the Cherry Hill Gambinos, and Angelo Ruggiero, John Carneglia, Gene Gotti, and John Gotti. It was a decision the diplomatic, gun-shy boss would have considerable difficulty making.

As tensions within the Gambino family escalated, the family and its underboss were hit with still another federal indictment, this one from the Organized Crime Strike Force of the U.S. Attorney, eastern district. A RICO case, it charged Aniello Dellacroce and the middle ranks of the Gambino family, including John Gotti, with operating an illegal criminal enterprise, namely the Gambino crime family.

Not long after this bombshell exploded, the FBI informant within John Gotti's crew, known as Wahoo, told the FBI that he had learned at the Our Friends Social Club in Ozone Park that John Gotti, Angelo Ruggiero, Gene Gotti, and John Carneglia had received reliable reports from one of their informants close to Castellano that Big Paul was "contemplating contract murders on them," in part "because of internal strife within the Gambino family" and in part "because John Gotti is being promoted as Big Paul's successor." Wahoo went on to tell the FBI that Castellano wanted "to make Tommy Bilotti the new boss of the Gambino family and therefore is considering wiping out a strong portion of the Gotti faction. Gotti is contemplating striking first before Castellano can formulate his own plan."

Gotti gave an indication of how he was feeling at the time in a brief conversation with an associate picked up by an FBI bug near the Bergin on June 19.

GOTTI: I know what's goin' on. See, you don't, Mike. You're oblivious to this, guys like you, your brother and certain other soldiers, God bless ya, you're oblivious to what's goin on, but I ain't, I'm in the fuckin' hunt.

Thus by June 1985 it appeared that the Gambino crime family was both at war with the government and at war with itself.

The civil war within the Gambino family was coming to a head on several fronts. On the burning question of whether Angelo Ruggiero should turn the tapes recorded in his home over to Big Paul, the FBI bug in Dellacroce's house picked up a lecture from Dellacroce to Ruggiero and John Gotti:

DELLACROCE: Now what do you want me to tell him?

The guy says "Fuck you," he don't wanna give you those fuckin' tapes. . . . I've been tellin' [Castellano], "the guy can't give you the tapes because his family is on there." I've been trying to make you get away with these tapes, but Jesus Christ Almighty, I can't stop the guy from always bringin' it up. Unless I tell the guy "Why don't you go fuck yourself?" . . . Then we, we, go and roll it up and go to war . . . I told you that's the last stage. Let's wait. Let's take it easy. That's the last stage. If it has to come to that, it'll come to that.

The last stage was drawing near. On June 12, as Big Paul was contemplating his retirement in prison and his underboss lay mortally ill in his Staten Island home, Big Paul and John Gotti had a sit-down at the White House to discuss Big Paul's plans for a "peaceful transition" after the feds had removed him from the scene.

The bug in the White House had been taken out by then, so all we know about the sit-down is what John Gotti told an associate at the Bergin Hunt and Fish Club within earshot of another FBI bug.

Certain of going to jail either because of the DeMeo crew car-theft case or the Commission case or both, and equally certain that the ailing Dellacroce was not long for this world, Castellano told Gotti that, in the event he had to go to prison, he was going to turn over day-to-day power in the family to Tommy Gambino, Tommy Bilotti, and John Gotti, while he would call the ultimate shots from confinement.

It was an unrealistic solution. Although Gotti got along well enough with Tommy Gambino, he detested the impetuous Tommy Bilotti, whom he once referred to as a "fuckin' lugheaded scumbag," and it was absurd to imagine that the three of them could run the family in troika.

Actually, Castellano's selection of his doglike boy

Friday Tommy Bilotti as future underboss showed how deteriorated the old man's judgment had become. The squat, muscle-bound, toupeed Bilotti lacked brains, tact, shrewdness. He had no political sense whatsoever.

Gotti informed his associate at the Bergin: "He [Castellano] told me again last night, 'Well, I'm gonna try to make a peaceful transition, switch the family over to two, three guys.' . . . But we ain't gonna get nothin."

Castellano's actual words, according to Gotti, were: "You come with me, Tommy, and the other guy." To which Gotti replied that Gambino and Bilotti were very different and probably wouldn't get along.

When his associate at the Bergin asked Gotti what would happen if he were not included in the succession, Gotti replied firmly: "You know what we're gonna do then? Tommy and the other guy will get popped."

John Gotti had good reason to feel so confident. For some time his power and influence had been growing. Gotti received a strong signal that his power in the Gambino family had multiplied considerably in August 1985, at the wedding reception of Gambino mobster Frank DeCicco's son.

An FBI bug near the Bergin picked up Gotti bragging to an associate about what had happened.

GOTTI: Whose wedding was that this weekend that we went to?

PELLEGRINO: Ah, Frankie DeCicco's son.

GOTTI: Whose wedding did it look like it was?

PELLEGRINO: Yours.

GOTTI: How many people come and bothered me? Ah, ah, till what time in the morning?

PELLEGRINO: Till about . . .

GOTTI: They put a chair next to me.

PELLEGRINO: . . . three o'clock, three-fifteen.

GOTTI: Every goodfella, every skipper, and every nongoodfella came up to me. My brother Pete said he clocked seventy-five guys. I says he, he undersold me. I says it's more than seventy-five guys that came and talked to me.

As the summer of 1985 wore on, tensions within the Gambino family were exacerbated by the four federal indictments that had been brought against various members. Big Paul had to confer continuously with his attorneys, led by James LaRossa, about the DeMeo crew and Commission cases. Angelo Ruggiero and Gene Gotti had to huddle with their attorneys continuously about their heroin-trafficking case. And now the ailing Dellacroce had to confer with his attorneys at his bedside and John Gotti had to start preparing for his RICO trial. All these indictees had to cope with the embarrassments of their taped conversations, especially Big Paul, who repeatedly insulted his fellow Commission members and everyone associated with the Dellacroce faction within range of the White House bug.

With Aniello Dellacroce out of action, John Gotti became the de facto leader of the Dellacroce faction within the Gambino family, which meant that not only did he give orders to the Fatico crew at the Bergin but also to several other crews, some of which operated out of the Ravenite Club in Little Italy. By the fall of 1985 FBI agents and State Organized Crime Task Force investigators stationed along Mulberry Street noticed a steady stream of Gambino men and mobsters from other families converging on the ailing Dellacroce's old headquarters, the Ravenite Club, which John Gotti had taken over. Gotti was recorded complaining about having to cope with "goodfellows from all over the country" who were coming to confer with him. "They all come to me," Gotti griped. "I ain't got nobody here. I got to listen to everybody. I forget what things there are. I write notes to myself."

With Dellacroce dying and Gotti taking over his power, with Big Paul brooding over his coming probable imprisonment, and the two Tommys contemplating their future roles as boss and underboss, the autumn of 1985 promised to be a momentous one for the Gambinos. The pivotal event, everyone knew, would be the death of Dellacroce. The ailing mobster's physicians had predicted it would occur in December.

28

The Plot to Kill Castellano

On Todt Hill the fall air is full of cascading yellow and russet leaves, the cries of gulls, the calls of crows, and clouds of briny fog drifting in from the Atlantic. As the daylight shortens and the trees turn gray and bare, a dark pall of melancholy gradually envelops the hill and begins claiming the moods of its residents.

Isolated in his mansion on Todt Hill, in a household torn by the rivalry between his mistress and his wife, Big Paul Castellano, his future now clouded with federal indictments and spreading dissension within his own Mafia family, did not need anymore melancholy than that which already pervaded his being.

During the fall of 1985 the boss kept to himself in the White House, separated from the rank and file of his family, but not from his attorneys, who kept him busier than he would have liked with their incessant calls. The car-theft-ring trial was already under way. The Commission trial would be next. Two others would follow. Four indictments, four complex cases, four trials to prepare for and then endure in the courtroom.

About the only pleasures remaining to Big Paul, other than the balm Gloria poured on his wounds, were occasional lunches with his businessmen clients at the Palm or at Sparks Steak House in Manhattan. For these meetings Big Paul would don one of his expensive tailor-made, double-breasted suits and one of his tailor-made mohair overcoats, climb into his Lincoln Town Car, and be driven by his chauffeur and intended underboss, Tommy Bilotti, over the Verrazano Narrows Bridge to his Manhattan appointment. It was a pleasant drive. It felt good to be suspended over the entrance to New York Harbor, with all that sea and sky around him, then plunge into Bay Ridge and onto the Gowanus Expressway to Manhattan, where Bilotti would take him up the FDR Drive and off at the Forty-second Street exit to his rendezvous over a thick, juicy steak at Sparks. But after that brief respite from his troubles it was back to the heavy gloom of his violated fortress on Todt Hill, the falling leaves, and the calls from his attorneys.

Sharing Big Paul's gloom was his Staten Island neighbor and family underboss Aniello Dellacroce. Dying of cancer, the seventy-one-year-old veteran mobster was scheduled to go on trial on RICO charges along with John Gotti, and other Gambino men, on December 2. Already pretrial hearings had been held at his bedside in the presence of the judge scheduled to hear the case, Eugene Nickerson.

Dellacroce, former gunman for Albert Anastasia, loyal capo, underboss to Carlo Gambino, and mentor to John Gotti, had been keeping the peace in the family. The young Turks—the Gotti brothers, Angelo Ruggiero, Tony "Roach" Rampino—had wanted to go to war against Big Paul. Dellacroce had restrained them, telling them over and over again, "The boss is the boss is the boss." You do not strike down a boss no matter how irksome he has become. Big Paul did not realize it, but all that was keeping him alive was his failing underboss. The irony, of course, was that Big Paul wished Dellacroce dead.

How had Big Paul gotten himself into such a gigantic mess? A witness at the car-theft-ring trial was already fingering him as the monster who ordered the contract murders. Soon his ordering of his son-in-law's murder would come up in court. How was that going to look in the papers? Soon, also, pretrial hearings for the Commission trial would be held. The transcripts of the tapes recorded in his house would be turned over to his fellow Commission members and Fat Tony Salerno and Tony Ducks Corallo would learn what he really thought of them. As fall settled over Todt Hill, and the trees surrounding the White House shed their last leaves, Big Paul brooded in his kitchen dining nook. Glancing around, he wondered where the FBI had installed its bug. Agents Kurins and O'Brien had not told him.

He would go to jail. That was now certain. There was an outside chance that he could beat the car-theft-ring case, because some of the witnesses against him were such disreputable lowlifes, but there was no chance he could beat the Commission case. The evidence was there, and it had come from his own mouth.

Consolations? Gloria and his blood family were about all he had left, but they were at war. He took pride that his three sons were doing well in business, that all three had become millionaires, but resented their opposition to his relationship with Gloria. He also took pride in how well his nephew, Tommy Gambino, was doing in his trucking business. He trusted Tommy. Tommy would be a good acting boss after the feds took Big Paul off to jail. He was smart, hardworking, and fair. A solid businessman, a man of good sense. And he would do what he was told. The orders Big Paul would give him from prison would be respected. Of that he had little doubt.

Tommy Gambino had never succeeded in becoming his own man. He had always done as he was told. Agents Kurins and O'Brien had recorded Tommy's feelings about his personal predicament while they were monitoring the White House bug. Addressing his remarks to his uncle Paul he had said:

> Me, I never had the chance to say, "Well, I'm going to do something I want to do." I always did it for my family, for my children, for my father, for my mother. Matter of fact, always, even when I spoke, it was always, how does it affect other people? I wish I had your independence, Paul. In my life, in my fifties, I still haven't reached it. Where I could do something that I want to do and the hell with anybody else. Understand, I don't begrudge it to you. I'm glad you have that leverage, that privilege. You wear it well, God bless you, Paul.

Thomas Gambino, eldest son of Carlo Gambino, was a man whose life spanned two worlds. His father had wanted him to be a legitimate businessman, and in a sense he had become one. He owned four profitable trucking companies that virtually monopolized the trucking business in Manhattan's busy garment district. But he nevertheless maintained a connection with the crime family his father had led for nineteen years. He was, strictly speaking, also a capo in the Gambino family answerable to his uncle Big Paul Castellano. This was one of the reasons why his trucking companies prospered so robustly. Ninety percent of all finished garments picked up from the cutters and sewing contractors and then delivered to the showrooms and retailers was done in Gambino trucks. Out of fear of Gambino reprisals, the clothing manufacturers who used his trucks went along with his exorbitant prices, which were from forty to seventy percent higher than that charged by independent truckers. This meant that for every $100 garment shipped in New York the mob pocketed from $3.50 to $7.50. This was nothing less than a mob tax on the consumer. The cumulative value of this tax was so great that Tommy Gambino was able to send up to his uncle Paul as much as $2 million a year out of his garment district trucking profits.

Tommy Gambino lived with his wife in a luxurious penthouse apartment in a town house located in the most fashionable and expensive residential area of New York, Lenox Hill, at East Sixty-eighth Street, just off Fifth Avenue. The couple also owned a beach house on Pinehurst Street, Lido Beach, on Long Island's north shore.

Gambino's wife, the former Frances Lucchese, was the daughter of Cosa Nostra boss Tommy "Three-Finger Brown" Lucchese, a close friend of Carlo Gambino and once one of the most powerful bosses in New York, founder of the family that still bears his name today.

Tommy Lucchese had brought up his attractive daughter to be an educated lady. He had sent her to school at the fashionable Sacred Heart Convent on East Ninety-first Street, near Fifth Avenue, where she was educated by Catholic nuns.

Tommy Gambino had also been sent to expensive private schools by his father: prep school at the New York Military Academy, then Manhattan College. In marrying Frances Lucchese, not only did he unite with a peer in terms of education, but also with a family that could promote his business interests: His father-in-law, Tommy Lucchese, a master extortionist, had wielded enormous power in the garment district, and Tommy Gambino had inherited much of that power upon his father-in-law's death in 1967. The Gambino-Lucchese marriage was a mid-twentieth-century version of the dynastic unions medieval kings delighted in arranging for their heirs.

Big Paul had a special fondness for his Gambino nephew. Since Tommy's father had been responsible for making Big Paul boss, he felt a special obligation to him. He would repay his late cousin Carlo by naming Carlo's son as his successor.

All this was known to Aniello Dellacroce, John Gotti, and other members of the Dellacroce faction. They had been made aware that when Dellacroce died and Big Paul went off to prison, Tommy Gambino would become acting boss and Tommy Bilotti underboss. Thus there would be no room at the top for the likes of John Gotti.

Gotti was an ambitious man. Already he had acquired the ailing Dellacroce's power, which meant that he was in control of around ten of the Gambino family's twenty-three crews. To get control of the remaining ones and attain maximum power in the family, he decided he had no choice but to have Big Paul Castellano eliminated before the boss went to prison.

Knowing that things would eventually come down to this, John Gotti had been cultivating friendly relations with two of Big Paul's most trusted capos, Frank DeCicco and DeCicco's mentor, James "Jimmy Brown" Failla, who had once served as chauffeur to Carlo Gambino. Gotti had always thought these Castellano loyalists could become useful to his designs.

Those designs were suddenly galvanized on December 2, when Dellacroce died, as predicted, on the day his and John Gotti's trial was supposed to commence in Brooklyn Federal Court.

The next day New York police detectives patrolling Mulberry Street spotted John Gotti and Castellano loyalist Frank DeCicco, strolling together near the Ravenite Club, talking animatedly. The detectives, aware for some time that Gotti had occasionally been meeting with DeCicco, nevertheless thought it curious that Gotti would be seeing a Castellano man immediately after the death of his anti-Castellano mentor.

Dellacroce's wake was held the following day, December 4, and both the city detectives and the FBI were out in force to find out who was in attendance and who was not. They observed that practically the entire Gambino crime family had turned out to pay their respects to "Uncle Neil," with the notable exception of the family boss, Big Paul Castellano. And they observed that the capos and soldiers were paying their respects not just to Dellacroce's blood family, but also to John Gotti.

Later it was learned that the Gambino capos and soldiers who attended the wake had expressed shock and anger over the absence of their boss, Big Paul. According to the Cosa Nostra code it was unthinkable that a boss would not attend his underboss's wake, especially when the two had worked together all their adult lives, as had been the case with Castellano and Dellacroce.

Investigators believe that Big Paul did not attend the wake because he feared the resultant publicity, if he had attended, would hurt his chances for acquittal in the ongoing car-theft-ring trial that was causing him so much embarrassment.

Whatever the case, Castellano's deciding not to attend his underboss's wake turned out to be a grave miscalculation. For not only did his absence cause him to lose even more respect among his own men, it also caused his fellow members on the Commission to be disgusted with him.

Those Commission members, who were about to

go on trial with Big Paul in Manhattan Federal Court, had grown very concerned about their chairman. They were suspicious that Castellano, at seventy, might be tempted to exchange retirement in prison for retirement in his White House by offering to open his mouth to the feds. There was a weak streak in Big Paul Castellano. He liked his creature comforts, his luxuries, too much. He had worked too hard, and endured too much, to have to give up his Staten Island mansion, his expensive wardrobe, his Lincoln Town Car, Gloria, and those delicious meals at Sparks and the Palm for Mafia Row at Lewisburg.

Yes, who knew what sort of a deal Big Paul might try to cut with the feds?

Seemingly unconcerned about these suspicions and the angry reaction of his men to his not showing up for Dellacroce's wake, Big Paul quietly went about his business announcing to his capos that Tommy Bilotti would be his new underboss, filling the vacancy that had opened up upon Dellacroce's death.

When John Gotti learned this news he flew into a rage. As Dellacroce's protégé he felt he should have been named his successor. Bilotti, an official in Castellano's Staten Island–based Scara-Mix Concrete Company, had had nothing to do with Dellacroce and his crews. In Gotti's eyes he was a hotheaded fool who had scant experience with the Brooklyn and Manhattan rackets. Now Gotti realized his worst suspicions had come true: Big Paul was trying to freeze him out.

If Big Paul had not been as fatuous a man as he was, if he had been more street smart, if he had been a genuine Cosa Nostra boss who had fought for his position, not merely inherited it, he would have realized that the ambitious John Gotti would not have abided by Big Paul's plans for his and Dellacroce's succession, that he would have gone on the warpath over them. And, realizing this, he would have swiftly ordered his ambitious capo executed.

But Big Paul felt he was invulnerable. He was the boss. He chaired the Commission. No one in his family, or outside it, would dare topple him. You don't kill bosses like himself. It can't be done without getting permission from the other bosses on the Commission. Seemingly unaware of the extent of John Gotti's dissatisfaction, and latent power, Big Paul decided to discipline his unruly capo. According to the federal indictment brought against Gotti on December 12, 1990, for conspiring to murder Paul Castellano between December 2 (the date of Dellacroce's death) and December 16, 1985, "Paul Castellano informed John Gotti of his intention to break up Gotti's crew and reassign its members to other crews in the Gambino family." He would arrange a sit-down with Gotti to discuss this and other proposals. Conferring with his trustees Frank DeCicco and Jimmy Failla, Castellano decided that the three of them should meet with Gotti on Monday, December 16, over dinner at Sparks Steak House in Manhattan.

Meanwhile, Big Paul had to endure his arraignment in federal court in the Commission case. It would be held not far from the courtroom in which the car-theft case was being tried.

While Big Paul was being arraigned in the Commission case, John Gotti and his men were preparing for the sit-down at Sparks. First on Gotti's agenda was to get Castellano loyalists Frank DeCicco and Jimmy Failla on his side. By pointing out to DeCicco and Failla that they were never going to make much money under the greedy, aging Castellano and his "fuckin', lugheaded, scumbag" underboss Tommy Bilotti, Gotti lured the two capos away from their loyalty to Big Paul and into a plot to kill him.

Gotti, who prided himself on knowing "what's goin' on" and on being "in the fuckin' hunt," was confident he could get away with knocking off his boss because, among other things, he knew he would receive tacit approval of the hit from the Commission. For it was well known in the underworld that the other bosses hated and distrusted Big Paul and would be only too happy to be rid of him.

And so a plot was hatched. DeCicco, Failla, and two people who were not in on the plot, Tommy Gambino and Armond Dellacroce, son of Aniello, along with an as yet unidentified man, would go to Sparks before Castellano and Bilotti were due to show up and occupy a table for six. Then a team of eight gunmen, later identified by Gotti underboss turned government informant, Sammy Gravano, as John Carneglia, Eddie Lino, Salvatore Scala, and Vinnie Artuso—along with backup gunmen Anthony "Tony Roach" Rampino, Iggy Alogna, Joe Watts, and Angelo Ruggiero—would be dropped off a half block from the restaurant. By five P.M. they would be stationed in ambush near Sparks, waiting for Big Paul and his new underboss to arrive. Other Gotti men would stand guard nearby. John Gotti himself would remain in the vicinity of Sparks in case the plot somehow failed. In that event he would simply keep his dinner appointment with Big Paul. After the deed was done, the killers would be picked up by Gotti henchman Sammy "the Bull" Gravano, and DeCicco, Failla, Armond Dellacroce, and their other companion would quietly leave the restaurant and disappear into the night.

29

End of a Boss

It was a cold, rainy morning on Todt Hill when Big Paul arose to confront the business scheduled on his agenda for December 16.

Since the court in the car-theft-ring trial was in recess for that day, Big Paul had the morning off. His first appointment was scheduled for noon at a nearby Staten Island diner. There he would meet with his trusted capo Jimmy Failla and John Riggi, boss of New Jersey's DeCavalcante crime family, to discuss a labor problem. After the meeting Tommy Bilotti would drive him into Manhattan for a 2:30 P.M. visit to the offices of his attorney, James LaRossa, at 41 Madison Avenue near Twenty-fifth Street. If he had time he would do a little Christmas shopping before his next appointment, a dinner meeting at Sparks Steak House at 210 East Forty-sixth Street. There he was scheduled to have a sit-down with John Gotti and four other members of his family. A table for six had been reserved at Sparks in the name of a Mr. Boll for 5:00 P.M.

Big Paul had a lot on his mind the morning of December 16 as he shaved, had breakfast with Gloria, and dressed for the day. The car-theft-ring case had been gnawing at him for weeks. He hoped James LaRossa had some encouraging news for him. So had the problem of the unruly and overambitious John Gotti been gnawing at him. It had become particularly vexatious in the last fourteen days following Aniello Dellacroce's death. This evening, at Sparks, he was going to settle his differences with Gotti and his followers once and for all. Among other things he was going to try to make up for his not attending Dellacroce's wake by apologizing to Dellacroce's son Armond. Essentially a peace-loving man, Big Paul wanted to establish a lasting truce between himself and his power-hungry capo from Queens.

By 11:30 Big Paul was dressed and ready to be picked up by Tommy Bilotti. He would wear a raincoat and carry an umbrella, for, judging from the pounding of wind and rain on the White House windows, it promised to be a particularly nasty day.

Tommy Bilotti arrived at 11:45 in his black Lincoln Town Car and took Big Paul to his meeting with Jimmy Failla and John Riggi at the nearby diner. By 1:30 the three had completed their business and Big Paul was ready for the drive into Manhattan. Both he and Bilotti were unarmed—Castellano had not carried a weapon in years—and they had not taken the precaution of bringing bodyguards with them.

Over the Verrazano Narrows Bridge, onto the Gowanus Expressway, into the Brooklyn-Battery Tunnel, up the FDR Drive, out at the Twenty-third Street exit, and by 2:30 Big Paul was at the law offices of James LaRossa.

There he conferred briefly with LaRossa about the ongoing car-theft-ring trial and gave out Christmas envelopes stuffed with cash to the law firm's secre-

taries who were working on his case. He was gratified
to find LaRossa generally upbeat about the trial. The
attorney did not think the testimony of the prosecution's chief witness against his client was going to
hold up in court. The witness, the "Gay Hit Man"
who had recently demanded to have his lover transferred to his cell, was just too disreputable. Big Paul
was also pleased by the effusions of gratitude
expressed by the secretaries as he placed the bulging
envelopes in their hands and gave each a hug and a
kiss. James LaRossa was regarded as New York's premier criminal defense attorney at the time, a man
who never deceived his clients, and so it was most
pleasing to Big Paul to hear his reassurances. Leaving
the law offices at 4:00 P.M., Big Paul found himself in
a reasonably good mood for his sit-down with Gotti
an hour later. To pass the time before the dinner at
Sparks, he decided to do a little Christmas shopping,
directing Tommy Bilotti to take him up to a store on
East Forty-third Street.

While Big Paul's black Lincoln was battling the
Christmas season rush-hour traffic in midtown
Manhattan, buffeted by icy winds and a driving rain,
a group of eight to ten armed men, all wearing
trenchcoats and fur hats, were taking up positions
around Sparks Steak House on East Forty-sixth
Street between Third and Second avenues, waiting
for the boss to show up for his appointment. Some
were in parked cars along Third and Second. Three
were seated on benches in front of the Sam Flax
office supplies store on the north corner of Forty-
sixth and Third. Others walked up and down East
Forty-sixth Street in the vicinity of Sparks and the
Parisian-Chinese restaurant Chez Vong, next to the
steak house. Some time before 5:00 P.M., Frankie
DeCicco, Jimmy Failla, and Armond Dellacroce had
entered Sparks and occupied their table.

After buying some perfume for a secretary, Big
Paul and his driver began making their way through

heavy traffic up Third Avenue, bound for the appointment on Forty-sixth Street. Sparks Steak House stood on the right side of the eastbound street about a third of the way down the block. A dark green canopy adorned the restaurant's entrance, and just beyond it, two gigantic gilded Chinese lions, with cannonballs in their mouths, flanked the entrance to Chez Vong. Big Paul, whose father had been a butcher in Brooklyn, owned a wholesale meat business that sold cuts of choice beef to Sparks, and Big Paul had also bestowed labor peace on the steak house. Big Paul felt comfortable there. In keeping with the image of a respectable businessman he had striven so hard to project, the atmosphere at Sparks was in quiet good taste, redolent more of the nineteenth century than the roaring 1980s. Its walls were a medley of dark wood paneling and coffee-colored stucco hung with paintings of English landscapes and such favorite nineteenth century scenes as a nymph looking at her reflection in a spring. Grandfather clocks were scattered here and there about the large main room and the subdued lighting bathed everything in a soft amber glow. The place gave the impression of being part London men's club, part English pub. There was nothing Italian about it or, God forbid, Sicilian. It catered to an older, largely male crowd of local businessmen and diplomats from the nearby United Nations. There was absolutely nothing about the place that bespoke of the Mafia.

Big Paul had been going to Sparks for years, a loyal customer, but a conversation of his, taped by the White House bug, revealed he was not all that happy with the restaurant. Apparently during the entire time he had been patronizing Sparks the restaurant never offered him so much as a free drink. Where, he asked, was the respect?

As the seventy-year-old Castellano and the forty-seven-year-old Tommy Bilotti labored through the all-but-blocked traffic on Third Avenue, and as hundreds of pedestrians poured out of offices and onto the sidewalks and streets, the men in trenchcoats took up their final positions for the coming ambush.

Third Avenue and East Forty-sixth Street were so congested with rush-hour traffic and hordes of Christmas shoppers that Castellano and Bilotti did not arrive at Sparks until almost 5:30. As the black Lincoln pulled in front of the restaurant's canopy and came to a halt, a fusillade suddenly broke out that was witnessed by dozens of passersby.

A married Rabbi from Brooklyn accompanied by a stunningly beautiful call girl, on their way to a 5:30 dinner reservation at Sparks, saw six to eight men in identical trenchcoats, one carrying a walkie-talkie, converge on the parked Lincoln and open fire on its two passengers. From descriptions of the shooters given by these and other witnesses, including one pedestrian who witnessed the shooting from only a few feet away, police detectives believe it was John Gotti associate Tony "Roach" Rampino who gunned down Tommy Bilotti as he was getting out of the car, and John Carneglia who pumped six shots into Big Paul as he was struggling to lift his considerable weight out of the Lincoln's backseat. An eyewitness told the police that one of the hit men walked over to Castellano's bullet-ridden body, which had fallen out of the car and into the gutter, and fired a coup de grace at point-blank range into the boss's head. Another witness, dining in the restaurant when the shooting broke out, told the police she saw three men leave Sparks immediately after the shooting. From police mug shots, the woman identified two of the men as Frankie DeCicco and Jimmy Failla. Another witness identified Failla as the man he saw come out of the restaurant after the shooting and lean over Castellano's crumpled body and feel his jugular vein, apparently to make sure Big Paul was really dead. A trained nurse, who went to Bilotti's aid in a vain attempt to revive him, told the police she saw only two shooters, that the others present at the massacre, at least one of whom was carrying a walkie-talkie, appeared to be backup men protecting those actually doing the shooting. A witness who had taken refuge behind one of the gigantic golden lions in front of Chez Vong told police he saw the entire assassination team walk rapidly east after the shooting toward Second Avenue, and another witness, standing on the corner of Dag Hammarskjold Plaza, on the northwest corner of Second Avenue and Forty-sixth Street, saw three men in trenchcoats walk up rapidly and get into a Lincoln in front of the plaza and then take off southbound down Second Avenue. Still other witnesses on the corner of Second Avenue and Forty-sixth saw two other trenchcoated men get into another car and also head southward down Second Avenue.

More than likely Castellano and Bilotti had recognized their attackers as they approached them from the sidewalk with guns drawn. And in the split second between that instant of recognition and the first shots, Big Paul must have realized what had happened: that Jimmy Failla and Frankie DeCicco had betrayed him to John Gotti.

Meanwhile, as the crime scene was being analyzed, pandemonium had broken out in a room at NYU Law School. The beepers carried by Organized Crime Task Force Director Ronald Goldstock and the police officers and FBI agents attending a reception for Professor Robert Blakey began going off in chorus throughout the room as word of the Castellano hit reached their offices. They rushed out of the reception to public phones and car radios to find out what had happened.

Before long, scores of police officers, in an explosion of revolving cartop lights, were at the scene of the crime on East Forty-sixth Street, examining the two corpses, scratching out diagrams of their positions on the street and sidewalk, interrogating eyewitnesses, and confiscating the contents of Bilotti's and Castellano's pockets and what they had left behind in the car. Big Paul was found to be carrying $3,300 in cash, and his underboss $6,300. In the abandoned Lincoln, police found a parking ticket whose time stamp indicated Bilotti had incurred the violation while Big Paul was shopping for perfume on Forty-third Street. The bottle of perfume, gift-wrapped, was found, along with the sales slip. No weapons were recovered.

Word of the murder soon reached the Staten Island White House. According to agents Kurins and O'Brien, Connie Castellano, within an hour of the shooting, handed Gloria Olarte a sealed envelope containing $18,000 in cash, telling her that her father had wanted her to have the money and that she should now get out of the house.

Big Paul had been raised a Catholic and he and his wife had raised their children as Catholics. Nevertheless, John Cardinal O'Connor declined to grant permission to the Castellano family to have a funeral mass said for Big Paul. A spokesman for the cardinal told the press that "holding such a mass was ruled out because of the notoriety of Castellano's death and his alleged—and I underline the word alleged—connection to the organized crime syndicate." Citing canon law, the spokesman added: "A person who has not led a Catholic life or has been involved in a public life not in keeping with the teachings of the church . . . would be denied the liturgical farewell of the church." The cardinal did, however, grant permission for a priest to say prayers at Castellano's wake in Brooklyn and at his graveside on Staten Island.

Paul Castellano's wake was held at the Cusimano and Russo Funeral Home in the Gravesend section of Brooklyn three days after his death. Among those present were Castellano's widow, Nina, her sons Paul,

Jr., Philip, and Joseph, daughter Constance, and nephews Joe and Tommy Gambino. To the insistent demands of broadcast and print reporters outside the funeral home for information on who had attended the wake (they were particularly anxious to learn whether John Gotti was present), one of Castellano's sons told the reporters that the wake was "just for the family." Castellano's attorney, James LaRossa, added, "I can assure you Gotti is not in there. It was a private affair for the family only." One of the attendees at the wake, an elderly man with an Italian accent, commented that Castellano's predecessor, Carlo Gambino, had been waked at Cusimano and Russo and that many more people had attended that wake in 1976 than were present at his successor's wake nine years later.

Another huge crowd of reporters and photographers showed up at the old Moravian Cemetery at New Dorp, near Dongan Hills, Staten Island, where Big Paul was to be interred. They were held at bay by a force of twenty-five policemen under strict orders not to let anyone but Castellano's family enter the burial grounds. Big Paul was to be buried in a secret unmarked grave and no one was to know where it was save for the members of his immediate family.

The Dongan Hills section of Staten Island, a high, wooded area spotted with expensive, secluded homes, includes Todt Hill. And so Big Paul's final resting place lay, in a sense, in the shadow of his White House.

The Moravian Cemetery in Dongan Hills is one of the oldest in New York City, containing tombs from as early as the mid-seventeenth century when "Staaten Eylandt" was part of the Dutch colony of "Nieuw Amsterdam." The cemetery's chapel was built long before the Revolutionary War. Among the notables buried in the Moravian's vast wooded grounds are the great steamship and railroad magnate Cornelius Vanderbilt and his descendants, who occupy a 110-acre plot, surrounded by a wall and dominated by a huge mausoleum, built on a scale worthy of a Roman emperor.

Today the Moravian Cemetery surrounds a pond overhung with willows and beeches and filled with splashing ducks and geese and gulls. On the far side of the pond the grounds climb toward the Dongan Hills and the huge Vanderbilt plot that occupies the summit of the cemetery's grounds.

On December 20, 1985, the remains of Big Paul Castellano were carried to a pink marble crypt that stood somewhere between the pond and the hill bearing the Vanderbilt dead. There, with his wife and children and grandchildren and nieces and nephews looking on, Big Paul was laid to rest, in an unmarked section of the crypt. Not far away his unlucky, short-lived underboss, Tommy Bilotti, was interred in a grave later marked by a tombstone bearing his name.

Those who were aware of the impossible bind Big Paul was in at the time of his death knew that, in the end, fate had been merciful to him. When in 1986 the verdicts came down in the Commission case, for which he was due to stand trial, Big Paul's fellow godfathers—Fat Tony Salerno, Tony Ducks Corallo, et al.—received sentences of one hundred years each plus fines of as much as $250,000. If Big Paul had received such a sentence—and he would have certainly received one—he would have been condemned to spend the rest of this life behind bars, with no hope of parole. For the luxury-loving crime boss it would have been a devastating retirement.

Part VI

Drawing Fire

The Rule of John Gotti (1986–1992)

30

The Crowning of
John Gotti

While the remains of Big Paul Castellano were being interred in an unmarked grave in the old Moravian Cemetery at New Dorp, John Gotti was making his first moves toward taking control of the family Big Paul had bossed for the past nine years.

Thanks to its informants within the family and the FBI and State Organized Crime Task Force bugs planted in various family haunts, law enforcement was able to follow closely the transition process from Paul Castellano to John Gotti. Almost nothing escaped their hidden eyes and ears.

Since the evening of December 16, when Castellano was gunned down, the police and the FBI had been concerned that warfare might break out between the Gambino family's two contending factions. They were relieved, then, when an informant within Brooklyn capo Ralph Mosca's crew, Dominick Lofaro, reported to the FBI that on December 20, the day on which Castellano was laid to rest, Ralph Mosca told his crew at a meeting, "Johnny says everything's goin' to be all right. . . . We won't have to carry no guns around."

John Gotti seemed to be in control. He seemed to know enough about the murders of Castellano and Bilotti to know there would be no power struggle in their wake. The police and the FBI had expected as much from the beginning. The day after the Castellano hit, undercover men were out in force on Mulberry Street near the Ravenite to find out who Gotti was seeing. There, the morning of the seventeenth, they beheld Gotti and Frankie DeCicco walking up and down the street talking animatedly. Suspecting that DeCicco must have been part of the conspiracy against Castellano, the police then tailed the mobster out to Brooklyn to find out who *he* was seeing. To their great interest, they observed DeCicco entering the Veterans and Friends Social Club, then emerging from it with his mentor and fellow Sparks patron the night before, Jimmy Failla. The dimensions of the plot to kill Castellano were beginning to come into focus.

John Gotti's importance to the Gambino family was also beginning to come into focus. On the afternoon of the seventeenth, FBI and police surveillants, covering activity around the Bergin Hunt and Fish Club in Ozone Park, observed a dozen or so Gambino capos, including several from New Jersey, enter the club to confer with John Gotti. No other member of the Gambino family was receiving such attention on the day following the Castellano rubout.

Two days after the murders, all the captains in the Gambino family met at Caesar's East Restaurant on Fifty-eighth Street and Third Avenue to discuss the killing of Castellano and the election of a new boss. Joe Gallo, in his position as family *consiglière*, presided over the meeting. He told the captains that no one knew who killed Paul, that the murder was being investigated, and soon a new boss would be elected.

In the days that followed, the police and the FBI stepped up their surveillance of Gotti. On December 22, a detective spotted John Gotti, Frankie DeCicco, and Jimmy Failla in Brooklyn shuttling back and forth between the Veterans and Friends Social Club and Tommaso's Restaurant as if they were conducting a series of secret meetings and were concerned about being overheard.

Then on Christmas Eve everything came to a head at the Ravenite in Little Italy, where undercover investigators and detectives witnessed, and recorded, a remarkable spectacle: a steady procession of cars pulling up in front of the Ravenite and disgorging their passengers at the club's entrance on Mulberry Street. New York Police Detective John Gurnee, stationed in a police surveillance van not far away, photographed at least two hundred men arriving at the Ravenite, charging up to John Gotti, standing in the doorway, and embracing him and kissing him on both cheeks. Prior to that scene, Manhattan district attorney investigator Andrew Rosenzweig, tailing Gotti undercover along Mulberry Street, overheard the prospective new godfather telling Frankie DeCicco: "They've got to come to me."

Then, on December 30, Joe Gallo called another meeting of all the captains, plus Angelo Ruggiero, Sammy Gravano, Gene Gotti, and Georgie DeCicco, in the basement of a lower Manhattan apartment complex and an election was held to determine who the new boss would be. It was then that Frankie DeCicco stood up and nominated John Gotti. "They went right around the table," Sammy Gravano was to later tell a rapt courtroom. "Everybody nominated John. John was the boss."

In view of Gotti's newly attained high status, the State Organized Crime Task Force saw fit to install a bug in an annex to the Bergin Hunt and Fish Club between the club and the Nice N EZ Auto School, the better to learn what the new boss was up to.

Immediately the task force eavesdroppers were rewarded with several intriguing tidbits from the tongue of John Gotti and other Bergin denizens.

In response to an unknown male commenting on an article in the *New York Times* about Bilotti, not Castellano, being the intended prey of the shooters on December 16, Gotti dismissed the idea, saying, "Whoever it was, whoever went there, was gonna get shot."

When Angelo Ruggiero asked whether the other New York bosses had approved of the Castellano hit, Gotti replied, "One half sanctioned us, the other half said they're with them, we sanction ya."

It wasn't long before the bug in the Bergin annex overheard Gotti reorganizing the leadership of the family he now bossed.

"Frankie's an underboss at least," Gotti told Angelo Ruggiero, referring to Frank DeCicco.

As it turned out, DeCicco profited considerably from his treachery. In addition to naming him under-boss, Gotti also made him captain of the Staten Island crew once led by Tommy Bilotti.

The Bergin bug soon recorded Gotti expressing his new sense of self-importance. To an unknown male he was recorded saying:

> Me and you may socialize, but I can't socialize
> with these guys, I can't bring myself down,
> I'm a boss, you know what I mean. . . . I
> gotta isolate myself a little bit.

As to the role that Paul Castellano's nephew, Thomas Gambino, would play in the family, the Bergin bug recorded Gotti telling one of his soldiers:

> I told Tommy, "Whatever we do, I want you
> to know. Even if it's bad off color, I want you

to know from us. This way you know you're
a part of it."

Later the bug recorded Gotti telling the same soldier:

> I'm gonna suggest to Tommy, we're gonna
> beef up his regime, Tommy Gambino, but
> we're not giving him no fuckin' hotheads or
> any of those scumbags, we can't fuck his
> mind up with these bullshit street sit-downs.
> I don't want to hurt Tommy.

The Mafia has its own values, its own code of
ethics. Tommy Gambino and his uncle Paul had been
close. They had been related by blood and marriage.
Uncle Paul had told Tommy he would become acting
boss of the family if Castellano had to go to prison.
Yet, knowing John Gotti had had his uncle killed and,
in so doing, had upset Big Paul's plan of succession,
Tommy Gambino still had to maintain cordial relations with his uncle's killer.

Keeping watch outside Thomas Gambino's Manhattan apartment building at 6 East Sixty-eighth
Street, New York police detectives observed John
Gotti and his wife, Victoria, enter the building one
Saturday evening around 7:00 P.M. Later, in testimony before a grand jury, Thomas Gambino admitted that he and his convent-educated wife, Frances,
had entertained the Gottis at cocktails and dinner in
their penthouse apartment that evening and that all
four had taken a stroll down Park Avenue afterward.
The Neapolitans have a proverb for this sort of
behavior: "*Bisógna fàre buon vìso a cattìvo guivoco*"
("You must show a happy face to a dirty trick").

John Gotti was feeling pretty good about taking
over the family. "It's gonna be nice, you watch," he
told one of his soldiers within range of the Bergin
bug. "Nice," to put it mildly; later an FBI bug would
pick up Gambino capo George Remini explaining

how each of the family's twenty-three crews would pay a tribute of $10,000 to Gotti at Christmas.

Personnel administration was very much on Gotti's mind as he set about reorganizing the family. The Bergin bug recorded him discussing family matters with Remini.

GOTTI: And they come at me, and they say we're telling you now, what about this and what about that, move this guy are you gonna move us all? I said, "Let me tell you fellas something, I'm right in what I just done, I could break every one of you captains right now, and not overstep bounds," a new boss does that. As soon as he's done he gets up and makes a speech. He says I'm asking all you people to resign, all the captains, and then he puts them back in place the next day. That's the rules, and the rule. So Joe Gallo [Gotti's *consiglière*] makes a speech, he says, "He's right. Hah," he says, "he can break all the captains, he can break his underboss anytime he wants. The only person he can't break . . ."

REMINI: *Consiglière.*

GOTTI: . . . Is his *consiglière.* I says, "Joe, don't flatter yourself," I says, "you ain't no Paulie." He says, "What are you talking about? . . . I'll getcha voted in or voted out, you think you're dealing with a fool?"

REMINI: Who's gonna go against ya?

GOTTI: No, no, no, no, "You think you're dealing with a fool," I told him. "I break those twenty-three captains. I put ten captains there that I promote tomorrow. Georgie, Louie, Freddie, and Tom, they vote you down, I break them, put my original captains back and you ain't no *consiglière.*"

Reveling in the opportunities that were now available to him as boss, John Gotti was soon thinking of the future of the family he had taken command of. On January 18, 1986, a little over a month after the Castellano murder, the bug in the Bergin annex picked up a conversation between Gotti and an unknown male in which the new boss discussed his plans for that future:

UNKNOWN MALE: It's gonna be tough.

GOTTI: No, it will be tough with the, with the law now.

UNKNOWN MALE: That's the only, the only thing I want to tell ya.

GOTTI: The law's gonna be tough with us, okay. If they don't put us away . . . if they don't put us away for one year or two, that's all we need.

UNKNOWN MALE: Yeah.

GOTTI: But if I can get a year run without being interrupted. Get a year gonna put this thing together where they could never break it, never destroy it. Even if we die, be a good thing.

UNKNOWN MALE: It's a hell of a legacy to leave.

GOTTI: Hmmm.

UNKNOWN MALE: It's a hell of a legacy to leave.

GOTTI: Well, you know why it would be, ah, because it would be right. Maybe after thirty years it would deteriorate, but it would take that long to fuckin' succumb.

UNKNOWN MALE: It's a long haul . . . and you were thinking long before everything was done.

GOTTI: Yeah, but you can't, so we got some fuckin' nice thing if we just be careful.

But, as it would turn out, it was not in John Gotti's makeup to be careful, especially with the law. He was just too hotheaded and impetuous.

In March 1986, about two and a half months after he had taken over the Gambino family, he was called to account, in court, for his incautious involvement in a fracas back in September 1984.

A thirty-five-year-old refrigerator mechanic, Romual Piecyk, driving his car down a side street in Maspeth, Queens, found his way blocked by a double-parked car outside two gambling joints operated by John Gotti and his Bergin crew, a social club and the Crazy Corner Bar. Honking his horn in exasperation, the mechanic soon drew the owner of the double-parked car, Frank Colletta, out of the bar. Colletta, an associate of John Gotti, promptly punched Piecyk in the face through the driver's-side window and, noticing he had a wad of bills in his shirt pocket, plucked it out and counted $325. The burly, six-foot-two mechanic then got out of his car and started scuffling with Colletta. At this point John Gotti, noticing the brewing fight from the bar, erupted out of the place, went up to Piecyk, and punched him in the face, yelling at him to get lost.

The mechanic retreated and went to the police. Before long Frank Colletta and John Gotti were under arrest on felony assault and theft charges. About a year and a half later the matter went to trial in state supreme court.

Meanwhile the Castellano and Bilotti murders had occurred and John Gotti had been touted in the New York papers as the most likely successor to Big Paul Castellano. Gotti's face was beginning to show up regularly in the *Daily News* and the New York *Post* and the national tabloids, where he was described as vicious and ruthless.

Knowing now who his attacker really was gave Piecyk second thoughts about testifying against John Gotti. The trial did eventually take place, but when it came time for Piecyk to recognize defendant Gotti in court, the frightened mechanic suddenly claimed to have forgotten what his attacker looked like. Since the victim was unable to identify Gotti in the courtroom as one of the two men who had assaulted and robbed him, the case collapsed and the new Gambino boss was acquitted of all charges brought against him.

Later, unsubstantiated rumors began circulating that Gotti had threatened Piecyk before the trial began. Piecyk told reporters at a post-trial press conference, "I think any human being would lie to save his life."

The Piecyk trial was a relatively insignificant event in the life and career of John Gotti, but it did have one important result. It focused the public's attention on New York's latest godfather.

Reporters commented on Gotti's immaculately coiffed bluish gray hair, his $2,000 hand-tailored, double-breasted suits, his white-on-white shirt collars and French cuffs, his jeweled cuff links, his matching silk tie and pocket handkerchief, his gleaming $300 Italian leather shoes. They dubbed him the "Dapper Don." Here was a new breed of godfather—or rather, a throwback to the flamboyant dons of old, to Al Capone, Frank Costello. Certainly Gotti's style and demeanor had little in common with that of the bosses of the other New York families with whom he had to deal at meetings of the Commission: vulgar, overweight men like Fat Tony Salerno and Tony Ducks Corallo.

Reporters also noted that the well-groomed John Gotti was an intimidating presence in a courtroom. He stood out among all others, making the government prosecutors and the judge look drab and uninteresting and the members of the jury look utterly insignificant. Then there was Gotti's swaggering walk, the imperious way he carried himself, back straight, head up, chin out. Change his haircut and drape a toga over him and he would recall those marble figures of ancient Roman emperors and generals that fill up several halls in the Vatican Museum.

In the courtroom, Gotti showed unfailing good cheer. His big, winning smile. His occasional flirtatious glances at female jurors and ladies of the press. What juror would not be intimidated by such a defendant? Especially if the juror knew about the permanent disappearance of John Favara and the sudden loss of memory of Romual Piecyk.

John Gotti's acquittal for assaulting and robbing Piecyk gained him widespread notoriety, but he did not become nationally famous until he went on trial again in a much bigger case, the federal RICO case that had been brought against Aniello Dellacroce, John Gotti, and the middle ranks of the Gambino crime family in March 1985. When that trial began in Brooklyn Federal Court on April 7, 1986, three and a half months after the murder of Big Paul Castellano, the media was out in force. Television cameramen from all the major networks were on hand to greet the charismatic new godfather as he arrived in the federal courthouse in Brooklyn's Cadman Plaza, resplendent in his tailor-made overcoat and wide-lapelled, double-breasted suit, sporting a diamond ring on his left pinkie finger.

That evening John Gotti entered millions of American households coast-to-coast. A major mob celebrity, the likes of which the public had not seen since Frank Costello defied the Kefauver Committee on a national television network, was born.

As John Gotti was consolidating his hold on the Gambino family and becoming something of a media star, his victims, the Castellano and Bilotti families of Staten Island, were dealing with their respective losses. Big Paul had died intestate and his widow, Nina, had been named administratix of his estate. The surrogate fixed the value of Castellano's estate at $620,000, consisting principally of two meat markets in Brooklyn, the Meat Palace and Butcher Boy, which in 1985 had combined total gross revenues of $4.46 million. Among Big Paul's assets were four hundred shares of the Instanet Corporation worth $10,000, jewelry and personal effects valued at $20,000, and $7,000 in cash. By far the most valuable of Big Paul's known assets was his Todt Hill mansion, the White House, which his widow placed on the market for $3.5 million. Under New York State law when there is no will an estate is apportioned one third to the widow and two thirds to the children. In addition to his widow Castellano was survived by his sons Joseph, Paul, Jr., and Philip, and a daughter, Constance, all residents of the Dongan Hills and Todt Hill section of the island.

A palatial home, a couple of meat markets, and, most probably, several stashes of cash here and there that escaped the surrogate: not a very substantial legacy for a man through whose hands millions of dollars in ill-gotten gains flowed every year. But what had been Big Paul's true legacy? Had it not been a legacy of ruined lives and relentless pillage? All the murders. Twenty-five connected to the car-theft ring alone. How many more had there been under Big Paul's rule? And what about the sufferings of all the murder victims' families?

And then there had been the ceaseless plundering of the people of the city of New York. The tax Big Paul had demanded and received for the tons upon tons of concrete poured every year at construction sites throughout the city; the tax he received on all the clothing trucked in and out of the garment district. All the other kickbacks he had taken over the years. The waterfront payoffs. The exorbitant loan shark interest he had been collecting all his life. In the end Big Paul's White House had been built by money stolen from the people. It was a monument to murder and thievery.

31

The Gambino Legacy

The criminal enterprise John Gotti inherited upon the assassination of Paul Castellano had been growing steadily for the past fifty-four years. By the time it fell under Gotti's control, it had achieved a stranglehold on many New York industries—from meat distribution and building construction to waste disposal and garment trucking—and was grossing at least $500 million a year, probably much more. As one former Gambino associate told me: "You have no idea how much money keeps pouring in. It's unbelievable. It's like twenty-three mighty rivers all emptying into one lake."

How was this conglomerate organized, how did it operate, what were its major activities? Was John Gotti capable of running it successfully?

According to the New York State Organized Crime Task Force and tapes of Gambino wiseguys' conversations recorded by FBI bugs, the Gambino family in 1986 consisted of twenty-three *regimes*, or crews of soldiers, each headed by a *caporegime*, or captain, who reported to the family underboss, who in turn reported to the boss. The family's *consiglière*, or counselor, dispensed advice to the boss and underboss and also to the captains and soldiers. The money earned by a given crew would travel upward, with each level in the hierarchy collecting its share of the spoils. Thus the boss, the underboss, and the *consiglière* would each receive cuts from the profits of all twenty-three crews after the crew captains and soldiers were paid off. Twice a year, on his birthday and at Christmas, the boss would receive a tribute from each of his crews that totaled around $100,000. With an average of twenty to twenty-five soldiers in each crew, the Gambino family numbered almost five hundred men. Affiliated with them were several thousand "associates," mostly from the labor unions, political machines, and industries the family controlled or did business with.

Some of the crews were highly specialized. Thomas Gambino's crew was wholly concerned with racketeering in the garment trucking industry. The crew once headed by Tony Scotto was wholly concerned with labor racketeering on the New York and New Jersey waterfront. Robert "Di B" DiBernardo's crew specialized in pornography. Carmine "The Doctor" Lombardozzi's crew specialized in securities theft and stock market swindles. James "Jimmy Brown" Failla and his crew monopolized private waste carting in New York and were masters at illegal waste disposal. Pasquale Conte, a member of the board of directors of the Key Food supermarket chain, was also a Gambino capo. As we know, the crew run by Nino Gaggi and Roy DeMeo specialized in car theft and the selling of stolen cars in the Middle East. For most of the crews the standard staples were loansharking, gambling, hijacking, and shakedowns, with the specialty being carried on by only a few members of a given crew.

Paul Castellano had been recorded by an FBI bug telling one of his captains, "Our job is to run the unions." The reasoning behind the dictum was that if you controlled the labor supply of a given industry, you controlled that industry. Thus the Gambinos had for many years been heavily involved in labor racketeering, notably in the waterfront, hotel and restaurant, construction, garment, meat, and waste disposal industries. Through control of key locals and district councils of the International Longshoremen's Association they were able to dominate most of the Manhattan and Brooklyn waterfront. Likewise their control of key locals of the Hotel and Restaurant Employees International enabled the Gambinos to shake down restaurants, bars, nightclubs, and hotels in return for guaranteeing labor peace. By occupying key positions within the unions serving New York's construction industry the Gambinos, in conjunction with the other New York families, were able to charge contractors a two percent fee on their overall construction projects' budgets again in return for guaranteeing labor peace, but also for guaranteeing the safe and prompt arrival of essential building materials, such as concrete, to construction sites. The division of the fees among the five families would be decided at meetings of the Commission. Some of the construction unions in which the Gambinos exercised considerable influence were, according to the State Organized Crime Task Force, the International Brotherhood of Teamsters, Local 282; the Cement and Concrete Workers Union, Local 20; the Mason Tenders Union, Local 23; and the Steam Fitters Union, Local 638. Mob control of the construction industry was directly responsible for construction costs in New York being the highest in the nation.

But the Gambinos' influence in the construction industry was not confined to the unions serving the industry. Various Gambino men owned, controlled, or held employment with important construction companies. Paul Castellano and his sons owned the Scara-Mix Concrete Company on Staten Island. John Gotti's former *consiglière*, Salvatore "Sammy the Bull" Gravano, was president of the JJS Construction Company of Brooklyn and the owner of half a dozen companies serving the construction industry. John Gotti, Jr., is president of the Sampson Trucking Company. Alphonse Mosca, a Gambino family capo, was the owner of Glenwood Concrete Flooring, Inc. John Gotti held the position of salesman with the ARC Plumbing Company of Queens, a firm holding contracts with the city of New York worth $20 million. According to public testimony given before the New York State Investigation Commission in 1985, Frank DiCicco, Gotti's underboss, was on the payroll of the Leon DeMatteis Construction Corporation, a major New York State builder.

The Gambinos were also active in industries allied to the construction industry. In 1990 John Gotti's older brother, Peter, was indicted for allegedly splitting, with the Lucchese family, a $2 fee from Local 580 of the Architectural and Ornamental Ironworkers Union on each of over a million replacement windows union workers put up in New York public housing projects. Peter Gotti was later acquitted of these charges.

Another legitimate business in which the Gambino family wielded considerable clout was the meat business. Twenty percent of all the meat sold in the United States changed hands on the New York meat market, which was controlled by three organized crime families: Genovese, Lucchese, and Gambino.

Since the 1930s Paul Castellano and various members of his family had been involved in both the wholesale and retail meat business. Big Paul had owned two large retail meat markets in Brooklyn and controlled the Ranbar Meat Packing Company; the

Dial Poultry and Meat Company, which distributed chicken and meat to three hundred retail butchers and several supermarket chains; and Quarex Industries, a major meat distributor. He also had influence with two big supermarket chains, Key Food and Waldbaum's, that bought large quantities of meat. And, as might be expected, he had representatives within the Amalgamated Meat Cutters Union, the Butcher Workmen of North America, and the United Food and Commercial Workers Union, which bargained in behalf of 525,000 meat industry workers.

According to author Jonathan Kwitny, in his book *Vicious Circles*, the Castellano meat businesses had a long record of "suffering suspicious hijackings, which can lead to insurance claims; and of selling meat products that were later found to have been stolen off docks and trucks."

In 1977 Castellano's Ranbar Packing, Inc., was indicted by a federal grand jury in Brooklyn on charges of defrauding the government with counterfeit or stolen food stamps. According to Jonathan Kwitny's book the company apparently made $660,000 worth of fraudulent claims to the government.

Waste disposal was another business in which the Gambinos were active. As has been noted, this was Jimmy Failla's specialty. Failla, an officer in the Manhattan Trade Waste Association, controlled Rosedale Carting and the National-Stage Carting Company. Rosedale disposed of most of the waste it collected at a Staten Island landfill near the Arlington Railroad yard. In 1989 it was discovered that among the waste deposited in the landfill were hypodermic needles, catheters, and surgical gloves. In 1991 federal investigators found out that Failla's trucks were dumping toxic waste from the New York metropolitan area as far away as the mountains of West Virginia.

Pornography was a major earner for the Gambino family. It was the specialty of the crew headed by

Robert "Di B" DiBernardo, who controlled a huge network of Times Square area "adult" peep shows and bookstores that sold pornographic books, videos, and photographs at considerable markup. An FBI investigation of DiBernardo revealed he was the biggest pornographer in the United States. His company, Star Distributors, the nation's largest pornography distributor, was located in a building in downtown Manhattan owned by former vice-presidential candidate Geraldine Ferraro's husband, John Zaccaro. According to reliable sources, Ms. Ferraro collected $350,000 in rent from DiBernardo which she used to finance her political campaigns.

Eventually the FBI ensnared Di B in a sting operation and he was indicted and convicted. Not long after he appealed his conviction, Di B DiBernardo disappeared. Police detectives now suspect he was murdered and that John Gotti and his underboss, Salvatore Gravano, were involved in the crime. Apparently Gotti had heard that Di B was talking against him behind his back.

Then there was the narcotics trade, specifically the heroin business. As we have seen, both Big Paul Castellano and his underboss, Aniello Dellacroce, profited off the Sicilian heroin pipeline through their association with the Sicilian Zips. And we know that three members of John Gotti's crew, his brother Gene, *gumbah* Angelo Ruggiero, and John Carneglia, were deeply involved in heroin trafficking. Dealing heroin was the most dangerous and lucrative of all the family's operations.

But these criminal activities in and around New York did not define the limits of Gambino operations. The Gambinos were also active throughout Long Island, Connecticut, Pennsylvania, and New Jersey, especially in Atlantic City, and in Fort Lauderdale and New Orleans.

Loan-sharking, running illegal gambling casinos, stealing cars, stealing securities, hijacking trucks, selling heroin, distributing pornographic materials, labor racketeering, construction job shakedowns, waterfront shakedowns, garment trucking rackets. What qualities must a man have to successfully lead such a risky, intricate, and inherently unstable enterprise as the Gambino crime conglomerate? As Big Paul Castellano had once told Joe "Piney" Armone: "This life of ours, this is a wonderful life. . . . But it's very unpredictable. There's so many ways you can screw it up. . . ."

He must possess a rare combination of traits. Like the CEO of a large corporation, or the commanding general of an army, he must be courageous, aggressive, energetic, shrewd, resourceful, intelligent, and have the ability to inspire unquestioning loyalty in his subordinates. But he must also be cunning, ruthless, vengeful, violent (on occasion), clever, treacherous, and remorseless in his willingness to use murder to further his and his family's ends. He must be an administrator, a judge, a politician, a diplomat, a general, a businessman, and a lawless schemer and killer, not a combination of traits often found in one individual.

In reviewing the careers of John Gotti's predecessors we observe that to be seriously deficient in one or two of these traits can precipitate a boss's abrupt downfall. Albert Anastasia was an effective leader and organizer, but he was not very clever and was decidedly too violent. It was these two flaws that led to his assassination in a barber's chair at the Park Sheraton Hotel. Anastasia's violence antagonized too many of his subordinates and he was not clever enough to realize some of them were plotting against him.

His successor, Carlo Gambino, was able to keep the personality traits necessary to be a successful Mafia boss in a sounder state of equilibrium than any of his predecessors or successors. Carlo rarely lost his temper. Though he could coolly order a contract murder with a nod of his head or the raising of an eyebrow, he was never personally violent. Above all, Gambino was supremely clever. He possessed that quality so prized in his native Sicily, *furberìa*, which, loosely translated, means a kind of sly cleverness, a craftiness. Proof of Carlo's ability to lead a crime family effectively lies in the fact that by successfully waging continuous war for nineteen years he built the largest and most prosperous crime family in the United States and survived the long battle to be able to die peacefully in his own bed.

Not so for his nephew and brother-in-law Paul Castellano. We recognize in Big Paul the able diplomat, businessman, and administrator, Big Paul the imposing leader who was ruthless in doing away with anyone who threatened the success of his criminal activities, as he did in the car-theft-ring operation, which, as we know, resulted in at least twenty-five murders, probably many more. But we also see a Big Paul who lacked *furberìa*, who lacked shrewdness, a man who trusted his enemies too much. A man who was so unclever as to be under four federal indictments at the time his lack of *furberìa* resulted in his murder.

Did John Gotti possess the necessary traits to be able to successfully manage the Gambino crime family and lead it into the future? To, in his own words, "put this thing together where they could never break it, never destroy it"?

For a while it appeared that he did. He proved himself to be a natural leader of men and showed he could be sufficiently ruthless when he wanted to be. Consider the nerve it took to knock off his boss in a midtown Manhattan ambush at rush hour. But as his rule as boss unfolded he began displaying character flaws so marked one wondered how he could ever manage to survive. There was his extreme vanity, his publicly displayed arrogance and bravado, his total lack of prudence.

Gotti seemed oblivious to the fact that all his public

posturing, his posing and preening, his immaculately coiffed hair, his $2,000 suits, his black Mercedes, his diamond pinkie ring, would goad law enforcement to get him at any cost.

But it was his imprudence, above all, that was destined to bring about his downfall. Gotti knew how devastatingly damaging the FBI tapes had been to Neil Dellacroce, Paul Castellano, Angelo Ruggiero, and the members of the Commission. And yet he repeatedly demonstrated a total lack of caution in his conversations with his subordinates at the Bergin Hunt and Fish Club and later at the Ravenite Club. Did he think the FBI was so incompetent that it would not bug him in his inner sanctums the way it had done in those of Dellacroce, Ruggiero, and Castellano? "Don't say anything you don't want played back to you someday," he had told one of his men within earshot of an FBI bug, and then proceeded to say things that could, if picked up by a bug, destroy him utterly.

To hear New York police detectives, federal prosecutors, and State Organized Crime Task Force investigators talking about John Gotti is to sense the full measure of detestation law enforcement held for the "Dapper Don." Gotti's arrogant posturing and big mouth made him the law's principal target. Their determination to put him out of business became implacable.

That determination came to partial fruition in April 1986, when John Gotti went on trial in Brooklyn on federal racketeering charges. The case was designed to put Gotti behind bars for the rest of his useful life.

32

Beating the Rap, Round One: The RICO Trial

No sooner had John Gotti assumed control of the Gambino crime family than he found his new authority challenged on several fronts. First, a goon squad, on orders from a corrupt carpenters union official, brazenly trashed the construction site of a restaurant owned by a Gambino associate. Then, two months later, the government finally brought Gotti to trial on federal racketeering charges.

Gotti's reaction to the first challenge was taped by a bug in the Nice N EZ Auto School next to the Bergin on February 7, 1986:

"We're gonna, gonna bust him up."

His reaction to the commencement of his trial was shouted to a crowd of reporters outside a federal courthouse in Brooklyn on April 7:

"We're gonna beat this rap."

John Gotti's retaliation for the trashing of the Bankers and Brokers Restaurant construction site in

Battery Park City can be reconstructed from the FBI tapes of his conversations during February and March 1986.

John O'Connor, business agent of the United Brotherhood of Carpenters and Joiners of America Local 608, had paid a call on the construction site of a new facility the Bankers and Brokers Restaurant was building at Battery Park City in downtown Manhattan, and had noted with displeasure that nonunion construction crews were being employed at the site. O'Connor notified the contractor that the situation presented a "problem," but that the contractor could enjoy labor peace for a price. After $5,000 was paid, O'Connor came back for more and was rebuked. O'Connor then struck back by having a union goon squad inflict what turned out to be $30,000 worth of damage on the restaurant construction site.

Upon being notified of the sacking of his soldier's restaurant, John Gotti observed wryly that O'Connor was acting "overconfident" and announced his intention to punish him, to "bust him up." He then sent *caporegime* Angelo Ruggiero to enlist the Westies aid in teaching O'Connor a lesson he would not forget. Jimmy Coonan, boss of the Westies, agreed to accept the contract and began planning the shooting of John O'Connor.

Gotti's preoccupation with settling the score with O'Connor was then interrupted on April 7 with the commencement of his trial in Brooklyn Federal Court. The racketeering case had been painstakingly assembled by Assistant U.S. Attorney for the Eastern District Diane Giacalone, who had been investigating Gotti nonstop for the past four years. The defendants were to be the middle echelon of the Gambino crime family hierarchy, including John Gotti, capo of the Bergin crew at the time of the indictment. The principal defendant was to have been Aniello Dellacroce, but when he died on December 2, 1985, and when Paul Castellano was murdered two weeks later, Gotti, the emerging boss, automatically became the principal defendant.

As the trial got under way Gotti was free on $1 million bail, but then, six days after the trial began, something happened that abruptly affected his status. His underboss, Frank DeCicco, was killed by a remote-control bomb that had been planted in his car, parked near Tommaso's Restaurant in Brooklyn. DeCicco had just left a meeting with his mentor, Jimmy Failla, at the nearby Veterans and Friends Social Club. As soon as he got into his car a tremendous explosion erupted which blasted DeCicco's body through the roof of the car and onto the street. The resultant publicity gave the court second thoughts about having John Gotti free on bail. The murder of his underboss had complicated the jury selection process. It intimidated prospective jurors.

Back at the Bergin, Gotti and his men were at a loss to explain the hit on Frankie DeCicco. The police detectives were, too. The Mafia did not ordinarily use remote-control bombs to effect rubouts. Although the murder has never been solved, investigators believe it must have been perpetrated by associates of Thomas Bilotti, the Castellano protégé DeCicco had betrayed.

To replace DeCicco, Gotti named veteran *caporegime* Joseph "Joe Piney" Armone as underboss. Armone had been around since the days of Carlo Gambino and enjoyed near universal respect in the family.

A huge crowd turned out for Frank DeCicco's wake. Police detectives, stationed outside the funeral home in Brooklyn, noted that the attendees showed a great deal of respect to John Gotti. Gotti paid particular attention to Thomas Gambino. At one point the detectives observed Gambino get into a car with Gotti, drive off, and return forty minutes later. The pax between the new boss and the former boss's nephew seemed to be intact.

After the wake, jury selection for Gotti's RICO trial resumed under a cloud. Prosecutor Diane Giacalone moved to revoke Gotti's bail because she was convinced the publicity generated by the DeCicco murder had intimidated many prospective jurors. In addition, she produced a witness who testified convincingly that the refrigerator mechanic Romual Piecyk had been intimidated by Gotti into not recognizing Gotti in court. Would not Gotti also seek to intimidate witnesses scheduled to appear at the present trial if he was allowed to remain free on bail?

The matter was hotly debated by the defense and the prosecution as jury selection proceeded. Gotti did not help his cause when he and his defense counsel, Bruce Cutler, burst into laughter over some of the statements certain prospective jurors made during their questioning, and were reprimanded by the judge for doing so. Finally, on May 13, Diane Giacalone prevailed and Gotti's bail was revoked. He surrendered on the nineteenth and was jailed forthwith at the Metropolitan Correctional Center in downtown Manhattan. The trial was then postponed and would not resume for three months.

Not everyone in law enforcement rejoiced over the revocation of Gotti's bail. The State Organized Crime Task Force, installers of the Nice N EZ bug next to the Bergin, were against it because it meant that there would be no more opportunities to secretly record Gotti's conversations.

Meanwhile, on May 7, a band of Westies, acting at the behest of John Gotti, had shot carpenters union official John O'Connor four times in his thighs and buttocks, in front of the building at 1650 Broadway that housed the offices of Local 608 of the United Brotherhood of Carpenters and Joiners of America. The assault would return to haunt John Gotti two and a half years later.

On August 18, after a three month recess, the drama of *The United States v. John Gotti et al.* resumed. The principals in the contest were Judge Eugene H. Nickerson, Prosecutor Diane F. Giacalone, Defense Counsel Bruce

Cutler, defendant John Gotti, and, of course, the jurors, who would decide the outcome of the trial.

Judge Nickerson was a sixty-seven-year-old millionaire WASP patrician from the north shore of Long Island, otherwise known as the Gold Coast, who had been educated at Harvard and Columbia, lived in a walled estate, was a member of the exclusive Piping Rock Club, and was securely listed in the social register. At one time he had been Nassau County Executive and he had once run, as a Republican, for the U.S. Senate. A tall, courtly, silver-haired gentleman, who spoke in the distinctive upper-class drawl of the North Shore, Judge Nickerson was uncomfortable in the presence of street-smart toughs like John Gotti and Bruce Cutler.

As it would turn out, Judge Nickerson would also feel uncomfortable in the presence of lead prosecutor Diane Giacalone, an idealistic young assistant U.S. attorney of Italian ancestry who had made it her mission in life to get John Gotti. Ms. Giacalone was often irascible and consistently stubborn. And within a month of the resumption of the trial she would conceive an intense dislike of her chief adversary, Bruce Cutler, an aversion she would openly express in the courtroom.

The thirty-six-year-old assistant U.S. attorney was dedicated to her work as a government prosecutor. Born in a middle-class Italian community in Ozone Park, Queens—John Gotti's future fiefdom—Ms. Giacalone had gone to a Catholic parochial school for girls, Our Lady of Wisdom, and then on to Queens College Law School and a job as an assistant U.S. attorney with the eastern district. Once on the job, she became outraged by reports she received of the criminal activities emanating from the Bergin Hunt and Fish Club in her native Ozone Park. Soon she developed a special antipathy for the Bergin's *caporegime* John Gotti and made it her personal crusade to investigate and eventually prosecute him. Beginning her investigation in September 1981, she completed it in early 1986, in time for the racketeering trial of John Gotti *et al.*, which she, more than anyone else in law enforcement, had pushed for.

If Bruce Cutler was prosecutor Giacalone's nemesis, he was Judge Nickerson's antithesis.

Cutler was a Brooklyn tough guy. Bullet-headed, bullnecked, with a powerful physique filling out his expensive double-breasted suits, which sometimes appeared to be identical to those worn by his client, Mr. Gotti, Cutler had been a champion wrestler at Brooklyn Poly Prep and an aggressive lineman on the Hamilton College football team. Although he identified with John Gotti, and imitated the boss's style, Cutler was quick to point out that he was by no means as tough and street smart as his client. Coming from a comfortable Jewish family in Brooklyn—his father was a police officer, later a lawyer—Cutler called himself a "candyass" compared to John Gotti. As it would turn out, the patrician, well-mannered Judge Nickerson was no match for the rough, unscrupulous Bruce Cutler. (Repeatedly the North Shore WASP patrician would let the Brooklyn tough guy get away with courtroom mayhem. Repeatedly he would allow him to play theatrically to the jury rather than strive for judicial truth.)

As for Cutler versus Diane Giacalone, it would be a contest between an apprentice and a master, between a sparring partner and a champion. A former assistant U.S. attorney, who therefore knew both sides of courtroom warfare, Cutler would repeatedly seize the initiative, often succeeding in turning prosecution witnesses into *his* witnesses, making Giacalone look like a fool. He dominated the courtroom, upstaging everyone else with his flamboyant, combative style. He was much given to the mangling of prosecution witnesses, leading them into traps and then hitting them below the belt. And he was particularly adept at influencing jurors by directing improper questions at witnesses. Asking witnesses outrageous questions, which would be strenuously objected to by the prosecution, with the objections always being sustained by the judge, the question, though stricken from the court record, nevertheless would remain firmly lodged in the jurors' minds.

If the likes of Bruce Cutler made Judge Nickerson feel uncomfortable, one can imagine how the likes of John Gotti made him feel. During the trial Cutler, playing to the jury, would repeatedly remark that his client had been "denied Harvard," Judge Nickerson's alma mater. One wondered why Cutler did not follow through and complain that his client had also been denied Piping Rock.

The first exchange between the two would set the tone of the relationship between judge and defendant. It occurred at noon on August 18. The court was arguing the question of where the defendants would be eating lunch. At a certain point in the discussion Gotti piped up from the defense table: "Judge, why don't we just not eat? Why should we eat? We don't deserve to eat."

To which remarks the judge did not offer a reply.

By September 16 a jury of six men and six women had been selected from a pool of twenty-eight. At the insistence of the prosecution the jurors were to remain anonymous; they would be known only by numbers. Among the jurors were two Italian-Americans, two blacks, and two ex-Marines. All the jurors had heard about John Gotti and were familiar with his reputation as the boss of an organized crime family. A juror would have had to have been a marginal personality, a lunatic, an outcast, a dropout not to have heard about John Gotti, for in the early weeks of the jury selection process the media focused on John Gotti and his trial as if there were no other news to report. The process of media celebritification of Gotti would continue unabated throughout the trial. By the time opening statements were made, a portrait of godfather Gotti, painted by Andy Warhol, graced the cover of *Time* magazine.

Opening statements were made by the prosecution and defense on September 25 before a packed courtroom. Among the spectators was a vociferous group of Gotti supporters from Ozone Park, Howard Beach, and Bensonhurst, whose shouting, laughing, and yelling in support of their idol was a trial of another kind for the proper Judge Nickerson.

For her opening statement prosecutor Diane Giacalone chose to wear a bright firecracker-red suit. This prompted John Gotti to immediately dub her the "Lady in Red" and some of his groupies among the spectators to call her "Little Red Riding Hood."

Ms. Giacalone began her ninety-minute opening statement with an evocation of the 1973 McBratney murder in Snoope's Bar on Staten Island in which, it will be recalled, John Gotti had participated and for which he had been prosecuted and sent to jail. She raised the issue of the McBratney murder, she told the jury, because it was a crime John Gotti had committed in order to be ordained a made member of the Gambino crime family. After evoking the brutality of the attack on McBratney, and emphasizing Gotti's reward for his role in the crime, she marched over to a blackboard and quickly sketched a chart of the Gambino crime family's organization showing John Gotti at the top as boss and Joseph Armone and Joe N. Gallo beneath him as underboss and *consiglière*, with the various *caporegimes* and crews under them. That done, Giacalone launched into an explanation of what a RICO case was with reference to the present case against Gotti and his codefendants. She explained that the first count in the indictment charged Gotti and the other defendants with conspiring to commit crimes as part of an ongoing criminal enterprise, the Gambino crime family, and the second count charged the defendants with actually committing certain crimes, "predicate acts" as she called them. It was a strong opening statement. One could sense that it was delivered out of a sure conviction of

John Gotti's guilt. As Ms. Giacalone sat down, Gotti allowed a faint, sneering smile to appear on his handsome, sinister face.

No sooner had Giacalone resumed her place at the prosecution table than Bruce Cutler sprung into action as if he were in the wrestling ring. Sprinting across the courtroom on the balls of his feet, he paused before the blackboard and denounced what Ms. Giacalone had scrawled there as lies and pure fantasy.

There is no such thing as the Gambino crime family, he told the jurors. It was a fantasy concocted by the government. That said, he turned and quickly erased the prosecutor's organizational chart from the blackboard, a maneuver which should have drawn a censure from Judge Nickerson.

Cutler then launched into an impassioned defense of his client's character and activities. John Gotti was not connected to any organized criminal enterprise. That was a pure fiction cooked up by the government. The government was against John Gotti because of his flamboyant life-style. It did not like his tailor-made suits, his cursing, his gambling, and the friends he hung out with at the Bergin Hunt and Fish Club, which was just a plain neighborhood social club.

Cutler's oration was all theater:

> The prosecutor, the Lady in Red today, says, well, he associated with the same people. He hung around the same places. He was denied the country clubs of this world. . . . He was denied the fancy prep schools and the Harvard Business Schools and all the other places where the rich and famous go. So what did he do? Stayed with his friends. People he grew up with. . . . What's wrong with that? Is there some criminal charge about that—associating with people the government doesn't like? The Bergin Hunt and Fish Club is not some nefarious, behind-the-

scenes location. People come in and out. Sanitation men, civil servants. Nuns, women, and children. The Bergin is John Gotti's country club, if you will. If he were in some suburb, that's where he would spend his time. Spending time in a social club by playing cards, drinking coffee . . . that is the lifestyle that is indicted.

Trumpeting to the jury that the only family John Gotti belonged to was his own blood family, his wife and his kids, Cutler then picked up a copy of the indictment, held it up to the jury, and said:

This indictment is rotten to the core. . . . If you take stew with bad meat, and bad carrots, and bad potatoes, and bad onions, put on the fancy wine dressings that the government does and call it RICO, it still stinks. It still is rancid. It's still rotten. It still makes you wretch and vomit.

Then, still holding the indictment high, he strode over to a trash basket and exclaimed to the jury:

You can stop it. You can take this indictment and put it in here!

And crumpling the document, he tossed it into the trash basket shouting: "This is where it belongs. That's what it is. It's garbage."

Cutler's opening statement was a theatrical performance that made no judicial sense.

In her opening statement Diane Giacalone had warned the jurors that many of the key witnesses the prosecution would call would be "horrible people."

And horrible they did turn out to be. James Cardinali, heroin trafficker, five times confessed murderer, congenital liar, a frequent visitor to the Bergin Hunt and Fish Club. Salvatore "Crazy Sally" Polisi, hijacker, heroin trafficker, bank robber, and associate of John Gotti. Dominick Lofaro, heroin trafficker, gambler, confessed murderer, member of the Ralph Mosca crew and frequenter of the Bergin Hunt and Fish Club. And then there was Matthew Traynor, heroin dealer, bank robber, convicted perjurer, government informant, longtime friend of John Gotti, whom Giacalone had initially enlisted as a prosecution witness, but who then turned on her and agreed to become a witness for the defense.

The horribleness of these disreputable characters played right into the hands of the swaggering, supremely confident Bruce Cutler, who systematically "Brucified" them, as the press would term his ability to insult, humiliate, and pound witnesses into a pulp.

Before the mayhem of witness testimony and cross-examination began, Judge Nickerson reminded the jurors, in an ever so polite way, that questions to witnesses were not evidence. But, as it would turn out, Cutler's frequently improper questions would be asked so forcefully and so tellingly that they would have the force of evidence for the jurors.

The principal actors in this spectacle remained true to character from entrance to exit. Giacalone was earnest, legalistic, and often upset. The head of the defense team was brash, biting, explosive. The judge remained dignified, genteel, and overly patient. The star defendant was charming, sinister, and sartorially resplendent.

Enter Salvatore "Crazy Sally" Polisi, hijacker, bank robber, loan shark, jewel thief, heroin and cocaine dealer, currently residing in the Witness Protection Program after having been released from prison in exchange for his testimony against people like John Gotti. Ms. Giacalone leads him to tell the court he had come to know John Gotti in the early seventies when he was operating an illegal gambling casino called the Sinatra Club. Gotti used to come in often. He was a heavy bettor. After getting to know Gotti, Polisi took to dropping in at the Bergin Hunt and

Fish Club. At both clubs, Polisi testifies, he had over-heard conversations which implicated Gotti in a variety of crimes: loan-sharking, illegal gambling, hijacking, and car theft.

So as not to hand Cutler and his cohorts a side of meat they could hack to pieces at will, Giacalone gets Polisi to admit he had faked insanity to obtain a discharge from the Marine Corps, then embarked on a life of crime that included armed robbery, hijacking, bribing policemen and judges, loan-sharking, and trafficking in heroin and cocaine. With that out of the way, she turns Polisi over to the defense attorneys for cross-examination.

Bruce Cutler had many weapons in his arsenal, one of which proved to be particularly deadly when trained on Diane Giacalone's witnesses. It was Vic Juliano, a former police detective who had become a private eye in his retirement. Juliano possessed a special talent for sniffing out unsavory activities in a witness's past. What he turned over to Cutler on Polisi was devastating.

Striding over to the witness stand, Cutler looks up at Polisi and begins with a few routine questions.

"How many lies have you told in your life, Mr. Polisi?"

"An untold amount of lies."

"How many drugs have you sold; if we piled them up in the witness stand, how high would it go?"

"I'm not sure."

"How much money have you stolen in your life?"

"Millions of dollars."

"How many people have you stuck up in your life, sir?"

"Many."

Then Cutler took out the ammunition Vic Juliano had given him and stuck it in his clip.

Firing away, he asked:

"Isn't it a fact that during your days at the Sinatra Club you had two fifteen-year-old girls working as prostitutes entertaining your clientele?"

"That's not correct."

"You knew Eddie P's sister Barbara and not only did you know her, but in the late seventies when you were heavily involved in heroin trafficking, you used to beat her up, didn't you? You used to force her to have sex with you for heroin, did you not, sir?"

"No, I didn't."

"Didn't you get your wife involved in heroin in the late 1970s sir?"

"No."

"Did you have wife-swapping deals going on with your friends?"

"No, I didn't."

"Isn't it true that you photographed your wife committing forcible sex acts on other men at your directions?"

"That is not correct."

After this barrage, Judge Nickerson reminds the jury once again that questions are not evidence.

No matter. The damage has been done. Certain images of Crazy Sally's activities have lodged in the jurors' minds and there they will remain.

But Cutler is not finished. He sees an opportunity to convert Polisi into a witness for the defense.

"These neighborhoods where you applied your heroin and cocaine, these are neighborhoods that you lived in, frequented, and spent time in, is that correct?"

"That's correct."

"These are the same neighborhoods where John Gotti is loved and revered as far as you know? Just yes or no."

"Yes."

Enter handsome young James Cardinali, the prosecution's star witness, currently serving ten years for murder. Ms. Giacalone coolly gets him to admit to his relationship with John Gotti and to link Gotti to various crimes organized in the Bergin Hunt and Fish Club and to the three murders named in the indictment. So far, so good.

Now it is the defense's turn. First Cardinali is cross-examined by Jeffrey Hoffman, attorney for defendant Gene Gotti. Hoffman gets Cardinali to admit that the primary reason why he is testifying for the government is to "save his own ass." Then it is the turn of defendant Tony Roach Rampino's attorney, David DePetris. DePetris gets Cardinali to admit to committing murder, and to using hard drugs in prison while in the Witness Protection Program. Then it is defense attorney Barry Slotnick's turn. Slotnick, who had represented the late Aniello Dellacroce, gets Cardinali to say, "Yes, I lie a lot." Finally, it is Bruce Cutler's turn. Cutler, charging up to the witness stand like a bull, gets Cardinali to admit he once pistol-whipped a priest and killed three drug dealers in Florida after he made his agreement with the government to be a witness against Gotti.

Then, alluding to a dispute Cardinali is alleged to have had with the Lady in Red, Cutler thrusts his big chin out to Cardinali and says: "You made up with Ms. Giacalone, did you?"

"Yes."

"In other words she's no longer a slut, a blow job, a liar in your mind?"

"Correct."

At which Judge Nickerson admonishes: "Please don't make these comments and please keep your voice down." Nickerson is the only actor in the courtroom drama who says "please." None of the attorneys ever go near the word.

At a certain point even John Gotti gets into the act. From the defense table he accuses Giacalone of lying. Pointing to Cardinali, he shouts, "She's trying to protect that murderer, she's the murderer, that mother!"

"Please," Judge Nickerson says.

Cutler saves his masterstroke for the end of his questioning of Cardinali. Suddenly converting him into *his* star witness, he asks him what he thinks of John Gotti and Cardinali replies, "He is the finest man I ever met."

By the end of December James Cardinali as a credible witness is finished. It is clear from the quizzical expressions on the jurors' faces, as he steps down from his final testimony, that they didn't believe a word he said, except, perhaps, his praise of John Gotti.

January 1987 arrives and word comes to the courtroom that the Commission case, starring the likes of Fat Tony Salerno, Tony Ducks Corallo, and Carmine "The Snake" Persico has ended with guilty verdicts and sentences of one hundred years for each of the defendants. Gotti's reaction to this news is to go over to the reporters crowding the rail and exclaim: "Those cases got nothin' to do with us. We're walkin' outa heah!"

Now it is Dominick Lofaro's turn. Lofaro, soldier in Ralph Mosca's crew, who often visited the Bergin with his boss, confessed murderer, government informant, wearer of a body wire for the State Organized Crime Task Force, a major witness against John Gotti. By the time Cutler gets through with him, Lofaro has admitted to two murders, trafficking in multikilo heroin shipments, and being allowed to keep drug money upon his last arrest in return for his testimony against Gotti. More quizzical looks on the jurors' faces and some knowing nodding of heads. Who would believe such a man?

In all, Giacalone called seventy-eight witnesses, one more "horrible" than the other, before she rested the government's case on January fourteenth.

It was now the defense's turn to assure John Gotti's acquittal. In an ingenious maneuver Bruce Cutler managed to win an intended prosecution witness over to his side. He was Matthew Traynor, an old friend of John Gotti, a heroin dealer, bank robber, convicted perjurer, and FBI informer against Gotti and his Bergin crew. He was serving time for a bank robbery and wanted to get his sentence reduced.

Diane Giacalone had been preparing Traynor to testify against Gotti when, to her acute consternation, she caught him in a lie and dismissed him. Later he tried to get back into her good graces and she had ignored him. It was then that Traynor phoned Bruce Cutler to tell him that he had a few stories to tell about Giacalone that could severely embarrass her in the courtroom. Quickly seizing the opportunity, Cutler recruited Traynor as a defense witness.

With Matthew Traynor's testimony the trial sank to a new low.

Once on the stand, Traynor told the court that Diane Giacalone had given him drugs to induce him to tell lies about John Gotti. He was often stoned when they were together in her office preparing his testimony. During one session Traynor told Giacalone that he wanted "to get laid" and she then "gave me her panties out of her bottom drawer and told me to facilitate myself. . . . She said: 'Make do with these.'"

Giacalone's intent, according to Traynor, was to get him to frame John Gotti for various crimes he did not commit. To placate him, Giacalone allegedly had DEA Agent Edward Magnuson give him drugs, and prescriptions for Valium and codeine were also allegedly obtained for him through a doctor who was associated with assistant U.S. Attorney John Gleeson's wife, a nurse.

To this testimony the prosecution raised such impassioned objections, with Diane Giacalone calling all Traynor's allegations lies, that even the gentlemanly Judge Nickerson was moved to assert, "This case is not going to turn into any more of a circus than the defendants' attorneys have already made it."

Yet when Diane Giacalone moved to have all of Traynor's testimony stricken from the record, Judge Nickerson denied her request.

In or out of the record, damage had been done to Diane Giacalone's reputation by Matthew Traynor's testimony. It would be difficult for the jurors to extirpate from their minds the impression of Giacalone bribing a prosecution witness with drugs and offering her panties to relieve his sexual frustrations.

The defense rested on February 11 and immediately Diane Giacalone petitioned Judge Nickerson to allow her to call seventeen witnesses to rebut Traynor's testimony. The seventeen were called and their testimony added three more weeks to the trial. When they were through, Ms. Giacalone's reputation had not been fully rehabilitated. Certain images remained in the jurors' minds.

On March 6 a tired and somewhat confused Diane Giacalone presented her summation of the prosecution's case. Her peroration lasted five hours and contained several mistaken names and some errors of fact.

Then it was Bruce Cutler's turn to sum up for the defense. Abandoning his usual combative stance, Cutler allowed himself to speak in as reasonable a tone of voice as his passionate temperament could muster. Very simply he told the jury that no credible witnesses had come forth and stated they saw John Gotti commit a crime or order a crime to be committed, which, in a way, was true. It all depended on which witnesses you believed and which you didn't.

On March 6 the case went to the jury and a week later its verdict was announced in court: For John Gotti and all the other defendants it was not guilty on all counts. From now on the press would start calling Gotti the "Teflon Don."

33

Between Trials: The Gambinos Under Siege

John Gotti's victory over the U.S. government elevated him to new heights of celebrity, greatly enhanced his prestige in the underworld, and made him and the crime family he led more of a target than ever to law enforcement.

During the remainder of 1987 and throughout all of 1988, while Gotti cavorted around town in his black Mercedes and $2,000 suits, attracting extensive media attention wherever he went, prosecutors waged continuous war against the Gambino family and planned their next assaults on its boss.

Although he appeared outwardly confident and unworried in public, Gotti knew that it was only a matter of time before he would be called to account for the murder of Big Paul Castellano and the shooting of John O'Connor.

After the initial flush of his court victory subsided, Gotti soon found himself in a sea of vexations. One of his most acute problems was what to do with all the wiseguys who had ratted on him or who had talked too much within earshot of FBI bugs.

A month after Gotti's acquittal, one of prosecutor Giacalone's witnesses, Crazy Sally Polisi, was released from prison and given five years probation on heroin trafficking for his testimony against Gotti. He had obtained his freedom (he had been facing twenty-five years to life) by telling lies about the Gambino boss. The penalty, of course, for ratting on a boss was death without trial. To maintain discipline among his troops Gotti had to make an example out of Polisi. But Polisi was now in the Witness Protection Program, living in an undisclosed location under a new identity. The only way to get to him would be to bribe someone in the U.S. Marshals Service and that was very risky.

But what to do about Polisi turned out to be a minor problem compared to other personnel matters Gotti had to cope with. Two weeks after Crazy Sally got off with probation, three of Gotti's most trusted and valuable men went on trial for peddling heroin: his brother, Gene, and Bergin brethren Angelo Ruggiero and John Carneglia.

These three had been indicted largely because of Angelo Ruggiero's leaky mouth. It was the Ruggiero tapes that formed the government's principal body of evidence in the case. The whole thing was acutely embarrassing to John Gotti, for, among other things, the indictment suggested that he himself was involved in the heroin trade, whereas he was known to be a boss who had forbidden his men to deal drugs. For running off at the mouth Angelo had endangered half a dozen Bergin wiseguys, including the boss. The Ruggiero tapes had been causing a lot of havoc in the family. They had been partly responsible for the rift between the Bergin crew and Castellano. By the time of his indictment Angelo was in a hospital dying of cancer. Perhaps nature would spare Gotti having to inflict the maximum penalty on his closest friend.

Then, about two months later, another one of Gotti's closest associates at the Bergin, Anthony "Tony Roach" Rampino, was arrested for selling heroin to an undercover cop. Rampino posed a threat to Gotti, for he knew too much about his boss's crimes and, facing hard time, might be induced to start singing. As it turned out, Tony Roach did not even have to be coaxed to talk. No sooner was he behind bars than he was promising detectives he would tell all he knew about the Castellano murder, including his own participation in the crime. "I'll give you the names of all the shooters," he told his captors.

By mid-October, as John Gotti approached his forty-seventh birthday, the Gambinos had taken another punch, this time a double whammy. Gotti's underboss Joseph "Joe Piney" Armone and *consiglière* Joe N. Gallo, both in their early seventies, were convicted of racketeering in the so-called Gambino hierarchy case, and both were sentenced to long prison terms. Armone and Gallo were veterans going back to the days of Albert Anastasia and Carlo Gambino. Gotti needed their experience. Now he was forced to name two relatively untried men as their replacements, Frank Locascio, who would be underboss, and Salvatore "Sammy the Bull" Gravano, named *consiglière*.

The two veteran mobsters, Armone and Gallo, ended their service to the Gambinos as bitter, disillusioned men. More than likely both would die in prison.

At his sentencing, Armone, a shriveled, lame old man, was given a chance to go free on bail if he would talk to the feds about the Gambinos. The former underboss remained loyal to the code he had lived by all his life, chose silence, and was given ten years.

Not long before Gallo received his ten years, at the age of seventy-four, the White House bug had picked up a conversation between Castellano and his white-haired *consiglière* that revealed the depth of Gallo's bitterness.

GALLO: It's all turning to shit, isn't it?
CASTELLANO: (Silence)
GALLO: I mean, you spend your life working on this thing, this thing of ours. You think you're doing right. Then something happens, something goes off track, you get old, it don't look as it used to look. Disappointed. You end up disappointed. And the bitch of it is, you can't put your finger on what went wrong. You're doing good, you're doing good, you're doing good. But somehow, the way it all ends up, you ain't done shit. It all ends up small. It all ends up sour.

It was around the time of Armone's and Gallo's trial that Walter Mack, assistant U.S. attorney for the southern district, was in the midst of conducting a joint state and federal investigation of the murders of Big Paul Castellano and Tommy Bilotti. Over fifty witnesses were being interrogated. It was now only a matter of time before John Gotti would be charged with the two killings.

With so many important members of his organization either dead or in jail—DeCicco, Cardinali, Ruggiero, Carneglia, brother Gene, Rampino, Armone, Gallo—one would have thought John Gotti would be lowering his profile a bit, or at least would be acting concerned. But no. As 1988 dawned, Gotti was often spotted in his favorite haunts acting like a royal. The most impressive spectacle he would put on would be in Little Italy. He would arrive at the Ravenite in his black Mercedes, resplendent in one of his $2,000 suits, diamond pinkie ring glistening in the sun, disappear inside, then emerge with a couple of his associates and begin strolling down Mulberry Street, waving like a monarch to his adoring Little Italy fans, as if he hadn't a care in the world.

But, unbeknownst to the Gambino boss, Gotti did have reason for concern and it had nothing to do with law enforcement's designs on him. As he was swaggering around Manhattan, regularly getting himself and his wardrobe into the tabloids, the bosses of the other four families were worrying about the heat his high visibility threatened to bring down on them. One of the most concerned was Vincent "The Chin" Gigante, eccentric boss of the powerful Genovese family. It had been The Chin who had forced Frank Costello into retirement by grazing his scalp with a bullet back in 1957. Now Gigante was hatching a plot to assassinate John Gotti. Fortunately for Gotti, the Genovese conspirators were recorded plotting the hit by an FBI bug in Cassella's Restaurant in Hoboken, New Jersey, a favorite meeting place of the Genovese mob's New Jersey division. Gotti was duly warned of the plot and was then given FBI protection.

Throughout 1988 tensions mounted between the Gambino and Genovese families, resulting in several skirmishes which saw two men killed, one a Genovese underboss, the other an innocent bystander.

Throughout 1988 also, a grand jury continued hearing testimony on the murders of Paul Castellano and Tommy Bilotti, and the Manhattan district attorney, working closely with the State Organized Crime Task Force, began preparing a case against John Gotti, Angelo Ruggiero, and Gambino soldier Anthony "Tony Lee" Guerrieri for conspiring to assault carpenters union official John O'Connor.

Then, suddenly, in mid-January 1989, as Gotti and around ten of his men swaggered onto Broadway out of Spring Street, a squad of plainclothesmen, some of whom had been posing as street peddlers along Gotti's route, pounced on the Dapper Don, pinning him against a building near Dean and DeLuca's Food Emporium, handcuffing him, and telling him he was under arrest for ordering the shooting of O'Connor. At his arraignment on January 25 Gotti told reporters, "Three-to-one odds I beat this case."

The indictment charged John Gotti, Angelo Ruggiero, and Anthony "Tony Lee" Guerrieri "with assault and conspiracy in connection with the May 7, 1986 shooting of John O'Connor, business agent of Local 608 of the Carpenters Union."

Specifically the indictment charged that Gotti, Ruggiero, and Guerrieri had conspired with certain members of the Westies gang to punish John O'Connor for wrecking the construction site of the Bankers and Brokers Restaurant at Battery Park.

"The goals of the conspiracy," the indictment alleged, were "to punish John F. O'Connor, and thereby reaffirm the authority of the Gambino Crime Family over all others who might challenge it, by causing serious physical injury to John F. O'Connor in retaliation for his role in the destruction of a Gambino affiliated location, Bankers and Brokers."

The indictment cited a February 8, 1986, tape-recorded conversation between John Gotti and codefendant Anthony Guerrieri in which, referring to O'Connor, Gotti told Guerrieri, "We're gonna, gonna bust him up."

The indictment then alleged, on the basis of the tapes, that Gotti ordered Angelo Ruggiero to contact the Westies' leader Jimmy Coonan "to carry out the punishment of O'Connor." Coonan then "recruited Kevin Kelly, Kenneth Shannon, James McElroy, and Joseph Schlereth to perpetrate the assault."

Finally the indictment concluded that "on May 7, 1986 co-conspirators Kevin Kelly, Kenneth Shannon, James McElroy, and Joseph Schlereth, acting in concert, shot John F. O'Connor causing him serious physical injury."

This time Gotti was allowed to go free on bail. As it

turned out, almost an entire year would elapse before he would stand trial.

Free on bail, Gotti remained as conspicuous as ever throughout 1989, swaggering through the streets around the Ravenite Club, dining with much panache in his favorite Manhattan restaurants, at Joe Corrao's Taormina in Little Italy, and in midtown at La Camelia on East Fifty-eighth Street and Sandro's on East Fifty-ninth Street, where his appearance would invariably reduce the awestruck diners to furtive whispering as the don made his way to his table.

Meanwhile, the government kept pounding away on the Gambinos. In February John Gotti's older brother, Peter, was arrested for participating in a replacement window scam that had defrauded the city Housing Authority out of tens of millions. In May Gene Gotti and John Carneglia were convicted of heroin trafficking and were each sentenced to fifty years in prison. Death from cancer spared co-defendant Angelo Ruggiero their fate and the boss's punishment. Finally, toward the end of the year, nineteen of John Gotti's Connecticut wiseguys were arrested and indicted for racketeering. "These arrests will basically put them out of business," commented the U.S. attorney in Hartford, Stanley Twardy.

The FBI and the State Organized Crime Task Force also kept up their around-the-clock electronic surveillance of John Gotti throughout 1989. When Gotti, fearful of being bugged, decided to hold his meetings in a hitherto unused upstairs apartment in the Ravenite, the FBI promptly installed a bug there in November that was destined to reap a rich harvest of information on Gotti and also on his lawyers.

And there were developments in the Castellano murder case in 1989 which would affect John Gotti in 1992. On May 11, 1989, Philip Leonetti, underboss in the Scarfo crime family of Philadelphia and Atlantic City, was convicted in a RICO case, along with eighteen others in the Scarfo hierarchy, including Boss Nicky Scarfo, and sentenced to forty-five years in prison. Not relishing the prospect of spending the rest of his life behind bars, Leonetti, despite his high rank, turned stool pigeon and, in return for a possible reduction of his sentence, began talking to the authorities about John Gotti.

For three hours on November 30, 1989, Philip Leonetti testified before a Manhattan federal grand jury charged with investigating the 1985 murder of Paul Castellano and his driver, Thomas Bilotti. During his testimony Leonetti told of his contacts with Castellano and Gotti and the relationship between the Gambino family and the Philadelphia–Atlantic City family headed by Leonetti's uncle Nicodemo "Little Nicky" Scarfo.

According to Leonetti, not long after the Castellano murder Gambino captain Sammy the Bull Gravano met with Nicky Scarfo in a Trenton restaurant and informed him that John Gotti was now boss of the Gambinos and Frankie DeCicco was underboss. Soon thereafter Gambino soldier Arnold Squitieri visited Scarfo in Atlantic City to arrange a meeting between Scarfo and John Gotti. The meeting then took place in late February 1986 in the Staten Island home of Gambino soldier Edward Garafola. Leonetti testified that he and Scarfo were escorted by Sammy Gravano to a back room in the house, where they found sitting around a table John Gotti, Frank DeCicco, *consiglière* Joe N. Gallo, and captains Angelo Ruggiero and Joe "Butch" Corrao. "Before we sat down," Leonetti testified, "the first thing John Gotti said to my uncle was, 'I got the okay from the Commission to kill Paul Castellano. . . . I just want you to know that, Nick, I did everything the right way.'" Whereupon Scarfo said: "I know, John. I'm sure you did." Later on in the discussion Gotti and Scarfo compared notes on their former bosses. According to Leonetti, Scarfo told Gotti that his former boss, Angelo Bruno, discriminated against the younger men in his family, stealing business ideas from them, whereupon Gotti said: "Jesus, Paul was the same way, the same type of guy. He did the same thing with us. He wouldn't let us make a living and on top of everything else he wanted to kill me."

Leonetti went on to tell the grand jury that he and Scarfo tried to check out whether Gotti had, in fact, obtained approval from the other bosses on the Commission and had met with limited success. Genovese family *consigliere* Bobby Manna told Nicky Scarfo: "Yes, he did get the okay. He did everything the right way." And Leonetti was told by Bonanno boss Joseph Messina that he "supported John Gotti in killing Paul." Leonetti further testified that he and Scarfo were unable to find out whether the heads of the Colombo and Lucchese families had sanctioned the hit.

One sidelight of Leonetti's grand jury testimony that particularly interested Assistant U.S. Attorney Walter Mack was a conversation Leonetti reported between Gambino soldier Dave Iacovetti, Nicky Scarfo, and himself. "Iacovetti was telling us about John Gotti taking over, and that he's a great guy," Leonetti testified, "and that he was telling my uncle, 'Just like you, Nick, he's a real gangster, always for the underdog.'"

At this Walter Mack asked Leonetti what Iacovetti meant when he said "a real gangster." And Leonetti replied: "It means he's not like Paul Castellano. Like, Paul Castellano was considered a businessman. John Gotti is considered a gangster. . . . He kills people. . . . If you're wrong and you keep doing it you're going to have a big problem with him. He don't hem and haw with you."

Those in New York who were building the government's case against Gotti in the Castellano assassination were most interested in what Leonetti had to say. Leonetti did not come across on the witness stand like the "horribles" who dogged Diane

Giacalone's RICO case or those who would sabotage the forthcoming district attorney's assault case. Handsome, articulate, well dressed, and even well mannered, Leonetti had recently helped prosecutors win guilty verdicts in three trials at which he testified. Those who would be prosecuting Gotti for the murder of Castellano would more than likely use Leonetti when, and if, the case went to trial. But before then Gotti would have to stand trial on other charges.

34

Beating the Rap, Round Two: The Assault Trial

It wasn't much of a case to try a Mafia boss on. Mobsters of John Gotti's rank are not usually tried for such lowly crimes as ordering an assault without intent to kill. But the Manhattan district attorney and the State Organized Crime Task Force believed they had put together a case that would put the Teflon Don out of business for some time to come. Since he had already suffered two felony convictions, a conviction for ordering an assault on carpenters union official John O'Connor could put Gotti away for twenty-five years as a "persistent felon."

The trial was to be held in state supreme court in lower Manhattan on Centre Street only a few blocks away from John Gotti's Ravenite Club headquarters.

Where Centre Street intersects Canal and travels north it forms a boundary between Chinatown and Little Italy, two opposing camps that have little use for one another. The streets in this area, teeming with vendors and pedestrians, are a blend of Shanghai and Naples. Here are Chinese selling rice noodles, Canton cabbage, shiny red Peking duck, glistening carp, egg rolls, fortune cookies, reels of shiny silk cloth; and here are Italians selling *zeppole, sfogliatèlle,* cannoli, espresso, salami, mozzarella, olives, sausages, flowers. The streets are narrow and twisting, crowded and noisy. Restaurants in the shape of miniature Chinese pagodas flourish a block away from Gambino capo Joseph "Joe the Butch" Corrao's San Gennaro Social Club, with its small terra-cotta statue of the fourth century martyred Neapolitan saint adorning the entrance. Italian and Chinese restaurants abound. Often prosecutors and defendants find themselves eating lunch in the same place during the midday recess.

For this trial Manhattan District Attorney Robert Morganthau assembled a prosecution team headed by Assistant District Attorney Michael Cherkasky, chief of the organized crime investigative division, assisted by State Task Force Attorney Barbara DiTata and Assistant District Attorney Jeffrey Schlanger. They were to prove no match for Gotti's attorney, Bruce Cutler, and Anthony Guerrieri's defender, Gerald Shargel, who also assisted Cutler in defending Gotti.

The media was out in full force for John Gotti's first appearance in court on January 8, 1990. "Live" video vans sprouting bushes of antennae and satellite dishes from all the major networks were parked outside the courthouse and scores of cameramen and photographers and reporters with walkie-talkies crowded the main foyer of the building waiting for the don to arrive.

When Gotti breezed in around nine-thirty, wearing a beige fitted double-breasted topcoat, dozens of flashbulbs popped in unison and incandescent klieg lights froze the don in a blinding white glow that took away the colors of his clothes. With the aplomb and sense of theater of a seasoned politician or movie star, he waved to the cameras and flashed that big winning smile of his, then strode briskly into a special elevator, one barred to the public.

When Gotti arrived at the courtroom he entered it not with the attitude and bearing of an accused man, but with the panache of a victor, a man full of himself, greeting the court artists with winks and smiles, acknowledging the admiring glances of the few spectators who had showed up early enough to witness his grand entrance.

Once the jury of seven women and five men was selected, forty-three-year-old Judge McLaughlin, a tall, thin, bespectaled man, with a cherubic face younger looking than his years, instructed the jurors to abide by the doctrines of presumption of innocence and proof beyond reasonable doubt and reminded them that an arrest, or an indictment, "means nothing" and that they should render their decision solely on the basis of what went on in the courtroom. It was imperative that Mr. Gotti be given a fair trial.

The stage was set. Once again John Gotti would face the prosecutorial zeal of government attorneys. Only this time it was not the United States that was after him but the people of New York. In this case Gotti's ultimate adversaries were Manhattan District Attorney Robert Morganthau, who had brought the charges against him, and Ronald Goldstock, whose agency, the State Organized Crime Task Force, had helped assemble much of the evidence in the case.

In this trial the clash between the prosecution and the defense would not be as strident as it had been in the Brooklyn racketeering trial. Although Bruce Cutler was his usual pugnacious self, his adversary, prosecutor Michael Cherkasky, a lanky man of forty-two, whose tortoiseshell glasses gave him a somewhat professorial look, never approached the level of nastiness Diane Giacalone had attained in Brooklyn. Nevertheless, enormous differences in style and battle tactics separated the two sides. The defense side of the courtroom was much more colorful, much more relaxed, more congenial even, than the prosecution. The prosecution was prosaic, overserious, dull, even dour, and nowhere near as confident as the defense. There was no one on the prosecution team who could come close to Cutler in histrionics. Although Cutler was frequently outrageous, he was never boring. At times the prosecution was boring in the extreme.

That is not to say that the prosecution was never exciting. It was, for one brief moment, at the very beginning of the trial. In his opening statement, Michael Cherkasky made one dramatic move that for a few seconds electrified the courtroom.

He moved toward center stage and told the court that in the "early morning hours of May 7, 1986," members of the Westies gang "shot John O'Connor four times in the back," wounding him so severely that he "barely survived."

That said, Cherkasky turned, approached the defense table, and, pointing a long, bony finger at Gotti, cried out, "This man, John Gotti, the head of the Gambino family, ordered that assault."

Gotti met Cherkasky's eyes without flinching, then turned slowly toward Cutler, a faint smirk on his lips. Cutler nodded.

Cherkasky resumed. John O'Connor, a carpenters union official, had led a goon squad to trash the Bankers and Brokers Restaurant construction site in Battery Park City because he was furious that the restaurant, which was being managed by a Gambino associate, used nonunion labor.

Turning again toward Gotti, Cherkasky, raising his voice, cried, "Like all bullies, Gotti could not let an affront to his authority go unpunished." And so he hired "a bunch of brutal, vicious killers from Hell's Kitchen to shoot O'Connor."

Cherkasky then outlined the state's case against John Gotti and his codefendant Anthony "Tony Lee"

Guerrieri. He told the court about the Gambino family's long-standing association with the Westies. He mentioned the tape of Gotti telling Guerrieri about what he wanted done about O'Connor: "We're gonna, gonna bust him up." He referred to the tape on which Gotti told Angelo Ruggiero to call on the Westies to carry out the actual assault. And he recounted the Westies' May 7, 1986, shooting of O'Connor in the thighs and buttocks in front of the union official's office at 1650 Broadway.

Cherkasky then launched into an explanation of who the players were in this drama. In considerable detail he explained what the Gambino family was, how it was organized, and what its rules were. "Break the rules and you die," he told the jurors. The purpose of the family, he went on, was to make money—from numbers, loan-sharking, and labor racketeering—through "terror and intimidation," through "threats of violence."

What forms of evidence would the prosecution present to prove its case? It would play tapes to the jury in which Gotti and his coconspirators would be heard plotting the assault on O'Connor. It would play a tape of a discussion between Westies Kelly and Featherstone recorded nine days after the shooting, acknowledging that they shot O'Connor at the behest of John Gotti. "O'Connor has a new asshole"; "We did it for the greaseballs," they had said.

Prosecution witnesses would testify to the structure and criminal activities of both the Gambino family and the Westies, and a witness would testify that the Gambinos and Westies were so close that members of the Westies gang attended the wake of Gotti's slain underboss, Frank DeCicco. Among the witnesses who would be called were mobster turned informant Vincent "The Fish" Cafaro, and Westy James McElroy. The tapes and the witnesses were designed to prove conclusively that John Gotti ordered the assault on John O'Connor.

Now it was Bruce Cutler's turn to make the opening statement for the defense.

Rising from the defense table, Cutler moved toward the jury rapidly, springing, it seemed, on the balls of his feet, and began his response to Mr. Cherkasky.

He told the seven women and five men that the government had brought John Gotti to trial three times in recent years in what had become "a modern-day vendetta, persecution, and witch hunt." Paraphrasing John F. Kennedy's inaugural address, he continued, "They will pay any price, they will bear any burden, they will forgive any foe in their quest to put John Gotti in jail."

"The state employed one hundred policemen," Cutler complained, "to arrest Gotti on the street. They came to shake up the neighborhood pretty good. They came with football helmets, with all these flak jackets and shotguns. It looked like they invaded Panama. Yet the state has no money to help the homeless." (Of whom there were fifteen lying in rags in front of the courthouse.)

"The government says it has tapes of John Gotti's conversations," Cutler went on, walking back and forth before the jury, swaying from side to side, crouching, then rearing up.

> We had one president who was taped for about a week and got fired. Mr. Gotti has withstood *twelve* years of surveillance and they haven't got anything on him yet. No one has ever seen him commit a crime. . . . The government isn't at all interested in O'Connor, the man that got shot, it's only interested in Gotti. . . . Gotti is one of eleven children. Fifty years ago he was born destitute and dirt-poor in the Bronx. The family was on home relief. . . . John Gotti is the opposite of a bully. He has stayed with the same people all his life. His qualities are loy-

alty and perseverance. He's self-educated. . . .
Mr. Goldstock's tapes are four years old.
Why didn't he do something about them
back in 1986?

After that jumbled introduction Cutler turned to
the subject of the government's witnesses.

They plea-bargain Vince Cafaro. When he
wouldn't cooperate with them they put him
back in jail. Cruel and unusual punishment.
Seventeen months in the hole at Otisville.
Finally Cafaro says: "I'll do anything you
want me to do. I'm losing my mind." They let
him out and he starts telling lies about John
Gotti. . . . As for these Westies, if Gotti is
who they say he is [the head of the Gambino
crime family] he wouldn't go to these
drunken, crazy madmen they call the
Westies to get *anything* done. . . . As for the
Westy witness, James "Studs" McElroy, he's
a convicted killer who has broken each of the
ten commandments over and over again. . . .
He is a drug-addicted killer who enlisted as
one of the soldiers in the *Morganthau* family.
He would do anything, say anything, to stay
out of jail. He's in for sixty years.

After that dismissal Cutler then launched into his
most dramatic gesture of the day. Observing that the
charges against Gotti had been brought by "the people of New York," he asked, "Who are the people of
New York? Where are they?" And he went over to the
prosecution table and, bending down, looked under
it. "I don't see the people of New York here!" he cried.
Then, standing up: "I'll tell you who the people of
New York are. They are Robert Morganthau, Ronald
Goldstock, and Rudolph Giuliani, that's who they
are!"
Time for Cutler's peroration.

All this Mafia stuff, La Cosa Nostra stuff is
fluff, wrapping. The core of this case is
McElroy and he's rubbish. Vince Cafaro is a
no-good rotten bum who married the prosecution to stay out of jail. . . . I know I'm
brash. I don't want to offend you. But I will
prove that the tapes prepared by the prosecution were prepared the way *they* want them
to be. The government invents people to fit a
crime. The Westies are not valid witnesses.
They are soldiers of Morganthau, Goldstock,
Giuliani. McElroy is a soldier in the *Morganthau* family. They are not interested in justice. All they are after are headlines, votes,
their careers.

On Monday the twenty-second the prosecution
called its first witness, Vincent "The Fish" Cafaro.

The fifty-six-year-old Cafaro had been a made
member of the Genovese family for most of his life.
For much of his criminal career he had worked
directly under Genovese boss, Anthony "Fat Tony"
Salerno. Among other things he had been responsible
for "controlling" Local 608 of the carpenters union.
He was called as a witness by the prosecution
because of his knowledge of the inner workings of a
Cosa Nostra family and a carpenters union local, his
knowledge of Paul Castellano's alliance with the
Westies, and his contact with John Gotti while the
two were inmates in the Metropolitan Correctional
Center.

Arriving in court to hear Cafaro rat on him, Gotti
handed his hand-tailored double-breasted beige overcoat to soldier and codefendant Anthony Guerrieri,
who dutifully carried the garment across the courtroom to a coatrack near the jury box, a courtesy he
would extend to his boss at every court session for
the remainder of the trial. Once relieved of his topcoat, Gotti took his place at the defense table, his sil-

ver blue hair—not a strand out of place—and diamond pinkie ring sparkling under the overhead spots, and muttered some obscenity about the morning's witness to Bruce Cutler who appeared to be champing at the bit in anticipation of his coming chance to bone The Fish from gills to tail.

Michael Cherkasky, fully aware of what his adversary intended to do with his first witness, sought to blunt Cutler's attack by eliciting from The Fish his confession of the sins of a lifetime.

When Cafaro finally appeared and took the stand Gotti glanced at Cutler and smirked. Cutler nodded knowingly as The Fish was being sworn in.

Cafaro, a thin, tallish, balding man wearing dark shades and a loose fitting nondescript suit, glanced furtively at Gotti and sat down, a look of resignation on his weary face. He was about to rat on a boss, but he was being paid $4,200 a month in Witness Protection Program money to do it and he was out of jail. Things could be worse.

In contrast to the smiling, self-satisfied defense, the prosecution appeared dead serious. Cherkasky and his two assistants huddled over a stack of papers, apparently discussing something of immense importance, before Cherkasky rose and confronted the man he hoped would help him win his case.

Cherkasky first got Cafaro to review his career in crime. How as a teenager he had been arrested for possession of heroin, burglary, bookmaking, gambling, extortion, and shylocking. How he subsequently became a made member of the Genovese family at an initiation ceremony presided over by his sponsor Fat Tony Salerno. The ceremony took place in the basement of a restaurant. There, laid on a table was a gun, a knife, a piece of paper, a bottle of alcohol, and some cotton. One of the wiseguys then pricked Cafaro's trigger finger with the knife, dripped some of The Fish's blood on the paper, and set the paper on fire.

"If I should betray the Cosa Nostra I should burn like this paper," Cafaro was made to chant.

Then he was told of the rules. "You can't fool around with an amico's wife. You can't fool around with junk. No pornography and no government bonds."

Cherkasky then got Cafaro to tell the court how a Cosa Nostra family was organized and how much money its members could make. Cafaro astonished his audience by telling them that from numbers alone he earned anywhere from $500,000 to $2 million a year, and he was just one soldier among many.

Things began to turn sour for The Fish in 1986 when he was arrested for a variety of crimes, was convicted, and sentenced to prison.

Soon he was breaking his oath of silence and cooperating with the FBI to obtain a reduction of his sentence. But then, when he began contemplating the retribution the Cosa Nostra could inflict on him, he refused further cooperation. After this he was condemned to solitary confinement in the "hole" at Otisville Prison in upstate New York. His cell was only six by eleven feet and had no heating in winter or air-conditioning in summer. Sometimes in July and August the temperature in his cell reached 110 degrees and he thought he might lose his mind. Finally after seventeen and a half months of this torture, he couldn't take it anymore and agreed to cooperate with the FBI again.

After gaining this admission, which, of course, Cherkasky knew Bruce Cutler would have fun with, the lanky prosecutor led The Fish into testifying about Paul Castellano's alliance with the Westies. As an aide to Fat Tony Salerno he had attended a sitdown between Salerno and Castellano at which Fat Tony had chided Big Paul about hiring the Westies to do dirty work for the Gambinos in contradiction of the Cosa Nostra rule prohibiting a family from hiring outsiders to commit crimes. Castellano admitted he used the Westies now and then, but, by way of disculpating himself, told Salerno he had inherited them from Carlo Gambino.

Cafaro then told of a meeting he had attended between members of the Genovese and Gambino families at which an agreement was reached that the two families would divide the kickbacks from the construction company that was building a new Bankers and Brokers Restaurant in Battery Park City. Later, while an inmate in the Manhattan Correctional Center, to which he had been transferred from Otisville, he had run into fellow inmate John Gotti who told him that he was "looking to play Paul's end of the Bankers and Brokers deal." How much might that net Gotti? Around $2 million.

Having gotten Cafaro to testify to the Gambinos' connection with the Westies and Gotti's involvement with the Bankers and Brokers Restaurant construction site, Cherkasky turned his witness over to Bruce Cutler and Gerald Shargel.

Cutler opened by reiterating the crimes Cafaro had been charged with: extortion, numbers, racketeering, bid rigging, mail fraud, loan-sharking. "Were all these charges true?" Cutler asked. "Not all," replied Cafaro. Cutler then asked whether it was true Cafaro had been declared at his last trial "a danger to the community"? The Fish replied that it was true.

Cutler then got Cafaro to describe how pleasant life was at the MCC. "It wasn't bad," Cafaro admitted, "the food was O.K., you could stay out of your cell as many as eighteen hours a day, you could work out on the exercise equipment, watch TV, use the telephone as much as you wanted, and receive visitors every day."

"But life wasn't that good in the hole at Otisville, was it?" Cutler asked.

"No," the Fish admitted.

"You didn't have access to the phone, TV, other people, did you?"

"No, in the summer of '86 it was 110 and there was no fan and at night ants would crawl on my face. I couldn't breathe. Someday I'm gonna write a book about it."

"You're going to write a book about John Gotti?"

Silence.

"I guess it would be a big bestseller, wouldn't it?"

Silence.

"So you were seventeen months in solitary at Otisville. You lost weight but you didn't lose your mind?

"No"

"Did you cry?"

"No, but I had a lotta dreams. Sometimes I thought my mind was shot."

"Your mind after seventeen months in the hole was shot?"

Silence.

"So you signed an agreement with the government to wear a wire and rat on your friends to get you out of your misery?"

"You could get forty years in jail if you didn't testify, couldn't you?"

The Fish nodded.

"What do you expect or hope is gonna happen when you get sentenced again?"

"I'm gonna not go to jail."

On this note Cutler returned to the defense table and turned the witness over to his associate Gerald Shargel.

"What would you do if you didn't go to jail, Mr. Cafaro?" Shargel asked.

"I'd open a numbers operation in a black area," replied The Fish. "I'll take out a businessman's loan to get it started," he added.

"You mean you want to get a businessman's loan to open up a numbers racket?"

"Why not?"

Whereupon the entire court, the jury, the prosecution, Gotti, Guerrieri, the press, and the spectators burst into laughter.

"Using Cafaro as a witness is a tactic better suited for a Soviet gulag than an American courtroom," observed Shargel.

Shargel told the court that Cafaro was "a born liar whose testimony was extorted by the same government that kept him locked in a freezing cell in Otisville for seventeen months."

Time for Cutler to return and finish The Fish off.

"So, Mr. Cafaro, you're not in jail, you're a free man being supported by the Witness Protection Program, right?"

"That's right."

"You remember what happened before when you wouldn't testify for the government? You had to go into the hole."

Cafaro did not respond. Cutler went in for the kill. "Your deal with the government has nothing to do with this case, does it? The deal you made was for your *freedom*, wasn't that it?" All The Fish could do was nod in agreement.

With Vinnie Cafaro's testimony out of the way, it was time for the prosecution to introduce in evidence the first batch of tapes. The State Organized Crime Task Force had obtained 750 hours of taped conversations between John Gotti and his associates as a result of the installation of court-authorized bugs and telephone taps in a room occupied by the Nice N EZ Auto School next to the Bergin Hunt and Fish Club from April 1985 to May 1986. The prosecution believed that the tapes would show conclusively that John Gotti was the boss of an organized crime family and that he had ordered the Westies to assault John O'Connor in retaliation for O'Connor's trashing of the Bankers and Brokers Restaurant construction site on May 7, 1986.

To present John Gotti's secretly taped conversations, the prosecution furnished the judge, jurors, attorneys, and defendants with wireless headsets while the press had to make do with transcripts. As for the multitude of spectators, including a large contingent of raucous Gotti groupies, who packed the spacious, high-ceilinged courtroom, they had to rely on their imaginations, or intuitions, to figure out what was going on.

The twelve jurors listened with varying degrees of concentration and interest. Two or three of them alternately smiled, winced, scowled, strained, and even laughed. Others remained expressionless. One or two appeared in danger of dozing off.

Hints as to what was on the tapes were signaled by the jurors' changing expressions, and an occasional audible outburst of Mr. Gotti's on tape that pierced through the headset filters—"He don't give a fuck, this fuckin' scumbag, he never throws a fuckin' punch!"—and, now and then, the appearance of a knowing smirk on the face of Bruce Cutler.

To show that John Gotti was indeed a Mafia boss, the prosecution unleashed a barrage of boasts from the Dapper Don:

JOHN GOTTI [Referring to his former haunt, the Bergin Hunt and Fish Club]: I ain't comin' here no more. I'm the boss now. I'm goin' right to New York every fuckin' day. Go to the barber, then right to New York.

JOHN GOTTI: I know what's goin' on. See, you don't, Mike. You're oblivious to this, guys like you, your brother and certain other soldiers, God bless ya, you're oblivious to what's goin' on, but I ain't, I'm in the fuckin' hunt. . . . Me, I'll always be all right.

JOHN GOTTI: We got some fuckin' nice thing here, if we just be careful.

JOHN GOTTI [Describing to an associate how he was

treated at a recent wedding]: Every goodfella, every skipper, and every nongoodfella came up to me. My brother Pete said he clocked seventy-five guys. I says he, he undersold me. I says it's more than seventy-five guys that came and talked with me.

There followed taped dialogues between John Gotti, Anthony Guerrieri, and Westy boss Jimmy Coonan that clearly indicated there was a relationship between the three, though they fell short of demonstrating some conspiracional activity directed at John O'Connor.

Rather than refute what was on the tapes, Cutler and Shargel challenged their validity, the question of whether they had been tampered with, the question of in what ways the FBI had "enhanced" several of them.

The two defense attorneys launched their major attack on Detective Edward Wright, principal investigator for the State Organized Crime Task Force, one of whose duties had been making transcripts of the tapes that were eventually played to the jurors.

Detective Wright, who had been investigating organized crime for the past seventeen years, had illustrated some of the tapes played to the court by presenting what amounted to a history and analysis of New York's five organized crime families. He told of their origins, their growth, their structure, their criminal activities, while Bruce Cutler sat at the defense table shaking his head.

Rising after Detective Wright was finished, Cutler began his cross-examination of the witness by belaboring, once again, his contempt for the government's "fantasies" it called Mafia, Cosa Nostra, organized crime.

"All we ever hear from the government is *Mafia!*" he shouted, pacing the center of the courtroom stage. "Cosa Nostra! . . . *Organized crime.* . . . But these are pure fantasies. They are constructs of the government. They are imaginary entities they use to categorize people. I say they don't exist. I've never seen one. No one on this jury has ever seen one. You know what they are? They are convenient labels the government can pin on a defendant to prejudice you against him. I ask the jury to ignore these labels. They don't mean a thing."

Then, turning to Detective Wright, Cutler asked him why so many of the tapes were barely audible, why they were so garbled. "Don't you people use state-of-the-art equipment?" he asked.

Wright acknowledged that the recording equipment the State Organized Crime Task Force used was not the last word in technological advance, and added that the hoods being bugged often turned up their televisions, ran faucets, and flushed toilets to avoid being overheard, but that he and his assistants had ironed out the rough edges and garbles so that the printed transcripts faithfully represented what was heard on the tapes.

This led Cutler, and then Shargel, to rip into the validity of the tapes. If Detective Wright's version of a tape was the only valid one, who was checking Detective Wright? Detective Wright then admitted the recordings were of such poor quality he had to listen to them ten, twenty, thirty times before he was able to make an accurate transcript of them. By the time Cutler and Shargel got through with Detective Wright, they had succeeded in shaking the jurors' confidence in the accuracy of many of the transcripts. After the trial one juror told an interviewer that she was often confused because what she heard on a tape was not what she saw on a transcript.

As it turned out, the playing of the tapes was not the bonanza for the prosecution the government hoped it would be. It was on to another live witness.

The three-day government tape show was followed by the testimony of key prosecution witness Westy enforcer James Patrick "Studs" McElroy, the man the government hoped would provide the glue to cement the case against Gotti. It would be McElroy's role to testify that Gotti gave the job of assaulting John O'Connor to the Westies.

James McElroy had been billed by the press as a ruthless, cold-blooded murderer, and so it was somewhat of a surprise when the deceptively mild-mannered forty-five-year-old Westy appeared on the stand in his horn-rimmed glasses, glen plaid jacket, and black slacks, looking more like a sporty accountant than the fiend he had been made out to be.

But McElroy would horrify the courtroom in a way no one had expected. It had to do with the bland, casual way he would recount his hideous deeds. He would talk of shooting someone in the face as lightly and inconsequentially as he would tell of buying a tube of toothpaste from his neighborhood druggist.

Michael Cherkasky began his direct examination of the witness by asking him a few questions about his life. In subdued, somewhat self-deprecatory tones McElroy told the court he was born and brought up in Hell's Kitchen, the son of an Irish longshoreman, and that he had dropped out of school early. "I wanted to be an interior decorater. But they put me in a shoemaker class, so I quit," he explained.

After that he worked as a laborer in a wire factory, then as a bartender, a bouncer, a bellhop, a doorman, and a stagehand, until he joined the Westies in the late sixties, where he began as a bookmaker and soon became an enforcer. "I knew how to box, to fight," he told the court. "I used to work out at the P.A.L. . . . The Westies was a good outfit to work for," he went on. "They controlled the neighborhood."

Cherkasky then got McElroy to identify Jimmy Coonan as the boss of the Westies, Mickey Featherstone as another enforcer, and Kevin Kelly, Tommy Collins, Kenny Shannon, and Joe Schlereth as soldiers.

When asked where these Westies were now, McElroy replied, "In jail."

Before getting to the nut of McElroy's testimony, Cherkasky got him to tell the court about his career as a Westy.

"Have you ever lied at a trial?" Cherkasky asked.

"Yes, and other Westies have lied at trials," replied McElroy.

"Have you ever lied to the prosecutor in this case?"

"Yes, about some of the things I did."

"Why?"

"Because I felt ashamed."

"But you're telling the truth now?"

"Yes."

"Why?"

"Because I have no reason to lie."

At Cherkasky's urging McElroy told of the Westies' dealings with the Gambinos, how Jimmy Coonan and Mickey Featherstone had met with Paul Castellano at Tommaso's Restaurant in Brooklyn and cut a deal. "The Westies and the Gambinos are friends," observed McElroy. "Danny Marino [a Gambino capo] told me, 'anything you need you can have.'"

"Did you ever kill anyone?" Cherkasky asked.

"Yeah. If Jimmy Coonan told me to take care of this guy, to whack him, I'd kill him. . . . I killed a number of men for Coonan, without pay, to show that Jimmy Coonan had men who would kill." McElroy's tone of voice was casual, nonchalant.

In the same offhand way McElroy recalled some specific murders he had committed.

> I killed William Walker after he insulted me. I shot him in the mouth.

> I killed Vincent Leone, who I'd known all my life. He was a loan shark. He owed us, so we whacked him. I cut his throat. Later I told Danny Marino, "Nobody steals from us."

Once at a bar some guy started with me, so I stabbed him in the face.

I also killed a drinking buddy of mine who told me he was going to kill me.

I killed a guy in a pet store once. I walked into the store and asked the guy if he had any flea collars. He didn't pay me no attention so I shot him in the head. He bounced off the wall so I shot him in the neck. He went out the door.

Citing a presentencing report on McElroy, Cherkasky told the court that McElroy once told an undercover police officer that he was a "professional assassin" who "enjoys killing people." The same presentencing report asserted that McElroy once threatened "to kill one member per week of Teamsters Union Local 817 unless he received a no-show job."

Bruce Cutler was in a fighting mood when he rose to cross-examine James McElroy. He looked genuinely angry, not merely combative, as he approached the witness stand. And when he first uttered McElroy's name he pronounced it with utter disdain.

Cutler began by reminding McElroy that earlier he had told the court he had lied to the prosecutor about his past, that he had held back some things because he felt ashamed of them. "But then here in court you stopped holding back and told us some of the things you did, as if you were *not* ashamed of them.

"As a kid in Hell's Kitchen you robbed bakeries and candy stores. But you're not ashamed of that. . . . When you grew up you stabbed people in the face, but you're not ashamed of that. . . . You broke a guy's jaw over fifty dollars, but you're not ashamed of that.

"Then there was William Walker. You spent all night drinking with him in a bar, then Walker drove

Michael Gedell of the Standard Drywall Corporation. Gedell had told grand jury investigators that defendant Anthony Guerrieri had brought a business card John O'Connor had left at the Bankers and Brokers to him at the Brooklyn office of Standard Drywall and started asking him questions about O'Connor. When Gedell asked Guerrieri why he was so interested in O'Connor, Guerrieri replied that the Gambinos were "going to put a rocket in his pocket." For the prosecution's case Gedell's testimony neatly complemented Gotti's remark in regard to O'Connor: "We're gonna, gonna bust him up." But at the last minute Michael Gedell backed down and refused to testify because he feared retribution.

But the government still had a few more cards to play. It was back to the tapes.

The tapes, the prosecution contended, would establish John Gotti's position as boss of the Gambino crime family, his plans for the future of that family, his relationship with the Westies, and his involvement in the Westies' assault on John O'Connor.

Throughout the trial defense attorneys Cutler and Shargel had insisted that Gotti was not the head of an organized crime family and that the Mafia, the Cosa Nostra, was a fiction invented by the government. That in reality organized crime did not exist.

To rebut Cutler's and Shargel's contention, the prosecution played a succession of tape-recorded conversations between Gotti and his associates in which Gotti clearly referred to himself as the boss, talked about his relationship with the Westies, talked with Westy boss Jimmy Coonan, and discussed retaliating against John O'Connor for the trashing of the Bankers and Brokers construction site.

And so once again a hush fell over the courtroom as the judge, the jurors, and the attorneys put on their wireless headsets and Assistant District Attorney Schlanger got ready to play a tape. And once again John Gotti declined to put on a headset or even read from the printed transcripts. Instead, still resplendent in his expensive suit and accessories, he leaned over the defense table and stared at the jury.

To show that Gotti and Jimmy Coonan did know each other:

GOTTI: When he told me "you know you're an unindicted coconspirator," first time, I'm indicted. When we used to be kids an unindicted coconspirator was a rat. Fuck him, too, buddy; it's a joke. You know they don't give a fuck, you know what I mean? In other words every time our name is picked up in a conversation, you're in it, in the soup.

COONAN: Yeah, I know.

GOTTI: How could people talk, without talkin' about us kinda guys?

COONAN: Yeah, that's right.

GOTTI: We're young, we're active.

COONAN: Yeah.

GOTTI: Me, I curse everybody on the fuckin' phone. I don't give a fuck. Not like, not like, like when we get pinched today, now, it ain't like years ago—they put you in a fuckin' cell, they beat ya for three fuckin' days—but today ya get locked up they tell ya ya got a right to remain . . .

COONAN: Heh, heh.

To show that Gotti believed Jimmy Coonan was his friend:

GOTTI (to an unidentified male): They put Jimmy, put my friend, Jimmy Coonan, you know he's like the leader of the West Side gang, the Irish guys. He's pretty good, a good kid, a good ballsy kid. . . . They put him down. He's on the payroll.

To show what another mobster thinks of John Gotti:

GOTTI (to an unidentified male): He says, "Know this is the way it should always be." He showed me how grateful he was. "When they says God's gift to the underworld, you are it!"

To show that Gotti considers himself a boss:

GOTTI (to an unidentified male two weeks after he took control of the Gambino crime family): Me and you may socialize, but I can't socialize with these guys. . . . I can't bring myself down. I'm a boss. You know what I mean.

To show what plans Gotti has for the crime family he now runs:

GOTTI: The law's gonna be tough with us, okay: If they don't put us away . . . for one year or two, that's all we need. . . . But if I can get a year, gonna put this thing together where they could never break it, never destroy it. Even if we die, be a good thing.

UNKNOWN MALE: It's a hell of a legacy to leave.

GOTTI: "Well, you know why it would be, ah, because it would be right. Maybe after thirty years, it would deteriorate, but it would take that long to fuckin' succumb.

On January 30 the prosecution played the February 7 tape it believed showed Gotti intending to have O'Connor assaulted and the tape, recorded three months later, on May 7, of the news of the shooting reaching the Bergin Hunt and Fish Club.

The February 7, 1986, tape:

GOTTI: You think you could find out [about John O'Connor]?

GUERRIERI: Well, I don't know if I'll find out tonight, John.

GOTTI: Even if you find out by the weekend, ya know.

GUERRIERI: Yeah, what local is it?

GOTTI: Six-oh-eight. John O'Connor. John O'Connor, 608, at 16 somethin', Broadway, 1694, somethin' like that. Carpenters.

GUERRIERI: In other words, you want to see if . . .

GOTTI: Ah, he's a business agent.

GUERRIERI: To talk, or somebody who could talk with him.

GOTTI: No, we want to see who he is with.

GUERRIERI: Oh, oh.

GOTTI: We're gonna, gonna bust him up.

Five days later Gotti and Guerrieri discussed whether carpenters union shop stewards might have been behind the trashing of Bankers and Brokers.

GUERRIERI: Well, according to what, I got one kid that works up there, he said he's, he's almost positive he wasn't there. He said he, he, he thinks it's like a lot of shop stewards got together.

GOTTI: I don't believe that.

GUERRIERI: He said, "Tony, he wasn't there."

GOTTI: I don't believe no shop stewards would take it upon themselves no more than I believe. . . .

GUERRIERI: Oh, no, maybe they didn't . . .

GOTTI: . . . that my mother would go down on Ronald Reagan.

At this the jury suddenly erupted into laughter and Judge McLaughlin commented, "Some things we're not going to clarify." Gotti then turned to Cutler and asked him what they were laughing about. Cutler pointed to the transcript and Gotti smiled.

On a March 8, 1986, tape Gotti and Angelo Ruggiero are discussing the evident embarrassment of a Genovese family member by the name of Dom over the trashing of the Bankers and Brokers by John O'Connor, a man the Genovese controlled. The question of who was going to punish O'Connor boiled down to whether it would be the Genovese or the Gambinos who would carry out the assault.

RUGGIERO: He came out and admitted, said, "I'm embarrassed." I said, "Remember when ya come back, it only, only the two options I want; it's either we give this guy it, or yous do.
GOTTI: You tell them yous do it. Let them do it, a smack in the face, Angelo, you, you, we can't, ya know, ya can't undo the fuckin' thing.

The May 7, 1988, tape told of the news of the shooting reaching the Bergin Hunt and Fish Club.

GOTTI: Did ya read the paper yesterday where they said I get paid for seeing people?
RUGGIERO: You get paid for it.
UNIDENTIFIED MALE: Twenty-five thousand, that ain't bad.
GOTTI: Hey, excuse me, excuse me.
GENE GOTTI: John O'Connor's been shot four times. They (whispering) hit him in the legs. I heard it on the news, Angelo. It went off just like that.
RUGGIERO: Oh, yeah.
GENE GOTTI: [Laughter] Heard it on the news.

Although the tapes proved that John Gotti and Jimmy Coonan did know each other, defense attorneys Cutler and Shargel argued that nothing presented on the tapes indicated that Gotti had hired Coonan's Westies to assault John O'Connor.

They challenged the relevance of the "Gonna, gonna bust him up" tape, arguing that the conversation was held a full three months before the shooting of O'Connor and it was unclear on the tape whether Gotti had said "bust him up" or "bust 'em up." If it was "bust 'em up," Gotti might have been referring to some organization, such as the Genovese family.

"Bust 'em up" could have meant bust up the relationship between O'Connor and the Genovese.

When Detective Edward Wright, chief investigator of the State Organized Crime Task Force, took the stand to defend the relevance of the "We're gonna, gonna bust him up" tape, Bruce Cutler asked, "Did you know what was meant by that?"

"Yessir," Wright replied.

"Do you know what was on Gotti's mind?"

"Yes."

Cutler raised his voice. "You can read his *mind*? Take a look at him over there and tell me what he's thinking about."

"I wish I knew," said Wright.

At which Gotti, the jury, and everyone else in the courtroom, but the prosecution team, burst into laughter.

Cutler and Shargel then got Detective Wright to admit that the conversations on the tapes in question were so difficult to make out that he himself had to listen to them fifty times to be able to make a transcript of them.

But the tape that aroused the most controversy was one the prosecution was holding for last. It was a recording of a conversation about the shooting of O'Connor held on May 16, nine days after the shooting, between two Westies, Mickey Featherstone and Kevin Kelly, in a visitors' room in Rikers Island Prison.

Federal and state authorities had set up two recorders behind a painting in the Rikers Island visitors' room. The conversation that was taped was used at two federal trials that convicted Kevin Kelly of racketeering, including the shooting of O'Connor as a favor to Gotti.

As it turned out, the federal transcript of the conversation differed slightly from the state version, giving rise to a fierce debate.

In the federal version, Kelly made no mention of

Joe Schlereth, who, according to McElroy's testimony, had been the triggerman in the assault, whereas in the state version Joe Schlereth *was* named by Kelly as the triggerman. It was the state's version of the tape that had been introduced as evidence in the trial. Both versions had Kelly telling Featherstone that the attack on O'Connor was done "for the greaseballs." The prosecution contended that "greaseball" was a slang expression the Westies used to describe an Italian, specifically an Italian mobster. Both versions also had Featherstone remarking that the plot to attack O'Connor had been hatched at Frankie DeCicco's wake, just as McElroy had testified.

After the trial Gerald Shargel told the journal *Manhattan Lawyer* that the state Rikers Island tapes "scared the hell out of me," because it tended to corroborate McElroy's testimony. "It was what McElroy said coming from another source. It scared me because when jurors hear something twice, sometimes they start to believe it."

But Shargel was able to cast doubt on the state's version of the transcript during his cross-examination of Steven Mshar, the state investigator who had prepared the transcript. Telling the court that "the transcripts were changed to fit the prosecutors' accusations," Shargel got Mshar to admit that the tape was barely audible and that it had been "enhanced" at an FBI laboratory. Furthermore, Shargel pointed out that the government had already convicted Kevin Kelly of shooting O'Connor, giving the lie to McElroy's contention that it had been Schlereth who had pulled the trigger.

Then Shargel stunned the prosecution by producing a sentencing memorandum in another case, written by Assistant District Attorney Robert Mass and filed a month before the Gotti trial began, stating that according to grand jury testimony, the Bankers and Brokers Restaurant had been destroyed at the order of Pascal McGuinness, president of the United

Brotherhood of Carpenters and Joiners of America and O'Connors "main rival." O'Connor had been accepting money from Italian mobsters, the memorandum read, "in order to allow non-union carpenters to build the Bankers and Brokers Restaurant . . . McGuinness found out about these payoffs and decided to teach both O'Connor and 'the guineas' a lesson by ordering a goon squad to destroy the restaurant."

This was indeed a blow to the prosecution, but it was not the last blow the defense was to deliver.

For its last witness the defense called none other than the victim of the May 7 assault: John O'Connor.

Taking the stand, the fifty-three-year-old former carpenters union official described his shooting at his union local's headquarters and went on to suggest that union strife, not John Gotti, was probably behind the attack. "At the time we were having some problems," he admitted.

O'Connor, in fact, was facing imminent trial in state supreme court on a 127-count indictment charging him with bribery, extortion, coercion, and grand larceny in connection with his union activities.

O'Connor went on to inflict another wound on the government by pointing out that if the State Organized Crime Task Force was so certain that John Gotti's remark "We're gonna, gonna bust him up" referred to an impending assault on him, they were duty-bound, by law, to warn him in advance, but did not. In fact, O'Connor pointed out, state task force investigators did not mention the plot against him when they picked him up for questioning the day before the shooting, the implication being that they must not have placed much significance on the "We're gonna, gonna bust him up" remark until after he was shot.

"When has there ever been an assault case when the defense subpoenaed the victim?" asked Gerald Shargel.

Referring to O'Connor's testimony about foes in his union, not John Gotti, possibly ordering his shooting, Michael Cherkasky addressed the jury and asked, "If you get shot by John Gotti for breaking up a restaurant, what happens if you testify against him?"

On to the closing arguments.

Michael Cherkasky summed up the prosecution's case step by step, emphasizing that the charges "are the result of four separate investigations that all point to the guilt of Gotti and Guerrieri."

Referring to the tapes, Cherkasky said they show beyond a reasonable doubt that Gotti is a crime boss, "arrogant, egotistical, power-hungry, and insulated from the dirty work that his minions do."

Witness Vince "The Fish" Cafaro was necessary to the case to establish the context of organized crime and what were its structure, chain of command, purposes, and rules. He also gave valuable testimony about Gotti telling him he "was looking to play Paul's end" in regard to the Bankers and Brokers Restaurant.

The tapes clearly indicated, Cherkasky went on, that Gotti intended an assault on John O'Connor to punish him for trashing the Bankers and Brokers and that he ordered the Westies gang to actually carry out the assault.

The testimony of McElroy about Gotti hiring the Westies to assault O'Connor was independently corroborated by the taped conversation between Mickey Featherstone and Kevin Kelly in which Kelly explains how he and Kenny Shannon set up the ambush of O'Connor and accomplished it "for the greaseballs . . . who needed somethin' real quick." The two Westies also corroborated McElroy's testimony that the Westies' initial contact with Gotti about assaulting O'Connor occurred at the wake of Frankie DeCicco, something that had been much disputed by the defense.

In considering the evidence in this case, Cherkasky pointed out that each element of evidence should be considered in the general context of the case. "The whole here is much stronger than any of its parts," Cherkasky told the jurors. "One fact corroborates another."

If Cherkasky took a reasonable approach to the evidence in his summation, Bruce Cutler took a decidedly emotional approach.

"The assault case against John Gotti is a Hollywood production," thundered Cutler, "scripted by cops and starring a psychopathic killer" as its chief witness. "If this were John Q. Citizen it wouldn't take five minutes for the jury to say 'Not guilty.'

"McElroy joined this law firm," Cutler roared, pounding on the prosecution's table, "as the star. The screenplay is written around him, written around a man who is a snake, a rat, a lying bum, nothing but swill.

"I tell you," Cutler continued, prancing around in front of the jury, "that my client John Gotti is being persecuted. The prosecutors wrote a screenplay for their witnesses and the transcribers of the taped conversations.

"The majesty of this courtroom," Cutler ranted on, "is being sullied by the corruptions of this case. . . . You don't have to love my client. I don't ask you to do that. You may, but you don't have to. All I ask you folks to do is look at their case, look what they did with this case in an American courtroom. . . . The tapes meant nothing four years ago and they mean nothing now. The investigators rewrote the transcripts of the tapes to fit the prosecution's theory of the case. The motive and purpose is to poison your mind so you think you're hearing what you're seeing."

Turning the floor over to Shargel, Cutler returned to the defense desk with a self-satisfied, almost smug smile on his face. Gotti gave him good marks with his eyes and a nod of his head.

In his summation Gerald Shargel centered his venom on James McElroy, whom he called a drug addict, a killer, a psychopath, and a maniac, emphasizing that the jailed Westy enforcer would lie about anything to regain his freedom.

Referring to Vince Cafaro, Shargel insisted to the jury that he "was put on the stand to fill your head with visions of gangsters like in a movie."

Shargel turned and faced the jury. "When the smoke clears, you'll recognize that there was no proof, let alone proof beyond a reasonable doubt that John Gotti and Anthony Guerrieri had anything to do with this assault."

"I was waiting for them to put a case on," Gotti told a reporter as he exited the courtroom after final arguments.

Judge McLaughlin's instructions to the jury were a model of judicial probity and good common sense.

First he told the panel of seven women and five men that although the judge instructs on the law, the judge's opinion does not count; only the jury's opinion counts.

An indictment, he went on, is not evidence of anything. Evidence is sworn testimony and exhibits. The jurors are not allowed to speculate about things that are not evidence. The jurors will determine the credibility of witnesses in accordance with certain tests. Is the witness neutral or hostile? Does the witness have a good reason to falsify? What is the past history of the witness? What is the witness's behavior on the witness stand like?

Turning to the doctrine of reasonable doubt, McLaughlin told the jurors that a doubt is based on reason and a logical and coherent doubt is based on evidence or lack of evidence.

Audible tapes are evidence, but transcripts of tapes are not evidence, the judge went on, they are merely an aid.

As for Mr. Cafaro and Mr. McElroy, their convictions for crimes can be taken into account when deciding whether their testimony is credible or not. He told the jury to remember that the testimony of an accomplice is suspicious without further corroboration.

He said membership in an organized crime family, a Mafia family, is not a crime in itself.

He told the jury that to convict the defendants in this case the prosecution had to prove that the defendants acted with mental culpability, that they acted intentionally and recklessly.

As Judge McLaughlin intoned these precepts, intended to assure the defendants of as fair a trial as possible, the jurors sat silently and respectfully, while John Gotti leaned back from the defense table, wearing his perpetual smirk, and impatiently tapped a ballpoint pen on a pad. Was the civilized majesty of the law being wasted on the likes of John Gotti?

It took the jury three days of deliberations to arrive at its verdict. When the foreman began reading the not guiltys, the courtroom was hushed. By the time he recited the twelfth not guilty, pandemonium had broken out among the Gotti supporters in the spectators' section and Judge McLaughlin had to cry out from the bench, "Any more of this and it's thirty days in jail, and I mean it!"

Gotti's reaction to the verdict—letting his head drop, then jabbing the air with his right fist, then kissing defense attorney Bruce Cutler—was witnessed by a national television audience. It was Gotti's third consecutive victory over the government and it was obvious to all that he and Cutler were savoring it.

The triumphant exodus of the Gotti entourage from the courthouse degenerated into a headlong charge through a wall of reporters and cameramen backed up by a seemingly impenetrable formation of tanks sprouting attennae and satellite dishes. There were scuffles between Gotti's bodyguards and assorted media types thrusting hand-held mikes and videotape cameras into the victor's face until finally Gotti was in a Cadillac plunging into the dense conjestion of Centre Street on his way to the big celebration that awaited him a few blocks away in Little Italy.

By the time the hero's car had begun climbing the narrow confines of Mulberry Street, with its scores of sidewalk cafés and Italian stores, bars, and restaurants lining the way, hundreds of well-wishers had gathered along the sidewalks shouting, "Viva Gotti," "Way to go, Johnnie," "Attaway, Johnnie Boy," "Gotti! Gotti! Gotti!"

Then, as the car stopped in front of the Ravenite Club and Gotti got out, the don was pounced on by a crowd of supporters, most of whom appeared to be local middle-aged women bent on kissing him on his lips. "I love this man. He's good for the neighborhood," cried one heavyset Italian lady as she threw her arms around the don. Once inside the Ravenite, Gotti sat down at a big round table in the rear of the club and, lighting up a cigar and accepting a glass of Asti Spumanti, began holding court. For several hours a steady stream of his men, the capos of his twenty-three crews, and many soldiers and associates, came to pay their respects and congratulate him on his victory. As darkness fell, the rockets' red glare lighted up the buildings north of the Ravenite as hundreds of fireworks were exploded from balconies and rooftops. It was at the height of the fireworks display around 7:45 P.M. that Gotti emerged from the Ravenite, a grinning Sammy Gravano by his side, got into his Mercedes, and headed home to Howard Beach.

Meanwhile, back at the Bergin Hunt and Fish Club, flags and balloons had been strung up in front of the club and cars had been honking their horns all afternoon in the neighboring streets to celebrate their hero's triumph. Nearby, along the storefronts up and down 101st Street in Ozone Park banners streamed proclaiming, CONGRATULATIONS JOHN AND TONY—WE LOVE YA.

When Gotti arrived back at his Cape Cod house at Howard Beach, he found clusters of balloons tied to his fence, ribbons fluttering everywhere, and a group of around thirty neighbors out in front of the house cheering his return. Leaping out of the car, Gotti waved to the cheering crowd, then ran up to embrace his wife, Victoria, and his two pretty redheaded daughters, Vicky and Angela, and his little grand-daughter, before disappearing inside.

During the next few days John Gotti was the talk of New York as he made conspicuous appearances in some of Manhattan's top restaurants and the Gambinos kept up nonstop celebrations in Little Italy, Ozone Park, and along East Eighty-sixth Street in Brooklyn.

While this was going on, investigators and prosecutors from the office of the Manhattan district attorney and the State Organized Crime Task Force were wondering what had gone wrong and the jurors in the case were preparing to tell them.

In an interview for New York *Newsday* Michael Cherkasky insisted that he believed the prosecution had established a convincing case against John Gotti but that "as far as the trial of emotion and sympathy, we lost the case."

"On evidence and reason, we won, but the prosecution never understood the role that emotion and sympathy would play in this trial. We did not have sympathetic witnesses or even a sympathetic victim. . . . We tried to keep emotion and sympathy out of this trial but we obviously failed."

Later, in interviews for *Manhattan Lawyer*, some of the jurors gave their opinions of the government's case and how it was prosecuted at trial. Initially, they told *Manhattan Lawyer* the twelve members on the panel were split three ways, six for acquittal, four for conviction, and two undecided. Three days later, after repeatedly reviewing the government's tape recordings, the twelve jurors agreed they did not have sufficient evidence to convict Gotti and codefendant Guerrieri of any of the three felony charges they faced.

Critical to their decision was the March 8, 1986, tape in which Gotti and Angelo Ruggiero were discussing who should carry out the assault against John O'Connor. Ruggiero said he told a member of the Genovese family, "Either we give this guy it, or youse do." Then Gotti said, "You tell them youse do it."

While the prosecutors thought the tape suggested the Gambinos should carry out the assault, five of the jurors thought just the opposite, that Gotti was actually refusing to play a role in the assault, that he was washing his hands of it, letting others do it.

Six of the jurors never wavered in their belief that the state did not prove its case. The foreman, William Buchanan, a retired Newark schoolteacher, said, "I have to admit that voting not guilty was a very unpleasant result for me. I felt truly that he was guilty as hell, but I have to admit that the evidence just didn't hold up. It was thin to begin with."

All five jurors interviewed by *Manhattan Lawyer* said the tapes convinced them that Gotti was the leader of an organized crime family. "I definitely had that impression," said juror Virginia Hill. "I don't believe he's a plumbing salesman."

Apparently the jurors were much less impressed by the relevance of the "Gonna, gonna bust him up" tape than the prosecution had hoped. Juror Richard Silensky, an aspiring actor, said: "Does he mean he's going to bust the union up, bust O'Connor up, bust the union offices up? It wasn't clear."

Almost all the jurors were convinced that the testimonies of Vince Cafaro and Jimmy McElroy were not believable and that the Rikers Island tape of the conversation between Westies Mickey Featherstone and Kevin Kelly was barely audible and too confusing to be taken seriously. And why was the "We did it for the greaseballs" supposed to be so significant? As one juror put it: "Who are they? *Which* greaseballs, if you'll parden me?"

Apparently the jurors were not overly impressed by John Gotti or, for that matter, even afraid of him.

Juror Silensky was particularly firm on this issue. "If anything," he said, "nobody expressed any sympathy or identification with Gotti." During their deliberations he and the other jurors kept calling Gotti and Guerrieri "thugs and mobsters."

John Gotti was acquitted of the assault charges on February 9, 1990. Now he was free again to "put this thing together where they would never break it, never destroy it."

"The law's gonna be tough with us, okay," Gotti had told an unknown male in early 1986. "If they don't put us away . . . for one year or two, that's all we need."

As it would turn out, Gotti would be granted a little over ten months "to put this thing together," for by December 23, 1990, he would be back in prison, with bail denied, charged with, among other things, ordering and planning the murder of Big Paul Castellano.

35

Toward the Showdown

Four days after his acquittal, with the media's proclamations of his invincibility still ringing in his ears, John Gotti and his wife, Victoria, left for a vacation in Florida, driving down, since Gotti has a phobia about flying.

Day-to-day operations of the Gambino crime family were then left to underboss Frank "Frankie Loc" Locascio, a veteran bookmaker and loan shark formerly based in the Bronx, who had been with the family for thirty-five years. Gotti had made Locascio underboss upon the incarceration in December 1987 of Joseph "Joe Piney" Armone, underboss since the murder of Frankie DeCicco in April 1986. No sooner had Gotti left for Florida than detectives assigned to surveil Gotti's Little Italy haunts began observing Frankie Loc and his Armenian bodyguard, Zev Mustafa, entering the Ravenite Club with increasing frequency. Taking a new interest in Locascio's activities, investigators found that he managed two large illegal gambling casinos for the family, one in the Bronx and another in southern Connecticut, that were destined to get him and his boss into considerable trouble by the end of the year.

Although Gotti had emerged unscathed from his confrontations with the law, the Gambino family had taken some hard blows over the past few years and would continue to be severely battered in the near future.

Underboss Joseph Armone and *consiglière* Joe N. Gallo, both in their seventies, had each been sent to prison for ten years. On May 23, 1989, John Gotti's brother, Gene, had been sentenced to fifty years in prison for heroin trafficking. In February, John's other brother, Peter, had been arrested for participating in the replacement window scam. In January 1990, John Gambino, the leading Sicilian associate of the New York Gambinos, was indicted for heroin smuggling and released on $2 million bail. Then, as Gotti's assault trial was winding down, former Gotti associate Salvatore Reale was arrested at a Texas-Mexico border checkpoint for carrying nearly $4 million in cash in the trunk of his car.

Reale, a handsome, suave former private eye turned racketeer, had been convicted of extortion in Brooklyn Federal Court and given probation in return for information on his mob connections. One condition of his probation was that he get out of New York and never return. Another was that he refrain from dealing in drugs. Now he was caught with $3.8 million in drug money at the Mexican border. Soon he would be indicted for violation of parole and sentenced to ten years in prison. For the Gambino family this was a serious matter because Reale knew too much about John Gotti and his family's criminal activities.

Meanwhile, federal prosecutors had zeroed in on two mob-dominated Teamsters locals at JFK Airport and had indicted John Gotti's man at JFK, codefendant in the assault trial, Anthony "Tony Lee" Guerrieri, for labor racketeering and extortion. And before long the government would bring a RICO case against the International Longshoremen's Association, specifically targeting Brooklyn Local 1814, controlled by John Gotti. The government's war on the Gambinos was relentless and John Gotti felt the full pressure of it upon his return from Florida. Being boss of the Gambinos meant he had to ride into battle every day.

But there were lighter moments to the Teflon Don's life. One of them was the marriage of his eldest son, John A. "Junior" Gotti, on April 22, 1990.

Junior Gotti, twenty-six at the time of his wedding, was a stocky bodybuilder, trucking company executive, and fledgling Gambino capo who appeared to have no other discernible ambition than to emulate his notorious father. Like his father, he had shown himself to have a short fuse and a readiness to use his fists to make a point. Arrested twice for assault, Junior, following in his father's footsteps, beat both raps. Junior also displayed a fondness for tailor-made, double-breasted suits.

Gotti Junior was educated at New York Military Academy, a private prep school at Cornwall-on-Hudson, noted, among other things, for taking in the sons of powerful New York mobsters. Carlo Gambino had sent his son, Thomas, there, as Joe Colombo had done with his son, Joe, Jr. After his son's graduation, Gotti Senior set Junior up in business with a Brooklyn firm, Samson Trucking, which specialized in construction-related trucking. Junior became president of the company. According to Queens law enforcement authorities, Gotti Senior also had his son formally inducted into the Gambino family when he turned twenty-five. Junior was given a small crew that is involved in labor racketeering, principally at construction sites, loan-sharking, auto parts theft, and drug trafficking.

In early 1986 federal wiretaps picked up a conversation between Gotti Senior and Junior that revealed the father exercised considerable control over his son.

JOHN GOTTI: You tell Anthony next time don't be mentioning no fuckin' names on the phone or I'll put him in the fuckin' hospital. . . . And before you do anything or he does any fuckin' thing you tell me first.

JUNIOR: Okay.

Until his engagement to Kim Albanese, the twenty-two-year-old daughter of a carpet installer from Valley Stream, Long Island, Gotti Junior liked to spend his evenings hitting the night spots in Brooklyn and Long Island with a band of young toughs, including John Ruggiero, son of Gambino capo Angelo Ruggiero; and Vincent Corrao, capo of a Gambino crew in Little Italy and son of Joseph "Joe Butch" Corrao. The gang had a reputation for roughing up customers at bars and clubs and getting away with it, due to the reluctance of witnessess to testify against young Gotti.

Junior Gotti's wedding fell six days after John Gotti associate Anthony Guarino, president of the Arc Plumbing Company, where Gotti Senior held a no-show job, was convicted of obstruction of justice, and four days before another John Gotti associate, Ravenite Social Club owner Joseph "The Cat" LaForte, was sent to prison for obstructing the grand jury probe of the murder of Paul Castellano.

For his son's wedding John Gotti spared no trouble or expense. He had arranged for a lavish reception to be held for the bridal couple in the grand ballroom of the Helmsley Palace Hotel in midtown Manhattan.

The Helmsley Palace, incorporating the old Villard mansion, a historic landmark, and situated between two other historic landmarks, St. Patrick's Cathedral and the residence of the archbishop of New York, had become a much-favored locale for important wedding receptions, surpassing in desirability even the Plaza and the Pierre.

In honor of the bride and groom and their respective families, hotel president Leona Helmsley had ordered that an Italian flag be flown to the right of the hotel's main entrance, a gesture usually made only when a high dignitary of the Republic of Italy was in residence.

Judging from the large number of Gotti seconds on the sidewalk in front of the main entrance, in the main lobby, and in the hallway leading to the ballroom, one would almost believe a head of state *was* in residence in the hotel. Gambino soldiers were everywhere, greeting and screening the wedding guests, fending off crashers and photographers, trying to keep all the FBI agents and state and city police detectives under surveillance.

By 8:00 P.M. some 240 invited guests had assembled in the grand ballroom for a sumptuous wedding feast that included tenderloin of beef tips, stuffed veal loin, fettucine Alfredo, seared medallions of veal and lobster, chocolate mousse, cake, wine—a 1984 Pouilly-Fuisse—and champagne.

Since both hotel security forces and squads of Gambino soldiers prevented the media from getting anywhere near the festivities, details of the Gotti wedding party went unreported. The press did, however, report the outrage of the Helmsley flying the Italian flag at its entrance. For the hotel to have displayed the flag of Italy for the wedding of a mobster's son was an insult to every honest, hardworking Italian-American in the United States, to every friend and lover of Italy, and to the Republic of Italy itself.

For John Gotti the wedding festivities were a welcome respite from the government's relentless assault on the Gambinos. Two of Gotti's closest associates, Guarino and LaForte, were going to prison. In May, former associate Salvatore Reale was sentenced to ten years in prison, and brother Peter Gotti was indicted in the window replacement case. And the press kept publishing articles on the Castellano murder case linking Gotti to that crime.

On the Fourth of July John Gotti held his annual
Independence Day outdoor barbecue bash in Ozone
Park, Queens, defiantly setting off fireworks despite
the police ban on them, and on the following day
Junior Gotti's wife produced a son, whom the press
quickly dubbed "*il bambìno di tùtti i bambìni*."

The fall saw the murders of two Gotti associates,
Louis DiBono and Eddie Lino. DiBono's body was
found in his car parked in the World Trade Center's
underground garage. Lino had been found in
Brooklyn shot in the head, execution style. In both
killings John Gotti was a lead suspect. Between the
DiBono and Lino killings, the Gambino brothers,
Thomas and Joseph, Carlo's sons, were indicted on a
RICO charge of enterprise corruption related to the
monopolistic stranglehold they exerted on the multimillion-dollar garment district trucking industry, one
of the family's most lucrative rackets.

Then, on December 12, 1990, amid persistent
rumors of an impending federal case against him, the
ax again fell on the boss of the Gambino crime family—an eleven-count federal RICO indictment against
Gotti, underboss Frank Locascio, *consiglière* Salvatore
Gravano, and garment district capo Thomas
Gambino. The principal counts were racketeering and
murder. Gotti was charged with five murder conspiracies, including the killing of Paul Castellano and
Thomas Bilotti. Other counts in the indictment were
for bribery, illegal gambling, loan-sharking, extortion,
obstruction of justice, and tax fraud.

Fifteen FBI agents arrested Gotti, Locascio, and
Gravano on the evening of Wednesday, December 12,
at the Ravenite Club, where twenty-seven Gambinos
had gathered. Thomas Gambino was arrested at his
office in the garment district. At the time of their
arrest Gotti had $6,000 in cash on him and Gambino
$11,000. Gotti, Locascio, and Gravano were ordered
to be held until Monday, when prosecutors were
scheduled to play tapes of their bugged conversations

in court to show that they would intimidate jurors or witnesses if released on bail before trial. Gambino was released after posting a $500,000 bond.

The indictment went into considerable detail on each count. In the conspiracy to murder Paul Castellano the indictment alleged that from April 1982 through December 1985, Castellano had imposed the rule that "any member or associate of the Gambino family found to be involved in narcotics trafficking would be murdered." It further alleged that conversations intercepted in Gambino soldier Angelo Ruggiero's home "revealed extensive narcotics trafficking by members of John Gotti's crew, including Angelo Ruggiero, Gene Gotti, and John Carneglia." The indictment went on to state that Paul Castellano had made frequent requests that Ruggiero provide him with transcripts of the taped conversations but that underboss Aniello Dellacroce took steps to prevent the transcripts from being turned over to Castellano. "Dellacroce, Ruggiero, and John Gotti were concerned about turning the tapes over to Castellano because they included conversations about narcotics trafficking and references to Commission meetings," the indictment stated. Finally, "In or about late 1985 Paul Castellano obtained copies of the Ruggiero tapes." Then Aniello Dellacroce died on December 2, 1985. "Between that date and December 16, 1985," the indictment alleged, "Paul Castellano informed John Gotti of Castellano's intention to break up Gotti's crew and to reassign its members to other crews in the Gambino family." After learning of this intention, "John Gotti and others conspired to murder Paul Castellano." The indictment went on to allege that "On December 16, 1985, arrangements were made for a meeting with Paul Castellano at Sparks Steak House," and on that day John Gotti, Anthony Rampino, and John Carneglia "went to the vicinity of Sparks Steak House and shortly thereafter Paul Castellano was murdered in front of Sparks Steak

House." Although the indictment did not specifically name Castellano's and Bilotti's killers, it implied that Rampino and Carneglia had done the shooting on orders from John Gotti. Gotti "went to the vicinity of Sparks Steak House," in case the murders were bungled. In such an event Gotti would have had to have met with Castellano in the restaurant as planned.

In addition to the Castellano and Bilotti murders, the indictment charged John Gotti with conspiring to murder two made members of the Gambino family, Liborio "Louie" Milito and Robert "Di B" DiBernardo, and a reputed member of the DeCavalcante crime family of New Jersey, Gaetano "Corky" Vastola, who was warned of Gotti's intentions by federal authorities in time to escape death. The indictment further alleged that Salvatore Gravano requested John Gotti "to authorize and direct the murder of Louis DiBono," the Gambino associate whose body was found in a garage at the World Trade Center. The motive the indictment assigned for these murder conspiracies was "for the purpose of maintaining and increasing their [the defendants'] positions in the Gambino Family, an enterprise engaged in racketeering activity."

But according to law enforcement authorities close to the grand jury probe, there were more specific reasons why Gotti and his men wanted these people killed. The pornographer DiBernardo, whose body has never been found, was eliminated, they believe, because he had angered Gotti when he failed to show up for an important meeting of all the capos at the Ravenite Club shortly after the bombing to death of Frankie DeCicco, an unpardonable offense when coupled with DiBernardo's well-known ambition to muscle in on DeCicco's construction industry racketeering. As for Staten Island soldier Louie Milito, whose body has also never been found, sources contend that he was done away with because he had been too close for comfort to the late Paul Castellano. The killing of

Gambino soldier and construction contractor, Louis DiBono, sources believed, might have had something to do with an ongoing federal and state investigation of labor racketeering in the construction industry. And the plot to kill Corky Vastola, a New Jersey racketeer with whom John Gotti did business, who was facing twenty years in prison for a narcotics conviction, was probably to silence him before he cracked and ratted on John Gotti.

Beside participating in the murder conspiracies, the indictment charged, Gotti conspired to bribe an as yet unidentified public official while on trial for the assault on John O'Connor and attempted to obstruct the investigations of the Castellano murder, the Gambino family, and Thomas Gambino.

Additionally the indictment charged Gotti and his codefendants with operating two illegal gambling casinos, one in New York and the other in Connecticut, and with "extortionate extensions and collections of credit."

Finally, the indictment charged Gotti with income tax fraud, since he claimed that his sole sources of income were his jobs as a salesman for the Arc Plumbing Company and for the Scorpio Manufacturing Company, whereas, in reality, these were no-show jobs designed to make Gotti appear legitimate.

Commenting on the indictment to the press, the U.S. attorney for the eastern district, Andrew J. Maloney, stated that the government now had "the strongest case ever against John Gotti."

At the closed bail hearing held in Brooklyn Federal Court on the Monday following John Gotti's arrest, six FBI tapes were played that were explosive enough to persuade Judge I. Leo Glasser to postpone his decision on whether to grant bail for another week.

During the week of waiting, major newspapers, magazines, and television networks petitioned Judge

Glasser to release the content of the tapes, and the judge refused. Finally, on Monday, December 22, the judge held a three-hour hearing, closed to the public, at which the six tapes were played again.

After the hearing was over, spectators and journalists were allowed into the courtroom to learn Judge Glasser's decision:

"I have concluded the government has sustained its burden by clear and convincing evidence. . . . There are no conditions of release that will reasonably assure the safety of any other persons in the community."

That, of course, meant that Gotti, Locascio, and Gravano were denied bail and therefore were compelled to remain behind bars until at least the conclusion of their trial.

The decision did not seem to bother John Gotti very much. Smiling at the judge while receiving his decision, Gotti then got up, went over to his brother, Peter, and wished him a merry Christmas.

Later, in the corridor outside the courtroom, Bruce Cutler told reporters: "We will fight the case from jail. . . . We have done it before, we will do it again."

And so Gotti and his underboss and *consiglière* had to return to the Metropolitan Correctional Center for the duration, causing the Gambino crime family to be leaderless for months.

Who would fill the void? Law enforcement authorities familiar with the structure and personnel of the Gambino family believed that Little Italy capo Joe "Butch" Corrao would call the shots in day-to-day street operations in Manhattan, while John D'Amico, a close confidant of Gotti's, and the seventy-one-year-old capo Jimmy Failla would run things in Brooklyn and Queens. Junior Gotti, in turn, would be the spokesman for his father. This would put Junior in a powerful position. He would be transmitting his father's orders to the troops. In a way, he would be an acting boss.

According to the FBI, Gotti was a lot safer in the

MCC than he would be on the outside. Since he was under a federal indictment, FBI agents would no longer be tailing him night and day and this lack of security might encourage some of Gotti's enemies to assassinate him. The FBI pointed out that one of the reasons it was relatively easy to assassinate Castellano was that he was under federal indictment at the time and therefore without FBI protection.

What was on the six tapes? This was the burning question for the news media. But despite repeated petitions and one joint lawsuit brought by several papers and networks, the tapes remained sealed.

Inevitably there were leaks. It was learned that Gotti had paid a police officer $10,000 to inform him where the government had placed its bugs. It was also learned that the government had taped several conversations between Gotti and his attorneys, Cutler and Shargel, in the apartment above the Ravenite Club. Apparently those conversations were so compromising to the two lawyers' reputations that the U.S. attorney's office was compelled to make a motion to Judge Glasser to have Cutler and Shargel removed from the case.

Pretrial hearings on the tapes were often tempestuous. At one hearing Bruce Cutler, annoyed at not being given a chance to speak, stood up and shouted, "I am not here as some sort of potted plant!" Then, facing Judge Glasser, he said: "I feel tension between us. . . . I said good afternoon to you and you didn't respond. What did I do to offend the court?"

To which Judge Glasser responded: "One more outburst from you and I will ask you why you shouldn't be held in contempt of court. . . . When I ask you to sit down and tell you that I will get to you in time I mean it."

Cutler then began grumbling over this and Glasser scolded him again: "I would appreciate it when I am talking that you keep quiet! . . . Do you understand that?"

As it turned out, the wheels of justice in the government's case against Gotti, Locascio, Gravano, and Gambino turned very slowly. Pretrial hearings on the tapes dragged on for months. It was conceivable that it would take almost a year to bring the case to trial. Meanwhile, Gotti and his top executives languished in the MCC, deriving a modicum of excitement from watching the Gulf War on television.

The Gulf War dominated the news so completely from January 16 to February 26, 1991, that the media almost forgot that the mob trial of the century was impending in New York.

It was not until April 13 that the media was suddenly shocked out of its forgetfulness. On that day Gotti's former personal bodyguard, confidant, and chauffeur, Bartholomew "Bobby" Borriello, was shot ten times in the head as he was getting out of his Lincoln Town Car in front of his Bensonhurst, Brooklyn, home. The news of the killing made the front page of every newspaper in the New York metropolitan area and prompted several days of speculation as to who might have been behind it.

Since Borriello was suspected by law enforcement of playing a key role in the slaying of Big Paul Castellano, there were rumors that Gotti himself had orchestrated the hit, that he had been worried Borriello might rat on him if he was prosecuted for another crime, and it was rumored that the feds were building a case against Borriello for drug trafficking.

But the lavish funeral given Borriello in a prominent Brooklyn church quickly dispelled that idea. Borriello was a low-level soldier in John Gotti's army, a chauffeur and bodyguard. As such he did not merit the grandiose obsequies he was given in Brooklyn. Fleets of shiny black limousines. Carloads of elaborate floral wreaths. All the Gambino capos, dressed in black surrounding the coffin as it was carried down the church steps. Junior Gotti conspicuously present near the veiled and grieving widow. It was a funeral fit for a *càpo di tùtti i càpi*—or a Don Vito Corleone.

The funeral was designed to tell the world that though the boss, underboss, and *consiglière* were temporarily out of action, the family was still very much intact and would stand together to honor the memory of a valiant soldier fallen in battle.

Though he was out of action, John Gotti could still order a big, expensive funeral for one of his men. Though out of action, he could still send a message to Borriello's killer that there were quite a few Gambinos around ready to avenge Bobby's death.

No, it was not John Gotti who had ordered the execution of Bobby Borriello. After the funeral it was widely reported, with law enforcement backing, that Borriello's murder was the result of a personal vendetta, the act of someone who felt he had been wronged by Borriello and simply took his revenge.

After the Borriello murder the New York press reawakened to the long-neglected presence of its most celebrated gangster in jail, awaiting a trial federal prosecutors were confident would put him away for the rest of his life. The dramatic potential of this countdown would generate a continuous stream of articles on John Gotti, his family, and his alleged crimes. Almost every week a new theory of who was behind the killing of Big Paul Castellano would be floated. It was not until the tempestuous pretrial hearings of June, July, and August that it was learned the final showdown would commence in January 1992.

But before then, the prosecution became convinced that John Gotti's attorneys, Bruce Cutler, Gerald Shargel, and John Pollok, had become "house consel" to the "enterprise" charged in the indictment, namely the "Gambino Organized Crime Family." It moved to disqualify the three attorneys from representing the defendants in the case at trial. This bombshell precipitated another clamor for the tapes to be unsealed and made available to the public.

Finally, in response to mounting pressures from the media, Judge Glasser released on August 1, 1991, transcripts of the tapes used to justify the pretrial detention of Gotti, Gravano, and Locascio, and to justify the disqualification of their counsel.

The release of the tapes caused an immediate uproar, for they clearly showed John Gotti admitting to and planning murders, tampering with the criminal justice process, insulting his attorneys, and treating those attorneys as if they were members of the Gambino crime family.

To justify the pretrial detention of Gotti, Gravano, and Locascio the government sought to demonstrate that "the defendants are violent persons" and "intend to operate the Gambino family as an ongoing enterprise if released on bail," adding that "no combination of conditions will assure that these defendants will not tamper with the judicial process" if released on bail.

Most of the tapes released had been recorded from November 1989 through March 1990 by bugs planted in three areas of Gotti's Little Italy headquarters, the Ravenite Club: the main room on the first floor, a hallway behind the main room, and in a third floor apartment, formerly occupied by the caretaker of the club, Michael Cirelli, whose death in January 1988 had left the apartment occupied by his widow, who was not always there. A fourth eavesdropping device had been installed at a curbside location on Mulberry Street near the Ravenite.

At first the FBI had bugged the main room of the club, but Gotti and his men discovered the device and neutralized it.

It was not until informants told the FBI that Gotti was holding high-level talks with his underboss and *consiglière* in the hallway and in the empty upstairs apartment that FBI technicians installed bugs in those locations. As it turned out, the recordings made from these two bugs were much clearer than those made from the bug in the main room. Often the ones recorded in the main room were blurred by the steady hum of thirty or so Gambino men all talking at once. Gotti thought he had outwitted the feds by holding talks in the upstairs apartment, but what he had done was give the FBI a soundproof room in which to record his most incriminating conversations.

To illustrate Gotti's propensity for violence the government cited taped conversations between Gotti and Locascio and Gravano about the murders of Robert "Di B" DiBernardo and Louis "Louie" DiBono.

GOTTI: When Di B got whacked they told me a story. I was in jail when I whacked him. I knew why it was being done. I done it anyway. I allowed it to be done anyway.

GOTTI: And anytime you got a partner who don't agree with us, we kill him. He kills 'em; okay, Sam? Said it's all right, good-bye.

GOTTI: Louie DiBono. And I sat with this guy. I saw the papers and everything. He didn't rob nothin'. Know why he's dying? He's gonna die because he refused to come in when I called. He didn't do nothin' else wrong.

In January 1990, Gotti instructed an associate, Peter Mosca, how to handle some unwanted competition from a Greek gambling operation.

MOSCA: This Spiro . . .
GOTTI: We got a game there for twenty years. Is this rat-fucking Greek's name Spiro?
MOSCA: That's right.
GOTTI: You tell this punk . . . I . . . me . . . John Gotti . . .
MOSCA: I'm meeting him tonight.

GOTTI: . . . will sever your motherfucking head off! You cocksucker! You're nobody there.

MOSCA: [Unintelligible]

GOTTI: Listen to me, tell him. Tell him, "Listen, you know better. He'll sever your motherfucking head off! You know better than to open a game there."

Other tapes recorded at the Ravenite released by Judge Glasser clearly showed that Gotti intended to run the Gambino family from jail, but was acutely worried that if underboss Locascio and *consiglière* Gravano were also denied bail the family might unravel into warring factions. In 1989 Confidential Source (CS) 1 learned that Gotti was grooming his son, John Gotti, Jr., to watch his father's financial interests in the family should he go to jail. In July 1990, CS-1 reported John, Jr.'s promotion to captain.

To justify its contention that Gotti's attorneys be disqualified from representing him because they had become "house counsel" to the Gambino crime family, the government released several tapes in which Gotti spoke about his attorneys and their roles in the Gambino crime family.

In regard to Gerald Shargel, Gotti told the attorney that his "friends" "would use him."

"Two guys took him on right away," Gotti later told an associate, "and I brought him six . . . I remember Gerry when Gerry was just an ambulance chaser," he added.

In a conversation between John Gotti, Gravano, and Locascio, Gotti expressed displeasure at the amounts of money he was having to pay lawyers Bruce Cutler, John Pollok, and Gerald Shargel for representing various members of the Gambino family.

GOTTI: Bruce, I don't know him all my life. I know him five years. . . . Without us he wouldn't be on the map.

GOTTI: You know these are rats, er, Sam. And I gotta say, they all want their money up front. And then you get four guys that want sixty-five, seventy-five thousand apiece, up front. You're talking about three hundred thousand in one month.

GOTTI: I paid a hundred and thirty-five thousand for their appeal. For Joe Gallo and Joe Piney's appeal, I paid thousands of dollars to Pollok. That was not for me.

Referring to Cutler and Shargel:

GOTTI: I gave youse three hundred thousand in one year. Youse didn't defend me. I wasn't even mentioned in none of these fucking things. I had nothing to do with none of these fucking people. What the fuck is your beef? . . . Before youse made a court appearance youse got forty thousand, thirty thousand, and twenty-five thousand. . . . That's without counting John Pollok. . . . You standing in the hallway with me last night, and you're plucking me. I'm paying for it. . . . Where does it end? Gambino crime family? This is the Shargel, Cutler, and who-do-you-call-it crime family.

Later in the course of this conversation, Gotti referred to his attorneys as "overpriced, overpaid, and underperformed. . . . You know and I know," he went on, "that you're taking money under the table. Every time you take a client, another one of us on, you're breaking the law."

In support of its motion for a court order disqualifying counsel, the government contended that Gotti's taped remarks about his lawyers clearly indicated that the lawyers did not simply represent him but dozens of other members of the Gambino crime family, and therefore acted as "house counsel" to that enterprise. To emphasize this contention, the government produced a list of Cutler's, Pollok's, and Shargel's clients within the Gambino family. Cutler had represented Gambino associates Michael Coiro and Joseph Gambino, and John Gotti's brother, Peter. Pollok had represented Gambino members or associates Angelo Ruggiero, John Carneglia, Joe N. Gallo, Joey Piney Armone, George Remini, Alphonse Sisca, Anthony Gurino, John Gambino, Joseph Gambino, and Edward Garafola. And Shargel had outdone them all, counting among his Gambino family clients, Gotti, Coiro, Carneglia, Ruggiero, Corrao, Remini, Gravano, Squitieri, Armond Dellacroce, Tony Lee Guerrieri, Matteo Romano, Charles Carneglia, Thomas and Joseph Gambino, and the Gambino-affiliated Westy, Jimmy Coonan.

But the government even went further. It showed that Cutler and Shargel had become so much a part of the Gambino crime family that they even went along with some of its members' crimes.

Cutler and Shargel represented Gambino capo George Remini, the hulking, three-hundred-pound owner of the Top Tomato produce market on Staten Island, and knew that Gotti did not want Remini to testify at the 1989 trial of Thomas Gambino for obstruction of justice. If Remini refused to testify at the trial it meant he was committing the crime of contempt of court. Finally, as the government put it, "with Shargel at his side, George Remini committed the crime that John Gotti wanted him to commit." He refused to testify.

In its effort to show that the government had "ample probable cause to believe that these attorneys have complicity" in some of the crimes charged against Gotti, the prosecution released a tape recorded on March 29, 1990, that established that Bruce Cutler was assigned by Gotti "to be his conduit of information to and from the Patriarca Organized

Crime Family, which is based in Rhode Island."

"If I ever wanna get a message to them, or from them, we'll do it through you," Gotti told Cutler in one of the taped conversations.

The government also presented other tape-recorded evidence of Cutler's and Shargel's role as "house counsel" to the Gambino family. It demonstrated that "Shargel answered directly to John Gotti regarding the press coverage of Gambino family members and associates, and tried to be 'helpful' in that regard," and charged that Cutler and Shargel "were directed to obtain information about upcoming arrests, and complained about being 'high-priced errand boys.'"

In its long memorandum in support of its motion for an order disqualifying counsel, the prosecution also touched on the matter of Gotti's alleged murder of Paul Castellano and Thomas Bilotti.

The memorandum stated that "at trial we will play various conversations in which John Gotti discussed his fervent desire to murder Castellano and Bilotti and the fact that he had done so." The memorandum went on to state:

> We presently intend to also play [Gotti's] "denials" for two reasons. First their number and delivery will support our argument that John Gotti "doth protest too much." Second, and more important, these statements reflect Gotti's motive to murder Castellano and his bold arrogance in believing that an "I didn't do it" party line could save him from prosecution. Our argument will be based on the content and delivery of these "denials" which approached the level of a joke.

Noting that the nationally broadcast television program *America's Most Wanted* reported on November 26, 1989, that John Gotti was responsible for the murders of Castellano and Bilotti, the prosecution observed that "during the three days following the broadcast John Gotti littered his conversations with exculpatory statements about this event."

For example, on November 28, 1989, Gotti told Gravano and Locascio at the Ravenite Club: "Whoever killed this cocksucker, probably the cops killed this Paul. But whoever killed him, the cocksucker, he deserved it."

The following evening, when Shargel was summoned to the hallway in the Ravenite to join Gotti, Joe the Butch Corrao, and others, Shargel became a witness to a similar denial. "The shootout was in the paper today," remarked Gotti. "I wasn't there. It must've been a ball."

The next time John Gotti appeared in court, August 7, 1991, he and codefendants Salvatore Gravano and Frank Locascio were not represented by counsel. It was a pretrial hearing at which Gotti and the others were supposed to have introduced their new attorneys and a trial date was supposed to have been agreed on.

Curiously, before the defendants arrived from the MCC and the courtroom had barely filled up, the disqualified Bruce Cutler entered the room, strode briskly up the center aisle, and disappeared through a door to the left of the judge's bench, never to appear again. He was, however, duly noted, and filmed, by the television crews massed on the sidewalk in front of the courthouse as he entered the building. "The whole thing with Cutler is publicity, image," an assistant U.S. attorney, eastern district, later explained to me. "Everything he does is calculated in terms of its public relations impact."

Wearing one of his trademark finely tailored, double-breasted, navy-blue suits, with a flower-print tie and matching pocket handkerchief, Gotti, his hair considerably whiter than it had been at his last trial, stood up to face Judge I. Leo Glasser looking uncustomarily vulnerable and alone.

But as soon as he opened his mouth he proved to be the same old Gotti: combative, arrogant, perverse, and insulting.

When Glasser asked Gotti whether Bruce Cutler intended to be there that morning, Gotti shot back with: "He said you said he's not my lawyer anymore."

To which Glasser replied: "I disqualified Mr. Cutler from representing you at trial. I did not disqualify Mr. Cutler, or Mr. Shargel, or Mr. Pollok, from representing you with respect to pretrial matters."

"I thought the trial was on," said Gotti.

"The trial has been scheduled for September twenty-third," replied Glasser.

"If you put the TV on you can see the trial," Gotti returned, seeming to relish the irrelevance of his remark.

After Judge Glasser, in his steady monotone, repeatedly asked Gotti whether he had hired new counsel to represent him at the trial, Gotti lost patience and, pointing at the prosecutor, John Gleeson, said: "I'm not worried about their phony tapes or their phony transcripts this guy made up. He can't handle a good fight and he can't win a fair trial!"

Later on, in his protracted harangue with the judge, Gotti lost control again and called the prosecutor a "bum" and a "little Lord Fauntleroy."

On the subject of advising the defendants to hire counsel Judge Glasser was even less successful with Salvatore Gravano. "How much time do you think you would need to get a new lawyer?" Glasser asked Gotti's *consigliere*. Gravano shot back: "I have no idea. Jacoby & Meyers don't come there," referring to the Metropolitan Correctional Center in which he was being detained.

Finally the judge ordered a hearing on the matter

of new counsel for the defendants for August 21, later postponed until August 28.

Since Gotti, Gravano, and the others had hired new counsel by the twenty-eighth, the hearing was almost bland compared to the wild August 7 session at which Gotti, representing himself in court, had called prosecutor John Gleeson a "bum" to his face.

Gotti had chosen a prominent Miami-based lawyer, Albert J. Krieger, sixty-seven, to represent him, on the advice of James LaRossa, attorney of the late Paul Castellano and a scheduled prosecution witness in the upcoming trial. And Gravano had picked a New York lawyer who had once been an assistant U.S. attorney, Benjamin Brafman, forty-three, to defend him. Krieger, whose shaven head, stocky build, and tailor-made, double-breasted suit made him look like an older Bruce Cutler, had been a former president of the National Association of Criminal Defense Lawyers and had successfully represented several organized crime figures, drug dealers, and white-collar defendants in Florida. Among his most well known clients had been Joe Bonanno. U.S. Attorney for the Eastern District Andrew J. Maloney characterized him as "one of the premier criminal defense lawyers in the country." Brafman had recently scored a success in winning an acquittal for James Patino, one of the accused in the Bensonhurst murder case of 1990. He was currently helping Bruce Cutler defend Peter Gotti in the trial about bid-rigging on city window replacement contracts.

For the August 28 pretrial hearing all the principals in the case showed up. The disqualified Cutler and Shargel, allowed to attend pretrial proceedings, joined Krieger and Brafman at the defense table along with David S. Greenfield, representing Locascio, and Michael Rosen, on behalf of Thomas Gambino. Gotti, having endured prison for the past nine months, appeared somewhat shrunken and subdued. Huddling with Cutler repeatedly, he never raised his voice above a whisper during the hearing. Gravano, a short, stocky, square-jawed mobster in his forties, seemed curiously relaxed, smiling wanly at the spectators. Locascio, sixty-one, with his ashen face, sunken eyes, and stringy gray hair, looked tired, and a dour Tommy Gambino, sixty, with his father's hawk-beaked nose dominating his pinched face, appeared far more worried than his codefendants. Present in the courtroom were Gambino's brother, Joe, looking like Tommy's twin, Gotti's older brother, Peter, a defendant in the ongoing replacement windows trial, and various Gambino wiseguys, including the cherubic John D'Amico, believed to be substituting for his jailed boss in the Gambino family's Brooklyn and Queens theater of operations.

At the brief hearing, Al Krieger dominated the proceedings. Standing before Judge Glasser, he told him that his client, John Gotti, would rather be represented at trial by Bruce Cutler, but that, under the circumstances, Krieger would do his best. He also informed the judge that Gotti was prepared to stand trial as soon as possible, but that he, Krieger, needed time to familiarize himself with the case and asked that the trial date be postponed from September 23 to January 15.

"I told Mr. Gotti that I literally needed months to respond to the court in a realistic sense," he told the judge. Later to reporters he remarked that Gotti would compare his every move "with what Mr. Cutler would have done. It's a fact of life and it imposes a great burden on me." This appeared reasonable to all and so the showdown was set for January 15, 1992. By then Gotti, Locascio, and Gravano would have spent thirteen months and two Christmases in jail awaiting trial.

36

The Gambino Foundation

On September 29, 1991, on a bright sunny morning in Nassau County's New Hyde Park, a ceremony was held at the Long Island Jewish Medical Center to mark the opening of the Gambino Medical and Science Foundation's $2 million Bone Marrow Transplantation Unit. On hand for the ceremony, in addition to the hospital officials and the news media, were the donors of the new unit, the brothers Joseph and Thomas Gambino, sons of the late Mafia boss Carlo Gambino.

The Gambino brothers made their $2 million gift at a time when both were facing trials in state and federal court. Both brothers had been indicted in a forty-five-count state racketeering case that charged them with exerting a monopolistic stranglehold on the trucking industry in the garment district and Thomas Gambino had been indicted, as a capo of a crew in the Gambino crime family under John Gotti in a racketeering case that charged him with loan-sharking, extortion, and obstruction of justice. The brothers were due to face trial on the state charges on January 6 and Thomas was due to face trial with John Gotti and his underboss and *consiglière* on January 20. If convicted, both brothers faced the possibility of long prison terms and confiscation of their property.

For at least two decades the Gambino and Lucchese families, which had been united by the marriage of Tommy Gambino and Frances Lucchese, had maintained a chokehold on Manhattan's lucrative garment district trucking business by controlling the flow of goods and supplies in and out of the district through the trucking companies they owned.

A garment—let us say a woman's dress—is subjected to a good deal of trucking about in lower Manhattan before it ends up as a finished product in a garment district showroom. From a fabric warehouse a bolt of cloth is trucked to the cutting factory and from there to the sewers and then to the workshops that attach the buttons, zippers, and frills to the dress. All this movement of goods is carried on exclusively by Gambino and Lucchese trucks at exorbitant rates. Dress manufacturers were advised in subtle ways that if they attempted to use cheaper, independent trucks they would get into trouble. They would be reminded of who the Gambino brothers were and what kind of muscle they had behind them. A recalcitrant cloak and suitor might find himself confronted one morning by a squad of four or five goons in trenchcoats in the corridor outside his office. "We're from Tommy," they would tell him. "You know, Tommy Gambino."

The mere mention of the name Gambino would usually be sufficient to beat the recalcitrant manufacturer back in line. As prosecutor Elliot Spitzer put it in his opening statement at the trial of the Gambino brothers: "These defendants are businessmen. But they are businessmen with a powerful partner, organized crime. It wields an iron fist inside a velvet glove."

No one in the garment center was exempt from this sort of intimidation. And so even the big name labels of Calvin Klein, Ralph Lauren, Halston, and Liz Claiborne had to give in and have their goods transported exclusively in Gambino trucks. The Manhattan District Attorney's Office estimated that for every $100 a customer spent on a dress, coat, or jacket made and sold in Manhattan's garment center $10 went to the Gambino brothers and their associates, which added cost the manufacturers, in turn, would pass on to the consumer.

Among the four trucking concerns the Gambino brothers owned and operated, the biggest and most profitable was Consolidated Carriers. The Manhattan District Attorney's Office estimated that from 1988 through 1991 Consolidated earned $22 million. For their efforts on behalf of the company, as president and vice president, Tommy and Joe Gambino paid themselves annual salaries of $1.8 million each. In addition, each earned $2.8 million from the company's net profits, giving each brother total annual earnings of $4.6 million.

Assistant District Attorney Michael Cherkasky, who directed the state's investigation of the Gambinos' garment center trucking company business, estimated that while their uncle Paul Castellano was alive, around $2 million a year in illegal trucking profits was funneled up to him. Now the $2 million went to his usurper, John Gotti. According to state investigators, Tommy himself would carry the money down to the Ravenite every Wednesday evening and hand it over to Sammy the Bull Gravano, who in turn, would consign the cash to his boss.

In view of the seriousness of the charges against them, it was only natural that both press and public would raise the question of whether the Gambino brothers' gift was timed to get them sympathy, perhaps from jurors, at their forthcoming trials. It was not difficult to imagine a Gambino defense counsel standing before a jury and demanding, "Are you going to send this hardworking father and grandfather—who has donated $2 million of his hard-earned money to assist helpless young children to escape an agonizing death from cancer—are you going to send such a man to jail?"

To blunt a possible accusation that the Gambino donation was a public relations ploy, the Long Island Jewish Medical Center staged a press conference at its Schneider Children's Hospital, where the Gambino Bone Marrow Transplantation Unit had been installed. There a battery of television cameramen and print photographers focused on Long Island Jewish's president, Dr. Robert K. Match; Schneider Children's Hospital's Chief of Staff Dr. Philip Lanzkowsky; Herb and Linda Katz, parents of a cancer-ridden child who had been cured thanks to a bone marrow transplantation treatment; and Joseph and Thomas Gambino.

It was a serene and lovely setting. Long Island Jewish, which embraces also the Albert Einstein College of Medicine, is set in a spacious park of broad green lawns, stands of tall trees, bright flower beds, and scattered fountains. Through the window of the room in which the press conference was being held, one looked out over an expanse of lawn at a fountain spraying sparkling streams of mist into the air.

Inside the room, however, the mood was tense. The television cameramen and print photographers had only one thought in their heads: Get some good shots of the Gambino brothers as they entered the room from the corridor. No one seemed to be particularly interested in photographing doctors Match and Lanzkowsky.

Then, suddenly, someone from the corridor shouted: "Here they come! Here they come!" As Joe and Tommy Gambino entered the cramped room, the eyes of the major networks bore down on them, and as they took their seats to one side of the rostrum the brothers had to endure a merciless flashbulb assault that lasted several minutes. Meanwhile, the doctors had arrived in the room and were duly ignored.

The Gambino brothers, looking tired and drawn and distinctly ill at ease, were both wearing double-breasted gray pin-striped suits, white shirts with French cuffs, conservative ties, and highly polished black shoes. Tommy Gambino's worried expression and pinched face made his Gambino Pinocchio nose look longer than ever.

In his introductory speech Dr. Match urged the media to desist from asking questions of the Gambino brothers unrelated to cancer treatment. "To assume that because they have the name Gambino that they are involved in criminal activities is not the American way," Dr. Match said. "Many people are indicted on information that doesn't hold up before a jury.

"We've known these people a long time," Dr. Match went on. "I think the press has exaggerated the Mafia issue over their philanthropy and good." Besides, he added, the Gambinos' foundation was "strictly monitored by the state attorney general."

Dr. Match explained that since chemotherapy destroys white blood cells, leaving patients dangerously vulnerable to infection, an ultrasterile environment is crucial. The Gambino Foundation's Bone Marrow Transplantation Unit contained the most sophisticated means of protecting patients against infections.

Dr. Match concluded by stating that the Gambino unit was one of New York State's most significant and comprehensive bone marrow transplantation facilities and the only one in the state dedicated to pediatric procedures.

Dr. Match was followed by Linda Katz of Lawrence, Long Island, whose two-year-old daughter, Marlee, had recently undergone treatment in the Gambino unit for a potentially fatal stomach cancer. In a heartrending, highly emotional talk Mrs. Katz spoke of the agony of having a baby daughter stricken with apparently terminal cancer. She was saved, in the end, by the Gambino Bone Marrow Transplantation Unit. Turning to the Gambino brothers, Linda Katz thanked them for helping to save the life of her infant daughter. "It's a very noble thing what these people have done," she said. "They have set an example for others to follow. . . . I and my husband thank you from the bottom of our hearts."

It was now the turn of the Gambinos to take the floor. Thomas Gambino stood up first, looking frail and nervous. It was obvious that he was not accustomed to speaking in public. Immediately going on the defensive, the sixty-two-year-old Thomas said: "It was the choice of the press, not us, to publicize this gift. . . . I don't think I need any good publicity." He then pointed out that his family earned its fortune—estimated by the Manhattan district attorney to be in the neighborhood of $100 million—as "honest, hardworking people in the garment center—manufacturing, trucking, and that's where the money comes from."

Thomas went on to mention that cancer had ruined his mother's life and caused her death. "We feel if there is anything we can do to prevent this terrible disease, it would be the least we could do," he concluded.

Brother Joseph then rose, took the rostrum, and, repeating his older brother's remarks, said, "Cancer is a big thing in our life, because our mother died of cancer. We're going to do whatever we can to correct this terrible disease."

A lively question-and-answer session followed Joseph's brief remarks. Of course all the reporters in the room were champing at the bit to ask the brothers Gambino about their upcoming trials and whether their donation was a public relations gambit designed to eventually win the sympathy of jurors, judges, and the media. But by and large the ladies and gentlemen of the press held their tongues, confining their questions to the cancer treatment facility the brothers had financed. One reporter, however, badgered Tommy Gambino about the source of the money for the Bone Marrow Transplantation Unit and was met with a vigorous denial that the money came from ill-gotten gains. That exchange was then followed by a general discussion of where the money from some of the great philanthropic benefactions of the past came from. During the discussion everyone seemed to agree that the Rockefeller fortune had been amassed by means of business practices that would be considered illegal today.

The point was well made. The history of American philanthropy is marked by magnanimity resulting from illegal activity. Commodore Cornelius Vanderbilt amassed his enormous fortune from the steamship and railroad industries by means of extortion, watering of stock, and the economic ruin of his competitors. Much of that fortune ended up in the coffers of Vanderbilt University in Tennessee. The Joseph P. Kennedy Foundation is tainted by money made from illegal trafficking in liquor during Prohibition and stock market manipulations during the Roaring Twenties that would be illegal today. In 1991 former ambassador to the court of St. James's Walter Annenberg was praised for donating his large collection of French Impressionist paintings, worth around $50 million, to the Metropolitan Museum of Art. The original Annenberg fortune, founded by Walter's father, Moses, who died in prison, was based on Moses's illegal racing wire service boasting fifteen thousand clients in 223 cities, which he managed with the support of gangsters Al Capone and Johnny Rosselli.

After the press conference broke up I approached Tommy Gambino, introduced myself, and told him my sister had gone to school with his wife, Frances, at the Sacred Heart Convent on East Ninety-first Street. "Oh, yes," he said, "that's such a fine school. You know, I'm very much a family man. Four children and six grandchildren. That's why I like to do something for the poor children with cancer."

I observed that Tommy Gambino's mood was extremely defensive. He desperately wanted to appear upright and respectable. It tortured him to be associated in the press with the Gambino crime family. All his life he had striven to live down the image his father had projected to the world. All his life he had striven to distance himself from the crime family his uncle, Paul Castellano, had led for nearly a decade, and John Gotti had led since his uncle's murder.

In his grand jury testimony of September 1988, he had denied over and over again that such an entity as the Gambino crime family even existed. He had lamented over and over again that to be characterized in the press as a gangster's son had caused him untold misery. He himself had nothing to do with organized crime. He was just a hardworking trucking company executive in the city's garment center. He had worked there all his life since graduating from college.

But, as we know, FBI surveillance tapes of conversations in John Gotti's social clubs and Paul Castellano's White House told another story.

The White House bug revealed that one of Big Paul's most frequent visitors was his nephew, Tommy Gambino. Discussions between Castellano and Gambino were recorded concerning Big Paul's dislike of John Gotti, the Apalachin mob summit of 1957, Joseph Bonanno's autobiography, the Commission, problems Gambino was having getting his and his uncle's rightful share of the spoils from their garment center rackets—Castellano: "Look, we got a third of the jobs and I want a third of the money. I want a third of everything, get it? It's rightfully mine and I want it!"—and contract murder. In that last exchange Tommy Gambino had discussed the cost of killing a man: "Fifty to a hundred thousand to get someone killed. . . . Hey, that's too much money. . . . Don't say anything . . . because it's my ass if Tommy said a hundred thousand to kill a guy from Paul. It may sink us all."

Later, after Castellano's murder, the bug in John Gotti's Bergin Hunt and Fish Club overheard Gotti talking about Tommy Gambino with one of his soldiers:

Gotti: I told Tommy, "Whatever we do, I want you to know. Even if it's bad off color, I want you to know from us. This way you know you're a part of it."

GOTTI: I'm gonna suggest to Tommy we're gonna beef up his regime, Tommy Gambino, but we're not giving him no fuckin' hotheads or any of those scumbags, we can't fuck his mind up with these bullshit street sit-downs. I don't want to hurt Tommy.

Alas, Tommy Gambino was caught between two worlds. He had not been brought up to be a gangster and had not wanted to be a gangster. He had worked hard in what appeared to be a legitimate business that grossed $40 million a year, and had made enough money that he and his convent-educated wife could live an upper-middle-class life with a luxurious penthouse apartment off Fifth Avenue in fashionable Lenox Hill and a beach home on the north shore of Long Island. But, at the same time, he could never escape the milieu in which he had been raised. He had spent nineteen years of his life as the eldest son of the most powerful Mafia boss in the United States, with all that implied in terms of filial duties imposed. And he had spent the next nine years of his life as the favorite nephew of the most powerful Mafia boss in the United States, with all that implied in terms of the demands of blood loyalty. As much as he would have liked to escape his father's and uncle's world, he was unable to do so. He had been made the capo of a regime in the garment center by Big Paul because Big

Paul needed someone he could trust to oversee the family's lucrative rackets there: "I want a third of the money. I want a third of everything, get it? It's rightfully mine and I want it!" It was clear from the tape that it was Tommy's job to get the boss his money. And Tommy Gambino needed the muscle of the Gambino crime family behind him to reap the enormous profits his seven garment-center trucking companies, operating five hundred trucks, earned. Without that muscle, he could not possibly have maintained his companies' monopolistic stranglehold on trucking garments and supplies to and from the center. Without that muscle, clothing manufacturers would seek to cut costs by hiring less expensive independent trucking companies to transport their goods. Circumstances had trapped Tommy Gambino. He had no choice but to remain in the crime family his father and uncle had guided for twenty-eight years.

I had observed at the dedication ceremony at the Long Island Jewish Medical Center that Tommy Gambino appeared worried and ill at ease. Gambino had good reason to be worried. Although he probably had a genuine sympathy for cancer-stricken children, his donation of the $2.5 million Bone Marrow Transplantation Unit was, more than likely, the act of a desperate man. For, at the time he made the donation, Tommy Gambino was only three months away from the greatest crisis of his life, his two trials, one for extortion, price-fixing, restraint of trade, and enterprise corruption in the garment center, and the other for extortion, obstruction of justice, and loan-sharking as a capo in the Gambino crime family. If convicted in both trials, Gambino stood to spend the rest of his useful life in prison and, under the new state RICO law, have all his property confiscated.

37

The Gravano Defection

A month after the Gambino brothers announced their $2 million donation to Long Island Jewish Medical Center, the incarcerated head of the Gambino crime family, John Gotti, received two devastating blows.

The first came on October 29 when the office of the U.S. attorney, eastern district, revealed to the press that the prosecution would call a witness at Gotti's coming trial who would testify that he saw Gotti in the vicinity of Sparks Steak House on East Forty-sixth Street shortly before Thomas Bilotti and Big Paul Castellano were shot to death in front of the restaurant on December 16, 1985.

"What the fuck are you doing over there?" the witness heard Gotti shout to one of the members of the hit team that had assembled near the steak house waiting for Bilotti and Castellano to arrive. According to the witness Gotti barked out orders to at least two other men near Sparks shortly before Bilotti and Castellano showed up, then disappeared into the rush-hour crowd. A week later the witness picked Gotti out of a spread of one hundred police photos as the man he had seen directing the hit team near the restaurant.

For Gotti, fretting in the Metropolitan Correctional Center in anticipation of his trial, this new witness was bad news indeed. For he had already been informed the prosecution had tapes that clearly implicated him in the Castellano hit. Now the new witness would corroborate the tapes.

But an even bigger blow fell on Gotti eleven days later, when, to the astonishment of everyone, the government announced that Gotti's codefendant and newly appointed underboss, Salvatore "Sammy the Bull" Gravano, had turned against his boss and decided to testify against him at his coming trial. New York law enforcement officials concurred that Gravano's cooperation was "the highest-ranking defection ever." Never before had an underboss facing trial with his boss turned against his boss at the eleventh hour.

KING RAT! headlined the New York *Post*, in describing Gravano's defection. DON'S NUMBER TWO WILL SING THE HITS headlined the *Daily News*. "This defection is unprecedented in the annals of New York organized crime," declared Edward McDonald, former head of the eastern district's Organized Crime Strike Force.

Needless to say, the prosecution was delighted with the new turn of events. A spokesperson for the eastern district observed that Gravano had "access to everything and everybody," and that he could be expected to supply corroboration of "just about everything" on the over one hundred hours of taped conversations recorded at the Ravenite from 1988 through 1990 which the prosecution intended to introduce into evidence at the trial.

Salvatore Gravano had worked with John Gotti for fourteen years. They had been street thugs together after Gotti was released from Green Haven State Prison in 1977 in the early years of Big Paul's reign. Gravano, a weight lifter and amateur boxer, brash and arrogant like Gotti, had acquired his nickname Sammy the Bull from his compact muscular physique, featuring a thick bovine neck. Unlike Gotti, however, he dressed casually, often wearing just sneakers, jeans, and a black leather jacket. When Gotti became boss after the Castellano murder, Gravano, the alleged Sparks getaway driver, grew closer and closer to Gotti, eventually becoming his *consiglière* upon the imprisonment of his predecessor, Joe N. Gallo, in 1987.

Gotti liked Sammy the Bull, who was five years his junior, and Gravano held Gotti in such high esteem that he became the boss's most conspicuous yes-man, never failing to act on Gotti's wishes enthusiastically and with dispatch.

So close did Gotti and Gravano eventually become that before Gotti had been denied bail and sent to the MCC to await trial, he had made him his underboss and designated him as his successor should Gotti be convicted and sent away for the rest of his life. The FBI had caught this promotion and designation of succession on tape. The bug in the upstairs apartment of the Ravenite had recorded on January 4, 1990, a conversation between Gotti and Gravano that gave Gotti's intentions away.

GOTTI: Hopefully we got time. . . . Soon as anything happens to me, I'm off the streets. Sammy is the acting boss. He's our *cugin*. But I got something that's bothering me, Sammy. I don't wanna start like The Chin did with them people. Bad precedent. So I'm asking you how you feel. You wanna stay as *consiglière*? Or you want me to make you official underboss? Acting boss? How do you feel? What makes you feel better? Think about it. Think about it tonight.

GRAVANO: Ah, you know how exactly I believe that and even with some of the bullshit things. The case against me would be a massive RICO racketeering.

GOTTI: All right, yeah.

GRAVANO: So, it's probably gonna be like only a hundred, eighty, indictments . . . eh, counts.

GOTTI: *Sammy.*

GRAVANO: Of labor racketeering.

GOTTI: *Sammy.* First they got, they got more indictments. I don't know what they got for you. But they got more than that for you. It doesn't matter, Sam. This thing here . . . this is my wishes that if, if I'm in the fucking can, this Family is gonna be run by *Sammy.* I'm still the boss. If I get fifty years I know what I gotta do. But *when I'm in the can Sammy's in charge.*

Salvatore Gravano was flattered that John Gotti had chosen him to run the Gambino family in the event that Gotti was sent to prison. But when the indictments came down and Gravano found himself in the same boat as his boss, facing charges that could, upon convictions, send him away to prison for fifty years to life with no chance of parole, his love and admiration for John Gotti, and satisfaction over Gotti's evident high regard for his talents, began to lose some of its bloom. Then, when his attorneys showed him transcripts of the tapes of his conversations with Gotti recorded in the Ravenite's upstairs apartment—conversations clearly linking him to at least two, possibly three murders—whatever positive feelings he had nourished for his boss vanished in a nightmare of unrelieved dread. It was Gotti's big mouth and astonishing incaution that had gotten him into this mess.

For Sammy the Bull there was now only one way

out, only one way to avoid life imprisonment with no chance of parole, and that was to turn on his boss and be a witness against him at his coming trial.

In so doing, Gravano would be in a position to cripple the Gambino crime family perhaps beyond repair. Not only would he have the power to put Gotti away for good, but he could also destroy Frankie Loc Locascio and other high-ranking capos, people like Jimmy Failla and Joe Butch Corrao. In other words, he would be able to destroy the entire leadership of the Gambino family.

Sammy the Bull had more to lose than his freedom by sticking by Gotti and going to trial with him in January. Since this was a RICO case, he also stood to lose most of his ill-gotten property.

By the time of his indictment, Gravano had put together a small conglomerate of businesses, most of which were related to the construction industry. He owned S&G Construction, Rite Work General Construction, Gem Steel, Rebar Construction, and companies dealing in asbestos, Italian flooring, dry-wall work, and rugs. In addition Gotti had put him in charge of controlling Teamsters Local 282, which in turn had a monopolistic stranglehold on all construction trucking in New York.

Through his association with the Gambino family, Gravano had become a major power in New York's construction industry and a wealthy man. Now, because of certain provisions of the RICO statute allowing for the confiscation of mobsters' illegally acquired property upon a racketeering conviction, Gravano stood to lose all he had won over the past fourteen years.

And, given the evidence the U.S. attorney, eastern district, had assembled, it had become all too clear to Gravano and his attorneys that the government had a solid case against him.

It was all on the tapes. There was a conversation, picked up in early 1986, by the Ravenite apartment bug, between John Gotti and Salvatore Gravano, on which Gravano was heard asking Gotti for permission to "whack" Gambino capo Robert DiBernardo. Gotti gave Gravano his consent and DiBernardo has not been seen since. Apparently DiBernardo had had the nerve to try to muscle in on some of Gravano's construction rackets.

Then there was the Liborio "Louie" Milito murder. In early 1988 the Ravenite apartment bug picked up a conversation between Gotti and Gravano during which Sammy the Bull asked permission from Gotti to have Milito killed. Gotti granted permission and Milito, another threat to Gravano's construction rackets, was murdered on March 8, 1988.

Boss and underboss committed still another major indiscretion within earshot of the Ravenite apartment bug in late 1989. On this tape Gravano was caught pleading with Gotti to have construction executive and business partner Louis DiBono, a made member of the Gambino family, killed. Although the bug did not record Gotti authorizing the hit, DiBono was murdered several months later. His body was found in a car parked in the garage of the World Trade Center on October 4, 1990.

John Gotti knew full well what was going on, that the murders Gravano had requested him to authorize had directly benefited Gravano's businesses. The Ravenite apartment bug had picked up Gotti complaining of his *consiglière*'s murderous entrepreneurial style.

GOTTI: Where are we going here? Where the fuck are we going here? Where are we going here? Every fucking time I turn around there's a new company cropping up. Rebars. Building. Consulting. Concrete. And every time we got a partner who don't agree with us, we kill him . . . He kills 'em. He okays it.

But not only did the feds have the tapes of Gravano

asking Gotti for permission to kill rivals and associates, they also had corroboration of what was said on the tapes by confidential informants.

The office of the U.S. attorney, eastern district, maintained seven confidential sources on the activities of the Gambino family. CS-1, 2, 3, 4, and 6 had provided information for more than two years. CS-5 and 7 for the last six months.

CS-1 was able to corroborate that Gravano had been responsible for the killing of DiBono, and CS-6 confirmed that Gravano had urged Gotti to murder still another made member of the Gambino family, Edward Garafola, who was perceived to be a disgruntled former associate of the late Paul Castellano.

But the murders were only a part of Gravano's problem. In its indictment of him the government had also hit Gravano with charges of operating illegal gambling casinos in New York and Connecticut, loan-sharking, racketeering, obstruction of justice in the Castellano murder investigation, and bribery of a public servant.

The bribery of a public servant made headlines on December 12, 1991, with the eastern district's announcement of the indictments of former police detective William Peist and two Gambino men, capo Joseph Joe Butch Corrao and George Helbig, for leaking confidential information to John Gotti.

Behind the charges lurked the Great Defector, Salvatore Gravano, for it was he who had supplied enough damning information to the government to warrant the indictments of the three men. Sammy the Bull Gravano's career as King Rat had begun.

The indictments charged that Detective William Peist, through intermediaries Joe Butch Corrao and George Helbig, leaked confidential information from police files to John Gotti from the spring of 1987 to December 1990.

According to the indictment, Peist, a detective in the Intelligence Division, with access to crucial computerized law enforcement files, leaked information to Gotti on seventeen important state and federal investigations of Gambino family members. Peist furnished Gotti with information on the Castellano murder investigation, including the police sketch of the homicide scene and a top secret list of possible suspects in the Castellano hit. He also told Gotti where listening devices in his hangouts were located and he gave him the names of some of the government's confidential informants.

The indictment further alleged that Peist had been assigned to protect the jurors in Gotti's 1990 assault trial and that he had used this assignment to give Gotti the full names and addresses of the jurors.

For his delicate services Peist received regular weekly payments from Gotti through intermediaries, among whom was Sammy the Bull Gravano.

According to the indictment the route Peist's information took was from Peist to his wife's cousin, Peter Mavis, an associate of Gravano's, who passed it along to Gambino associate George Helbig, who then delivered the tips to Joe Butch Corrao and John Gotti.

Since Joe Butch Corrao was reputed to be Gotti's "street boss" or number four in the family hierarchy while Gotti awaited trial in the MCC, his indictment could mean that the entire top leadership of the Gambino crime family could be put out of action if convictions were obtained at the upcoming trials. The government already had number two, Gravano, on its side. Now Gotti, Locascio, and Corrao faced the possibility of long prison terms. Who would be left to run the family if all three were convicted? Tommy Gambino? But he and his brother Joe were due to go on trial in early January 1992 on very serious charges. If they were convicted and sent away to prison, who would be left to lead the Gambinos through the 1990s?

With the turning of Gravano, federal prosecutors now had a formidable array of witnesses to set loose against John Gotti. In addition to Sammy the Bull, they had mob canary Crazy Phil Leonetti, who claimed to be present when Gotti told Philadelphia boss Nicky Scarfo he had ordered the slaying of Castellano and had had it sanctioned by the Commission. Leonetti was also disposed to tell the world that Gotti had authorized the bombing wipe-out of underboss Frankie DeCicco.

The prosecutors, as we have seen, also had a reliable witness who would attest to the presence of Gotti in the vicinity of Sparks Steak House barking out orders to Castellano's and Bilotti's murderers.

And then there were all the tapes. The hundreds of hours of recorded conversations between a loquacious and unguarded Gotti and his men in the Bergin and the Ravenite throughout 1988, 1989, and 1990.

For the first time in its long, unrelenting, so far unsuccessful campaign to put Gotti behind bars, the government finally had the evidence it needed. Turning Gravano had been the prosecution's most telling ploy. If the jury would believe him, Gravano could send his boss away for the rest of his useful life.

Part VII

The Showdown

New York, 1992:
*The United States v.
John Gotti*

38

The Tapes

*This is a case about a Mafia boss being brought down
by his own words, his own right arm, and
in the course of it bringing down his whole family.*

U.S. Attorney Andrew J. Maloney's opening statement to the twelve anonymous, sequestered
jurors was succinct and on the mark. For the principal evidence in the thirteen-count murder-racketeer-
ing case against John Gotti was to come from secretly
taped conversations between Gotti and his subordinates and the testimony of his former underboss,
Salvatore "Sammy the Bull" Gravano, recently turned
government informant.

"The unthinkable happens," Maloney went on.
"Sammy Gravano contacts the FBI and comes in and
makes a deal and confesses to all the murders in the
indictment and to his participation in the Paul
Castellano murder. He will tell you about horrible
crimes, confessing to a total of nineteen murders. We
have no brief with Sammy Gravano. He is no different
or better than John Gotti. Both of them kill people as a
matter of course in running the Gambino crime family."

Andrew Maloney's opening remarks in early February 1992 were made to a packed Brooklyn courtroom dominated by the huge bald eagle of the great seal of the United States hanging above the judge's bench.

To the left of the center aisle sat a large contingent of Gotti supporters. Among them were several Gotti captains, the most conspicuous of whom was the slim, brisk, silver-haired John "Jackie Nose" D'Amico, who functioned as a sort of cheerleader for the group, and some relatives, notably Gotti's stocky ex-sanitation worker brother, Peter, and three rows of Gotti groupies, many of whom had waited in line since dawn to get a glimpse of their hero.

To the right sat the media—the newspaper-radio-television press—and the courtroom artists. As a media junkie, Gotti enjoyed playing to this audience, especially to CBS Television's Mary Murphy, NBC Television's John Miller, ABC Television's Pablo Guzman, CBS Radio's Eileen Cornell, *Daily News'* gangland columnist, and co-author, with Gene Mustain, of a biography of Gotti, Jerry Capeci, and New York *Newsday'*s columnists Murray Kempton and Jimmy Breslin. Once when Gotti noticed Mary Murphy was missing from the press section he was so upset he asked one of his supporters to find out why she had not come to the courtroom that day. It turned out that she had been up all night covering the abortive takeoff of a US Air jet at La Guardia Airport.

In the left well of the court John Gotti and code-fendant Frank "Frankie Loc" Locascio sat with their attorneys and assistants, led by the noted Miami-based criminal lawyer, short, stocky, hairless, bullet-headed Albert J. Krieger, who had replaced the disqualified Bruce Cutler. In the right well sat the prosecution team led by the tough, combative U.S. attorney for the eastern district of New York, Andrew J. Maloney, looking every inch the West Point boxing champion he once was. Assistant U.S.

Attorney John Gleeson, who had unsuccessfully prosecuted Gotti at his last federal trial, sat beside him.

Facing the jurors in their box on the right side of the courtroom, opposite the prosecution table, Maloney continued his opening statement, turning to the centerpiece of the government's case: Gotti's alleged murder of boss Paul Castellano in order to seize control of the Gambino crime family. Maloney told the jury that according to certain taped conversations and the testimony of Sammy Gravano, it was learned that Gotti was head of a faction within the Gambino family that hated Paul Castellano and feared him because he had issued an edict that any member of the family that dealt in drugs would be killed. That marked John Gotti for execution because two weeks before Castellano's murder Big Paul had received a batch of transcripts of FBI tapes that clearly showed that John Gotti's brother Gene and several other close Gotti associates had been involved in a huge heroin-smuggling operation which Gotti could not have been ignorant of. It was right after John Gotti learned Castellano had received the transcripts that he and his partners, Salvatore Gravano, Angelo Ruggiero, Anthony Rampino, John Carneglia, and others decided "to take out the boss," Maloney told the jurors.

"This is a compelling case coming out of the mouth of John Gotti and his associates," Maloney went on. "You will hear five extraordinary conversations between John Gotti, Frank Locascio, and Sammy Gravano secretly recorded by the FBI in a widow's apartment above the Ravenite Club. In these conversations you will hear Gotti say how much he hates tapes and you will hear him badmouth others who have been caught on tapes because he knows how devastating tapes can be.

"Your task will be quite simple," Maloney informed the jurors. "It will not be that complex because these defendants in their own words will tell you what it is all about."

His voice rising, Maloney then told the jurors of a tape on which Gotti is heard expressing an intention to sever the head off a Greek gambler who had dared set up a game in Gambino territory. As he pronounced the words "sever the head off" Maloney suddenly wheeled around and, pointing his right index finger at Gotti, made a simulated pistol out of his hand and pulled the trigger. Gotti smiled back.

"Now we will let John Gotti's own words and those of his former underboss tell you the story of the crimes set forth in the indictment," concluded Maloney as he turned and walked back to the prosecution table, his face a mask of stone.

Albert Krieger was quick to pounce on the significance of Sammy Gravano's coming testimony for the prosecution. In his opening statement for the defense he called the turncoat witness a "little man full of evil, connivance, manipulation, and vanity who has tried to clean his own slate by admitting to nineteen murders."

Turning around to pound his fist on the prosecution table, Krieger said: "This table has the power of absolution. We will prove to you that what has happened is the government is engaged in the equivalent of a body-snatching trade, that they are trading in currency, so to speak—dead people for testimony."

"Nineteen murders!" thundered Krieger in his ringing baritone, staring at the twelve jurors and six alternates sitting in the jury box. "We don't have enough chairs to put the victims in!" "What we have here, ladies and gentlemen, is a contingency fee, pure and simple," roared Krieger. "Deliver, you get it. Don't deliver, spend your life in jail for the crimes you committed. That's Gravano, pure and simple."

Turning his attention from Gravano to the tapes,

Krieger told the jury: "We are not afraid of the tapes. You will hear on these tapes that Mr. Gotti has been through two trials where similar tapes were played and the jury rejected them as not supportive of the case charged."

Krieger then warned the jurors that "the profanity you will hear on the tapes might be staggering for some, bizarre for others, and shocking to others." But, Krieger reminded them, the jurors had to realize that Gotti learned to speak the English language "on the streets, not in college. . . . He wishes he could say three words without cursing." Apparently not satisfied with the impact this remark had on the expressionless jurors, Krieger unwittingly caused the spectators to break out laughing by adding "Although profanity laced every sentence, it never intruded upon his conversations with children or women," which, of course, the jurors could not confirm, since the government would not play any tapes of conversations between Gotti and women and children.

Finally Krieger sought to dismantle the linchpin of the prosecution's case against Gotti: the charge that Gotti planned the killing of Paul Castellano out of fear Castellano was going to kill him and some of his associates because they violated his edict against dealing in drugs. That theory is "all wrong," Krieger told the jurors. "Gotti never had anything to do with drugs," and one of the tapes proved it, Krieger contended. Since Gotti had no reason to believe Castellano was going to execute him he "had no reason to launch a preemptive strike against him. . . . No," Krieger reiterated, "we are not afraid of the tapes."

Throughout the opening statements John Gotti appeared extraordinarily relaxed, even cheerful, considering the enormity of the charges against him and the possible penalty of life imprisonment with no possibility of parole he would have to pay if convicted. To some he seemed resigned to his fate from the very beginning. Reliable sources claimed that Gotti's lowest moment had come in November 1991, when he was told that his buddy and most trusted aide, Salvatore Gravano, had turned against him. It was then that he knew he could not beat the case and that he would probably have to spend the rest of his life behind bars. Despondency had overcome him then in his cell in the MCC, but by the time the trial began three months later, that despondency had turned to a calm resignation.

Although Andrew Maloney, as the official leader of the prosecution team, presented the government's opening statement, he let his young assistant U.S. attorney, John Gleeson, take over the day-to-day chore of presenting the government's case. Gleeson immediately began playing the tapes.

Gleeson's first order of business was to demonstrate to the jury that the Gambino crime family did exist, that John Gotti ran it, and that he and Gravano and Locascio discussed running family business together.

Let the tapes roll.

GOTTI (to Gravano): Tomorrow I wanna call all our skippers in. I'm gonna tell them I'm the *representate* till I say different. Soon as anything happens to me, I'm off the streets, Sammy is the acting boss. He's our *consiglière*. But I got something that's bothering me, Samm. . . . I'm asking you how you feel. You wanna stay as *consiglière*? Or you want me to make you official underboss? Acting boss? How do you feel? What makes you feel better? Think about it. Think about it tonight.

GOTTI (to Gravano and Locascio on making new members): I wanna make it a short and sweet

list, Frankie. This is not the time to make
twenty guys. And where are we gonna find
them, these kinda guys? Frank, I'm not being a,
a pessimist. It's gettin' tougher, not easier! We
got everything that's any good. Look around . . .
I told you a couple a weeks ago, we got the only
few pockets of good kids left. Look at this fucking bum. Your father's a cop, the uncle's a cop,
the mother's a pain in the ass.

GOTTI (to Gravano and Locascio): The lawyers . . .
GRAVANO: I hate them.
GOTTI: You know these are rats, er, Sam. And I gotta
say, they all want their money up front. And
then you get four guys that want sixty-five, seventy-five thousand a piece, up front. You're
talking about three hundred thousand in one
month, you cocksucker. Take it easy, you
motherfucker. I don't give a fuck, Frankie. . . .
They plucking me. I'm paying for it. You got
Sammy, you got one hand in his pocket. You
got both your hands in Joe Butch's pocket.
Where does it end? Gambino crime family?
This is the Shargel, Cutler, and whattaya call it
crime family. . . .
GRAVANO: They wind up with the money.
GOTTI: The fuckin' you kiddin'? You know what I
mean?
LOCASCIO: They're overpriced, overpaid, and, and
underperformed.

GOTTI: And this is gonna be a Cosa Nostra till I die.
Be it an hour from now, or be it tonight, or a
hundred years from now when I'm in jail. It's
gonna be a Cosa Nostra. This ain't gonna be a
bunch of your friends are gonna be "friends of
ours." It's gonna be the way I say it's gonna be,
a Cosa Nostra. A Cosa Nostra! . . . Just saying,
you might being a guy brings you a basket

makes him a good guy. It makes him a mother-fucker to me. Don't make him a good guy. It makes him a good guy when he's one of us and he proves he's right for us. And I'm the best judge a that, I think right now.

Throughout the playing of the tapes John Gotti never put on his headset and only occasionally glanced at the transcripts in front of him. He was trying to be nonchalant about them, but was obviously uncomfortable. On a January 24, 1990, tape about remarks Gotti had made in 1985, Gotti had spoken of his chagrin over the tapes to Gravano and Locascio:

GOTTI: But these, only thing bad about these tapes, only thing I can, I comfort myself with, I was just telling Frankie, I says to myself today. Thank God this is 1985. If this tape, 1988, '89, I would've thrown myself off a fuckin' bridge for embarrassment.

But if Gotti was embarrassed about what was crackling over the headsets, he did not show it. Wearing a slight smirk most of the time, Gotti would only betray emotion when John Gleeson would rise from the defense table to elucidate a tape. Then his smirk would disintegrate into a sneer and he would pretend to dismiss what Gleeson was saying with a flick of the back of his hand.

It would be hard to imagine a personality more different from John Gotti than John Gleeson. With his dark, horn-rimmed glasses and thin, ascetic face, Gleeson looked scholarly and deadly serious. Wearing plain navy-blue, single-breasted business suits and regimental stripe ties, Gleeson gave the impression of being modest and unpretentious. Speaking in a measured monotone, Gleeson's questioning of witnesses and remarks to the jury, thorough in the extreme, evinced a methodical and logical mind. Nothing could be more foreign to John Gleeson's personality than Gotti's arrogance and vanity, his flashy clothes, obscene language, and blatant air of invincibility.

On with the tapes. The "five extraordinary conversations" between Gotti, Gravano, and Locascio promised by Andrew Maloney came through the headsets accompanied by background music from a phonograph playing "O Sole Mio," "Mona Lisa," and "Strangers in the Night."

They were indeed extraordinary. On them Gotti talked freely about the problems of running a crime family, discussing business that required him to "whack" partners occasionally who stood between him or Gravano and a dollar, or who had shown him disrespect. Some of these clearly indicated that despite Gotti's professed love for his underboss, by December 12, 1989, he was beginning to get fed up with Gravano's greed and his increasing need to have rivals and disloyal partners eliminated.

Referring to Robert DiBernardo, a Gambino soldier active in some of Gravano's construction projects, who disappeared on June 5, 1986:

GOTTI: When Di B got whacked they told me a story. I was in jail when I whacked him. I know why it was being done. I done it anyway. I allowed it to be done anyway.

GOTTI: Di B, did he ever talk subversive to you?

LOCASCIO: No.

GOTTI: I took Sammy's word. Louie DiBono. And I sat with this guy. . . . He didn't rob nothin'. You know why he's dying? He's gonna die because he refused to come in when I called. He didn't do nothin' else wrong. . . . He's gonna get killed because he, he disobeyed coming.

DiBono's body, shot seven times in the chest and face, was discovered in a locked car parked in a

World Trade Center garage on October 4, 1990.

GOTTI (to Locascio): Who's gonna defy me? What are you gonna do? Take a hot, sleeping, like I did to the other guy. No! Frank, I'd welcome that. I'll kill their fuckin' mothers, their fathers.

In the same monologue Gotti turned his attention to a third man Gravano asked him to have murdered, Liborio "Louie" Milito, owner of Gem Steel, a Gambino-controlled construction company.

GOTTI (to Locascio): Louie had Gem Steel. You, you told me that the guy talked behind my back. Now *you* got Gem Steel. The other thing, you told me Di B cried behind my back. Now you got all that!

You know, Frankie, you could love me, he loves me, he loves me, I know he does. But Jesus fuckin' Christ, this is not your candy store!

And I tell him a million times, "Sammy, slow it down. Pull it in a fuckin' notch. Slow it down! Pull it in a notch."

You, you, you come up with fifteen companies, for chrissake! You got Rebars, you got concrete pouring, you got Italian floors now. You got construction, you got drywall, you got asbestos, you got rugs. What the fuck next?

Clearly Gotti believed his underboss's greed was getting out of control and that Gravano was preventing other Gambino capos and soldiers from making money in the process. Nevertheless he, Gotti, was taking the blame for his underboss.

GOTTI: And I keep telling people it's my fault. I told him to do that. I told him to do this. . . . What the fuck, am I nuts here? If I go to jail, they'd be happy.

Later on in the conversation Gotti accused Gravano of being as greedy as Paul Castellano.

GOTTI (to Locascio): And more important, I don't believe in that fuckin' bulldozin'. That's what made me hate, really, fuckin' Paul. You, ya, you couldn't even get a fuckin' ham sandwich [from him]. Everyone is right. He sold the *borgàta* out for fuckin' construction company. And that's what we're doing right now. I don't know if you could see it, but that's what we're doing right now. Three, four guys will wind up with every fuckin' thing. And the rest of the *borgàta* looks like fuckin' waste.

Gotti went on to tell Locascio that Gravano was getting to be like Castellano—that, for example, he was using his influence over a Teamsters official to steer construction jobs to a company controlled by him, even to the extent of forcing a company controlled by Gotti out of business.

GOTTI (to Locascio): He's using my fucking flag to conquer the fucking market. Who the fuck are you? You're creating all these things here. I got made guys that want this business. Where am I going? What do I do with the rest of the *borgàta*? Throw 'em in the fucking street?
    He could turn the whole fuckin' industry into a private playpen.
Locascio: You know what I gotta say. You're telling of all the businesses that he's got, you don't get nothin'.
GOTTI: I would be a billionaire if I was lookin' to be a selfish boss. That's not me. . . . All I want is a good sandwich. You see this sandwich here?

This tuna sandwich? That's all I want, a good sandwich.

Having demonstrated to the jury via the tapes that the Gambino crime family existed, that John Gotti ran it, and that he and Salvatore Gravano and Frankie Locascio discussed family business together, including murder, prosecutor John Gleeson turned the jury's attention to the centerpiece of the trial: the murder of Paul Castellano.

Gleeson told the jury that John Gotti's principal role in the murder of Castellano would be proven by the tapes and the testimony of Salvatore Gravano.

That John Gotti had no use for Paul Castellano was amply demonstrated by the tapes:

GOTTI (to Gravano): Paul, let me tell you about Paul, Sammy. He didn't . . . he was a fucking fish on the desert. He was fish outa water! He don't know this life! . . . You fuckin' . . . he was a piece of shit! Rat, rat, cocksucker. Yellow dog! Yellow dog, yellow dog!

GOTTI (to Gravano and Locascio): You know what got me sick?

GRAVANO: [Laughs]

GOTTI: I curse people. Everybody does it. We're human. We're bums. We bums in the street.

LOCASCIO: That's right.

GOTTI: Every fucking time I went there [to Castellano's Staten Island mansion] on a Saturday or Sunday I hated it, Frank. I hated the fucking world. Because whoever was there before me, as soon as he left, he cursed out. "Scumbag." "Asshole." "Motherfucker." *Minchia!* I mean, ain't there nobody good here? No, you know when you leave that door, he's gonna say it about you.

The tapes revealed that not only did Gotti have no use for Castellano, he also had nothing good to say about his predecessor, Carlo Gambino.

GOTTI: [Carlo Gambino] was a rat motherfucker. A back door motherfucker. People don't know what this fucking guy done. He was the one who started these temporary positions, and nobody in positions. There was never no such thing in "this thing of ours."

Why did John Gotti want to kill Paul Castellano? John Gleeson asked the question of the jury, then proceeded to answer it.

Gleeson explained that the tapes revealed a growing tension between the two factions within the Gambino crime family, that led by Castellano himself and that led by underboss Aniello Dellacroce and his protégé, John Gotti.

This tension derived from several conflicts within the family. One was over drug dealing. Paul Castellano had issued an edict that any member of the Gambino family caught dealing in drugs would be sentenced to death without trial and by 1985 Castellano had become aware that at least three members of Gotti's crew were dealing in drugs and the feds knew it. Gleeson cited some tapes to prove his point. One was a conversation between John Gotti's brother, Gene, and his closest friend, Angelo Ruggiero.

GENE GOTTI: Oh, Paul is thinking about doing something.
RUGGIERO: Him and Chin made a pact. Any friend of ours that gets pinched for junk, or that they hear anything about junk, they kill him. No administration meetings, no nothing, just gonna kill him. They're not warning nobody, not telling nobody because they feel the guy is gonna rat.

As tensions mounted between the two factions of

the Gambino family over drug dealing on the part of Gotti's crew, Gotti was taped at the Bergin Hunt and Fish Club expressing his disgust with Castellano.

GOTTI: This cocksucker's got me so fuckin' hot. . . . You know who's happy with them? Absolutely nobody's happy with them. . . . Absolutely nobody's happy with them.

Tapes reveal that Castellano was equally unhappy with Gotti and his crew. On June 8, 1985, Castellano was taped telling his underboss, Aniello Dellacroce, that he knew Angelo Ruggiero and his attorney, Michael Coiro, had the 1982 tapes of discussions of drug dealing between Ruggiero, Gene Gotti, and Eddie Lino. "I gotta get them," he told Dellacroce, implying that if he did not get them there would be trouble.

The next day Ruggiero was recorded telling Dellacroce and Gotti he could not turn over the tapes.

RUGGIERO: I'm gonna tell you somethin'. If you two never bother with me again, again in the rest of my life, I ain't givin' them tapes up. If you never bother with me, again, for the rest of my life. I can't. I can't. There's good friends of mine on them fuckin' tapes.

There followed a heated discussion between Ruggiero, Dellacroce, and John Gotti during which Dellacroce and Gotti urged Ruggiero to turn over the tapes to avoid war.

GOTTI (referring to Castellano): While he's the boss, while he's the boss, you have to do what he tells you.
DELLACROCE: That's what I'm tellin' you. That's what we wanna hear. You see, that's why I says to you before, you, you, you don't understand Cosa Nostra.

GOTTI: Angelo, what does Cosa Nostra mean?

DELLACROCE: Cosa Nostra means that the boss is your boss. You understand? Forget about all this nonsense.

Later on in the discussion Dellacroce repeated his definition of Cosa Nostra to Ruggiero with added emphasis. Unconsciously parodying Gertrude Stein's definition of a rose, he intoned: "La Cosa Nostra. The boss is the boss is the boss."

With Castellano repeatedly insisting to Dellacroce that Ruggiero surrender the tapes or else, and Ruggiero repeatedly refusing to do so, the two Gambino family factions had reached an impasse. It was now a question of who would kill who first.

Then, on December 2, 1985, Dellacroce died of cancer and shortly thereafter, in the words of the government's indictment, "Paul Castellano informed John Gotti of Castellano's intention to break up Gotti's crew and to reassign its members to other crews in the Gambino family." It was then, the prosecution contended, that Gotti and his men went into action and began plotting the murder of Castellano in earnest.

After making this point, the prosecution called its first witness to the Castellano slaying. He was Jeffrey Davidson, a thirty-year-old public relations executive whose office in December 1985 had not been far from Sparks Steak House on East Forty-sixth Street.

Davidson testified that he had just left his office and was walking east along Forty-sixth Street at the start of the rush hour on December 16, 1985, when he heard "a volley of gunfire, shots . . . several pops, kind of clustered together."

"Well, I stepped out onto the street," Davidson continued, "looking to see what was going on. I looked up Forty-sixth Street between Second and Third avenues, because that's where I heard the shots. I saw a body in the street next to a car with its driver's side door open. It was lying flat on its back.

"And then I saw a man come from around the front of the car," Davidson went on, "and stand over the body in the street.

"Then I saw this man extend his arm over the body in the street and saw his arm recoil three times. . . . When the arm recoiled," he added, "I heard the sound of gunfire."

Elucidating Davidson's testimony, prosecutor Gleeson remarked that it was clear the body in the street, near the driver's side of the car, was that of Thomas Bilotti, Castellano's chauffeur. Castellano had been ambushed on the passenger side of his black Lincoln.

And who delivered this deadly coup de grace to Tommy Bilotti? Jeffrey Davidson, upon looking over dozens of mug shots police detectives had shown him, identified the gunman as John Carneglia, a Gambino soldier and close friend of John Gotti, currently serving fifty years in prison for heroin trafficking.

Davidson testified he had a clear view of the gunman's profile when he walked around the car after firing three shots into the body on the street, observing he had a prominent nose and protruding lips. Davidson went on to testify that the gunman was joined by two other men dressed, like him, in long overcoats. "They kept going down Forty-sixth Street until they disappeared into some construction work," Davidson concluded. "That's the last I saw of them."

It was during the testimony of Jeffrey Davidson that an incident occurred at the defense table that revealed how tense the seemingly imperturbable John Gotti had become.

Since February 6, as jury selection in Gotti's trial was nearing completion, Tommy and Joe Gambino had been standing trial in Manhattan state court charged in a forty-five-count indictment for maintaining a monopolistic stranglehold on the garment center's trucking industry. During the first three weeks of the Gambino trial some of the thirty-five thousand secretly taped conversations between the Gambino brothers and their associates and certain clothing manufacturers were played that clearly showed the Gambinos were forcing sewing, cutting, and fabric concerns to use Gambino trucks exclusively at exorbitant rates and were having their men threaten the manufacturers in subtle ways if they dared use independent trucking companies to move their goods. So obvious had their guilt been revealed by the tapes that Tommy and Joe finally broke down on February 26 and pleaded guilty to one count of restraint of trade, agreeing to pay a fine of $13 million and get out of the industry if it would keep them from being sent off to jail. The government had agreed and signed the deal with the Gambinos.

When news of the Gambinos' deal with the government was conveyed to John Gotti, via a written memorandum passed to him in Brooklyn Federal Court during a break in Davidson's testimony, Gotti, who had strenuously urged all his capos to never plea-bargain with the government, scowled more contemptuously than he had been observed to do since the trial had begun, rolled the memorandum into a ball in his right fist, and threw it toward the prosecution table. In that instant Gotti realized that the Gambino brothers were betting against him, or else they would never have copped a plea. For Gotti to have Tommy Gambino betting against him was almost as brutal an act of treachery as Gravano's stab in the back of several months before.

By the time of Jeffrey Davidson's testimony, presented on February 26, and his cross-examination on the twenty-seventh, everyone in the spectators' and press sections was speculating on when turncoat Salvatore "Sammy the Bull" Gravano was going to take the stand. It had been widely rumored that

Gravano's testimony would be so thorough and so compelling that having other witnesses testify to the plotting and slaying of Castellano would be superfluous. When, on Friday, February 28, it was announced in court that Philip Leonetti, the former Scarfo family underboss, would not testify, everyone concluded that Sammy the Bull would take the stand at the beginning of the following week.

The tapes played during the first two weeks of the trial had been terribly damaging to the defense. John Gotti's own words did what very few live witnesses could have done. They had shown conclusively that Gotti was boss of the Gambino crime family, that he discussed his family's criminal activities with his subordinates, and that he had admitted to participating in at least three murders. This alone should have been enough to assure his conviction on the principal counts in the indictment. Now all that remained to send him away for the rest of his life was the traitorous testimony of Sammy the Bull Gravano.

39

Gravano

I was a good, loyal soldier. John barked and I bit.

With these words Sammy the Bull Gravano described the halcyon days of his relationship with his former boss, John Gotti. Times were good then. The big money flowed in. Mutual enemies were quietly eliminated. So rosy did Sammy's relationship with Gotti become that Gotti was moved to remark within earshot of an FBI bug, "Soon as anything happens to me, I'm off the streets, Sammy is the acting boss."

Then came that December evening in 1990 when the feds swooped down on Sammy Gravano, John Gotti, and Frank Locascio outside the Ravenite Club, arrested them, handcuffed them, and hit them with a thirteen-count indictment on charges of racketeering and murder. And before long Sammy found himself in a cell in the MCC reading transcripts of taped conversations between himself, John Gotti, and Frankie Locascio that he quickly realized could send him away to a maximum-security federal prison for the rest of his life.

Now the halcyon days were over and Sammy had begun brooding in his cell over the transcripts and what he and John Gotti and Locascio had said on them.

"Where are we going here? . . . Where are we going here?" Gotti had asked Locascio on one tape, alluding to Gravano's entrepreneurial exploits. "Every fucking time I turn around there's a new company popping up. . . . And every time we get a partner that don't agree with us, we kill him. You go to the boss and your boss kills him. He kills him."

On another tape Gotti, referring to Gravano, had told Locascio: "He's using my fucking flag to conquer the fucking market. Who the fuck are you? You're creating all these things here. I got made guys who want this business. Where am I going? What do I do with the rest of the *borgàta*? Throw 'em in the fucking street?"

This was a John Gotti that Sammy Gravano had not known before. This was a John Gotti who appeared to disapprove of what Sammy was doing, even though it resulted in Sammy sending cash payments up to Gotti amounting to $100,000 a month.

Brooding in his cell, Sammy the Bull recalled his and Gotti's bail hearing in mid-December 1990, when, after the government played a tape about the DiBernardo murder, he realized Gotti had lied about him. On the tape Gotti had complained to Locascio that Gravano's greed had urged him on to "whack" Robert "Di B" DiBernardo, who Gravano allegedly said was talking ill about Gotti behind his back. Later Sammy had confronted Gotti in the MCC about the tape and told him that what Gotti had said on the tape wasn't true, that it was a lie, that he never asked permission to kill Di B, that Gotti had ordered him to kill Di B and he had simply obeyed the order. When Gotti responded with a cold sneer, Sammy realized for the first time he had been a fool to have trusted Gotti, whose big mouth had gotten him in so much trouble that he now faced spending the rest of his life behind bars.

For months Sammy had brooded in his cell about the tapes and Gotti's unwary mouth and his lies and what a bleak and empty future now lay before him, until one day his despair overwhelmed him to such an extent that he secretly placed a phone call to the FBI and told the agent on duty he was willing to turn state's witness and testify against his boss at his upcoming trial.

For the FBI's Gambino Squad, the office of the U.S. attorney, eastern district, and the State Organized Crime Task Force, Sammy the Bull Gravano's defection was a godsend, the key to convicting the criminal they detested more than any other. It was, in fact, an unprecedented act. Gravano was the highest-ranking Cosa Nostra mobster ever to become a government witness at a trial of a Cosa Nostra boss. When he took the stand and testified against John Gotti, Sammy the Bull would be making history. He would go down in the annals of organized crime alongside that notorious turncoat of 1963, Joe Valachi.

Salvatore Gravano had had a spectacular career as a Gambino family mobster. Born into a poor working-class family transplanted from Caltanissetta, Sicily, to Bensonhurst, Brooklyn, he had dropped out of school at the age of sixteen and began supporting himself with armed robberies and burglaries. After a two-year stint in the Army from 1964 to 1966, he joined a Colombo family crew in Brooklyn and began to make valuable contacts in construction companies and unions connected to the construction industry. In 1970 he established his reputation as an accomplished killer by committing his first murder. At least eighteen more would follow, perhaps as many as thirty-six according to his cellmates at the MCC. After a dispute with his Colombo crew captain he was released to a Gambino crew, where he rose quickly working with construction unions. After Paul Castellano took over the Gambino family, Castellano formally inducted him into the family in recognition of his reputation as a fearless killer and big "earner." As a made man in the early 1980s he entered the drywall construction and plumbing business with two partners and began making his first big money bribing union officials to allow nonunion labor onto a job site, then taking kickbacks from construction companies that saved money from hiring nonunion labor.

After the murder of Paul Castellano, Sammy the Bull formed Marathon Construction, a concrete company, and began taking over Castellano's former interests in the construction industry. If one of his partners became unruly or too greedy, as did Liborio Milito and Louis DiBono, he had them killed. By 1989 his reported annual income was $764,000, up from $55,000 in 1984. By then he had gained complete control of the huge Gambino concrete interests and had been made family underboss by John Gotti. At the time of his arrest with Gotti and Locascio in December 1990, he had become one of the most powerful Cosa Nostra leaders in the nation.

Day One

The atmosphere in Brooklyn Federal Court was taut with anticipation when, on March 2, 1992, prosecutor John Gleeson informed the court that Salvatore Gravano would be the next witness.

After four long minutes Sammy the Bull entered the courtroom from a back door near the judge's bench. The short, brisk Gravano, wearing a gray double-breasted suit and a red tie instead of his usual T-shirt and jeans, looked subdued and sad-eyed as he took the stand and shot a quick glance at the elegantly attired John Gotti, who allowed a smirk to appear on his face and then turned to his lawyers and said audibly, "Look, he's all dressed up."

The courtroom was packed. Every inch of seat room had been taken up. Fifteen hulking FBI agents and federal marshals filled the first two rows of the spectators' section, forming a thick high wall between Gotti supporters Jackie Nose D'Amico, Peter Gotti, Joseph DeCicco, and the witness stand. No, no one was going to be able to stare down Sammy the Bull Gravano.

Also present among the spectators were noted trial lawyer, F. Lee Bailey, New York FBI boss James Fox, and Special Agent Bruce Mouw, head of the FBI's Gambino Squad, located in Queens, and the man most responsible for putting Gotti in the position he was in.

On the other side of the aisle the courtroom artists and the press were crowded together in too little space. Frantically the artists were attacking their drawing boards, trying to capture a likeness of Sammy the Bull that would appear on television in time for the five o'clock news and illuminate the pages of the *Daily News*, the New York *Post*, and *Newsday* the following morning.

As Gravano took the stand, newly released transcripts of a tape began circulating in the press section.

The transcript featured a conversation between John Gotti, Frank Locascio, and Sammy Gravano about Paul Castellano receiving FBI agent Joe O'Brien and Organized Crime Task Force Investigator Joseph Coffey at his Staten Island White House, and how only "rats" allowed feds and cops into their homes.

GOTTI: He [Castellano] goes to the door. He sees on the TV, O'Brien and the other guy. He goes there, "Hello, Joe." Tells, calls the agent by the first name, "Come on in." Make Nina make coffee for you. You fucking rat motherfucker! My wife gotta' make coffee for the fucking agents? "Hello, Joe." Come in my house? . . .

Coffey came to him one night, told him, "These Irish guys are dragging you down!" . . . He's an FBI. He's, he's a cop, whatever the fuck he is. What does he do? What are you talking to this motherfucker? What a potential rat yourself. You fucking bum! . . . You fucking bum! You're a fucking rat. You let a cop in, in a half second, but two friends you won't let in. You fucking . . . he was a piece of shit! Rat, rat cocksucker. Yellow dog! Yellow dog, right? What, Sammy? All this guy needed was a little whack in the fucking mouth.

The ladies and gentlemen of the press were trying to digest this latest glob of Gotti sewage when prosecutor John Gleeson began interrogating witness Gravano.

In response to John Gleeson's initial, perfunctory questions the courtroom heard the diminutive, frowning Sammy the Bull say in a hoarse, barely audible voice:

"John was the boss," Sammy the Bull said in a hoarse voice. "I was the underboss. . . . I ran the construction industry and I helped John run the family. I spoke with some of the captains and I took care of some of the problems in the family."

It had been Paul Castellano himself who had inducted him into the family in 1976, Sammy testified, adding that when Castellano asked him during the induction ceremony if he would kill if asked to, he quickly replied yes, he would.

The preliminaries taken care of, Sammy the Bull proceeded to present an appalling narrative of day-to-day operations of the Gambino crime family, a tale of violence and depravity, of armed burglaries, loan-sharking enforcement, extortion, and murder. During the course of his narrative Gravano admitted to participating in nineteen murders, eleven of which, including the killing of Paul Castellano, he claimed were either ordered or sanctioned by John Gotti.

"*Nineteen!*" The collective whisperings from the press section could be heard.

At the conclusion of his narrative prosecutor Gleeson asked Gravano why Mr. Castellano was killed.

"There were quite a few reasons," Gravano replied. "He was selling out his family for his own basic businesses," having even entered into partnership in some enterprises with captains of the Genovese family. "He was having a lot of problems with a number of people. . . . We were wondering if and when Castellano had the tapes, he might make a move, he might strike. We were worried, especially about John and Angelo."

Gravano went on to testify that a small group of disaffected soldiers, calling themselves "the fist," led by Gotti, had begun to conspire against Castellano eight to ten months before the December 16, 1985, hit in front of Manhattan's Sparks Steak House. Before long the conspirators were approaching the heads of the city's other families and certain captains in the Gambino family for their support. The bosses of the Lucchese, Colombo, and Bonanno families were quick to give their blessing. The Genovese family was not approached because Castellano had gone into partnership with some of its members, and its boss, Vincent "The Chin" Gigante, could not be trusted.

The plot gained momentum when Castellano allowed a disobedient Gambino captain in Connecticut to be killed by a member of another crime family. "You just don't let people from another family kill a captain in our family; that's against the rules," observed Gravano.

Then on December 2 Aniello Dellacroce died and

Castellano did not attend the funeral and wake. "Paul showed total disrespect," observed Gravano. This enraged the conspirators and spurred them on to go forward with their plans to assassinate Castellano, he explained.

To a hushed and expectant courtroom, straining to hear what witness Gravano was saying in his hesitant, expressionless, monotonal voice, Sammy the Bull then outlined in detail the plot to kill Paul Castellano.

"We were wondering if and when Paul might make a move—if he might strike," Gravano went on. Castellano said he was going "to wreck John's crew" because members of that crew had violated·a family rule against drug dealing.

According to Gravano, Gotti suggested two possible plans for killing Castellano—shoot him at his Staten Island home or at a Staten Island diner he used to eat at before meetings with his lawyer, James LaRossa—both of which were rejected.

Finally Frankie DeCicco, the Castellano loyalist turned traitor, informed Gotti and Gravano that he and Tommy Gambino would be meeting Castellano and Bilotti for dinner at Sparks Steak House on December 16 and the three agreed that Castellano would be ambushed there.

The final planning session was held the night before Castellano and Bilotti were killed. Gotti, Gravano, and Angelo Ruggiero sat down with eight other Gambino capos and soldiers in the basement of Gravano's drywall construction company on Stillwell Avenue in Brooklyn and discussed how the murders would be carried out.

By now at the defense table John Gotti's right hand had formed a clenched fist and he had fixed Gravano in a steady stare. The testimony that would send him to prison for life was about to come down.

At the Brooklyn meeting Gotti and DeCicco did the talking, Gravano continued. They designated Eddie

Lino, Salvatore Scala, Vinnie Artuso, and John Carneglia to be the shooters. Gravano and Anthony "Tony Roach" Rampino would be the backup shooters, along with Iggy Alogna, Joe Watts, and Angelo Ruggiero. Not all of these were told the victims would be Castellano and Bilotti, Gravano continued, to avoid a tip-off.

Another meeting was held the afternoon of the shooting in a small park overlooking the East River on Manhattan's Lower East Side.

"I brought a gun and a walkie-talkie . . . so we could communicate with one another," Gravano said. "We told them exactly who was going and that it had to be done, so don't miss. At that time we told them Paul and Tommy were going."

There were ten Gambino men stationed around East Forty-sixth Street between Second and Third avenues as the Christmas rush hour began, Gravano continued. The designated killers—Carneglia, Lino, Scala, and Artuso—were in front of Sparks Steak House. Backup shooters Iggy Alogna, Joe Watts, and Angelo Ruggiero were up the block near Second Avenue. Tony Roach Rampino, the fourth backup shooter, was stationed across the street from Sparks opposite the four gunmen who were lying in wait. "If they got away and ran across the street, or if somebody tried to interfere, then Tony would whack them," Gravano explained.

As for himself and John Gotti, Gravano went on, "Me and John got in the car and parked on the Third Avenue side of Forty-sixth Street.

"We had Sparks Steak House sandwiched in," observed Gravano dryly as he concluded his testimony for the day.

His first day of testimony at the Gotti trial was just the beginning of a long period of service to the U.S. government for Sammy Gravano. Under the agreement he had made with the U.S. attorney, eastern district, Gravano would be testifying at trials for the next two years. In exchange Gravano was to face a maximum twenty-year prison term and pay a $250,000 fine. Had he not turned government witness, Gravano would have faced life in prison without parole. Under the agreement, Gravano's sentence would not be pronounced until he fulfilled his two-year period of testifying for the government. At that time Judge I. Leo Glasser could give Gravano less than twenty years at his discretion. If, however, Gravano did not abide by his agreement and gave false or misleading testimony he could be prosecuted for any crime to which he admitted.

Day Two

By nine o'clock the following morning the hallway outside Judge Glasser's courtroom was more jammed than usual. The doors to the courtroom would not open until nine-fifty, yet both the spectator and press lines were overflowing. Various Gotti supporters patrolled the space between the two lines. "Ya ready to get sick again?" Jackie the Nose D'Amico yelled at the press line. "Ya ready to get *really* sick today, eh?"

"*Nineteen murders,*" everybody in the press line was commenting on Gravano's sensational confession, "and for this he's only going to get twenty years or *less!*"

"Don't worry. If Gotti walks, they'll give him the max," commented a reporter.

When the doors finally opened, the two lines emptied into the courtroom in one jostling rush. Within minutes the artists were poised to start in on Sammy the Bull's broad, bony face, his small, sad eyes, perpetual frown, and occasional boyish grin. And, pads and ballpoints at the ready, the press was chomping at the bit for things to get under way. Today Sammy was going to relate the gory details of the Castellano assassination and the murders of five Gambino family members.

Taking the stand, the short, stocky Gravano stared straight ahead while the man he betrayed looked him over, smiling knowingly.

Gravano began by telling the court that he and Gotti were parked in Gotti's black Lincoln sedan, which had tinted windows, on the northwest corner of Third Avenue and Forty-sixth Street, looking down Forty-sixth Street at Sparks Steak House, when a car drew up near them and stopped for a red light. Gravano recognized Thomas Bilotti and Paul Castellano inside. "I turned and told John they were right next to us," Gravano said. Then he picked up his walkie-talkie to tell the gunmen in front of Sparks that "they were stopped at the light and were coming through."

When the light changed, the black Lincoln carrying Castellano and Bilotti turned right across Third Avenue, went down Forty-sixth Street, and parked in front of Sparks Steak House, where Gotti's four gunmen were waiting for them. Castellano was shot first. He got hit as soon as he opened the backseat car door. Bilotti then got out of the car and was squatting down peering through the back window to see what was happening to Castellano when he was shot from behind. "He was actually watching Paul get shot," Gravano observed.

Soon the Lincoln bearing Gotti and Gravano was abreast of the murder scene and Gravano, looking out the right window, saw Bilotti lying on the pavement in a pool of blood. "I noticed, I looked down at Tommy Bilotti," Gravano continued, "I said he was gone. We drove a little faster to Second Avenue. We made a right. We went back to my office in Brooklyn."

The police determined that Thomas Bilotti had been shot four times in the head and four times in the chest and back, and Castellano had been shot six times in the head and once in the chest.

Later Sammy Gravano was told that Thomas

Gambino, Castellano's nephew, entered Sparks Steak House just after the shooting and immediately ran into Gambino capo Frankie DeCicco, Castellano's betrayer, who had been scheduled to dine with the boss along with capo James Failla and soldier Johnny Gammarino. According to Gravano, DeCicco told Gambino: "Your uncle just got shot. Just go back to your car and leave."

It was at about this point in Gravano's testimony that court proceedings were suddenly interrupted by the screams of a woman coming from the courtroom entrance. At first they were muffled by the courtroom doors. Then, after sounds of scuffling, one of the doors burst open and an older woman in black appeared shrieking into the courtroom: "I spit on him! . . . Sammy Gravano! I spit on him!"

Sammy the Bull winced and shifted his weight in the witness chair while John Gotti turned and peered at the distraught woman as half a dozen marshals wrestled her out of the courtroom. Back in the corridor the woman kept shrieking, then fell to her knees and sobbed uncontrollably. New York *Post* columnist Mike McAlary was on the scene and he asked a young woman who appeared to be with the older woman what the outburst was all about.

"Murder!" replied the young woman, who identified herself as the older woman's niece. "Murder! Sammy Gravano killed her sons, the Carino brothers. The mother comes for revenge!"

As the marshals dragged the still screaming woman to the elevator, Sammy Gravano resumed his testimony. Murder was in the air in courtroom number five. Sammy the Bull had just recounted two. Anna Carini had just lamented two more. Now Sammy would relate five more grisly killings. But before he did, he enlightened the jury on how John Gotti was elected boss of the Gambino family.

Two days after the murders of Castellano and Bilotti, all the captains met in a back room at

Caesar's East Restaurant, a place Sammy Gravano owned on East Fifty-eighth Street in Manhattan. The men sat down at one long table presided over by Joe N. Gallo, the family's *consiglière*, who was flanked by John Gotti and Frankie DeCicco. According to Gravano, Gallo told the captains that he was temporarily in charge and that there would not be any trouble, that their men were not in any danger and should not carry guns or "overreact to anything."

Gravano went on to testify that a week later another meeting of all the captains was called in Brooklyn to elect a successor to Paul Castellano. The captains were all seated around a large conference table with an armed Gravano and an armed Angelo Ruggiero standing watch over them, "for intimidation purposes," Gravano explained. DeCicco nominated John Gotti to be boss, and, according to Gravano, "They went right around the table. Everybody nominated John. John was the boss."

Now it was time for Sammy to recount some of the achievements of the new Gotti administration, beginning with five murders.

Robert "Di B" DiBernardo was the first. DiBernardo, the family's chief pornographer, was also active in the construction trade and did a good deal of business with Sammy Gravano, seeing him at least twice a week. Gravano testified that Gotti, who was in jail awaiting trial at the time, was so "steaming hot with rage" over slights and insults from Di B, he ordered Gravano to kill him. At first Gravano tried to talk Gotti out of it, but Gotti remained adamant. In the end Sammy had no choice. He had to follow the boss's orders.

One day Gravano summoned DiBernardo to the offices of his drywall company on Stillwell Avenue in Brooklyn to meet with him and his crew, Gravano testified. In a lifeless monotone Gravano told the jury, "Di B came in. He came downstairs. He sat down. The old man Joe Paruta got up and I told him to get Di B a cup of coffee. He got up. In the cabinet there was a .38 with a silencer. He took the gun out, walked over to Di B, and shot him twice in the back of the head." Gravano and his men then loaded DiBernardo's body into the trunk of Gotti codefendant Frank Locascio's car and DiBernardo was never seen again.

Gravano insisted to the jury that he was ordered to kill DiBernardo by Gotti and had not asked permission to murder a man he considered a friend.

Liborio Milito, a member of Gravano's crew, was next. Gravano believed Milito had betrayed him by "badmouthing our administration," and asked Gotti if he could have him killed. "Gotti gave me permission to take him out," Gravano told the jurors, and specifically asked that his brother, Gene Gotti, be given the assignment.

Milito was then told to come to a club Gravano owned, Tali's, in the Bensonhurst section of Brooklyn, on the pretext that he was to discuss killing someone else. Gravano was sitting with two other men playing cards when Milito walked into the club.

"Johnny Carneglia went to the other room. Had a gun with a silencer on it. Came out. Shot him one time behind the head. When he fell down he put the gun under his chin and pulled the trigger," Gravano testified in his customary matter-of-fact tone of voice.

With the relating of each killing Sammy the Bull was adding additional years to John Gotti's all but inevitable prison term. Gotti seemed to sense this, for he abandoned the steady, smirking stare he had fastened on Gravano during his account of the Castellano and Bilotti slayings, in favor of displaying a number of dismissive gestures toward the government's star witness, accompanied by whispered remarks into his attorney's ears, instead. Had he begun to squirm? members of the press corps asked each other.

Time for Louis DiBono, a partner in one of

Gravano's construction companies whose bullet-ridden body was found in October 1990 in his car in a World Trade Center parking garage.

DiBono had given Gravano problems for months over their construction partnership and Gravano had appealed to Gotti more than once to get rid of him. Finally Gotti himself became fed up with DiBono and gave the job to get rid of him to the head of DiBono's crew. A few weeks later "John told me he was gone," testified Gravano.

Gotti's next victim was Wilfred "Willie Boy" Johnson, a codefendant in Gotti's earlier racketeering trial, who had betrayed Gotti day in and day out as a paid government informant for sixteen years. Gravano testified that Gotti gave the job of killing Johnson to Eddie Lino, who had helped with the Castellano slaying. Willie Boy's body was found riddled with fourteen bullets on August 29, 1988.

Finally there was the murder of Francesco Oliverri. According to Gravano's testimony, Johnny Gambino, a captain in the Gambino family, had asked permission from John Gotti to kill Oliverri because Oliverri had killed Giuseppe Gambino, a Gambino family soldier. Gravano then assisted Gambino soldier Bobby Cabert in killing Oliverri one morning as he was moving his car from one side of the street to the other to comply with alternate-side-of-the-street parking regulations.

After Gravano recounted the Oliverri murder, prosecutor Gleeson started questioning him about Gotti's mole in the New York Police Department, Detective William J. Peist of the intelligence squad.

For over a year the FBI's sixteen-member Gambino Squad had suspected someone in the New York law enforcement community was passing highly confidential information to John Gotti, items such as the location of FBI and OCTF bugs, the names and addresses of jurors, and the dates on which the government intended to indict various members of the Gambino family.

A lengthy and intricate investigation eventually turned up the name of Detective William J. Peist, who, it was found, was connected to two Gambino family associates, Peter Mavis, a gambler, and George Helbig, a major bookmaker in the Little Italy crew run by capo Joe "Butch" Corrao. Among the intelligence Peist turned over to Joe Butch and John Gotti, through Helbig, was the location of two ongoing bugs directed at Sammy Gravano, one in a trailer office of one of Gravano's Brooklyn construction companies, and another in Gravano's Brooklyn social club, Tali's, in Bensonhurst. As it turned out, Gravano was the payoff man between Gotti and Helbig and Peist.

By March 1991 the FBI had developed a fairly strong circumstantial case against Peist, Mavis, and Helbig, but needed a witness to their espionage activities to obtain an indictment. In November that witness was found. He was Salvatore Gravano. On the basis of Gravano's testimony Peist was indicted in December, along with Joe "Butch" Corrao and George Helbig, for racketeering and obstruction of justice. They were due to stand trial in Brooklyn Federal Court. Sammy Gravano was to be the government's star witness.

So there it was. Sammy Gravano's testimony had corroborated the tapes of Gotti discussing his murders. It looked worse than ever for John Gotti. It would be difficult indeed for Albert Krieger to significantly demolish the evidence arrayed against his client. After the second day of the trial it appeared all but certain that the prosecution would prevail. John Gotti seemed to sense this, for on the third day of the trial he abandoned his grimacing and gesturing for a more composed demeanor. From now on a subdued look of resignation began to suffuse his face. It was all over. He might spend the rest of his life in the can. But somehow Gotti's facial expression seemed to indicate that he did not really care. One of the last true believers in La Cosa Nostra, he had done the right thing, according to his lights. On the first day of his trial Gotti was heard on one of the tapes reciting the litany of his credo: "And this is gonna be a Cosa Nostra till I die. Be it an hour from now, or be it tonight, or a hundred years from now when I'm in jail. It's gonna be a Cosa Nostra. . . . It's gonna be the way I say it's gonna be, a Cosa Nostra."

Day Three

On the third day of his testimony Sammy the Bull gave the jurors an inside glimpse of the day-to-day workings of a Cosa Nostra family. Speaking in a quiet voice and showing no emotion, Sammy painted a portrait of the Gambino crime family as a violent, highly lucrative enterprise in which murder, loan-sharking, and extortion were routine activities. Making money was the ultimate goal of the enterprise and all money made eventually trickled up to the boss, John Gotti. Testifying proudly that he was the biggest earner in the family, Gravano said that from profits off his construction industry rackets alone he sent $100,000 a month up to Gotti, or $1.2 million a year.

Then there were the payments (called "turn-ins") Gotti received from the capos who controlled the private garbage collection industry, the loan-sharking industry, the garment trucking industry, the skimming of gasoline excise taxes, and the shipping industry on the Brooklyn docks. These payments were in addition to the cash gifts each of the twenty-three capos were expected to give the boss on his birthday and at Christmas. Averaging $3,000 from each capo (Gravano usually gave $5,000), Gotti took in around $150,000 a year from his men in gifts alone. John Gotti, it was clear, was making millions of dollars a year, yet for income tax purposes he declared only the modest income he earned from two no-show jobs at Arc Plumbing and Scorpio Manufacturing.

Murder was the ultimate engine behind this moneymaking machine. The threat of murder loomed over the heads of all Gambino associates in the industries the family controlled or exerted influence over. And it was the omnipresent threat of murder that kept the Gambino capos and soldiers in line. Step out of line and you got killed; it was as simple as that. To illustrate this point prosecutor Gleeson got Sammy Gravano to testify on all ten murders in which he claimed Gotti was involved.

After briefly alluding to the already mentioned murders of DiBernardo, DiBono, Milito, Johnson, and Oliverri, which names caused a set frown to appear on Gotti's face, Gravano went on to describe the murders of Michael DeBatt (he had a drug problem), Thomas Spinelli (for testifying before a grand jury), Edward Garafolo (for showing disrespect), Frank Fiala (for cheating Gravano out of money), and a man known as Tommy Sparrow who was done in by Louie Fats and Philly Dogs (for testifying before a grand jury).

As an aside Gravano testified that sometimes he would help out the family of one of his victims. After killing Liborio Milito, a member of his own crew, Sammy gave his widow some money and spent $20,000 in construction work to finish building her house.

According to Gravano's testimony, John Gotti was not above murdering even his closest associates. When his Bergin buddy and coconspirator against Castellano, Tony Roach Rampino, got busted in 1988 for selling heroin to an undercover cop, Gotti told Gravano he would have him killed if he made bail.

Another crime routinely committed by the Gambino enterprise was jury tampering. Gravano testified that Gotti authorized him to pay a $10,000 bribe to a member of the jury in the 1990 heroin-smuggling narcotics trial of capo Eddie Lino, who won an acquittal. Gravano said he had been told by another mobster that the daughter of a good friend was on the jury and could be reached with a $10,000 gift.

"Gotti was elated with it and whatever it had to be it was okay and I was to handle it," Gravano testified. After winning his case, Lino reimbursed Gravano for the payoff.

But that was nothing compared to what Gotti pulled off during his 1986–1987 federal racketeering trial. That trial may not have been won for Gotti by Bruce Cutler, but by a bought juror. According to Gravano, Gotti found out from a friend of a Gambino capo that the foreman of the anonymous jury, George H. Pate, of East Norwich, Long Island, could be reached for $60,000. Gotti then ordered Gravano to deliver three payments of $20,000 each to an intermediary, Bosko Radonjich, head of the Westies gang, who would turn the money over to Mr. Pate. Gravano did what he was told. As a result of the jury's not-guilty vote, Gotti and his codefendants were acquitted.

In February 1992, George Pate was indicted along with Radonjich for conspiracy and obstruction of justice. Radonjich fled to his native Yugoslavia in 1991 and remains a fugitive, and George Pate pleaded not guilty at his arraignment, then stood trial in Brooklyn Federal Court. Largely as a result of Sammy Gravano's testimony he was convicted of obstruction of justice in November 1992.

During the third day of Gravano's testimony Judge Glasser excused a second juror, number 9, and ordered the reasons for the dismissal sealed. Earlier in the week the judge dismissed juror number 7 and sealed the reasons. These dismissals bothered both the defense and the media, both of whom petitioned that the reasons be unsealed.

In the hallway after the third day there was much talk of the dismissal of the two secret jurors.

"I bet the two jurors woulda found John not guilty," yelled a Gambino soldier at a clutch of reporters. "Tell your readers that!"

There was also much embittered talk about Gravano. One of Gotti's most ardent supporters, capo John D'Amico, also addressed a bunch of reporters.

"He [Gravano] touches everybody. That's the devil and the government wants to sleep with him."

"I can't wait until Krieger cuts him up tomorrow," offered another Gotti groupie. "Too bad Brucie ain't here. That's another thing this Glasser did that was not right, firing Brucie from the case."

Day Four

Now, on the fourth day of Gravano's testimony, it was defense attorney Albert Krieger's turn to cross-examine the government's star witness.

KRIEGER: When you got out of the Army it was said to you, Sammy, there's only one road open for you. That's go out with a gun and rob people. That never happened, did it?

GRAVANO: When you grow up in a neighborhood like I grew in, and you grew with the people I grew with, it was an environment. I was a kid . . .

KRIEGER: Go ahead.

GRAVANO: When I was a kid, I was involved in gangs, dropped out of school in the eighth grade. It was the environment. . . . It didn't seem wrong, the whole life-style didn't seem wrong.

KRIEGER: In the society which you say you grew up and which shaped your life, a person who is playing the role that you are playing at this point would be called a certain name, isn't that so?

GRAVANO: Probably.

KRIEGER: And that name is?

GRAVANO: An informer.

KRIEGER: Some other word?

GRAVANO: Rat.

The first day of Albert Krieger's cross-examination

of Sammy the Bull Gravano lasted only two hours because bomb threats emptied the courtroom twice. In those two hours Krieger sought to rattle Gravano and get him to admit the deal he made with the government was to "deliver John Gotti's head on a platter" in order to eventually gain his own freedom.

Though Albert Krieger was a brilliant defense attorney possessing a commanding presence and a powerful voice, he failed to rattle Sammy the Bull and failed even to get the diminutive mobster to admit he had made a deal to deliver John Gotti's head on a platter.

Sammy Gravano, a former amateur boxer, rolled with Krieger's punches, and on several occasions parried the defense attorney's questions deftly, sometimes turning them to his advantage and on one occasion causing the spectators and jurors to laugh at the defense attorney.

Krieger devoted considerable time to questioning Gravano about his plea agreement, trying to get him to admit the government awarded him the task of destroying John Gotti. Often his questioning was bitingly sarcastic.

KRIEGER: Mr. Gravano, what you were looking for, were you not, was not to spend all of your remaining days on this earth in jail, correct?

GRAVANO: I would imagine part of the reason is that.

KRIEGER: Part of the reason?

GRAVANO: Yes.

KRIEGER: And another reason was you wanted to turn yourself around and be a model citizen, correct?

GRAVANO: Not exactly.

KRIEGER: You are not looking forward, are you, to getting out of jail and advertising that you would like to be the guardian of orphan children?

GRAVANO: No.

KRIEGER: Or a role model for the youth of this city?

The answer to that is no also, isn't it?

GRAVANO: No, that's not the answer. That's not the answer.

KRIEGER: The answer is that you want to be a role model?

GRAVANO: Maybe that some other kids don't get their lives destroyed like I did.

Judging from the expressions on some of the jurors faces, Gravano's retort appeared to play well. There was something strangely believable about the no-nonsense Gravano.

Krieger, undismayed, kept pounding away at Gravano's motives to enter into a plea agreement with the government.

KRIEGER: And in the federal system when you are sentenced to a life term without benefit of parole, you come out of jail in a box, correct?

GRAVANO: I guess so.

KRIEGER: But your guilty plea to a racketeering charge could result in a sentence ranging from a maximum of twenty years all the way down to probation.

GRAVANO: It's a possibility.

KRIEGER: Without your plea bargain and testimony for the prosecution, Mr. Gravano, you could have faced a life sentence in the system's toughest prison, where inmates are locked in cages twenty-three hours a day and are lucky to get one shower a week.

GRAVANO: I believe it's two times a week.

At this some of the spectators and jurors and most of the reporters burst out laughing.

One spectator who didn't laugh was Roseanne Massa, sister of Gambino mobster Michael DeBatt who Sammy the Bull had murdered in his Bensonhurst social club, Tali's, in November 1987.

Roseanne Massa was reluctantly allowed by the marshals to sit in the last row of the spectators' section. There she sat, with two marshals standing guard beside her, glowering at Sammy Gravano, never taking her eyes off him, trying to make him squirm. For a second she was successful. Although Sammy never flinched when Gotti looked at him, when he first caught Roseanne Massa's vengeful gaze he quickly turned away.

Albert Krieger did not appear to be bothered by the laughter and took no notice of the venomous eye play between Gravano and Roseanne Massa. Resuming his cross-examination of the government's star witness, Krieger, composed and dignified, asked Gravano some questions about his businesses and his income that seemed pointless to many. Always the gentleman, Krieger called Sammy the Bull "Mr. Gravano" and rarely punched below the belt. His dignified courtroom style contrasted stridently with that of Gotti's former defense counsel Bruce Cutler, who regularly bullied, insulted, and ridiculed witnesses. One could imagine what Cutler would have done with the nickname Sammy the Bull. "Hey, Sammy," he might have said, "how come they call you the Bull? Is it because you're such a bullshit artist?"

"Objection!" the prosecution would cry.

"Sustained!" Judge Glasser would rule.

Sammy would not have to reply, but the effect of Cutler's remark would have remained in the jurors' heads.

Day Five

On the second day of his cross-examination of Sammy Gravano, Albert Krieger sought to show that the murders of Paul Castellano, Tommy Bilotti, Liborio Milito, and Louis DiBono benefited Gravano more than they benefited John Gotti and that it was therefore more reasonable to believe it was Gravano, not Gotti, who had instigated the killings.

KRIEGER: My question directed to you, sir, is as of now we have an understanding that you were told by Frank DeCicco [then a Castellano loyalist] that Castellano had made a threat on your life?

GRAVANO: That I will agree with.

KRIEGER: And is it not so, Mr. Gravano, that you obtained more than $1 million from a construction firm after your business associate, Liborio Milito, was murdered?

GRAVANO: Yes, I did.

KRIEGER: Isn't it a fact that Louie Milito severed his relationship with you and went into business with Tommy Bilotti?

GRAVANO: Yes.

KRIEGER: And it is a fact, is it not, that you felt betrayed by Louis Milito for doing what he did with Tommy Bilotti, right?

GRAVANO: When all the facts came out, yes, you are right, I did feel betrayed.

KRIEGER: And is it not true, Mr. Gravano, that you had a falling out with a business partner of yours, Louis DiBono?

GRAVANO: Yes, I had a problem with him.

KRIEGER: You had a problem with him that you wanted to resolve by killing him?

GRAVANO: Yes . . . the murder of Louie DiBono had nothing to do with the taxes, the money, or the business. He didn't come when John had called him, when the boss had called him. In my role as underboss I agreed with John's decision on killing Louie DiBono.

Albert Krieger appeared quite pleased with the way his line of questioning had gone. Nevertheless, the fact remained that John Gotti had said on tape: "Anytime you got a partner who don't agree with us, we kill him. You go to the boss and your boss kills him." And in reference to Louie DiBono, Gotti had said on tape: "He died because he refused to come in when I called. He didn't do nothin' else wrong." Who was the jury going to believe was ultimately behind the killings of Castellano, Bilotti, Milito, and DiBono? Gravano or Gotti? More than likely the jury would name Gotti.

On the second day of his cross-examination Sammy Gravano appeared much more confident than on the first day and John Gotti lost the composure he had displayed earlier in the trial. Muttering to himself and his attorneys and glowering contemptuously at his betrayer, he repeatedly pointed a finger toward the witness stand, Judge Glasser, and the lead prosecutor, John Gleeson, saying audibly, "One, two, three."

Returning to Gravano's motives in entering into his plea agreement with the government, Krieger tried, unsuccessfully, to tie that agreement to an effort to destroy John Gotti.

KRIEGER: You see yourself, do you not, as a witness that will be of assistance to the government in obtaining the conviction of John Gotti?

GRAVANO: No.

KRIEGER: You see yourself then as a person who just has no interest whatsoever in what the outcome of this case will be, right?

GRAVANO: That I have no interest?

KRIEGER: That you have no interest. You don't care what happens. Let the jury come in guilty, let the jury come in not guilty. Means nothing to you.

GRAVANO: In a way. They're the jury. And I'm not a juror.

These words concluded Albert Krieger's second day of cross-examination of Sammy Gravano. The talk in the hallway outside the courtroom was that Krieger did little to hurt the prosecution's case against John Gotti. As each day of the trial passed, it was becoming more and more apparent to all that Gotti was going to lose, and lose big. Gotti's chief supporters at the trial—Peter Gotti, Jackie Nose D'Amico, and Joseph DeCicco—looked particularly upset. As soon as he left the courtroom Peter Gotti tore down the hallway to the elevators without talking to anybody, followed by a disgusted-looking Joe DeCicco. The voluble Jackie Nose D'Amico paused to ask a group of reporters if Sammy didn't make them sick and to observe that if Bruce Cutler hadn't been disqualified by Glasser, "John would be winnin' this case."

Day Six

The day before Sammy Gravano's final two days of cross-examination New York was outraged by a shooting unprecedented in the annals of organized crime. A thirty-eight-year-old woman, Patricia Capozzalo, a mother and sister of mob turncoat Peter "Fat Pete" Chiodo, a Lucchese capo, was shot twice as she sat in her car outside her Bensonhurst home.

Never before had the Cosa Nostra tried to rub out an innocent blood relative of a family capo. Never before had the Cosa Nostra tried to kill a woman. Suddenly the rules had changed. Now there was no code of honor left. As New York *Post* columnist Mike McAlary commented, "The only rule is that there are no rules." With this attempted murder, the families of all mob turncoats were suddenly at risk; the families of jurors, even, could be at risk.

As Judge Glasser's Brooklyn courtroom was filling up on Thursday, March 12, the talk was of the attempted murder of Patricia Capozzalo and what it could mean to the trial. "Who knows? Maybe Sammy's family will be next" was the thought on everyone's lips.

Albert Krieger chose to ridicule Sammy Gravano's account of the Castellano murder as he began his third day of cross-examination of the government's star witness.

Zeroing in on Sammy Gravano's testimony that he and Gotti drove by the murder scene on East Forty-sixth Street, Krieger sought to make Sammy's account appear implausible, without much success. By now Sammy was a veteran witness. He had learned how to put a defense attorney in his place. Krieger resumed his questioning in a voice heavy with sarcasm.

KRIEGER: Instead of leaving the scene as quickly as possible . . . you and Mr. Gotti drove, I think the word is "slowly," that is how you described it, didn't you?

GRAVANO: Yes.

KRIEGER: Drove slowly across Third Avenue over to where the homicide had taken place and you looked out the window—had to roll it down?

GRAVANO: No.

KRIEGER: You looked out the window and said, "By gosh, Tommy Bilotti is dead"?

GRAVANO: Without the "by gosh."

Unable to make his ridicule of Gravano's account of the Castellano assassination compelling, Krieger turned to other matters in an effort to make Gravano appear unconvincing.

KRIEGER: Is it fair to say, Mr. Gravano, that you were greedy in your construction industry dealings?

GRAVANO (proudly): I was a big earner in the family.

KRIEGER: But didn't your income become much bigger after the murder of Mr. Castellano?

GRAVANO: I grew.

KRIEGER: You grew after Paul Castellano was killed.

GRAVANO: I continuously grew.

Turning to tax matters, Krieger began asking Gravano whether he was worried that the Internal Revenue Service would investigate him because he and his partners did not pay income taxes for their construction companies.

KRIEGER: You did not want the Internal Revenue Service to look too closely at you, Salvatore Gravano, correct?

GRAVANO: Because of this deal?

KRIEGER: Because of anything you were doing.

GRAVANO: I don't think anybody wants the IRS to look at them.

KRIEGER: It is further a fact, is it not, that you hope to escape prosecution, not only from tax matters, but from all other matters as a result of your deal?

GRAVANO: I've never discussed tax matters.

KRIEGER: I didn't ask you what you discussed. I asked you what you hope.

GRAVANO: I hope to?

KRIEGER: To escape prosecution for tax matters and every criminal, scurvy act that you've committed in your life?

GRAVANO: I hope so, yes.

In subsequent questioning Albert Krieger got nowhere with Sammy the Bull Gravano. Sammy was too cunning and defiant to be successfully baited by Krieger. His quick, dismissive comebacks to Krieger's probings frequently won the respect of the press section, which conceded with near unanimity that Gravano's testimony was the hit the prosecutors had hoped it would be.

After Krieger concluded his cross-examination, Anthony Cardinale, Frank Locascio's attorney, rose to ask Gravano a few questions. For some reason Cardinale's facing the witness animated Gotti, who had remained quite subdued during Krieger's questioning.

Cardinale, taller and younger and brasher than Krieger, tried to demean Gravano by insinuating he took steroids in prison to seem tough when, in reality, he was a weak man who was overheard crying to his girlfriend on the MCC phone about how horrible prison life was.

Harping on Gravano's dislike of jail, Cardinale asked him if it was true what he had heard from Sammy's cellmates, that he tried to scrape through prison windows, smuggle in fishing tackle, loosen tiles, and dig a hole in his cell floor in an effort to escape.

"Things like that were discussed," replied Gravano.

"You couldn't escape," Cardinale insisted, "and it was then that you made a decision to become an informant."

"No," replied Gravano.

At one point Cardinale tried to question Gravano about murders he had confessed to that didn't involve Gotti and was prevented from doing so by Judge Glasser. An argument on the issue was held at a sidebar, without the jury present, at which Cardinale told Glasser he did not intend "to get into how he [Gravano] killed them, how he dismembered them," or tell the jury about how Gravano in 1978 killed his brother-in-law, Nick Scibetta, and "chopped him up into little pieces and how they had a funeral for the guy's hand."

During the sidebar, Gotti suddenly stood up and faced the reporters and television people covering the trial. Then, pointing toward Gravano and muttering the word "junk," he stuck a simulated syringe into his left arm.

It had become clear to all at this point that the defense had run out of ammunition, if it ever had any in the first place, and the cross-examination of Gravano was sputtering out. Cardinale's further attempts to demean Gravano, full of inadmissable innuendos and insinuations, soon came to no avail and it was time for Sammy Gravano to make his final exit. Springing off the witness stand and walking briskly behind two federal marshals, he disappeared through the door the jurors normally used, while John Gotti made the sign of the cross and feigned wiping a tear from his eyes.

The high point of the trial of John Gotti was now over and the prosecution was secretly rejoicing. Sammy Gravano's testimony had corroborated much of the evidence on the most crucial tapes. He had successfully linked Gotti to eleven murders, and to jury tampering and obstruction of justice. The heart of the government's case was now solidly won. It remained to clear up several relatively minor charges in the indictment: loan-sharking, obstruction of justice, illegal gambling, and income tax evasion. For Maloney, Gleeson, and company these would be mere bagatelles.

40

The Summations

*Get my cell ready. . . . Get Joe Butch's cell ready, and
get Fat Georgie's cell ready. And nobody is taking the
stand. Tell them to go fight. Don't worry about it.
Don't worry about us going to jail. Me, Number One!
I like jail better than I like the streets.*

JOHN GOTTI

After two weeks of riveting testimony from Sammy
the Bull Gravano, prosecutor John Gleeson
addressed himself to the lesser charges in the indictment, playing, among other things, tapes to prove
obstruction of justice charges against Gotti.

The tapes demonstrated that Gotti intended to
refuse to testify at the 1990 obstruction of justice trial
of Thomas Gambino and would order two of his captains to do likewise, even though in refusing to testify
all three would be cited for contempt of court and
sent to jail as a result.

On one taped discussion about the coming Thomas
Gambino trial between Gotti and his then attorney,
Bruce Cutler, Cutler advised Gotti to testify and Gotti
objected. Cutler then told Gotti, "My duty is to protect you."

To which Gotti replied, "No, your duty is to listen."

Bruce Cutler was on hand in Brooklyn Federal Court the day Gotti's trial resumed after Sammy Gravano's testimony. Sitting in the front row of the spectators' section alongside Gotti captains Jackie Nose D'Amico, Peter Gotti, and Joe DeCicco, he winked and smiled at Gotti and repeatedly whispered what appeared to be derisive comments about prosecutor Gleeson into D'Amico's ear. Later, in the hallway outside the courtroom, Cutler told reporters: "John Gotti feels great. He feels he will win, and so do I."

"You know, if I was in there," Cutler told Gene Mustain, coauthor of a biography of Gotti, "you'd write another book, you'd write five more books. . . . You know," he continued, "I don't have Albert Krieger's good manners. I don't have John Mitchell's intellect. But having fought three previous cases for John, I know all the facts."

The irrepressible Cutler blustered about the hallway, yelling greetings at various Gotti supporters, as if nothing had changed. Yet as far as his situation with Gotti and the current trial were concerned, everything had changed. Judge Glasser had disqualified him from representing Gotti in court and a special prosecutor appointed by Judge Glasser had recently recommended that Cutler be tried for misdemeanor criminal contempt of court for a series of public comments he made which the prosecution contended prejudiced the government's right to a fair trial.

The post-Gravano testimony lasted from Monday, March 16, to Monday, March 30. Much of it, coming on the heels of some of the most exciting testimony ever heard at a Mafia trial, was somewhat tedious. In connection with the charges of tax evasion against Gotti, three of Gotti's former employers—Anthony Gurino, boss of Arc Plumbing; Michael Coiro, president of Scorpio Marketing; and Ignaccio Minucci, manager of Capri Construction—told the court that Gotti held paying jobs with their concerns but did no work. The modest income from these no-show jobs was all that Gotti declared on the few tax returns he filed between 1984 and 1989, and after 1985 he was making hundreds of thousands of dollars a year in illegal earnings as boss of the Gambino crime family.

The most interesting events in the post-Gravano period fell outside the testimony. There was the shouting match between Gotti and Judge Glasser, the news of a Genovese family plot to kill Sammy Gravano's wife and two children, the appearance in court of celebrities Cindy Adams, Jay Black, Mickey Rourke, and Anthony Quinn, and more news of the plot to bribe juror Pate.

Judge Glasser's outburst at John Gotti occurred during prosecutor Gleeson's questioning of Anthony Gurino of Arc Plumbing. Gotti had been smirking and gesturing at Gleeson, mockingly blowing kisses off the palm of his hand at him, when all of a sudden Judge Glasser, whose impatience with Gotti's courtroom antics had reached the boiling point, jumped up and said: "Excuse me. Excuse me. I am going to excuse the jury for a few minutes."

After the jury had filed out of the courtroom, Glasser looked at John Gotti sternly and said: "Mr. Gotti, this is addressed to you. If you want to continue to remain at this trial and at that table, I am going to direct you to remain at that table without making comments which can be heard in this courtroom, without gestures which are designed to comment on the character of the United States attorneys and the questions which are being asked of the witnesses.

"If you cannot refrain from doing that, I will have you removed from the courtroom," the judge went on. "You will watch the trial on a television screen downstairs. I am not going to tell you that again."

At which Gotti stood up, smoothed out his double-breasted jacket, and said: "That's your prerogative.

They don't need me to make gestures to describe them for sure."

"Mr. Gotti, I don't want to engage in any debate about this with you."

"Neither do I."

"I am just putting you on notice," emphasized Glasser.

"Neither do I," growled Gotti. "I am not here for a paycheck," and he sat down.

Then, on March 19, news reached the courtroom that two members of the Genovese crime family had been overheard by an FBI listening device discussing a plot to kill Sammy Gravano's wife and children. Details of the plot were contained in a racketeering indictment that had been unsealed in Newark on March 18. The indictment charged that on January 22 at a meeting in Boston, Genovese mobsters John Marrone and Ralph Marino discussed killing Gravano's wife, Debra, and their two children, Gerard, nineteen, and Karen, sixteen, with James Martorano, a capo in the New England Patriarca family. The news struck the radio-television-newspaper press as odd, since it was well known that Debra Gravano had renounced her husband and left their Staten Island home when Gravano turned government informant. Nevertheless, gossip began circulating in the courtroom that Gotti had asked some of his friends in the Genovese family to take revenge for Gravano's devastatingly damaging testimony. However, the ever-vigilant Bruce Cutler, prowling the courtroom hallway, reassured reporters that "there's nobody safer in this city than Gravano's wife and children. They love John and he's devoted to them."

Contributing to the occasional circus atmosphere of the winding down of the trial were the visits of two Hollywood actors, Mickey Rourke, who gained a measure of notoriety for playing a wiseguy in *The Pope of Greenwich Village*, and Anthony Quinn, who gained worldwide fame playing gangsters on the screen.

Taking a seat in the press section, Rourke, dapper in a silver-gray double-breasted suit, told reporters: "John's a friend. I'm here because I'm interested. I do roles that are urban-type roles. Gotti knows that stuff. He is a very intelligent person who was generous in giving me his time." Rourke waved at Gotti across the well of the court and Gotti waved back. But the marshals would not allow the two to shake hands.

Later on in the day Anthony Quinn made a grand entrance into Judge Glasser's courtroom telling reporters he wanted to play Big Paul Castellano in a movie. Quinn also made an attempt to shake Gotti's hand and was thwarted by federal marshals. This led Gotti to rub two fingers together and remark, "See, we're this far away from Russia."

"This is the best drama going on in America right now," Quinn told reporters during a recess. "This is the greatest theater you can possibly see. . . . The heart of this drama is the friend who betrays a friend. . . . I'm not here to sit in judgment of Mr. Gotti, but in judgment of a friend who betrays a friend. Friendship is a sacred thing. When I was growing up in East Los Angeles, the worst thing was to be a snitch."

Quinn went on to tell reporters that he had made around thirty gangster films and "the boys" he portrayed liked him because he understood how to portray them. He was now looking forward to playing Paul Castellano because of the seventy-five-year-old mob boss's love affair with his thirty-year-old housemaid. "Now, *that's* a beautiful thing," the actor said.

On the road to the summations prosecutor Gleeson introduced a witness who had trailed Gotti for years, Detective Kenneth McCabe, who testified that six days after the murder of Paul Castellano he saw Gotti at the Veterans and Friends Social Club in Brooklyn, a club founded by Castellano and one Gotti was never seen at before, in the company of Gambino mobsters

Joe Messina, Joe Piney Armone, Angelo Ruggiero, and Tony Roach Rampino. McCabe was convinced the meeting had something to do with Gotti's impending coronation.

Addressing jury tampering charges against Gotti, Gleeson read a stipulation to the jury about juror number 11, George H. Pate, selling his not-guilty vote in Gotti's 1986–1987 racketeering trial which had resulted in the acquittals of Gotti and six of his associates. Gleeson said that Pate had visited Bosko Radonjich eleven times while the boss of the Westies gang and Gotti associate was serving a prison term in 1979.

Then there was the matter of the conspiracy to murder Corky Vastola, a member of the Genovese family, as a favor to a capo in that family. Gleeson played the relevant tapes.

GOTTI: Ya know, ya know what we gotta do. . .
GRAVANO: I wouldn't be surprised if this fucking kid . . .
GOTTI: . . . but if true . . . if it's him . . .
GRAVANO: He's gotta . . .
GOTTI: . . . he liaison, the liaison guy's gettin' whacked. Because . . .
GRAVANO: (clears throat)
GOTTI: . . . that's not, that don't belong to us. That's their fucking crew. And he's gotta get whacked! . . . You wanna, you wanna challenge the administration, we'll, we'll, you will meet the challenge. And you're going, you motherfucker.
GOTTI: You would've think he'd go along, right? I mean Corky. . . . I mean Corky, but I mean. You and all okayed it, the other guy ordered it, is what I'm saying, the brother-in-law. You okayed it.

Gleeson told the jury he admitted the tapes were somewhat unclear and ambiguous, but he reminded them that Salvatore Gravano had corroborated them, testifying that John Gotti had conspired to murder Corky Vastola.

Came time for Gleeson to go over the evidence for the other murder conspiracies, those against Castellano and Bilotti, and against Liborio Milito, Robert DiBernardo, and Louie DiBono. Again he played the relevant tapes to the jury and showed how Sammy Gravano's testimony corroborated what was on them. Then, at the end of his presentation, U.S. Attorney Andrew Maloney stood up and announced, "Your Honor, the United States rests."

A recess was then called by Judge Glasser and everyone poured into the hallway. Soon the members of the press were agreeing among themselves that the government's case was overwhelmingly strong. Some reporters, however, were predicting a hung jury. Meanwhile, the Gotti lawyers and supporters were looking glum as the lawyers prepared to mount their defense.

In the hallway melee there were a few writers scavenging for stories. One of these was Gay Talese, author of *Honor Thy Father*, a book about the Bonanno crime family. He was doing an article for the op-ed page of the *New York Times*. Fastidiously dressed in a hand-tailored three-piece suit that fit his slight frame to perfection, Talese tried to zero in on the burly Bruce Cutler, who was roaming around in an apparent hurry to go nowhere.

"But, Mr. Cutler, I'd just like to have a few words with—"

"Come on, don't bother me. I told you I'd talk to you later."

"But we haven't got much—"

"Did you hear me? Later. Later. Now get the fuck outa my way."

Back to the courtroom. It was time for the defense to present its case. Gotti's and Locascio's lawyers had petitioned Judge Glasser to let them call six witnesses to the stand: a tax attorney for John Gotti, a doctor who had prescribed steroids for Gravano, a hypnotist who had tried to help Gravano overcome fear, an acoustical engineer who would discredit the accuracy of transcripts of the FBI and OCTF tape recordings, an eyewitness who had testified for the prosecution about the murders of Bilotti and Castellano, and Corky Vastola, the New Jersey mobster Gotti was accused of conspiring to murder.

Of these six, Judge Glasser allowed only one to take the stand, Gotti's tax attorney, Murray Appleman, who testified he had advised Gotti not to file tax returns for the past seven years because during that period Gotti was either being investigated by law enforcement or under indictment. Judge Glasser ruled that the testimony of the five other defense witnesses was either irrelevant or extraneous. Thus the defense was prevented from addressing the major crimes of which Gotti and Locascio were accused: the five murders, conspiracy to murder, obstruction of justice, bribery of a public official, loan-sharking, and illegal gambling. In justifying his decisions, Judge Glasser ruled that the testimony of Gravano's physician and hypnotist was extraneous to Gravano's testimony, and Corky Vastola's intended testimony that he did not believe he was threatened by Gotti was irrelevant to the conspiracy against him the FBI tapes exposed and Sammy Gravano's testimony corroborated.

And so, after Murray Appleman's testimony Albert Krieger and Anthony Cardinale were compelled to rest for the defense.

As Judge Glasser strode out of the courtroom, his black robe swirling behind him, John Gotti stood up and, simultaneously pointing to the judge's chair and facing the reporters, asked: "What happened to our defense? Maybe I shoulda put on a little song-and-dance."

In the hallway outside the courtroom Bruce Cutler vented his frustrations to the reporters:

> One out of six is not a very good batting average. The other witnesses would be germane to Gravano's credibility and that is what John is angry about. We want to demonstrate Gravano's bad character. John would like the jury to know the whole story. John is not happy that we were not allowed to put on the case we wanted to. We wanted to expose Gravano for the lying coward he was, and that's why John feels frustrated.

Most of the media people in the hallway crowd were in agreement that Krieger and Cardinale had been faced with an impossible task. This time the government had too good a case. Gotti's own words on the tapes and the words of his betrayer were devastating.

On to the summations. Prosecutor Gleeson would go first. Locascio's lawyer, Anthony Cardinale, would go next. Then Albert Krieger, and lastly Andrew Maloney would give the rebuttal summation.

When Gotti's antithesis and prosecutor in two trials, John Gleeson, rose to present his summation to the jury, Gotti fixed him with his most deadly stare, eyes narrowed, contemptuous smirk on his lips.

Gleeson, wearing his usual conservative navy-blue suit and regimental striped tie, his pale, ascetic face adorned by his usual thick horn-rimmed glasses, began his summation in his usual grave and deliberate manner.

"This is not a media event. This is not a movie. It's not about movie stars. This is not a stage for oratory. This is a trial in an American courtroom, a trial in which your decision will be based on the evidence that came from the witness stand, from the tape recordings, the other physical exhibits, and on that alone.

"These two defendants, ladies and gentlemen, together with Salvatore Gravano, ran a crime family, La Cosa Nostra, the Gambino crime family.

"I submit to you, ladies and gentlemen, when you have this type of criminal committing this type of crime, there are only two ways to prove it. . . . There are only two ways to do it: One, catch them talking about their crimes. Figure out a way to find those secret meetings and record them. There's one other way. Get one of them to come in and tell you about the crimes. We did both."

Referring to the tapes, Gleeson said: "We caught six hours of it—and it's absolute mayhem: who they murdered, who they're gonna murder, why they had someone murdered, how much money they're making from the docks, construction. Six hours. That's all we needed. Those tapes convict these defendants."

That point made, Gleeson went on to address himself to Salvatore Gravano's testimony.

"The underboss decides to quit, a member of the inner circle with personal knowledge and participation, John Gotti's best friend decides to quit.

"The long and short of it is you have them on tape, you have their closest criminal ally, telling you what they did.

"I submit to you, ladies and gentlemen, you can and you should convict on the tapes alone. I submit to you that you can and you should convict on Salvatore Gravano's testimony alone. Together, as I have already mentioned, the proof is absolutely overwhelming."

Gleeson then explained for the jury what the racketeering and conspiracy charges were and urged the jury to accept Gravano's testimony on the Castellano murder. "He lived it with John Gotti and the other people who carried it out."

Gleeson also argued that the tapes show that John

Gotti authorized the other murders charged in the indictment: those of Robert DiBernardo, Liborio Milito, and Louis DiBono. He then played the relevant tapes, replete with all their obscenities.

"Murder is the heart and soul of this enterprise," Gleeson went on. "It's the way discipline is maintained, it was the way power was consolidated, it was the way to deal with people who had the audacity to speak with the government, and it was the way to deal with someone John Gotti thought might be a rat someday."

It was time for Anthony Cardinale, attorney for Frank Locascio, to stand up for the defense. A tall, robust man with a bushy mustache and dark hair, he was far more rhetorical than Mr. Gleeson, often raising his voice in impassioned defense of both Locascio and Gotti.

"This case is nothing but a glorified frame-up," he thundered, "a Hollywood production" directed by a vengeful prosecutor "who would do anything to get John Gotti at any cost, to do whatever it takes to win!"

Pointing to Gleeson, Cardinale went over to the prosecution table and, pounding his fists on it, said: "He wants to put his credibility on the line like that! Good, it's on the line."

While cleaning his glasses with his tie, Gleeson objected and at a sidebar Judge Glasser upheld the objection and told Cardinale, "I just think it's dead wrong and improper to personalize."

Addressing the issue of the credibility of Sammy Gravano, Cardinale told the jurors, "If anyone doubted Gravano's ability to successfully lie, they should talk to Gravano's wife, who for fourteen years did not know that he had murdered her own brother."

Cardinale went on to insist that the prosecution could never obtain a conviction of Gotti and Locascio on the tapes alone. "Without Gravano, good-bye case!" he shouted to the jury.

"Gravano is a tremendous survivor," Cardinale went on, "who repeatedly lied and tailored his testimony to fit bits and pieces of the taped conversations. He's not Mr. Gotti's best friend; he's *Mr. Gleeson's best friend!*"

Referring to Gleeson's contention that the tapes alone, or Gravano's testimony alone, was sufficient to convict Mr. Gotti and Mr. Locascio, Cardinale roared, "Either one is not sufficient, the two put together are disgusting."

Albert Krieger also zeroed in on Sammy Gravano and the deal he had made with the government to testify against John Gotti.

"All the court can do at sentencing—except maybe gagging at nineteen murders—is to give him twenty years," Krieger shouted as he began his summation. "And Mr. Gravano testified he expected to get less than the maximum. . . . Nineteen murders—eighteen years in jail—less than a year per murder. Where are we? Is that where our system of justice has dropped to? Award a sick, demented serial killer his freedom, in exchange for what?" Then, pointing at John Gotti, he exploded: "In exchange for *that man's head*! . . . It reeks that's what it does."

Albert Krieger was a robust, athletic man with a bull neck and a bald head, like his predecessor, Bruce Cutler; but unlike Cutler, who was twenty years his junior, he behaved like a gentleman in the courtroom, raising his voice, yes, but never indulging in such Cutlerian tactics as throwing the indictment in a garbage can or demeaning mob witnesses by calling them, sardonically, by their nicknames, and then commenting on them as he did in Gotti's 1990 assault trial: "Joe the Fish. . . . Do they call you that because you stink like a fish head?"

In general Krieger tried to keep the tone of his summation on a high plane. He told the jury:

"Ladies and gentlemen of the jury, Mr. Gotti, charged with a crime in this courtroom, is no different from, no better than, no lesser than any person, any citizen, be that person young, old, black, white, one social status, another social status, no different at all and entitled to the same representation. And that representation is the best.

"Make one thing clear to you. I try, as clear as it is to me: I walk into that door ten feet tall, three ax handles wide across the chest. My eyes shoot lightning, my voice is thunder. I represent the people. I speak to you on behalf of constitutional liberties."

At a sidebar after Krieger's summation, which concentrated almost wholly on discrediting the testimony of Sammy Gravano, John Gleeson asked Judge Glasser to be allowed to present a short rebuttal summation before that of Andrew Maloney, explaining that he wanted to address Cardinale's denunciation of him as the "Get-John-Gotti-at-any-cost" prosecutor. Judge Glasser assented and Gleeson began his rebuttal by telling the jury that "the defense had ranted and raved about star witness, Sammy the Bull Gravano, not because Gravano lied but because he is their nightmare."

At this Cardinale leapt to his feet and yelled, "Whoa, whoa, whoa!" at which Judge Glasser shouted, *"Excuse me!"* As Cardinale remained standing, Glasser continued shouting, *"Sit down. Sit down. Sit down!"*

It was clear that, as the trial was coming to an end, and jury deliberations were imminent, pressure had mounted in the courtroom. It remained for Andrew Maloney to set off the final explosion in his rebuttal summation.

The U.S. attorney for the eastern district made a strong presence in the courtroom. The former West Point boxing champion gave the impression of being composed and fearless. His facial expressions rarely changed. There were the steely eyes and the mouth perpetually set in a tight, determined line.

Toward the end of his ten-minute rebuttal summation, Maloney told the jurors that "the evidence in the trial has clearly established that Gotti is the leader of the Gambino crime family. . . . If you accept the proof of what you are dealing with here," he went on, "the boss of a murderous and treacherous crime family and his underboss, you would be less than human if you didn't feel some concern—"

At this all three defense attorneys—Krieger, Mitchell, and Cardinale—leapt to their feet and objected. Judge Glasser then sustained the objection and said he would tell the jurors to ignore Maloney's remark. Later the defense team let Glasser know their thoughts and feelings about what Maloney had said. "This was a purposeful effort to throw a hand grenade in this case," complained John Mitchell. "It was not a summation, but an attempt to influence and prejudice. It was done for one purpose—to pollute this case. The summation Mr. Maloney gave was nothing short of outrageous."

"This was a desperate attempt to win this case by trying to frighten the jury into doing what the government couldn't do," lamented Anthony Cardinale.

Albert Krieger was the most forceful of all. Raising his powerful voice, he told the court: "The damage cannot be undone. We have come too far to suffer from what Mr. Maloney has done," and he called for a mistrial.

Meanwhile, Gotti's supporters were complaining loudly in the first and second rows of the spectators' section and Gotti was heard calling Maloney "a drunken bum." Then he stuck a thumb to his mouth and muttered, "piece of shit."

Maloney, who later claimed he did not hear Gotti's insults, would not back off his remarks, saying he was only trying to point out that "if they accept the evidence, they'd be less than human if they did not have some fear about this kind of organization."

During a closed conference between Judge Glasser and the attorneys, Glasser denied the mistrial motion and asked the defense attorneys to draft "curative" instructions to the jury.

It remained for Judge Glasser to instruct the jury on the law, after which the anonymous, sequestered jurors would begin their deliberations.

But not long after this conference the judge summoned all the jurors and the attorneys for both sides to investigate a report that juror number 3 had exhibited a "mindset against the government."

Apparently juror number 3 had told one of the deputy marshals that she thought she saw an FBI agent who sat at the prosecution table signal to a government witness as he testified. The marshal had asked her to write a note about it to the judge if she felt very strongly about it, but juror number 3 decided not to. Then, later on in the week, a marshal who was searching through a bag of laundry the woman was sending home found some sheets of paper with the names and addresses of several other jurors along with a note about the FBI hand signals.

In a closed session Judge Glasser questioned juror number 3 about the note and also asked the other jurors about it. The woman told Glasser she didn't think that the hand signals she saw would affect her impartiality.

When Glasser interviewed the other jurors about juror number 3's allegation, at least one other juror told him that juror number 3 had talked about the supposed hand signals with them.

Since jurors are not supposed to talk with each other about the case, prosecutor Gleeson urged Judge Glasser to have juror number 3 removed from the trial and Glasser promptly dismissed her.

When word of juror number 3's dismissal reached the courtroom, just before the jury was set to begin its deliberations, it shocked John Gotti and his retainers. "Soon as they think a juror likes us, boom, they're gone," exclaimed Gotti audibly. Then, as the first two rows of the spectators' section began grumbling, Gotti turned toward the prosecutors and called out, in his gruff, coarse voice, "The 1919 White Sox"—referring to the notorious "Black Sox" scandal when the Chicago White Sox threw the 1919 World Series to the Cincinnati Reds.

41

The Fall

Judge Glasser's fourth floor courtroom was half-filled by 9:35 A.M., Wednesday, April 1. The defendants and their attorneys were at the defense table looking slightly edgy, although John Gotti managed to project a measure of good humor with his daily morning smirk. The prosecution team had taken its place at its table, with John Gleeson looking customarily impassive, and Andrew Maloney stony and cool.

By 9:45 Judge Glasser was seated and the jury had filed into the courtroom. Glasser had gone over the thirteen counts in the indictment with the jurors and had instructed them on the applicable points of law the previous afternoon. Now, as the seven men and five women prepared to deliberate the case, Glasser told them to remember what he had gone over with them the day before, advised them that if they wished to listen to any tapes or go over any testimony again, they could do so, and wished them well. As the jurors filed out, the courtroom fell silent. For all those present it would be a long, silent, agonizing wait.

The first sign of what the jury was weighing came early in the afternoon. They asked to have two FBI tapes replayed for them, one recorded on January 4, 1989, the other on November 30, 1989.

The conversation of January 4 was between John Gotti, Frankie Locascio, and Sammy Gravano about who would lead the family if Gotti went to jail.

GOTTI: This is my wishes that if, if I'm in the fucking can, this Family is gonna be run by *Sammy.* I'm still the boss. If I get fifty years, I know what I gotta do. But *when I'm in the can Sammy's in charge.*

The conversation of November 30 was between Gotti and Gravano and told of Gotti's suspicions that Castellano was planning to kill him and Angelo Ruggiero for not turning over to Castellano FBI tapes about a heroin ring run by Ruggiero and Gotti's younger brother, Gene.

GOTTI: He [Castellano] felt he hadda hit me first. But if he hits me first he blows the guy who really led the ring, Angelo and them. Supposedly that's on the tapes.

Later on in the afternoon the jury asked to hear the January 17, 1990, tape on which Gotti is heard declaiming his powerful soliloquy on the Cosa Nostra in front of Frankie Locascio and Sammy Gravano.

GOTTI: I'm not in the mood for toys, or games, or kidding, no time. I'm not in the mood for clans. I'm not in the mood for gangs. . . . And this gonna be a Cosa Nostra till I die. Be it an hour from now, or be it tonight, or a hundred years from now when I'm in jail. It's gonna be a Cosa Nostra. . . .

Finally, another conversation between Gotti, Locascio, and Gravano was replayed at the request of the jury. It was about an intention of Gotti's to reach a juror who had been selected to sit in Gotti's coming state trial on assault and conspiracy charges in Manhattan state supreme court.

GOTTI: We got one guy who's on, his name's Hoyle, or something. Irish, I guess, Boyle or something. He's a lineman. He lives in Gramercy. Works, like, the Lower West Side. . . . I don't want to talk with him. And I'm not crazy, either. . . . And we have plenty of mopes here. . . . Maybe we can reach him or send word out there if anybody knows him. And I won't feed them no information except name.

On the first day the jurors completed their deliberations at 8:05 P.M. and then returned to their secret hotel.

Deliberations resumed the following morning in Brooklyn at 9:30. Again the courtroom was only half full. Most people in the press section were predicting a verdict on the third or fourth day of deliberations and did not bother to even come in on the second day. After all, it was boring to sit there in a silent, empty courtroom reading newspaper and magazines, waiting, waiting. . . . Opinion was divided among the newspaper, radio, television press as to what the verdict would be. Several thought there might be a hung jury, but most felt that Gotti would be convicted on at least half of the counts and that Locascio, an all but invisible presence throughout the trial, would be found innocent of all charges against him.

Twelve-thirty came and still no signs the jury had reached a verdict or was even close to reaching one. Time for the lunch break. Everyone filed out of the courtroom, complaining of the boredom of waiting inside.

At 1:03 Albert Krieger was munching a bagel with cream cheese in the courthouse cafeteria with his wife, Irene, and *Daily News* reporter Gene Mustain, complaining to them how difficult it had been to defend John Gotti against the government's charges, when a pallid, obviously concerned John Mitchell suddenly came up to him. "Albert, we have a verdict," he said. Krieger realized then that, in his own words, "Gotti was a goner." The verdict was too swift in coming down to have gone the other way.

At the telephone booths on the main floor reporters were frantically calling their offices to alert photographers and camera crews that a verdict would be coming down within minutes. The jury had caught everyone unawares.

By 1:10 Krieger had reached the defense table and the courtroom was beginning to fill up. Many of the press had been just hanging around in and outside the courtroom waiting for the action to begin and had torn up to the fourth floor at the first whisper a verdict was about to come down. Soon the trucks of the TV networks and the press photographers were on station outside the courthouse ready to pounce on the defense attorneys and the Gotti supporters as they exited the building after the verdict.

At 1:13 John Gotti strode into the courtroom, acting more stiff than usual, but still wearing his confident smirk. When he reached the defense table he shook hands with his defense team and glanced toward his retainers in the spectators' section, nodding to them and smiling.

Two minutes later Judge I. Leo Glasser entered his courtroom looking stern, even angry. Everyone stood. Then came two knocks on the courtroom door to the judge's left and the jury filed in and took their places.

As everyone sat down, a near total silence fell over the courtroom.

Then Glasser stood up and read a note he had just received from the jury forewoman. "Judge Glasser, we have reached a verdict on all counts, as to both defendants."

The forewoman of the jury now rose. John Gleeson and Andrew Maloney stared at her stonily. John Gotti, the media junkie, managed to throw a wink at the press section. Codefendant Frankie Locascio sat in his usual caved-in posture, his horse face immobile. Krieger, Cardinale, and Mitchell, slumped in their seats, looked apprehensive, as if they already knew it was all over.

Courtroom clerk Louise Schaillat then read from the verdict sheet:

"Count one, RICO: Conspiracy to murder Paul Castellano and murder of Paul Castellano. How do you find, proven or not proven?"

"Proven," said the forewoman.

With this John Gotti's head jerked back, his face displaying an expression of disbelief, but he soon recovered his poise.

"Count one, RICO," continued the clerk. "Murder of Thomas Bilotti. How do you find, proven or unproven?"

"Proven," said the forewoman.

"Count one, RICO," the clerk went on. "Conspiracy to murder Robert DiBernardo, murder of Robert DiBernardo. How do you find, proven or unproven?"

"Proven," said the forewoman.

And so it went for all counts in the indictment.

Frankie Locascio received almost identical treatment: convictions on all racketeering and racketeering conspiracy charges, including one murder, innocent on only one minor charge, illegal gambling. Facing a sentence of life imprisonment with no opportunity of parole, Frankie Locascio did not smile.

Upon receiving the complete verdict, John Gotti leaned over toward a downcast John Mitchell, patted him on the back, and said: "It's all right; don't worry. It's not over." Later Albert Krieger told reporters that

Gotti was "shattered by the verdict" but was "holding up well."

Gotti's retainers in the spectators' section were not holding up nearly as well. Shouting "Fix! Fix! Fix!" they were only quieted when Gotti put a finger to his lips and whispered, "Shush."

Then, when it came time for John Gotti to depart from the courtroom and go down to the holding pens in the basement, he stood up with his chest out and his head held high, straightened his tie, smoothed his jacket, shot his cuffs, and walked out behind the marshal, still in the fullness of his vanity and pride.

To John Gotti, who had learned his trade from a traditional Sicilian capo, Aniello Dellacroce, La Cosa Nostra was still a way of life lived according to a code, a faith, a set of firm, unwavering beliefs and rules. He himself had never betrayed that faith, those beliefs, those rules. When he was a soldier he never disobeyed his capo. When he was a capo he never disobeyed the family's underboss, Dellacroce, who had been his direct superior, not Castellano, who almost seemed to run another family. And never during his entire career in the Cosa Nostra had he ever ratted on anyone. No, by his lights, John Gotti had always done the right thing, had always upheld the faith.

John Gotti may have been the last true believer in the way of life that had evolved in America out of the old Sicilian Honored Society. Many times had his enemy, the United State government, recorded his credo from secretly placed electronic bugs:

GOTTI: I know what's goin' on. . . . I'm in the fuckin' hunt. . . . Me, I'll always be all right.

GOTTI: The law's gonna be tough with us, okay: If they don't put us away . . . for one year or two, that's all we need. . . . But if I can get a year run without being interrupted. Get a year . . . gonna put his thing together where they could never break it, never destroy it. Even if we die, be a good thing.

UNKNOWN MALE: It's a hell of a legacy to leave.

GOTTI: Well, you know why it would be, ah, because it would be right. Maybe after thirty years it would deteriorate, but it would take that long to fuckin' succumb.

GOTTI: And this is gonna be a Cosa Nostra till I die. Be it an hour from now, or be it tonight, or a hundred years from now when I'm in jail. It's gonna be a Cosa Nostra. . . . It's gonna be the way I say it's gonna be, and a Cosa Nostra. A Cosa Nostra!

Yes, John Gotti, Cosa Nostra boss, may have lost his freedom, but he had kept the faith, and for that reason he was going to be all right.

*Today has been another milestone in the fight against
organized crime. The Teflon is gone from the don.
And now he is covered with Velcro
and every charge against the don has stuck.*

So proclaimed James E. Fox, head of the FBI's New
York office at a press conference shortly after the
verdict was announced.

> Today's verdict by a courageous jury is the
> end of a very long road. Justice has been
> served and it feels awfully good.

A victorious Andrew Maloney beamed as he
expressed his feelings about the verdict to the press
in a courthouse room that seemed to hold more television cameras and microphones than people.

The next day J. Bruce Mouw, head of the FBI's six-
teen-man Gambino Squad, revealed his feelings
about John Gotti:

> Media stories that glorify Gotti as the Dapper
> Don, the Teflon Don, that emphasize his
> two-thousand-dollar suits and picture him as

a colorful Robin Hood–like robber: We can't understand this. To us John Gotti is a psychopathic killer.

Speaking of the convicted Gotti, Ronald Goldstock, Director of the State Organized Crime Task Force, said: "In retrospect his leadership was marked by profound failure. His high points were his early acquittals and the fireworks he sponsored in Ozone Park. Nothing more."

William Barr, Attorney General of the United States, told a national television audience: "The conviction of John Gotti should send a signal. The mob, as we have known it in New York and across the nation, is on the way out."

John Gotti's lawyers were predictably upset. John Mitchell told the crowd in front of the courthouse: "I don't think they [the jury] even applied any analytical thinking to this case. They only asked for three stupid tapes."

And a harried, downcast Albert Krieger, surrounded by television cameras and newspaper photographers as he exited the courthouse, said: "I don't believe the jurors compared what was on the tapes with Gravano's testimony. We will appeal this verdict."

Gotti's supporters were vehement in their outrage over the conviction of their hero.

Cina Cecala, a housewife, told television reporters in Little Italy: "You let everybody know that everybody in Little Italy loves John Gotti. . . . The don kept this neighborhood safe. On Christmas he would give out twenty-dollar bills to anyone who asked."

"I hope that the judge and Maloney rot in hell," cried another denizen of Little Italy, "and they should shoot that stool-pigeon bastard Gravano. I'd do it myself. I swear to it."

Out in Howard Beach, Queens, near the Gotti home, a reporter encountered John Gotti, Jr., and was told: "Don't take a picture of this house. If you do I'll rip your head off."

Soon speculation about who would take Gotti's place as boss began circulating in the newspaper-radio-television press and the corridors of New York law enforcement. FBI man J. Bruce Mouw believed Gotti would try to rule the Gambino crime family from prison, conveying orders on key issues to various capos on his visitors list, but doubted whether the capos would respect his wishes for long. Sooner or later it would be necessary to have an accessible hands-on leader available to establish policy, control the unions, and enforce discipline.

But who would this leader be? The name of the seventy-eight-year-old capo Giuseppe "Joe" Arcuri was being bruited about by both underworld and law enforcement sources. A stern old man who owned liquor stores and buildings in Queens and Brooklyn and who had been with the family since the days of Mangano and Anastasia, Arcuri was well liked and respected but was perhaps too old for the rigors of bossdom. Other aging capos like Jimmy Failla were also mentioned, but it was known that the wily and wealthy Failla was not interested in the job.

Then, as speculation intensified, something happened that gave out a strong hint as to who the boss of the future might be. One of the family's great old capos, Carmine "the Doctor" Lombardozzi, died and FBI agents and police detectives observing his funeral and wake were quick to notice who among the mourners was being shown attention and respect and who was being merely tolerated or ignored.

Carmine Lombardozzi, eighty-one at the time of his death, had been known as the financial wizard of the Gambinos. Called the "King of Wall Street," "The Elder Statesman," and the "Italian Meyer Lansky," he had been for years the biggest loan shark in New York's financial district, making usurious loans to scores of brokers and hundreds of Wall Street back-office personnel needing funds with which to speculate on the market. He eventually became the biggest earner in the Gambino family, outside of the brothers Gambino, and a very wealthy man.

Lombardozzi ended his days in a mansion on the water at Mill Basin, Sheepshead Bay, with a Rolls-Royce in his driveway and a yacht tied up to his own dock behind the house. Active to the last, he would hold court during the week at a table in the Grotto d'Oro Restaurant on Emmons Avenue, Sheepshead Bay. Here, sitting with his nephew and apple of his eye, Danny Marino, he would dispense advice to all who would seek it, and there were many, especially the family loan sharks who were having trouble collecting their "vig."

When Carmine Lombardozzi died of heart failure in his own bed on May 10, 1992, a little over a month after his boss, John Gotti, was felled in Brooklyn Federal Court, the entire Gambino family showed up at his wake at the Cusimano and Russo Funeral Home in Gravesend, Brooklyn, to pay their respect. The big black limousines filled, it seemed, every parking space in Gravesend. Many of those present had attended Carlo Gambino's wake at the same parlor sixteen years before and Paul Castellano's wake there seven years after that. All the great ones in the family ended up, sooner or later, at Cusimano and Russo.

Stationed around the funeral home that day were several dozen FBI agents and New York Police Department detectives taking down license plate numbers and observing the rituals of respect that unfolded around the entrance to the funeral home. What they witnessed was a John Gotti, Jr., receiving what appeared to be perfunctory greetings from the mourners while Danny Marino, standing in the doorway of Cusimano and Russo, was receiving an apparent acclamation. There they were, in their black suits and white shirts, crowding around him, giving him big bear hugs and effusive kisses on both cheeks.

Several present recalled that it was a hotheaded young Danny Marino who had beat up spying FBI agent John Foley at the 1963 funeral of Carmine Lombardozzi's father, an episode that had provoked the only known interest in Carlo Gambino on the part of FBI Director J. Edgar Hoover.

Yes, it appeared on that cool May afternoon of big black limos and husky men in black suits grouped against the bright green lawns surrounding Cusimano and Russo that the Gambinos might have been coalescing around the tough, handsome, and reputedly smart Danny Marino, the man who had run the Westies for Paul Castellano back in the early eighties when Jimmy Coonan, John McElroy, and Mickey Featherstone were on the loose.

But it was still too early to tell who John Gotti's successor would be. The prevailing speculation among the press and law enforcement was that if John Gotti was sentenced to life imprisonment with no chance of parole, he would remain as the ultimate boss of the Gambinos, making the most important decisions from prison and leaving day-to-day operations in the hands of Joe Arcuri and Danny Marino.

Whatever the case, it was unlikely that the Gambinos, after the massive battering they had taken, could ever recover the power they had once wielded in New York. For one, their economic base had been severely eroded. With Paul Castellano dead and Sammy Gravano working for the government, their control of the concrete industry, their most lucrative racket, was now a thing of the past. As was their next most profitable enterprise, the city's garment center. With the recently chastened Gambino brothers out of the garment trucking industry for good, several million dollars a year in illicit earnings would dry up. Add to these devastations the imminent collapse of the family's long-standing hold on the International Longshoremen's Association locals of the Brooklyn waterfront and there would not be much money available to keep the family's rank and file prosperous and to finance the expensive criminal operations the family had been able to mount with such ease and impunity in the past.

What an alien and exotic enterprise the Gambino crime family had been in New York over the past sixty years. Here this huge, predacious growth, with roots deep in the social soil of rural nineteenth century southern Italy, had thrived to such an extent that it was able to impose an invisible tax on the people of the most powerful and influential city in the world.

And what a succession of alien and exotic monarchs had managed to rule this murderous predator for sixty years, men whose lives and values were the antithesis of all that the founding fathers of the nation that harbored them had stood for and had embodied in the Constitution of the United States.

The leaders of the Gambino family had not been chosen in free elections. They were despotic tyrants who seized power by violent means, mostly by murder. Within the Gambino family there was no such thing as human rights. Offending members had no right to a fair trial. Commit a serious offense against the boss or the organization, and the penalty was "death without trial." For the Gambinos those outside the family had no rights of any kind. They were fair game to rob, cheat, maim, and kill. If "Thou shalt not kill" was one of the cornerstones of the Judeo-Christian ethical tradition upon which American civilization was based, it was the opposite with the Gambinos. Willingness to commit murder was regarded as the most prized quality a member could possess. The Gambino code of values was a relic of Europe's Dark Ages, that period from the fall of the Roman Empire in the fifth century to the establishment of the Christian city-states in the eleventh and twelfth centuries. The Gambino code was a throwback to the time when tribal chieftains, later to be known as feudal lords, gathered their clans into fortified hilltop villages and plundered the trade routes and each other at will.

It took almost a century for the United States to come to terms with this invisible government, this "enemy within," as Robert F. Kennedy had characterized organized crime in 1961.

In the end it was the passage of the federal RICO statute in 1970 and the death of FBI Director J. Edgar Hoover in 1972, after forty-eight years on the job, that allowed the government to finally focus its energies and resources on confronting the menace of organized crime in the United States.

Hoover's legacy of inaction in regard to organized crime was so pervasive in the councils of the FBI that it took the bureau seven years after the old man's death to mount its first major offensive against a Mafia boss. It was in 1979, under the directorship of William H. Webster, that the FBI launched a sting operation against Louisiana Mafia boss Carlos Marcello, which ultimately resulted in two RICO convictions of the veteran Mafia chieftain and the subsequent destruction of the crime family he had bossed for thirty-four years.

Subsequently the FBI and local law enforcement agencies launched successful offensives against the mob in Los Angeles, Kansas City, Philadelphia, Atlantic City, Providence, and Boston that virtually destroyed the crime families in those cities.

The most sensational of these victories was the successful prosecution in 1988 of the entire leadership of the powerful Philadelphia–Atlantic City family headed by Nicodemo "Nicky" Scarfo. Through the combined efforts of the FBI, the United States attorney for the eastern district of Pennsylvania, and the district attorney of Philadelphia, the entire hierarchy of the Scarfo family was eliminated. No fewer than seventeen made members of the family—boss, underboss, *consiglière*, all the *caporegimes*—were convicted on charges of racketeering, conspiracy, and murder and were sent off to federal prison to serve sentences of from thirty to fifty-five years each.

This unprecedented victory coincided with the equally successful prosecutions of the Commission and Pizza Connection cases, which saw the Cosa Nostra's entire ruling body sentenced to hundred-year prison terms and the huge Sicilian pizza-parlor heroin trafficking operation put out of business.

There remained that last bastion of organized crime in the United States, the five Cosa Nostra families of New York. With the Colombo and Bonanno families severely crippled, the Lucchese family already under federal attack, and the Genovese family suffering from lack of leadership, the government had set its sights on the nation's largest organized crime family, the Gambinos, and after three trials of its flamboyant boss, spanning a period of almost seven years, had finally succeeded in dealing it a possibly fatal blow.

By the time of John Gotti's conviction in April 1992, the traditional Italian Mafia in the United States was indeed "on the way out," as Attorney General Barr had put it after Gotti's trial.

To be sure, a few of the Cosa Nostra families would continue to survive off their time-tested staples—loan-sharking, numbers, burglaries, and hijackings—but the days when a Cosa Nostra family controlled entire unions such as the Teamsters and the Longshoremen, or entire industries, such as construction in New York City, were now over.

While he was active in the middle to late 1980s, John Gotti epitomized the traditional Italian Mafia more than any of his contemporaries in organized crime. Here was a boss with swagger and style and panache who actually did wield considerable power. With his partner in crime, Sammy the Bull Gravano, he controlled the concrete industry in New York; and through his capos in private garbage carting, the garment district, and the Brooklyn waterfront, he exerted considerable influence on those industries as well. But, above all, he as the disciple of Anastasia's gunman Dellacroce, was perhaps the last true believer in La Cosa Nostra, the last of the dons to believe passionately in the codes and goals and rituals of the 120-year-old criminal brotherhood that had sprung up in nineteenth century southern Italy and was so successfully transplanted in most of the major cities of the United States.

As the day of John Gotti's sentencing approached, La Cosa Nostra was dealt still another crippling blow. Vittorio "Vic" Amuso, boss of the Lucchese crime family, the third largest of New York's five Mafia families, was convicted of all fifty-four charges against him in his murder and racketeering trial in Brooklyn Federal Court. He, like Gotti, faced a life sentence. Now there was only one family boss left free in New York, Victor Orena, head of the divided and battered Colombo family, and he was slated to stand trial in late November.

John Gotti's sentencing was preceded by a brief, last-ditch effort of the defense, spearheaded by one of Gotti's new attorneys, that perennial champion of the oppressed, William Kunstler, to nullify Gotti's trial. Two of the anonymous, sequestered jurors had suddenly spoken up, saying that they did not think Gotti received a fair trial and that they had been pressured by the government to convict Gotti. To Kunstler's motions Judge Glasser would turn a deaf ear.

An enormous crowd of John Gotti's supporters showed up in Brooklyn's federal courthouse for the sentencing of their hero on June 23. Most of them did not gain admittance to the courthouse and were thus compelled to loiter in and around the courthouse as they awaited Judge Glasser's sentences.

Judge Glasser entered the packed courtroom around 10:00 and quickly got down to business. He first conferred privately with attorneys for both sides and denied a defense motion to set aside the verdicts or to order a hearing into the matter of two jurors who had called the verdict unfair.

Asking the attorneys if they wished to make statements, both the defense and the prosecution said no, they would not make any statements.

Glasser then asked John Gotti and Frank Locascio if they wished to make any statements of their own to the court before sentencing. Gotti, looking spiffy in a navy-blue double-breasted suit, gleaming white shirt, and yellow and orange tie with matching hanky, merely shook his head. Bruce Cutler, standing by the defense table, provided the words. "No, Your Honor," he said.

Frank Locascio, however, did have a statement to make. Reading from a spiral notebook, Locascio declared in a strong voice, "First, I would like to say emphatically that I am innocent." He then denied each charge of the indictment against him. "I am guilty, though . . ." he went on, "I am guilty of being a good friend of John Gotti. And if there were more men like John Gotti on this earth, we would have a better country."

Turning to John Gotti, Judge Glasser told him, "The guidelines in your case require me to commit you to the custody of the attorney general for the duration of your life." This translated into life imprisonment with no possibility of parole. In addition, Glasser ordered Gotti to pay a fine of $250,000 plus court costs.

Glasser then imposed an identical sentence on Locascio and abruptly left the courtroom. The entire proceeding had taken only ten minutes.

Word of Gotti's sentence traveled rapidly down the corridors of the courthouse, into the main lobby downstairs, and out the revolving doors to the multitude on the sidewalk and street.

Soon a violent demonstration against the sentence erupted among Gotti's supporters, and several chartered buses appeared on the scene disgorging more angry Gotti partisans. Screaming "Justice for John" and "Free John Gotti," the angry crowd, estimated by the police at from eight hundred to a thousand, tried to storm the courthouse, were repulsed, and then took out their rage by attacking police officers and smashing parked cars. A gang of fifteen young men began rocking a Pontiac Grand Am belonging to a deputy U.S. marshal and succeeded in turning it over on its roof. In the melee eight police officers were injured and a dozen Gotti supporters were arrested, including one of Gotti's nephews, Joseph Gotti, twenty-two, of Ozone Park.

Later James Fox, director of the FBI's New York office, told the press: "That was an orchestrated and planned event, not spontaneous. It was directed by the crew of John Gotti, Jr."

As the crowd's rage subsided, Bruce Cutler grabbed a bullhorn and roared to them: "John Gotti's a man's man and he's somebody people love and he's somebody everybody looks up to in this city. . . . He became too big for them, and so they tried to take him down. But we'll win this on appeal."

Later defense lawyers Albert Krieger, Anthony Cardinale, and John Mitchell told the press that the convictions of Gotti and Locascio would be appealed.

Many observers believed there were some grounds for appeal: Keeping Gotti and Locascio in confinement for thirteen months before trial. Disqualifying Gotti's and Locascio's lawyers, Bruce Cutler and Gerald Shargel. Judge Glasser excluding several defense witnesses from testifying. Glasser intimidating the jury by ordering it to be anonymous and sequestered. Andrew Maloney's "inflammatory" closing summation. A juror that might have been improperly dismissed. Another who felt under intense pressure to convict. Another who felt the verdict was unfair.

For John Gotti a successful appeal was his only hope against being buried alive. For an unspeakably bleak fate awaited him. The government had decided to pack him off to the harshest prison in the federal system, the maximum-security U.S. penitentiary in Marion, Illinois. There Gotti would be confined to an eight-by-seven-foot underground cell for twenty-three hours a day. He would be allowed one hour of solitary exercise a day in a concrete yard and only two showers a week. He would be taken to his showers shackled in chains inside a moveable cage. Meals would not be communal; they would be delivered through a slot in his cell's door. There would be no communal recreation, no work, no communal education classes. This was virtual solitary confinement. The gregarious, talkative Gotti would have only a small black-and-white television set and a radio for company.

At Marion it is next to impossible for a boss to run his crime family from prison, for all his telephone calls are monitored and he is not allowed physical contact with visitors. The visitors' room is divided by a thick Plexiglas partition. Visitors sit on one side and inmates on the other and they communicate by phone. There are no slots through which notes and packages can be passed.

At 7:35 the morning of June 24, 1992, the day after his sentencing, John Gotti was delivered to the custody of the warden of Marion. There he joined some of the nation's most infamous prisoners, at least two of whom Gotti knew: Nicodemo "Nicky" Scarfo and Jimmy Coonan. Others included spies John Walker, the Navy warrant officer who sold classified information to the former Soviet Union; Jonathan Jay Pollard, who spied for Israel; and the traitor former CIA officer Edwin Wilson, who as an employee of the U.S. government sold weapons to Libya's Colonel Mu'ammar Qaddafi and conspired to murder eight witnesses to his crimes.

Four days after John Gotti's incarceration, his father, John Gotti, Sr., died of heart failure at eighty-five. The immigrant from San Giuseppe Vesuviano had been seriously ill for some time. Hope for his son John's acquittal had been keeping him alive. When word of the verdict reached him, he took a sudden turn for the worse. This was a calamity not only for his large family, but for his name. John Gotti, Sr., the hardworking mason and later city sanitation worker, who had fathered thirteen children in his adopted land, did not want to believe his son was a gangster.

By consigning John Gotti to the hellhole of Marion, the government, determined to destroy the Gambino crime family once and for all, had effectively decapitated the Gambino organization. If Gotti's orders could not be transmitted to his subordinates, he would lose control of the family and chaos and decline would inevitably ensue.

However, not long after Gotti was confined to Marion his prosecutors alleged in a motion filed in U.S. District Court on August 19, 1992, that they had evidence from confidential sources that Gotti was using his son, John Jr., and older brother, Peter, who had been visiting him in prison twice a month, "to relay messages between Gotti and the rest of the Gambino family." "We believe that John Gotti is still the boss of the family and is running it through surrogates," affirmed U.S. Attorney Andrew J. Maloney. Still others in the office of the U.S. attorney, eastern district, were not so sure Gotti could run the Gambino family from inside Marion. Assistant U.S. Attorney Laura Ward stated that what Gotti could communicate to his son and brother would be "minimal" but they, in turn, could embellish it and make it sound detailed and authoritative to the 'capos.'

Then, on October 8, 1993, Gotti's ability to control the Gambino family from prison was dealt a fatal blow. The 2nd U.S. Circuit Court of Appeals decided to uphold Gotti's racketeering and murder conviction, rejecting the don's contention that Judge Glasser unfairly disqualified his lawyer, Bruce Cutler, from representing him. The Court of Appeals ruled that Cutler's disqualification was warranted because Cutler had "entangled himself to an extraordinary degree in the activities of the Gambino crime family." ". . . Cutler's role of house counsel raised a credible issue of the ethical propriety of his representation of Gotti in this case," observed the three judge panel in their sixty-two-page opinion. "An attorney cannot properly serve two masters." The Appeals panel cited two tape recorded conversations of Gotti in particular to illustrate their point: "Where does it end? The Gambino family? This is the Shargel, Cutler, whataya call it crime family," and "Go find out what's going on, when the pinch is coming. We're making you an errand boy. High-priced errand boy, Bruce."

As it turned out, not only was Gotti's appeal denied, but his flamboyant attorney, Bruce Cutler, was convicted of criminal contempt of court on January 7, 1994, for comments he made to reporters during Gotti's trial. Cutler had, in fact, violated a court order barring lawyers for the defense from making statements to newspaper and television reporters that had a "reasonable likelihood" of influencing jurors sufficiently to prejudice the outcome of a case.

The denial of Gotti's appeal meant that the fifty-two-year-old don would never leave prison alive and would have to relinquish his control of the Gambino family. Now, most certainly, a violent struggle for power would ensue within the family. One detective predicted that "you're going to see the bodies fall and the first one will be Gotti's son. People have been waiting to see what would happen with the appeal."

When Judge I. Leo Glasser sentenced John Gotti to life imprisonment with no possibility of parole, he sentenced a whole way of life to oblivion. For Gotti was the last of a breed of mob bosses who would probably never appear again. Organized crime, to be sure, would continue to exist. Asian and Colombian gangs with structures, hierarchies, and codes had already emerged in New York. But the old brotherhood of southern Italian *amìci*, the Honored Society, and its American offshoot, La Cosa Nostra, with all their rituals, lore, and sacred vows, were now doomed.

Who had sealed that doom? Not the government. The government was but an instrument, not a cause. It was the hubris of "God's gift to the underworld" that had sealed the doom of La Cosa Nostra. It was the bravado of the man who had composed that hymn to the institution he worshiped: "This is gonna be a Cosa Nostra till I die. Be it an hour from now . . . or a hundred years from now when I'm in jail. It's gonna be a Cosa Nostra." It was he who, with his loose, bragging tongue and misplaced trust, had finally brought down the object of his veneration.

Sincerely believing himself to be a martyr to his creed, John Gotti would probably survive the horrors of Marion.

Afterword

On Sunday, January 2, 1994, Rudolph Giuliani, the man who had set in motion the government's onslaught against organized crime in New York, and who was therefore ultimately responsible for the successful prosecution of John Gotti, was sworn in as the 107th mayor of New York.

After an arduous year-long campaign, Republican candidate Giuliani had defeated the city's first black mayor, Democrat David L. Dinkins, by winning a whopping seventy-five percent of the white vote.

In an impassioned inaugural address, in which he alluded frequently to the "indomitable spirit" of the first Italian-American mayor of New York, Fiorello LaGuardia, Giuliani vowed he would fight crime without letup and would seek to build the city's future on its great cultural institutions—the Metropolitan Opera, the City Opera, the fashion industry, the ballet, the New York Philharmonic, Broadway's theaters, and the city's great art museums—which, he said, "bring in millions of visitors from all over the world every year."

Giuliani went on to emphasize the role of the United Nations headquarters in the life of the city. "It is time to enhance our unique position as the home of the United Nations," he exclaimed. "Think of this: Albany, the capital of New York State. Washington, D.C., the capital of the nation. And New York City will again be the capital of the world."

Seated in the audience before New York's 200-year-old City Hall were 140 members of the Giuliani family, including the mayor's eighty-four-year-old mother, Helen. The new forty-nine-year-old mayor recalled that his grandfather, Rodolfo Giuliani, had emigrated to New York from Italy one hundred years ago with only twenty dollars in his pocket. "Like so many of you and your ancestors, he knew fear—fear of a strange land, fear of learning to speak a new language, fear of the unknown. But he didn't let that stop him. He dreamed that life could be better for him and his children in New York City and lived that dream."

In a very real sense the election of Rudolph Giuliani as mayor of America's greatest city redeemed the reputation of all Italian-Americans, especially those who lived in New York. For the past ten years New Yorkers of Italian descent had to endure the images of such depraved "paesans" as "Fat Tony" Salerno, Carmine "The Snake" Persico, "Tony Ducks" Corallo, Big Paul Castellano, John Gotti, and "Sammy the Bull" Gravano on the front pages of the city's newspapers day after day, as they both defied the law and succumbed to it. It was a demeaning, and revolting, parade of Italian names and faces that culminated in the squalid figure of Salvatore Gravano, who, after admitting to committing nineteen murders, had turned against his boss, the man who had elevated him from a street punk to the second-in-command of the Gambino crime family, and sent him away with his treacherous testimony to prison for the rest of his life.

Now New York's one million Italian-Americans beheld one of their own as the supreme magistrate of their city, the man ultimately responsible for erasing the faces of "Fat Tony," Carmine "the Snake," "Tony Ducks," Big Paul, John Gotti, and "Sammy The Bull" from the front pages forever. This cleansing in itself had been a major accomplishment, achieved before Giuliani had even issued his first executive order as mayor. The election of Rudolph Giuliani had bestowed a new dignity on all Italians living in New York, had given them a positive new image.

The vanity and gall of the murderous John Gotti, strutting about New York in his tailor-made $2,500 double-breasted pinstripe suits as if he owned the city, would be replaced by the understated simplicity and integrity of purpose of this grandson of hard-working Tuscan immigrants who knew himself to be not the boss but the servant of all the people of New York.

June 1994

Notes on Sources

Not much was known about the Gambino crime family until the FBI and the New York State Organized Crime Task Force began their programs of electronic surveillance of Gambino family members in the early 1980s and certain members and associates of the crime family turned government informants in the same period. Prior to the 1980s, information on the Gambinos was scarce and unreliable, as might be expected when dealing with an organization based on secrecy and silence. It follows, then, that much of what we claim to know about the early history of the nation's richest and most powerful crime family must remain murky and conjectural. The sources in the list that follows must therefore not be regarded as providing us with a record of absolute historical accuracy. At best they provide us with an approximation of what happened to the crime family founded in 1931 by Charles "Lucky" Luciano and headed in 1992 by the imprisoned boss John Gotti.

I. PRIMARY SOURCES

1. *Transcripts of Tape-recorded Conversations*. The Federal Bureau of Investigation and New York State Organized Crime Task Force (OCTF) recorded over 600 hours of Gambino crime family conversations from 1981 through 1990.

    a. *The John Gotti Tapes* (1981–1990). Conversations intercepted by the FBI and OCTF at the Bergin Hunt and Fish Club, Ozone Park, Queens; at the room next to the Nice N EZ Auto School, Ozone Park; the Ravenite Club, 247 Mulberry Street, Manhattan; and the apartment above the Ravenite Club.

    b. *The Angelo Ruggiero Tapes* (1982–1983). Conversations intercepted at the home of Angelo Ruggiero in Cedarhurst, Long Island.

    c. *The Aniello Dellacroce Tapes* (1983–1985). Conversations intercepted at the home of Aniello Dellacroce, 597 West Fingerboard Road, Staten Island.

    d. *The Paul Castellano Tapes* (1983–1985). Conversations intercepted at the home of Paul Castellano, 177 Benedict Road, Staten Island.

2. *State and Federal Trials*

    a. U.S. District Court, Eastern District of New York. *United States v. John Gotti et al*. RICO indictment. April 1986–March 1987. Transcript of trial at U.S. District Court, Brooklyn.

    b. Supreme Court of the State of New York, County of New York. *The People of the State of New York v. John Gotti and Anthony "Tony Lee" Guerrieri*. January 8–February 9, 1990. Transcript of trial at State Supreme Court, Manhattan.

    c. U.S. District Court, Eastern District of New York. *United States v. John Gotti, Salvatore Gravano, Frank Locascio, Thomas Gambino*. RICO Indictment.

January 21, 1992–June 23, 1992. Transcript of trial at U.S. District Court, Eastern District, Brooklyn.

1. U.S. District Court. Eastern District of New York. The Government's Memorandum In Support of Its Motion For Pretrial Detention of Certain Defendants. Signed Andrew J. Maloney, U.S. Attorney, Eastern District of New York, December 12, 1990.

2. U.S. District Court. Eastern District of New York. The Government's Memorandum In Support of Its Motion For An Order Disqualifying Counsel. Signed Andrew J. Maloney, U.S. Attorney, Eastern District of New York, January 18, 1991.

3. U.S. District Court. Eastern District of New York Memorandum and Order disqualifying Gerald Shargel, Bruce Cutler and John Pollok from representing defendants John Gotti and Frank Locascio at trial. Signed I. Leo Glasser, United States District Judge, August 1, 1991.

d. U.S. District Court, Southern District of New York. *United States v. Paul "Big Paul" Castellano et al* (20 other defendants). RICO conspiracy. 1985–1987. (Castellano was murdered during early stage of trial.) Transcript of trial at U.S. District Court, Manhattan.

e. U.S. District Court, Eastern District of New York. *The United States v. Thomas Gambino.* The Grand Jury testimony of Thomas Gambino, September 15, October 4, 1988. Transcript (285 pp.) at U.S. District Court, Brooklyn.

3. *Congressional Investigations*
a. U.S. Senate. McClellan Subcommittee on Organized Crime. Hearings. The testimony of Joseph Valachi. September 25–October 1, 1963. (Valachi's version of the history of organized crime in the United States.)

b. U.S. House of Representatives. Select Committee on Assassinations. Investigation of the Assassination of President John F. Kennedy. Appendix to Hearings.

Volume IX. Organized Crime. U.S. GPO 1978–1979.
(History of organized crime in the United States.
Reports on Carlo Gambino and Thomas Lucchese.)

    c. U.S. Senate. *Organized Crime: 25 Years After
Valachi.* Hearings before the Permanent Subcommittee on Investigations of the Committee on Governmental Affairs, U.S. Senate. One Hundredth Congress.
April 11, 15, 21, 22, 29, 1988. U.S. G.P.O 1990.
(Contains organization and membership of Gambino
crime family.)

II. SECONDARY SOURCES

1. *Books* (NOTE: Limited to books used as background and sources of information for this book.)

Arlacchi, Pino. *Mafia Business—The Mafia Ethic
and the Spirit of Capitalism.* London: Verso, 1986.

Alexander, Shana. *The Pizza Connection: Lawyers,
Money, Drugs, Mafia.* New York: Weidenfeld and
Nicholson, 1988.

Blumenthal, Ralph. *Last Days of the Sicilians. The
FBI Assault on the Pizza Connection.* New York:
Times Books, 1988.

Bonanno, Joseph. *A Man of Honor. The Autobiography of Joseph Bonanno.* New York: Simon &
Schuster, 1983.

Cantalupo, Joseph, and Thomas C. Renner. *BODY
MIKE: An Unsparing Expose by The Mafia Insider
Who Turned on the MOB.* New York: Villard Books,
1990.

Capeci, Jerry, and Gene Mustain. *Mob Star: The
Story of John Gotti.* New York: Dell, 1989.

Chandler, David Leon. *Brothers in Blood: The Rise of
the Criminal Brotherhoods.* New York: Dutton, 1975.

Coffey, Joseph, and Jerry Schmetterer. *The Coffey
Files: One Cop's War Against the Mob.* New York: St.
Martin's Press, 1991.

Cummings, John, and Ernest Volkman. *Goombata:
The Improbable Rise and Fall of John Gotti and His
Gang.* Boston: Little, Brown, 1990.

Davis, John H. *Mafia Kingfish: Carlos Marcello and the Assassination of John F. Kennedy.* New York: McGraw-Hill, 1988.

English, T. J. *The Westies: Inside the Hell's Kitchen Irish Mob.* New York: Putnam, 1990.

Fox, Stephen. *Blood and Power: Organized Crime in Twentieth Century America.* New York: Morrow, 1989.

Gage, Nicholas. *Mafia U.S.A.* Chicago: Playboy Press, 1972.

Gentry, Curt. *J. Edgar Hoover: The Man Who Kept the Secrets.* New York: Norton, 1991.

Gosch, Martin A., and Richard Hammer. *The Last Testament of Lucky Luciano.* Boston: Little, Brown, 1975.

Katz, Leonard. *Uncle Frank: The Biography of Frank Costello.* New York: Drake, 1973.

Kwitny, Jonathan. *Vicious Circles: The Mafia in the Marketplace.* New York: Norton, 1979.

Maas, Peter. *The Valachi Papers.* New York: Bantam, 1969.

Maiuri, Amadeo. *Passeggiate Campane.* Firenze, Italy: Sansone, 1950.

Meskil, Paul. S. *Don Carlo: Boss of Bosses.* New York: Popular Library, 1973.

Navasky, Victor. *Kennedy Justice.* New York: Atheneum, 1977.

O'Brien, Joseph, and Andris Kurins. *Boss of Bosses: The Fall of the Godfather: The FBI and Paul Castellano.* New York: Simon & Schuster, 1991.

Pileggi, Nicholas. *Wiseguy: Life in a Mafia Family.* New York: Pocket Books, 1987.

Pistone, Joseph D. *Donnie Brasco: My Undercover Life in the Mafia.* New York: New American Library, 1987.

Reid, Ed. *The Grim Reapers: The Anatomy of Organized Crime in America.* New York: Henry Regnery, 1970.

Russell, Maude. *Men Along the Shore.* New York: Brussel and Brussel, 1966.

Scheim, David. *Contract on America: The Mafia Murder of President John F. Kennedy*. New York: Shapolsky, 1988.

Sifakis, Carl. *The Mafia Encyclopedia: From Accardo to Zwillman*. New York: Facts on File, 1987.

Sterling, Claire. *Octopus—The Global Reach of the Sicilian Mafia*. New York: Norton, 1990.

2. *Miscellaneous Publications*

Blum, Howard. "The Cop They Call the Mob's Mole." *New York Times Magazine*, May 3, 1992.

Blumenthal, Ralph. "When Mob Delivered the Goods." *New York Times Magazine*, July 26, 1992.

Brodie, John. "The Gambino Group 1990 Annual Report." *Spy* Magazine, November, 1990.

Krupa, Gregg. "No Plumbing Salesman But . . .: 4 Jurors Wanted to Convict Gotti but Found Evidence Thin." *Manhattan Lawyer*, April, 1990.

Goldstock, Ronald. *Corruption and Racketeering in the New York City Construction Industry: An Interim Report*. New York State Organized Crime Task Force, 1987.

Goldstock, Ronald, and G. Robert Blakey. "On the Waterfront": RICO and Labor Racketeering. American Criminal Law Review, 1980.

MacKenzie, Richard, Miles Cunningham, and Lt. Remo Franceschini. The New Face of the Mob. Insight section. *Washington Times*, January 20, 1980.

3. *Newspaper Coverage of Organized Crime in New York and Sicily, 1931–1992*. Brooklyn *Eagle*. Staten Island *Advance*. New York *Journal American*. New York *World Telegram*. *The Evening Sun*. New York *Daily News*. New York *Post*. *Newsday*. *New York Times*. *Il Mattino*. *La Gazzetta di Mezzogiorno*. *Il Giornale di Sicilia*.

4. *Interviews*. The author interviewed the following law enforcement officials in New York about the

Gambino crime family: Ronald Goldstock, director of New York State Organized Crime Task Force (OCTF); Edward Wright, principal investigator, OCTF; Remo Franceschini, commander of the Queens District Attorney's Detective Squad; Michael Cherkasky, assistant district attorney and chief investigator, Organized Crime, Office of the District Attorney, Manhattan; and Joseph Coffey, investigative coordinator, Construction Strike Force, OCTF.

Informal confidential conversations with Gambino family associates and friends of Carlo Gambino, Paul Castellano, and John Gotti were held in Bensonhurst, Brooklyn, Little Italy, Manhattan, and at the trials of John Gotti in Manhattan and Brooklyn.

The author interviewed Charles "Lucky" Luciano four times in Naples in 1952, 1954, and 1955, and numerous people in Italy who knew Luciano during the period 1952–1962.

The author attended the 1990 assault trial and 1992 RICO conspiracy trial of John Gotti.

Acknowledgments

M y thanks go first to those friends and acquain-
tances in southern Italy and Sicily who, during
the 1960s, first awakened me to the existence and
power of the Camorra and the Mafia and in particular to those who knew Lucky Luciano during his last
years of exile in Naples (1955–1962) and provided me
with stories and anecdotes about him during that
period. Next my thanks to those who helped me learn
about La Cosa Nostra in the United States while I
was writing my last two books, *The Kennedys:
Dynasty and Disaster* (1984) and *Mafia Kingfish:
Carlos Marcello and the Assassination of John F.
Kennedy* (1988), and in particular to G. Robert
Blakey, former Chief Counsel of the House Select
Committee on Assassinations and currently head of
the Institute of Organized Crime at Notre Dame
University, who schooled me in the mysteries of the

Cosa Nostra while writing two books. This education, commencing in Naples in 1955 and culminating in the writing of *Mafia Kingfish* forms the foundation for this book.

To get down to specifics. The principal primary sources for this book are government documents, notably transcripts of secretly taped conversations of members of organized crime, notably of Paul Castellano and John Gotti. My most immediate debt of gratitude, therefore, goes to the agencies that provided me with those documents. They include the offices of the United States Attorneys for the Eastern and Southern Districts of New York, the Eastern District's Organized Crime Strike Force, the Queens District Attorney's Detective Squad, the Manhattan District Attorney's Organized Crime Section, and the New York State Organized Crime Task Force. In particular I wish to thank prosecutors Laura A. Ward, Edward McDonald, Douglas E. Grover, Michael Chertoff, and S. Bruce Barton, District Executive for the Eastern District of New York.

My thanks also go to those law enforcement officials who agreed to be interviewed by me for this book: Ronald E. Goldstock, Director, New York State Organized Crime Task Force, Lt. Edward Wright, Principal Investigator, OCTF, Lt. Joseph Coffey, Investigative Coordinator, Construction Task Force, OCTF, Michael Cherkasky, Assistant District Attorney and Chief Investigator, Organized Crime, Office of the District Attorney, Manhattan, Lt. Remo Franceschini, Commander of the Queens District Attorney's Detective Squad, and Laura A. Ward, Assistant U.S. Attorney, Eastern District. To these should be added certain people I interviewed for my previous books who provided me with useful information for this book, in particular the late Aaron Kohn, former Director of the Metropolitan Crime Commission of New Orleans, Harold Hughes, former Special Agent,

FBI, and William G. Hundley, former Chief, Organized Crime and Racketeering Section, Justice Department, under Attorney General Robert F. Kennedy.

Others who had helped me with *Mafia Kingfish* who also helped me with *Mafia Dynasty* were James E. Lesar, President of the Assassination Archives and Research Center, Washington, D.C., and Kennedy assassination researchers and writers, David E. Scheim, Paul L. Hoch, and Scott Van Wynesberghe.

I also wish to thank all those men and women who agreed to talk with me informally about the Gambino crime family on a confidential basis.

Since this book is an attempt at an overview of the history of organized crime in New York—spanning a period of roughly seventy-two years—I have had to rely heavily on many books on organized crime by authors who have gone before me. It would have been an impossible task to have researched the entire panorama without the aid of these writers' books. Foremost among them are Paul S. Meskil, author of *Don Carlo: Boss of Bosses;* Jerry Capeci and Gene Mustain, authors of *Mob Star: The Story of John Gotti;* John Cummings and Ernest Volkman, authors of *Goombata: The Improbable Rise and Fall of John Gotti and His Gang;* Martin A. Gosch and Richard Hammer, authors of *The Last Testament of Lucky Luciano;* Jonathan Kwitny, author of *Vicious Circles: The Mafia in the Marketplace;* and Joseph O'Brien and Andris Kurins, authors of *Boss of Bosses: The Fall of the Godfather: The FBI and Paul Castellano,* with whom I have also had several enlightening conversations. To all of these authors my thanks for their important contributions to this book.

My thanks also go to my researchers, Julia Ai and Daniel M. Peragine. Mr. Peragine deserves much credit for assembling the illustrations for the book.

I also want to thank Tom Salzano, Art Weil, and Vinola Dillon of Chemical Bank for their personal attention to my often urgent financial needs.

I owe a primary debt of gratitude to Gladys Justin Carr, Vice President and Associate Publisher at HarperCollins, who saw me through two previous books, *The Kennedys: Dynasty and Disaster* and *Mafia Kingfish* as well as this book. And I wish to thank my editor at HarperCollins, Cynthia Barrett, for her many judicious suggestions as to how the original manuscript might be improved. My thanks also go to the book's copy editor, Dave Cole, whose meticulous reading of the manuscript substantially improved the factual accuracy of the book.

My thanks to Maude B. Davis for her moral support and to Barbara Watson Davis and her husband David Watson, in whose house much of this book was written.

Finally I owe an incalculable debt of gratitude to Sohodra Nathu who tolerated me during the writing and helped me in countless, unanticipated ways, a process that often involved much personal sacrifice on her part. To her I owe more thanks than dedicating this book to her can express. From beginning to end she has been a constant source of encouragement, help, companionship, and love.

JOHN H. DAVIS

Index

JOHN H. DAVIS is the author of several bestselling books, including *The Kennedys: Dynasty and Disaster; Mafia Kingfish: Carlos Marcello and the Assassination of John F. Kennedy; The Kennedy Contract: The Mafia Plot to Assassinate the President; The Guggenheims;* and *The Bouviers*. A graduate of Princeton, he studied in Italy on a Fulbright scholarship and served as a naval officer with the Sixth Fleet in the Mediterranean. He lives in New York City.